BELIZE
Adventures in Nature

BELIZE
Adventures in Nature

Richard Mahler
Steele Wotkyns
Photography by Kevin Schafer

JOHN MUIR PUBLICATIONS
SANTA FE, NEW MEXICO

John Muir Publications, P.O. Box 613, Santa Fe, New Mexico 87504

Printed in the United States of America.
First edition. First printing October 1997.

Portions of this book were previously published as *Belize: A Natural Destination*
© 1995, 1993, 1991 by Richard Mahler, Steele Wotkyns, and Kevin Schafer.

Library of Congress Cataloging-in-Publication Data
Mahler, Richard.
     Belize: adventures in nature / Richard Mahler, Steele Wotkyns; photography by
Kevin Schafer. — 1st ed.
               p.   cm.
     "Portions of this book were previously published as Belize: a natural destination"—
T.p. verso.
     Includes index.
     ISBN 1-56261-369-3
     1. Belize—Guidebooks. 2. Natural history—Belize—Guidebooks. 3. Outdoor
recreation—Belize—Guidebooks. I. Wotkyns, Steele. II. Schafer, Kevin. III. Title.
     F1443.5.M34   1997
     917.28204'5—dc21
                              97-22457

                              CIP

Editors: Dianna Delling, Marybeth Griffin
Graphics Editor: Steve Dietz
Production: Janine Lehmann
Design: Janine Lehmann
Cover design: Janine Lehmann
Typesetting: Marcie Pottern
Maps: Kathy Sparkes, White Hart Design
Printer: Publishers Press
Front cover photos: Goff's Caye, red-eyed tree frog—Kevin Schafer
Back cover photos: Passion flower, rainforest/karst hills—Kevin Schafer

Distributed to the book trade by
Publishers Group West
Emeryville, California

CONTENTS

CONTENTS

FOREWORD

The fact that Belize is a natural destination is undeniable. This book provides thousands of details to back up that statement. Belize has it all.

That's why we call Belize the "Jewel of the Caribbean." It is a small country with beautiful and abundant natural resources, including rainforests, reefs, caves, waterfalls, and wildlife. Our famous barrier reef has been named a "World Heritage Site," a gift for everyone on the planet to share. Belize offers the rich cultural and archaeological patrimony of the Mayan civilization, as well as continued evidence of all the people who came afterward: Spanish, English, Garifuna, Lebanese, East Indian, Asian, African, and Caribbean. Belize is a study in contrasts, offering the traveler charming colonial-style housing and hospitality; jungle lodges with simple, primitive elegance in a rainforest habitat; and island resorts with peaceful beaches and sparkling, fish-filled waters.

A visit to Belize is a journey back in time. This is a nation that, due to its low population density and the foresight of its early leaders, has not exploited its natural resources to the extent of neighboring countries. Pine and hardwood forests cover a large portion of the country and provide important biological corridors for wildlife. Often called the "Noah's Ark" of Central America, Belize boasts the largest contiguous forested area north of the Amazon, helping to form a critically important "green corridor" from North to South America. The Mesoamerican Biological Corridor Project, initiated by the Wildlife Conservation Society and funded by the United Nations Global Environmental Facility, is geographically linking private and public protected areas up and down the continents through the isthmus of Central America. The resulting exchange of genetic pools is ensuring biodiversity of wildlife species and helping prevent the decline of endangered species that is occurring in part due to the "island" effect that occurs when protected areas are surrounded by development and cleared lands. We are proud to provide an essential link in this chain of life.

Why does this relate to your decision to travel to Belize? Because ours is a country that believe in the concept of *ecotourism*. Ecotourism is responsible tourism, travel that promotes conservation. To be specific, it *seeks to reduce the negative environmental and cultural impacts of tourism, while working to achieve authentic, intimate, meaningful, and educational encounters between visitors and local natural and cultural phenomena.*

Visiting Belize can be more than a vacation. You have a chance to actively participate in the conservation and protection of Belize's natural resources the minute you enter the country. Government officials will ask that you pay a PACT (Protected Areas Conservation Trust) fee. Be assured that this money will help protect our beloved jewel. All Belizean conservation projects, large and small, are eligible to apply for grants issued from the PACT, entirely funded by tourist donations.

Some say that Belize is an expensive destination, but let us carefully analyze the validity of that statement. While high-dollar resorts are plentiful, one can also find many budget-to-moderately-priced lodges, guest houses, and small hotels. When comparing, remember the human costs that are involved. Belizeans are paid on a standard wage scale that is lower than that of the United States, but much higher than that of its less fortunate neighbors. The result is a much lower poverty and unemployment level than "cheaper" destinations. Logistics are another factor. Many Belizean lodges and resorts are on remote islands or in dense jungles; therefore, their operating costs are far higher than those of their counterparts in cities.

When contemplating a visit to Belize, don't forget the educational value of this destination. Many lodges specialize in educational tours, including archaeology, biology, zoology, ornithology, and Lepidoptera, as well as tropical and marine ecology. One can learn from the example of such community-based conservation projects as the Community Baboon Sanctuary and Slate Creek Preserve. Residents of the communities that are involved in these efforts work together to protect the natural resources of their area, combining conservation, education, and research. They in turn benefit from the ecotourism activities that these projects encourage.

Belize has shown how government agencies and nonprofit NGOs (non-government organizations) can work together for the common good. The Belize EcoTourism Association (BETA), for example, has organized a nationwide campaign against litter. Watch for the "Beta No Litta!" signs along the highway, sponsored by concerned businesses and individuals. Help us "Keep Belize Clean and Green!" Please, don't litter!

By now you may be wondering exactly how you can become a responsible visitor. First, be selective in your choice of hotel, tour operator, and guide, and base your decision, at least in part, on conservation ethics. Find out if the business or individual donates time or money to support organizations active in managing Belize's parks and wildlife. Do they use local workers? Do they try to teach you, the visitor, how to better enjoy your stay without leaving a visible impact? Are they using recyclable or biodegradable materials instead of Styrofoam and plastics? To learn more, you can find an updated list of the members of the Belize EcoTourism Association at BETA's Worldwide Web page: *http://www.belizenet.com/beta.html.* This Internet site also displays BETA's code of ethics, which all members have agreed to live up to.

We hope you enjoy this book and that you'll carry it with you during your visit to Belize. It is a veritable encyclopedia of information about our culture, history, and natural resources. Please remember that your visit will help us to ensure that Belize will always be a natural destination.

Jim Bevis
Past President, The Belize EcoTourism Association

ACKNOWLEDGMENTS

The authors wish to especially thank Rita Cadena for the inspiration to write this book and the warm, wonderful people of Belize for making it possible. We also thank everyone at John Muir Publications for their patience and assistance.

Richard Mahler wishes to thank (among many others) Wil and Susan Lala; Lionel "Chocolate" Heredia and Annie Seashore; Bruce Foerster and Neil Rogers; the staff and owners of Soulshine Resort; Alfredo and Yvonne Villoria; the Cesario Choco famiy; Ray Herbard and Clive Farrell; the late Stephen Smith; Jim and Marguerite Bevis; Charles Colby II; Therese Rath Bowman; the staff of the Belize Tourist Board; the Belize Tourism Industry Association; and last, but not least, my steadfast and supportive parents, Don and Mary Mahler. A special thank you also goes to Continental Airlines, for extending courtesies beyond the call of duty. My deepest appreciation goes to Kate Droney, my favorite traveling companion and best editor.

Steele Wotkyns wishes to thank his parents, particularly his father, Steele Wotkyns; his patient and supportive wife, Rita; his co-author, Richard Mahler; Winston Seawell; the Slickrock Adventures team, especially Lucy, Phil, Jim, Elmo, and Celestine; Johnny at Long Caye; Lisa at Middle Caye; Raymond and Brenda Lee at Ocean's Edge; Dr. Susan Hammen-Winn; Martin Spragg at Second Nature Divers; Francis and Gloria Reid at Over the Top Restaurant; Barbara Borland of the Woman Rising Bed and Breakfast Group; Ian Anderson and the entire crew at Caves Branch Jungle Camp; the Carrs, the Meiths, and other staff at Banana Bank Lodge; Vicki and Ray Snaddon at Pook's Hill Lodge; Bart and Suzi Mickler and the staff at Maya Mountain Lodge; Lucy and Mick Fleming and the team at Chaa Creek/Macal River Camp; Sergio Paiz; Raul at Tikal; Pacz Hotel's team; Tineke Boomsma and Jan Meerman; Jim and Marguerite Bevis, family, and staff at MET; Bob Jones at Eva's; Fred Prost at Parrot Nest; Rudy and Gloria Crawford and family of the Paradise; Donald Tillett; Israel Cruz in Sarteneja; Casper Bijleveld and Juan Aldana at Shipstern Nature Reserve; Fernando Alamilla; Joan and Henry Menzies and staff at Caribbean Village; Vincent Murray; David Landis; John and Madeline at Jungle Drift; Tony Read and staff of the Living Reef Dive Center; Victor Gonzalez; Lou Nicolait; Dora Weyer; Svea Dietrich-Ward; Tom Grasse; Rosita Arvigo and Greg Shropshire at Ix Chel; Nick Brokaw; Linden Kosub; and others whom we have neglected to mention.

Kevin Schafer would like to thank Sharon Matola and the staff of the Belize Zoo. Thanks also to Meb Cutlack and Katie Stevens, and Rachel and Rita Emmer, all good friends. An especially warm thanks to Ged Caddick, for his help and enormous patience in the field. Finally, an endless debt to my father, who introduced me to Belize and spent his last days there, happily.

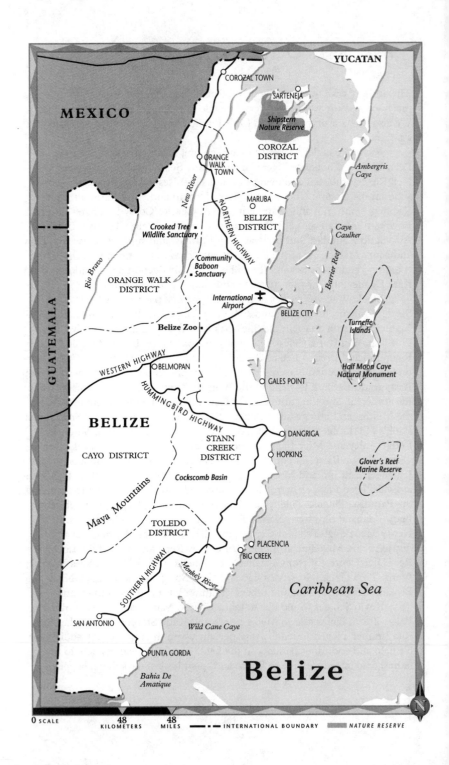

BELIZE: JEWEL OF THE CARIBBEAN

"Why would anybody want to go to Belize?" Chances are you'll be asked this question more than once before you get here. There are many answers, of course, and the one you select will depend on your interests and temperament. If you're a scuba diver, the offshore barrier reef is an obvious attraction. If you want to experience the unspoiled jungle, a trip to the interior of Belize makes perfect sense.

Perhaps the most obvious reason to visit Belize is to be able to experience the natural beauty and quiet ambiance of a relatively uncrowded and little-developed, subtropical destination. Whereas 80 percent of the native forests of Latin America have disappeared during the last two centuries, in Belize the opposite is true: nearly 70 percent of the original forest remains, and in a largely undisturbed form. Here you'll find hundreds of species of animals and plants that have largely disappeared from most of their original homes, yet are thriving in Belize. Offshore, meanwhile, one of the world's longest barrier reefs harbors exotic marine life in an underwater paradise unparalleled in the Western Hemisphere.

This sliver of Caribbean coastline remains the most sparsely populated nation in Central America, with less than 30 inhabitants per square mile. It is not the smallest country. With its 8,867 square miles, Belize is slightly larger than El Salvador. But whereas the latter is bursting with more than 8 million people, Belize had an estimated 1997 population of 250,000, about one-third of whom were crowded into a single town: Belize City. Stability is another obvious difference. Belize is a parliamentary democracy that has never suffered under the civil wars and dictatorships that have typified most other Central American countries. Belize enjoys a high literacy rate (93 percent of adults) and long life-expectancy (73 years for women, 67 for men).

Belize is divided into six political jurisdictions that roughly correspond to states or provinces. They are, from north to south, the Corozal, Orange Walk, Belize, Cayo, Stann Creek, and Toledo Districts. Most visitors will spend the bulk of their time in the Belize District, which encompasses the international airport, Belize City, and such northern islands as Ambergris Caye and Caye Caulker; and the Cayo District, where the town of San Ignacio and most jungle lodges are located. Of growing interest to visitors are the southerly Stann Creek and Toledo Districts, noted for their nature reserves, Mayan ruins, and pristine offshore waters. The northerly districts of Corozal and Orange Walk are the most agricultural areas of Belize and thus receive the fewest number of visitors.

A lobster fisherman and his helper rest in a café at Bluefield Range.

Ricardo Castillo

TRAVEL STRATEGY

Although this is a small nation, getting from one place to another takes some time: most roads are bad and the islands can only be reached by small airplanes or boats. In order to get the most out of the country, you should plan to spend at least a week in Belize.

The two areas of Belize that are of greatest interest to travelers are the Cayo District, in the country's west-central interior, and the offshore islands that arise along the barrier reef, particularly Ambergris Caye and Caye Caulker. Many visitors are content to spend all of their time on Ambergris Caye, taking an occasional day trip to a Mayan ruin or snorkeling and diving site. Although you'll probably enjoy yourself, this kind of trip won't give you a realistic look at the country. We recommend that you roam a bit from Ambergris to visit neighboring islands, or even spend a few nights on a caye or atoll that's less developed. In order to experience the best that Belize has to offer, we also urge you to spend at least two or three days exploring the area around San Ignacio, two hours west of Belize City via the Western Highway. Here you'll find comfortable jungle lodges, well-maintained nature trails, magnificent Mayan temples, cool mountain rivers, sacred limestone caves, and such unusual attractions as butterfly farms, rainforest medicine centers, and traditional Mennonite villages. Along the way you can take in the Belize Zoo, Community Baboon Sanctuary, and Crooked Tree Wildlife Sanctuary, or float on an inner tube through the underground grottos of the Caves Branch River.

If you have more time to spend in Belize, a journey south will reward you with fascinating destinations like the Cockscomb Basin jaguar reserve, Laughingbird Caye National Park, Garifuna villages, and Glover's Reef. The more adventurous traveler will want to take excursions into the rainforests and Mayan villages of the remote Toledo District. Others may want to head up the jungle rivers and through the wetlands of the Orange Walk and Corozal Districts to the north.

On the other hand, if your inclinations lean decidedly toward water recreation or Mayan archaeology, you may want to set up a Belize itinerary that concentrates exclusively on either offshore or interior travel, with a possible side trip to the ancient city of Tikal in neighboring Guatemala.

We recommend reading this book before you make any final decisions about your schedule so that you'll get the most out of Belize during the time you have available.

BELIZE HISTORY

Mayan Civilization

At the peak of the vast Mayan empire, archaeologists estimate that 1 to 2 million Native Americans lived within the borders of Belize, with an equal number dwelling nearby in what is now northeastern Guatemala and southeastern Mexico. Thousands more Maya were scattered across parts of Honduras and El Salvador.

The earliest Maya are believed to have spread into the confines of present-day Belize from Guatemala and Mexico about 2000 B.C., after their ancestors had crossed the land bridge from Asia many centuries earlier. There is evidence that archaic tribes roamed the area as early as 7500 B.C., at a time when Central America's climate and habitat were somewhat less tropical, given over to grassy savannas and broadleaf woodlands.

The early, or pre-Classic, Maya period extends from 1000 B.C. to A.D. 300. The Mayan civilization reached its height during the Classic era, from about A.D. 300 to 900. From around A.D. 1000 until the arrival of the Spanish 500 years later, the Maya were plunged into a precipitous decline (the post-Classic phase), and the underlying structure of their society fell apart.

No one knows for certain why the civilization disintegrated or why many of its members migrated north into the northern Yucatán peninsula and left many—but not all—of their city-states abandoned. Perhaps it was a prolonged war or a loss of faith in the priestly royalty who ruled with absolute authority. It is also possible that a series of droughts, earthquakes, or other natural disasters contributed to the breakdown. Archaeologists are collecting data that may someday help us settle such questions once and for all.

What is now generally agreed upon is that the area currently known as Belize was for many years the very heart of the Mayan empire. From A.D. 300 to 900, this was the center of their complex collection of city-states, linked by trails, rivers, and Caribbean trade routes. Recent excavations have shown that Caracol, the country's largest site, is even bigger than Tikal, long considered the most significant Mayan restoration. Archaeologists now believe that Caracol defeated Tikal militarily as the neighboring cities competed for dominance during the Classic period. Many aspects of the ancient Mayan civilization have disappeared from Belize (about 12 percent of the country's current population are descended from the Maya), but the

Richard Mahler

The temple of Canaa towers 140 feet above the ancient Mayan city of Caracol.

major archaeological sites at Xunantunich, Caracol, Altun Ha, and Lamanai still reflect its impressive achievements.

What distinguishes the hundreds of Mayan sites of Belize from those of neighboring countries is their relatively pristine character. For various reasons, Belize has left many of its ruins in much the same condition as they were found. Excavations and restorations are sporadic, only undertaken when funds and personnel become available—which isn't often.

In many ways, the ancient Maya were more advanced than their contemporaries in Greece, Italy, France, and England, reaching the zenith of their power during Europe's Dark Ages. These Native Americans were skilled astronomers and mathematicians, and accomplished farmers and engineers. They developed an elaborate religious system that incorporated many complex rituals and commemorated diverse natural phenomena. Their calendar system, for example, is precise within a matter of seconds in tracking phases of the moon, planets, and stars. Over the years, the Maya became expert artists and traders. Excavations in Belize have yielded seashells from the distant Pacific Coast, obsidian and gold from northern Mexico, pottery from South America's Andes mountains, and jade from the Central

5

American highlands. There is even physical evidence suggesting that Mayan trade routes extended as far as New Mexico, where the Anasazi civilization flourished during the same epoch.

Yet many dimensions of the Mayan way of life are dimly understood, and experts can only speculate on what the Maya's daily routine was like. By the time the first Europeans came to the region in the early 1500s, some Maya still lived in a few of the ancient cities. Their intricate civilization had largely dissolved by this time and the conquering Spanish tried to destroy much of what remained. Contrary to popular belief, however, the Mayan culture is still very much alive, particularly in rural areas of Belize, Guatemala, and the Mexican state of Chiapas. In Belize's southern Toledo District, Kekchí-speaking Maya still tell folktales that originated during the days of the Mayan empire and perform ritual dances held sacred by their ancestors. In the Cayo District, near Caracol, Mopan- and Yucatec-speaking Maya have revived the ancient art of slate carving, gathering stones from riverbeds their ancestors mined centuries ago.

The European Presence

European knowledge of Belize began in 1502, when Christopher Columbus sailed along Central America's coast and named the Bay of Honduras, which begins at the southern end of Belize's barrier reef. Other Spanish navigators followed throughout the 16th century, but few were willing to make the tricky crossing of Belize's reef, and none saw fit to establish a permanent outpost. Other than a successful, plunderous raid on the Mayan trading city of Santa Rita (now Corozal) in 1513, the initial Spanish presence was limited to a few minor explorations and some missionary work. Catholic churches were established at Lamanai and Tipú in the early 1500s, but the Spanish clerics were ejected around 1640.

Probably the first permanent settlement of foreigners in Belize began in the early 1600s when English-speaking Puritan traders, then based on the swampy Mosquito Coast of eastern Nicaragua, established outposts on strategic islands, including Tobacco Caye. The colonists ignored the fact that Vicente Yanez Pinzon and Juan Díaz de Solis, among other explorers, had already claimed the area for Spain. Despite their own lack of interest in starting a Belizean colony, Spanish forces routed the Puritans from their trading posts in 1641.

Seemingly unknown to the Spaniards, a separate group of ship-wrecked British sailors had started building their own tiny community on the coast some three years earlier. They were a motley crew,

How Did Belize Get Its Name?

The camp set up by Scottish sea captain, Peter Wallace, eventually became Belize City. Some say that the name "Belize" is derived from the Spanish pronunciation of "Wallace," which could sound something like the word. Others speculate that Belize comes from the Mayan words belix, *meaning "muddy water," or* belikin, *translated as "land that faces the sea." Perhaps it derives from the French* balise, *a reference to the beacons used to guide pirates back to port at night. Yet another theory is that the name comes from the old British verb* obelize, *which means to mark a map with an obelus, a sign that suggests a place is corrupt and undesirable. During its many years as a pirate haven, English mapmakers routinely obelized the camp founded by Peter Wallace.*

including many buccaneers who had learned of Belize through contact with the Puritan merchants. Gradually, over the next 150 years, more and more English settlers would move into the same area. They were later joined by a contingent of disbanded English sailors and soldiers who fought for the successful British liberation of Jamaica from Spain in 1655. Some of these early settlers were engaged in hardwood logging, others in piracy, and a precious few in farming. All would be forced to defend their primitive villages from sporadic attacks by Mayan Indians and Spaniards.

With few inhabitants, disease-infested backwaters, and a dangerous offshore reef, Belize was an ideal hideout for the raiders of the Caribbean. By the late 1600s, the most infamous Scottish, French, and English pirates had established permanent bases in Belize, from which they mercilessly attacked Spanish galleons carrying gold, silver, dyes, hardwoods, and other raw materials back to Europe.

Belize's first documented lumbering was undertaken by buccaneer Bart Sharp and his mates about 1660. The cutters were eager to remove logwood (a source of textile dyes) and mahogany (an excellent hardwood used to make fine furniture). Sharp and his cohorts

Kevin Schafer

Mayan children collecting firewood.

called themselves "Baymen," after the Bay of Honduras to the south. Unable to eject the Baymen by force, Spain finally signed treaties with Britain, in 1763 and 1786, which secured government cooperation in the suppression of piracy and protection of lumber interests. The British would be allowed to remain as long as they kept to certain areas and left the treasure-laden galleons alone.

As they gradually turned more of their attention toward timber cutting, the white settlers began importing hundreds of African slaves from Jamaica and other British-controlled islands of the Caribbean. They relied on the strength of their charges to accomplish the difficult task of cutting huge logs and hauling them to ships for export. By the 1700s, lumber was a booming industry and the English were going far into the Belizean interior to selectively cut the largest trees they could find.

Slowly but surely, British influence in Belize grew during the early 1800s. When Spain dismantled its New World empire and granted independence to Mexico and Guatemala in 1821, Britain's Foreign Office loudly rejected those countries' immediate claims to Belize; for separate reasons, each considered the "province" of Belize to be part of its own rightful inheritance from Spain.

By 1826, the Baymen woodcutters had extended their timber harvesting to the Sarstoon River, the present southern boundary of Belize, and had become so prosperous that England could not help but take notice. At the same time, Guatemala remained adamant in its determination to annex the region and periodically waged war against the "trespassing" settlers. In 1859, fearing continued political instability would be bad for its now-sizable business in the region, Britain finally signed a treaty with Guatemala in which the latter confirmed the present-day boundaries of Belize in return for British financing for construction of a road from Guatemala's capital to Belize City. For various reasons, this promise was never honored,

Why Belizeans Speak English

For almost 200 years, the legal status of the region now known as Belize remained vague. At one point, English authorities even ceded control over the area to Spain, with the understanding that its woodcutting concessions could remain. Other agreements barred the Baymen from erecting fortifications, governing themselves, and establishing plantations. The stouthearted settlers, true to the lawless spirit of their forebears, generally ignored such treaties and set up their own laws. Eventually, with great reluctance, London sent official representatives to the Bay Settlement during the late 1780s.

This action infuriated the Spanish, who felt Britain was overstepping the bounds of its treaties. The showdown came in a 1798 skirmish off St. George's Caye, near Belize City, where a few hundred angry settlers and a British schooner drove off a powerful, battle-hardened wing of the Spanish Armada. September 10 is still celebrated as Belize's "National Day," with a separate holiday on September 21 to mark independence from England in 1981.

thus explaining why Guatemala, which never formally ratified the 1859 agreement, remained hostile. (In 1991, Guatemala's newly elected president, Jorge Serrano, officially recognized Belize's independence in hopes of settling the long-running dispute, but there is still tension between the two countries.)

Similarly, Mexico's claim to Belize was not easily settled. Throughout the 19th century, the Mexican government insisted that the northern half—and perhaps all—of Belize was an extension of its Yucatán holdings. Tensions escalated during the Caste War of 1847 to 1858, when thousands of Indian and Mestizo (mixed-race) slaves in the Yucatán revolted against their masters and fled across the border in search of British protection. Mexican authorities decided not to pursue the renegades; thus, several thousand refugees became the nucleus for settlement in the northern districts of Belize, which remain largely Spanish-speaking. Mexico finally renounced any claim to Belize in an 1897 treaty with England.

The Colonial Period

In 1840, after establishing through various abolition-of-slavery acts that the Central American settlers were indeed its subjects, Great Britain declared Belize to be "the colony of British Honduras." But the declaration was in name only, and administration of the colony did not begin until 1862. It would be another nine years before British Honduras received formal recognition as a Crown colony, and it was not until the 1880s that the territory was administered separately from Jamaica.

With its formal establishment as a colony finally accomplished, development of Belize became more organized. Supervision was badly overdue, since a lack of diversification in industry and overdependence on imported goods had sent Belize into decline during the Victorian era. The concentration of land ownership made it difficult for entrepreneurs to start projects that might wean the colony from its motherland. By the late 19th century, a single London-based company (Belize Estate & Produce) owned more than a million acres of land, or one-fifth of the entire territory.

During this period, Belize went through a series of profound cultural changes, yielding a multiethnic society that remains remarkably cohesive. Many of the original English and Scottish settlers intermarried with freed slaves to form the Creole majority that still dominates the population. In the north, Mexican citizens crossed the border and began cultivating small farms. Many of their descendants now grow sugarcane, the country's most lucrative crop. To the south, Kekchí and Mopan Maya sought refuge from forced-labor plantations in Guatemala, and a small contingent of weary Confederate Civil War veterans arrived from the United States to found a plantation colony they called Toledo. From the Bay Islands off Honduras came a large number of Garifuna people. These blacks of mixed African and Carib-Indian ancestry had been forcibly expelled from the West Indies in 1797.

Others immigrating to Belize in smaller numbers during the 1800s included Chinese sugarcane workers and Lebanese shopkeepers. Ethnic Sepoys were conscripted to the colony from India after an 1857 rebellion, and many West Indian plantation workers were recruited to do

The face of this Benque Viejo boy reveals his Mayan/Spanish heritage.

fieldwork by the end of the century. A handful of expatriate Europeans and North Americans also decided to make Belize their home.

Early attempts to diversify the economy met with mixed success. The lack of roads, high transportation costs, and a limited pool of skilled labor stymied developers, and many new crops fell victim to exotic diseases and poor soil conditions. Periodic hurricanes devastated the country, uprooting trees and flattening houses. Then, as today, Belizeans were unable to produce enough food to feed themselves and had to rely heavily on expensive imports. Because their own food was cheap and labor plentiful, neighboring countries such as Honduras and Guatemala easily outproduced Belize in such valuable commodities as bananas, sugar, rubber, and chicle (a natural chewing gum base). Another problem facing Belize was its large population of freed slaves, who were legally barred from obtaining vacant Crown land that could be used for farming.

Early Twentieth Century

By 1900, British Honduras had grown to have a population of 37,000. Yet the economy was moribund, wages were low, and discontent was endemic. A destructive 1931 hurricane compounded the colony's problems. By the late 1930s, Belize's deteriorating economic conditions prompted some residents to begin calling for independence. (Sensing this unrest, Guatemala renewed its claims to sovereignty and to payment from Britain for the promised road to Guatemala City that had never been built. Over the next 20 years, Guatemala became more adamant in its demands, and several forays across the frontier had to be repelled by the British.)

During World War II, many Belizeans again volunteered to fight but returned to a land where living conditions were miserable, work opportunities were limited, and political power was concentrated in the hands of a wealthy and mostly white elite. Fearful colonial administrators responded to the growing unrest by passing restrictive laws and banning public marches. But in 1950, after a sharp devaluation of the local currency, Belizeans decided they'd had enough. The independence movement, led by George Price—an American-educated, cautiously liberal Creole divinity student—rapidly increased in size and influence. In 1954 voting rights were extended to all adults, and in 1955 a form of ministerial government was introduced. By 1961, London had agreed to begin the process of setting Belize free.

Meanwhile, the economy of the colony began to diversify. German-descended Mennonites began homesteading here in the late 1950s and greatly improved the domestic food supply. The first tourists began arriving about the same time, most of them divers and fishermen attracted by the offshore marine life. The economic diversification was matched by political change, part of an international move toward self-governance.

Full internal, elected self-government was instituted in 1964, modeled after the Westminster parliamentary system. Britain remained in charge of foreign relations, defense, and internal security. A bicameral assembly (House and Senate) was established, and its members were popularly elected. (After George Price's People's United Party, the largest political party is the more conservative United Democratic Party, in office from 1985 to 1989, and again beginning in 1993.)

In 1973 the colony's name was officially changed from British Honduras to Belize and on September 21, 1981, Belizean independence was formally declared. With British troops on full alert and the border sealed, the Guatemalan invasion that some had seriously feared never took place, and in 1992 Guatemala finally acknowledged Belize's sovereignty. The region was judged secure enough for Britain to withdraw nearly all of its armed forces from Belize during 1994, although the former colony is still a protectorate and a member of the British Commonwealth.

While Belize has successfully thwarted foreign claimants since

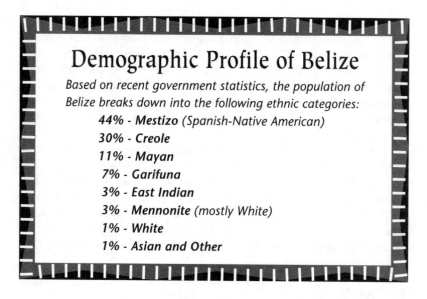

Demographic Profile of Belize

Based on recent government statistics, the population of Belize breaks down into the following ethnic categories:

44% - Mestizo *(Spanish-Native American)*
30% - Creole
11% - Mayan
7% - Garifuna
3% - East Indian
3% - Mennonite *(mostly White)*
1% - White
1% - Asian and Other

1798, it is quietly experiencing a subtle transformation into a Spanish-speaking country. Large numbers of Guatemalans, Salvadorans, and Hondurans have crossed its borders since independence, many of them illegally. In fact, during the early 1990s Mestizos reportedly replaced Creoles as Belize's largest single ethnic group. The vast majority of these newcomers are unskilled peasant farmers, attracted by an abundance of available land and relatively high wages, as well as a tradition of peace and political stability. The latter is a truly significant factor for people who have known only military dictatorships, political warfare, and genocidal terrorism.

Present and Future

Since 1994, when almost all British troops left, Belize has been on its own. Except for a token British force and a handful of U.S. Peace Corps volunteers, there's very little "official" foreign presence here, and as a result politics has evolved in a distinctively partisan Belizean-style. With the colonials gone and the border dispute with Guatemala settled, politicians have turned their attention inward, and there is more than enough to occupy their attention.

Thousands of immigrants have streamed into Belize in recent years, many of them Spanish-speaking peasants who harvest plantation crops or tend to their own homesteads. For the first time, Belize is reevaluating its centuries-old practice of welcoming hardworking newcomers with open arms and free land. Meanwhile, the nation's fragile economy limps along, crippled by high taxes and import duties as well as the vagaries of international commodity prices. The conservative United Democratic Party, in office since 1993, has made little headway in curbing unemployment and reducing Belize's enormous national debt. As this book went to press, there were signs that the opposition People's United Party might return to a political majority with its more liberal agenda.

The future of Belize may well depend on how its citizens and their leaders respond to the country's rapidly changing demographics—it is gradually becoming poorer and more Hispanic—and to the uncertainties inherent in an economy that remains largely dependent on fluctuating agricultural markets and the fickle tourist industry. The critical political decisions made during the next several years will likely determine the path Belize will follow for decades to come.

ECONOMY

Compared to other Central American countries, Belize enjoys relative prosperity, adequate health services, improving sanitation, a good public school system, and little of the income disparity that divides its neighbors into feuding factions of rich and poor. Still, Belize is heavily dependent on foreign aid—both governmental and private—for its survival. Out of necessity, most oil, food, manufactured goods, and consumer products are imported, and often paid for through loans and grants provided by aid programs from the United States, Great Britain, and other European Economic Community members. As a result, about 25 percent of the national budget goes to servicing the country's huge national debt.

While the country's economic base is broadening, progress has been painfully slow. In candid moments, government officials admit that illicit transport and trafficking in marijuana, cocaine, and heroin has been a major contributor to the bottom line. Major narcotic busts occur regularly in Belize but seem to have little impact on the drug business.

Although timber is still an important Belizean export (most of it pine and cedar now, not hardwoods like mahogany), the major agricultural crops are sugarcane and citrus, cultivated in the north and south, respectively. Bananas and fish products (mainly shrimp, conch, and lobster) are also important exports, along with honey, maize, pineapples, beans, mangos, papayas, cocoa, and rice. Poultry

Belizeans Abroad

Tens of thousands of Belizeans living in the United States and Canada remit millions of dollars to family members every year. Today, one-third as many Belizean citizens live outside the country as inside, with the largest concentrations in Los Angeles, New York, and Chicago, as well as Toronto and Vancouver. Because the average Belizean earns less than $500 a month, the money that relatives send home keeps the country afloat economically, providing the extra income needed to buy conveniences like refrigerators and TV sets.

and cattle are raised domestically, and light manufacturing (mostly clothing and furniture) now accounts for about 15 percent of the gross domestic product.

Observers consider the Belizean economy "fragile," since the country imports much more than it exports and remains vulnerable both to fluctuations in the price of plantation products and to trade preferences imposed by other countries. In an attempt to improve the situation, during the early 1990s Belize added powerful new incentives for investors, including duty-free export zones near the Guatemalan and Mexican borders. The possibility of an offshore banking industry similar to that of the Cayman Islands is also under discussion.

Tourism competes with agriculture as the biggest contributor to Belize's bottom line, thanks to steady interest among foreign visitors. The tourist industry is fickle, however, and has been subject to boom and bust cycles here during the 1990s. Nevertheless, the government of Belize and many in the hospitality business are openly and firmly committed to making natural history tourism a top priority for their country's future.

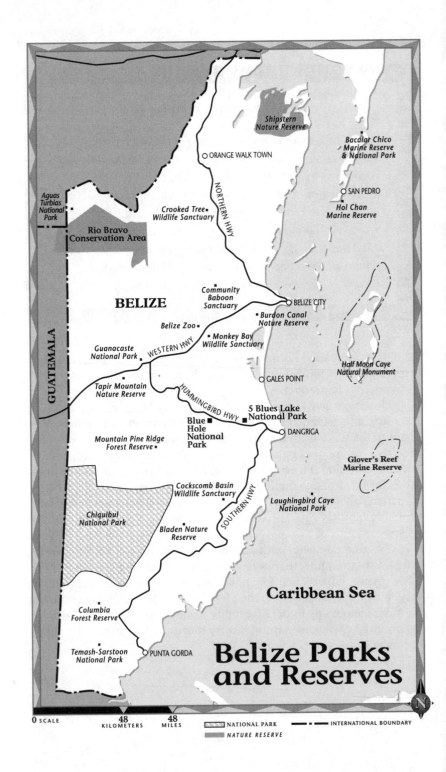

Belize Parks and Reserves

CONSERVATION AND RESPONSIBLE TOURISM

2

At one time or another, most of us entertain a tropical island fantasy. We dream about getting away from it all on an idyllic vacation in a remote, sunny paradise. We picture ourselves sprawled on a sandy beach under the shady fronds of a swaying coconut palm, sipping a rum punch, and staring hypnotically at a shimmering horizon. Or perhaps we see ourselves gliding through warm, turquoise water, sharing a dazzling marine environment with Technicolor coral, jaunty sea horses, and eye-catching stoplight parrot fish.

Maybe you've been lucky enough to take such a trip—only to return with the unsettled feeling that something vital was missing. Like eating a rich dessert full of empty calories, the experience was pleasing but not quite satisfying. Next time, we recommend an adventure in what we call "natural history tourism," which is exactly the sort of unusual vacation Belize has to offer. In the pages that follow, we'll take you to our favorite destinations in this plucky little country.

In many ways, Belize is far ahead of other less-developed nations in shaping tourism as an economic strategy that can preserve, rather than destroy, its priceless resources. Belize has won praise from international conservationists for the so-called sustainable development strategies it has implemented to protect its impressive treasures of nature and artifacts of Mayan history, while at the same time making sure that its people benefit from the public lands set aside

17

for environmental and other purposes. It has largely succeeded in this campaign despite constant monetary problems and growing pressure from agricultural and industrial interests. Many of Belize's government officials have looked around them to see the danger of following another path.

Large portions of neighboring Guatemala, Mexico, and Honduras are now completely deforested, with plantations, timber interests, and slash-and-burn subsistence farms quickly replacing the remaining tropical forests. In contrast, an estimated 70 percent of Belize's land area is still covered with forest, only some of which has been thinly and selectively logged in the past (compared, for example, to the barely 2 percent of intact forest remaining in nearby El Salvador, a bit smaller than Belize but with more than 30 times its population). More importantly, an impressively large proportion—about 30 percent—of Belize is under some form of officially protected designation.

PROTECTING NATURE'S TREASURES

Between 1990 and 1992, some 535,235 acres were put under permanent protection by Belize, including more than 200,000 acres of tropical forest in the Chiquibul region; 6,000 acres of mangrove wetlands in the Burdon Canal zone; and 97,000 acres of critical watershed in the Bladen Nature Reserve. During that same period, the Cockscomb Basin Wildlife Sanctuary (the world's only jaguar refuge) was expanded from 3,600 to 102,000 acres. Since then, Belize has added more parks and reserves, including designation of the entire 75-square-mile Glover's Reef atoll as a marine reserve and of the 23-square-mile Bacalar Chico area as a combination marine reserve and national park.

Belize has shown remarkable leadership in protecting tropical forests and marine resources, and many Belizeans deserve credit for these positive actions. Now Belize needs to shift attention from establishment of parks and protected areas to long-term, on-the-ground, natural area management. In order to accomplish this, the country's natural resources need to pay for themselves.

WHAT IS ECOTOURISM?

Nature-based tourism—often referred to as "ecotourism"—is strongly and officially encouraged in Belize. Politicians and bureaucrats are hopeful that Belize can learn from the mistakes of others, weighing the advantages of badly needed foreign income against the irreversible damage that unbounded traditional tourism and agriculture might inflict. But just as "it takes a village" to raise a child, it takes an entire country to carefully preserve and wisely manage natural resources. Hotels, tour operators, trade organizations, educators, individuals, and entrepreneurs throughout Belize have responded to the call for enlightened action.

"We in the private sector have a tremendous opportunity to do something for conservation in conjunction with government," Jim Bevis, past president of the Belize EcoTourism Association (BETA) and co-owner of Mountain Equestrian Trails, told us in a 1997 interview. "I see private enterprise as the facilitator to get things done." (Later in this book you will read about some specific, laudable environmental-protection projects undertaken by Bevis and other members of the business community, including the establishment of a private 4,000-acre nature preserve.)

BETA was formed in 1993 by a few members of the Belize Tourism Industry Association as a conservation-oriented branch of that trade group. BETA's mission is to promote environmentally responsible tourism, to be sensitive to the impacts of tourism, to promote education for locals and visitors, and to promote such concerns as pollution prevention. While Jim Bevis was president of BETA, many tourism businesses teamed with private citizens, schools, private industry, and community groups to carry out a successful nationwide "Adopt A Roadway" anti-litter campaign, dubbed "Beta No Litta." Visitors may notice green BETA signs bearing the names of sponsors of this program posted along major roadways.

SAVING TROPICAL HABITATS

Environmentalists are well aware of what can—and often does—occur when travel in the Tropics is promoted with little regard for natural resources: protective mangrove trees are stripped by builders from sandy shorelines; fragile coral reefs are damaged by inquisitive but uninformed divers and snorkelers; commercial marine species, such as conch and lobster, are depleted to meet restaurant demands; indiscriminate poaching may decimate wildlife populations; and oblivious amateur cavers may degrade speleothems formed over thousands of years. Despite its own best efforts, Belize has not escaped this long list of injuries. Yet many individuals, in government, academia, and

BELIZE - THIS IS OUR NATIONAL BIRD.
LIKE THE TOUCAN-OTHER WILD ANIMALS
AND BIRDS ARE PROTECTED BY LAW.
THE FINE IS $1000.00 FOR ILLEGAL
HUNTING. PROTECT OUR NATURAL
HERITAGE ! SPONSORED BY:
FOREST DEPARTMENT   H.R.I. EXPRESS

Richard Mahler

Conservation education is a popular theme on Belize billboards.

private industry, are making a determined effort to provide effective conservation education to each and every visitor.

Perhaps the part of the country facing the most intense development pressure is the marine environment, including coral reef formations immediately surrounding the most-visited cayes, Ambergris and Caulker. Coral reefs are the marine equivalents of tropical rainforests.

"In most coral species, each individual polyp lays down a skeletal container of calcium carbonate that surrounds and protects its soft body," biologist Edward O. Wilson wrote in *The Diversity of Life*. "Coral colonies grow by the budding of individual polyps, with the skeletal cups being added one on another in a set geometric pattern particular to each species. The result is a lovely, bewildering array of skeletal forms that mass together to make the whole reef—a tangled field of horn corals, brain corals, staghorn corals, organ pipes, sea fans, and sea whips." Some formations are thousands of years old.

Belize's barrier reef suffers injury every time a boat anchor is randomly cast and hauled in or a diver bumps against a piece of living coral. When these centuries-old marine architects are touched, they begin to turn black and die. Unfortunately, many collectors cannot seem to resist the urge to (illegally) collect sea fans, black coral, and even aquarium-bound fish. Commercial fishing throws the food chain out of balance when desired species are removed en masse. Important breeding and feeding grounds for lobster, conch, turtles, grouper, and waterfowl are destroyed by unrestricted fishing or when mangrove and sea grass beds are removed by developers. Over the long run, no one knows what the cumulative effect of all these changes will be.

PRIVATE SECTOR PARTICIPATION

A continuing trend in Belize, fortunately, is the active involvement of private citizens and tourism entrepreneurs in preserving and protecting their environment. On Caye Caulker, for example, tourist guide Lionel "Chocolate" Heredia has taught visitors and fellow boat operators how to proceed with caution and respect around Caribbean manatees, a shy and endangered species that is holding its own in Belize. "Chocolate" has taken the initiative of lobbying the government for designation of official manatee reserves and donates a percentage of his manatee-derived income to a nonprofit foundation that advocates on their behalf. He is one of many Belizeans who is willing to do something to keep his country the amazing natural wonderland that it is.

One of the greatest threats to Belize's remaining forests is the clearing and burning of land for citrus and sugarcane plantations.

21

Meanwhile, in Belize's interior, habitat destruction in the form of deforestation and selective woodcutting continues to cause serious damage to pristine ecosystems. According to the government, hundreds of refugees and migrant workers are entering Belize each year from other Central American countries, mostly Guatemala and El Salvador. They are drawn by Belize's relaxed attitude toward homesteading, and they bring with them a strong tradition of slash-and-burn agriculture. Unfortunately, this *milpa* approach quickly drains nutrients from the shallow soil, and new trees must be cleared every few years to secure fresh farmland. Many refugees also hunt wild game in order to supplement their meager diets.

Equally significant, owners of large citrus, banana, pineapple, and sugarcane plantations are lobbying government ministries to change the status of several forest reserves to allow more large-scale agriculture. The citrus industry in particular has charged ahead in recent years, clearing vast tracts of pristine tropical forests. Meanwhile, poorly regulated logging and oil-drilling concessions have created significant devastation of the Belize environment in recent years.

ECONOMIC TRADE-OFFS

Belizeans pay the price for this kind of development in the fouling of their potable water by acidic, pesticide-laden runoff from citrus fields. The sugarcane industry has dumped nutrient-rich effluent into rivers and wetlands that had become important wildlife habitats and popular tourist attractions. The removal of natural vegetation is also a factor in local and regional climate changes, upsetting the cycles of rain and drought. In many areas, large-scale farmers are rapidly clearing forests to plant grain and other crops. Cattle ranchers are also eager to increase their territory.

In a nation that still cannot feed itself, it is very tempting to give in to pressures for more agricultural exploitation. In many instances, however, the government of Belize, along with enlightened individuals and members of various tourism organizations, is operating under the premise that there are more long-term gains to be realized through nature-based tourism than through nonsustainable agricultural and industrial development. Visitors won't pay to see cultivated orchards and fields or poorly planned housing projects, but they will keep coming back to explore tropical forests, jungle rivers, and coral reefs.

Yet, with the opportunities of tourism come fresh challenges. Such growth forces decisions about establishment of a better infrastructure of

*Immigrant homesteaders' huts are a common sight
along the Hummingbird Highway.*

roads, communications, hotels, police protection, and food distribution.
One longtime tour guide, Winston Seawell, has expressed specific concern about the need for better tourist facilities (or at least *some* facilities)
at his country's most frequently visited natural and archaeological destinations. Deterioration of cultural institutions and ancient Mayan ruins
is an ongoing problem. Meanwhile, promotion of tourism must be carried out in a way that benefits Belizeans and is not detrimental to the
very sites that foreigners are being lured to visit.

CONSERVATION SOLUTIONS

As one of the world's most environmentally aware countries, Belize
has already set a standard of behavior that speaks for itself in big
and small ways. The Belize EcoTourism Association, for instance,
has successfully implemented an "Adopt A Roadway" project that
has yielded a noticeable decline in litter. Later on in this book you'll
read about the Community Baboon Sanctuary, the Cockscomb
Basin Wildlife Sanctuary, the Crooked Tree Wildlife Sanctuary, the
Shipstern Nature Reserve, and the Río Bravo Conservation Area.

Ecofriendly Exports

Herbal remedies. Natural chewing gum. Coconut soap. Cashew candy. Palm nut jewelry. Dried jungle fruits. These are some of the new Belizean products now being exported by environmentally aware businesses in an effort to make the country's tropical forests pay their way (an alternative to cutting them down).

Besides earning a profit and preserving natural habitat, a top priority of Rainforest Rescue Ltd. is "making jobs for local, indigenous people," company spokesman Roger Taylor told Profiles *magazine in a 1996 interview. Rainforest Rescue pays those who live in or near the forest to gather materials in a way that doesn't unduly harm the ecosystem, thus providing an alternative to timber cutting, hunting, and slash-and-burn agriculture. Native nuts, berries, and fruits, for example, are collected, washed, and dried, then packed for sale as a "jungle trail mix." Similarly, the hard nut of the cohune palm is collected and carved to make buttons and earrings. Six percent of all revenue is donated to the Belize Audubon Society, which manages many of the country's national parks.*

Rainforest Rescue is one of a growing number of ecofriendly exporters in Belize, ranging from Rainforest Remedies (a producer of plant-derived health supplements)

These are just five of the many innovative examples of how the demands of conservation can be successfully balanced with the fundamental economic needs of local people.

An innovative project in the southern part of the country demonstrates such sensitivity in action. In the largely undeveloped Toledo District, Mayan villagers have opened thatch-roof guest houses for travelers. Others have opened their simple homes to visitors who want a *to Programme for Belize (involved in the sustainable harvesting of chicle to make chewing gum) to Emerald Forest (which makes Siempre Bella skin care products). Some of these cottages industries are actively involved in community outreach.*

"We're training them," Audrey Wallace, senior project coordinator of Programme for Belize (PFB) told Profiles, *"but we're not going to hold their hands for ten years." For example, the non-profit PFB has been helping residents of four villages near its 229,000-acre forest conservation and management area learn how to tap chicle resin from sapodilla trees without harming them. The chicle is then sold to local entrepreneurs who package it and sell it as "100-percent natural" chewing gum.*

Emerald Forest's cofounder, Kate Priest, says her company "is committed to being a model of social and environmental responsibility," noting that indigenous people are employed to sustainably wild-harvest the ingredients used in its products, which include extracts from a plant called Siempre Viva. Also, a portion of profits are donated to effective rainforest protection programs through the firm's Emerald Forest Fund.

Thanks to investment laws that encourage the influx of foreign capital, Belize is able to successfully marry sustainable development with green exports, while keeping much of its undeveloped land under official protection.

firsthand look at a subsistence farming culture that has persisted for centuries. You can read more about this in Chapter 9, Southern Belize.

Similar community-level approaches are proving to be key models for long-term protection of Belize's forests. The Friends of Five Blues was formed to manage the spectacular Five Blues Lake National Park, with its 200-foot-deep inland lake surrounded by some 4,200 acres of lush, broadleaf tropical forest, interwoven with

Kevin Schafer

*Envrionmental education is a required part
of the curriculum for Belize schoolchildren.*

an otherworldly labyrinth of limestone caves. The Friends of Five
Blues' complementary goal is to ensure that the local community
directs and benefits from natural history tourism and that the people
living nearby realize financial rewards from tourism-related enterprises. (See details in Chapter 7, Western Belize.)

WHAT THE FUTURE HOLDS

While Belize's record of conservation achievements is admirable—
especially for such a young and impoverished nation—there is a clear
need for financial support from around the world to perpetuate the
country's successes and implement new strategies.

On-the-ground local management of protected areas is a top priori-
ty. The list of areas that need more patrols and boundary enforcement
includes the Bladen Nature Reserve, Sarstoon-Temash National Park,
Punta Ycacos Forest Reserve, Laughingbird Caye National Park, Tapir
Mountain Nature Reserve, Chiquibul National Park, Caracol
Archaeology Reserve, Guanacaste National Park, Glover's Reef Marine
Reserve, Half Moon Caye National Monument, and Bacalar Chico
Marine Reserve/National Park, all described in this book.

The Belize government has taken an important pioneering step to generate funds for protected areas by establishing something called the Protected Areas Conservation Trust (PACT). PACT's stated purpose is to "encourage and promote the protection, conservation, and enhancement of the natural and cultural resources of Belize." Every air traveler is required to pay $7.50 as they leave the country, with those funds earmarked exclusively for conservation and protection of Belize's natural and cultural resources, including operation of its many national parks and nature preserves. Taken together, these small individual contributions by foreign visitors will have a powerful and positive impact.

The Mussel Creek Example

Even with its impressive track record, Belize enjoys such a world-class abundance of natural treasures that new opportunities still exist to protect representative ecosystems. For example, one of Belize's most important freshwater ecosystems is the Mussel Creek/Mucklehany Lagoon wetlands in central Belize, about 20 miles west of Belize City. Dora Weyer, conservation leader of the Belize Audubon Society, the Belize Center for Environmental Studies, and other environmental/ conservation groups, has been interested in protecting this rich habitat

Steele Wotkyns

Mussel Creek is one of the country's most pristine (and least protected) wetland ecosystems.

27

for years. In 1994, Weyer wrote a proposal to designate the area as a wildlife sanctuary, a proposal that has allies within the government, but as of 1997 had merited no official action.

The Mussel Creek drainage literally teems with life: water lilies cover the rippling surface of its slow-moving stream, roseate spoonbills create pink mosaics along the water's edge, wood storks soar in tight formation up the winding channel, endangered hickatee Central American river turtles and threatened Morelet's crocodiles wait along embankments for their prey, while belted kingfishers plunge from tall kapok trees to snag tiny minnows from the waterway. In all, 12 officially threatened or endangered species have been recorded in the Mussel Creek drainage, including the fun-loving, but endangered Central American river otter. Weyer reports that some 31 mammal species, 44 reptiles, and 314 bird species are known to the area. During a brief 1997 visit, we identified howler monkeys, Caribbean manatees, and 18 bird species. As much as any natural wonder in Belize, the Mussel Creek wetlands call out for protection.

When asked, local guides in nearby Flowers Bank, Burrell Boom, and Bermudian Landing are eager to take travelers to the Mussel Creek area. At present, tourism in this particular domain is neither asset nor threat. With support from Belizeans, foreign visitors, and a commitment of management funds, it's possible that this fragile ecosystem will yet be protected.

HOW YOU CAN HELP

If you're interested in lending your support to ongoing conservation projects, there are many practical things you can do to help the environmental movement in Belize. One is to visit, learn about, and support the innovative but struggling community conservation efforts described in this book. You might also contact the established conservation groups in Belize City and contribute to the work they are doing:

Belize Audubon Society, 12 N. Fort St., Belize City; 2-34988, *http://www.belizeaudubon.org.*

Belize Center for Environmental Studies, 55 Eve St., Belize City; 2-45545.

Belize Tropical Forest Studies, 92-3310, e-mail *tfs@bcsl.com.bz.*

The Programme for Belize, 2 S. Park St., Belize City; 2-75616, e-mail *pfbel@btl.net.*

Slate Creek Preserve, 92-3310, e-mail *tfs@bcsl.com.bz.*

Many of these organizations have newsletters that you can subscribe to and their work is often described in *ECO*, a bimonthly Belize eco-tourism magazine sold at Go Tees/Go Graphics in Belize City. Another good information source is the World Conservation Monitoring Centre, e-mail *info@wcmc.org.uk,* which regularly updates Worldwide Web summaries concerning conservation practices and tracks the status of endangered species in Belize and other countries.

HOW TO TRAVEL RESPONSIBLY

Even if you make no direct contact with any environmental groups, it is important to know that simply visiting the destinations described in this book makes you a part of ongoing efforts to save a precious part of our planet. By financially supporting and/or volunteering with the groups or needy communities of your choice, you empower them to keep working to protect the natural heritage of Belize (and the world).

If you use the services of a so-called "ecotourism" hotel, guide service, or travel operator, we urge you to take a careful look at their practices. Do they hire local guides and book guests into locally owned hotels? Are they actively involved in training, conservation, or supporting local communities or field research in Belize? Are they a member of the Belize EcoTourism Association and do they subscribe to BETA's code of ethics? Do they display the toucan emblem of Belize's environmentally responsible tourism operators? We suggest you ask such questions before booking your trip.

In the meantime, while you are in Belize, we hope you'll keep in mind these guidelines to responsible travel published by BETA:

1. **Stay on the Trail**: Don't trample delicate vegetation.

2. **Plants**: Do not remove or disturb them.

3. **Marine**: Do not stand, touch, or kick sand on coral reef systems because sand raised by fins can suffocate coral or lower its disease resistance. Gloves increase chances of contact with coral. Enjoy the view without your hands.

Richard Mahler

The upper Macal River is one of the most popular whitewater streams in Belize.

4. **Wildlife**: Maintain a minimum distance of 30 feet from wildlife; stay on the periphery of animal assemblages; never surround an animal or group of animals or come between parents and their young; never follow or harass birds or animals for the sake of a photograph; keep decibel levels low; listen to the sound of the jungle; be unobtrusive when viewing wildlife.

5. **Sustainability**: Local guides, landowners, and conservation representatives should tell you their plans to ensure the sustainable use of wildlife habitats as you participate together in implementing these plans.

6. **Waste Disposal**: All trash must be contained and carried back to a designated landfill; no littering is tolerated.

7. **Wilderness**: Trips to wilderness areas must be led by experienced, well-trained, responsible naturalists and guides.

8. **Souvenirs**: Do not buy any sea turtle products, or any other products from wild animals, even if it is incorporated in artwork.

Here is an item of our own that we would like to add to this roster:

9. **Participate**: Become a positive contributor to Belize's experiment in developing a new, responsible tourism ethic. You help such a country's conservation projects succeed by joining, by visiting, or by volunteering to participate in them. Your presence is itself a vote of confidence in the difficult decisions government and business leaders must make.

The margay is a tree-loving nocturnal cat.

FLORA AND FAUNA OF BELIZE

3

Thanks in part to its diverse topography, soil characteristics, and weather patterns, Belize is blessed with several of the world's richest habitats. No fewer than 4,000 different species of native flowering plants are found within its borders, along with about 700 species of trees and several hundred species of other plants.

Scientists are only now beginning to perform an exhaustive inventory of Belize's plants. The task is daunting: more than 70 percent of the country is under some kind of forest cover, and almost half of Belize's primary forest is still standing. (Happily, a major part of this forest enjoys some degree of government protection.)

In the animal kingdom, the numbers are even more staggering. Literally thousands of varieties of insects are native to the five major ecosystems of Belize, along with hundreds of mammals, reptiles, amphibians, and fish. Some of the rare or endangered species found here in relatively abundant numbers are the tapir, howler monkey, anteater, ocellated turkey, king vulture, Morelet's crocodile, sea turtle, manatee, and jaguar, the hemisphere's largest cat. *Checklist of the Birds of Belize*, a pamphlet published by the Carnegie Museum of Natural History, lists over 540 species that have been sighted here, including more than 200 migratory birds from North America who winter in the Tropics. In many parts of the inland forest, it is not unusual to see as many as 120 different birds over a period of as few as four or five days. And of the world's more than 90,000 butterfly species, a very large percentage are found here. (See Appendix B for a list of scientific names of plants and animals in this book.)

Part of this species diversity is a result of Belize's relatively small population and the pristine quality of its wilderness. Another reason for the incredible assemblages of flora and fauna found here is the variation in habitat zones. The basic ecological regions include: northern hardwood, southern hardwood, mountain pine ridge, coastal savanna and pine ridge, and mangroves and beaches. Within these categories, distinctions can be drawn based on rainfall amounts (varying widely from north to south), altitude (from sea level to nearly 4,000 feet), and soil types (from very poor to very fertile).

Scientists are still finding plants and animals in Belize which are completely new to science or previously unrecorded in Belize. One expedition into the Maya Mountains, for example, sighted a bird in the latter category dubbed the scaly-throated foliage gleaner. Several new species of amphibians and flowering plants have been found during the 1990s.

Rather than attempt an exhaustive discussion of Belizean ecosystems and their native inhabitants in this limited space, we will simply provide thumbnail sketches of some of Belize's most intriguing flora and fauna. Many of these have one or more colorful names used by locals. Among our favorites is an unusually prickly jungle palm tree known as the "give-and-take palm" or "poke no dah boy."

BIRDS

KEEL-BILLED TOUCAN

You'll see this brilliantly colored creature, designated the national bird of Belize, on signs and symbols throughout the country. (The toucan is probably better known in the United States as "the Fruit Loops® bird" because of its association with the ad campaign of a popular breakfast cereal.) The keel-billed toucan is fairly common in Belize and prefers to live in tall trees, particularly those that bear nuts or fruit. The bird tends to swoop low as it flies, owing to the weight of its canoe-shaped bill. The toucan's stubby wings seem undersized for such a big load. The red-tipped beak is apple green with a triangle of orange on top and a streak of powder blue below. The toucan has green around its eyes, yellow on its collar, red under its tail, and its legs and feet are bright blue.

Belize's most famous keel-billed toucan, "Rambo," lives at the

Belize Zoo. He'll introduce you to the distinctive toucan call, a froggy *creek-creek* that is usually made during that flapping, soaring glide from one big tree to the next.

JABIRU STORK

The jabiru is the largest flying bird in the Western Hemisphere, standing up to five feet tall and with a wingspan reaching up to ten feet or more. It is also one of the rarest birds in Central America. Besides its size, the jabiru can be identified by its massive, slightly turned-up black bill, its all-white wings and body feathers, and its bare black head, which has a wide, inflatable crimson band at the base of the neck. It feeds on fish, snails, frogs, and snakes.

In Belize, where the jabiru is fully protected, a population of about 30 storks nests during winter months along swamp edges and roadside pools, as well as in wet savannas and lowland pine ridges. Considered "rare" in Belize and "imperiled" in other parts of its range, Belize's jabirus return from Mexico around November to make their nests, usually at the tops of tall, secluded trees. Breeding continues until early April, when the birds begin migrating back to Mexico for the summer. Crooked Tree Wildlife

Kevin Schafer

The toucan is Belize's national bird and conservation symbol.

Sanctuary is a favorite breeding ground of this enormous bird, and its nests are carefully protected. The jabiru is most commonly seen in Belize from December through March.

PARROTS

Seven species of parrots, one species of parakeet, and one species of macaw make Belize their home. Parrots have few enemies in the jungle except for larger predators, who tend to eliminate the weakest or most vulnerable birds. A far bigger threat is posed by humans, who continue to destroy the parrot's forest habitat, capture it for commercial purposes, or even kill it for food.

Red-lored parrot

Kevin Schafer

The capture of young parrots usually does considerable damage to the environment, since nesting trees are often cut down in the hope that chicks will somehow survive the fall. The species captured in greatest numbers here is the yellow-headed parrot, prized in North America as a fluent and easily trained "talker." Other vocal members of the same family are the Aztec (or olive-throated) parakeet and mealy (or blue-crowned) parrot. The latter mates for life and almost always flies in a two-by-two formation with its partner. These species are quite social and like to live near others of their kind.

The common names of parrots are inspired by easily identifiable head markings ("lore" refers to the area between eyes and beak, "crown" is the top of the head, and "front" is the forehead, while "hood" and "head" are self-explanatory). The less gregarious parrots found in Belize are the brown-hooded, red-lored, yellow-lored, yellow-headed, white-fronted, and white-crowned. Only sharp-eyed birders are usually able to tell the latter two species apart.

Like many tropical animals (and people), parrots usually nap during the heat of the day and are most often seen during later afternoon and early morning feeding periods. The birds roost in groups overnight.

SCARLET MACAW

One of the rarest birds in Belize is the scarlet macaw, the third-largest of the world's 16 surviving macaw species. It is one of eight such species in danger of extinction throughout much of its range, which extends from subtropical Mexico south to Bolivia.

A macaw sighting is an unforgettable experience. Mature birds, locally referred to as parrots, are over two feet tall and adorned with brilliant plumage, particularly bright red wing feathers speckled with dabs of yellow, orange, and blue.

The greatest threat to this magnificent bird is the destruction of its forest habitat, nest-robbing for the wild bird trade, and killing for meat and feathers. The first systematic study of scarlet macaws in Belize was carried out by the Center for the Study of Tropical Birds. It concluded that the bird has a relatively confined range in the dense central forests of the country, extending from the Maya Mountains divide, north to the Mountain Pine Ridge. A few individuals and small flocks have been seen in other areas from time to time. In recent years, however, no more than 30 birds have ever been seen at any given time or location.

"It is certain that the status of the scarlet macaw in Belize is precarious," concluded the final report of the Center. "Not only are there the persistent threats of habitat destruction . . . logging operations, plant collectors, etc., but the threat of wild birds being caught for the pet trade continues," despite the latter's illegality. There's at least some good news to counter this pessimistic outlook, however. In 1997 it was reported that scarlet macaws had begun to reinhabit the Cockscomb Basin, after disappearing for many years. The absence of hunting and logging in this wildlife sanctuary has apparently restored food trees favored by the birds and removed the threats once posed by humans.

BLUE-CROWNED MOTMOT

This beautiful and relatively large bird is sometimes called "Good Cook," because its deep-throated, *hoot-hoot* call (usually heard at dawn or dusk) sounds like those two words. It is also distinguished by its indigo head feathers and long tail. The latter acquires an oddly pointed shape through removal of central feathers by preening and wear. While the blue-crowned motmot is fairly common, its cousin, the keel-billed motmot, is one of the rarest birds in Central America, and only a few sightings have been documented. The bird is believed to be extinct in Mexico. There have been only two known sightings in Guatemala, and until mid-summer of 1994, the keel-billed mot-mot had not been seen in Belize for more than eight years. A recent sighting was made at the Tapir Mountain Nature Reserve, and there may be other individuals in remote protected areas.

MAMMALS

JAGUAR

The jaguar was among the most revered animals of the ancient Maya, and even today this jungle cat commands great respect among Belizeans, who often refer to it as a tiger, or *el tigre*. Up to six feet long and weighing as much as 250 pounds, its likeness turns up on modern T-shirts as well as eroded Mayan ornaments. Originally found from the southwestern United States to Argentina, the jaguar (largest cat in the Western Hemisphere) has become extinct or endangered throughout its range. In Mesoamerica, only a few hundred jaguar are believed to remain. In Belize, however, the animal is still seen in many areas, even within a 30-minute drive of Belize City. This nocturnal predator feeds primarily on peccary, paca, fish, or deer, along with an occasional bird, lizard, or turtle.

Kevin Schafer

The jaguar is the largest of five cat species in Belize.

Contrary to local belief, jaguars will not attack humans unless provoked and usually do not kill livestock unless their natural habitat has been destroyed and their natural prey replaced by cattle. The respected *Neotropical Rainforest Mammals* field guide recommends that humans never try to run from a jaguar, since fleeing may give it cause to chase. Human encroachment continues to limit the cats' territory, and hunters, operating illegally, occasionally kill perfectly healthy animals in Belize for their hides.

Jaguars are very territorial, ranging over vast areas of forest and savanna. The male, a solitary creature who partners with one female at a time, marks the boundaries of his kingdom with tree scratches and ground scrapings. The other four native cats of Belize are the puma, ocelot, margay, and jaguarundi.

BAIRD'S TAPIR

Called a "mountain cow" by locals, this largely nocturnal species is the national animal of Belize. Although it can grow as big as a small cow, the tapir is more closely related to the horse and hippopotamus. Still fairly plentiful here, the Baird's tapir has almost disappeared from the rest of its native Central America and Mexico, earning it a place on the endangered species list. It spends almost 90 percent of its waking hours feeding on fruits, browse, and grasses. Despite the fact that tapirs have thick hides and a disagreeable flavor, their ranks have been thinned by native hunters, many of whom mistakenly believe these docile vegetarians will attack and kill their domestic animals.

The tapir is adaptable to almost any Belizean environment, but today it is most plentiful in mountain forests where there is water nearby. Although it can weigh up to 650 pounds, the Baird's tapir is surprisingly agile and has splayed feet for navigating mud holes. The herbivore's long, flexible upper lip and strong molars are well-suited for foraging and swallowing twigs, nuts, and other tough plant tissues. The tapir has excellent senses of smell and hearing, although its eyesight is weak. The docile beasts are usually solitary and tend to avoid confrontation by steering clear of other large animals. Perhaps the best-known Baird's tapir is named April and lives in the Belize Zoo, where she has become both a favorite of visiting schoolchildren and a kind of national mascot.

DOLPHINS

Bottlenose dolphins are common off the coast of Belize, and research is now being done on these marine mammals at Blackbird Caye on the Turneffe atoll. Thanks to the media exploits of Flipper, the bottlenose is the most well-known dolphin species in the world. Individuals may be gray or whitish in color and can grow up to ten feet long. These very social animals can often be seen riding the bow wave of powerboats. They breathe air and give birth to live young, which they subsequently nurse.

The complexity of the social interactions among dolphins, scientists believe, may help explain the evolution of their large brains. The creatures emit a variety of complex buzzing, whistling, and clicking sounds that bounce off objects like sonar echoes and enable dolphins to "see" those objects. This process is called *echolocation.* The sound beams can apparently even penetrate living tissue, which seems to allow male dolphins to "see" when a female is approaching fertility.

Dolphins travel widely and have been seen along the Belize coast in almost every marine environment, including lagoons and jungle rivers. They sometimes show up off the coast of San Pedro, Caye Caulker, Hopkins, and Placencia, where they can easily be seen from the shore.

REPTILES

HICKATEE

The Central American river turtle is making one of its last stands along the waterways of Belize. Locally referred to as the hickatee, it can be found only here and in the most isolated parts of southern Mexico and northern Guatemala. Prized as a food source, this turtle spends almost its entire life in the water, except when it lays its eggs in rotting vegetation along the riverbanks, where the eggs incubate themselves. The hickatee is brown or olive drab on its back, with a cream-colored underbelly. Large males weigh as much as 50 pounds.

Unfortunately, the animal seeks out fish and aquatic plants by night, then sleeps or floats much of the day, making it an easy target for human hunters.

SEA TURTLES

Three of the world's eight species of sea turtles are known to nest in Belize: the green, loggerhead, and hawksbill. Although the situation is changing, many are still taken for their flesh, eggs, and shells.

Increasingly, turtles are being kept from their traditional nesting areas by fences, buildings, people, pets, bright lights, and loud noises. For these reasons, all three species found in Belize have been declared endangered. Visitors are urged to respect the nesting season (June 1 to August 31), refrain from buying turtle meat or products, and avoid throwing plastic bags into the sea in which turtles can easily (and fatally) become entangled.

No one knows how the female loggerhead turtle, called *lagra* in Belize, finds her way back to nesting beaches as many as 50 years after leaving that same stretch of sand to spend her life in the sea. Yet that is exactly what happens when this large turtle (up to 300 pounds) returns to Belize to lay up to 100 leathery eggs at a time. After a two-month incubation, tiny babies emerge from the shells and make a mad dash for the water. Most are caught en route by birds, crabs, lizards, and humans. Less than 5 percent typically survive to reproduce.

The green turtle is an even larger species, measuring up to four feet in length and weighing up to 600 pounds. Because its greenish meat and tender eggs are considered delicacies, this turtle has been hunted extensively. It also sometimes gets caught in shrimp nets while surfacing from the sea grass beds where it feeds.

One of the smaller sea turtles is the hawksbill, which gets its name from its sharp, hooked beak. The animal's top shell is covered with multicolored scales that have long been popular for use in combs, eyeglass frames, hair clips, and jewelry. The hawksbill is often killed before it reaches maturity, which has had a devastating effect on the species' ability to reproduce.

BASILISKS AND IGUANAS

Once you've seen a basilisk in action, you'll know why Belizeans have labeled it "the Jesus Christ lizard." The prehistoric-looking animal moves with such great speed—often on its hind legs—through its riverside habitat, that it seems to be able to skim right across the surface of a creek or river without sinking, disappearing into foliage on the opposite bank. Researchers have determined that the reptile actually forms a bubble of air beneath its feet that prevents it from sinking; extra flaps of skin across the toes of its enlarged rear feet make this water-walking trick possible.

While these omnivorous reptiles appear fierce—like a miniature *Tyrannosaurus rex*—they prefer to munch on leaves, flowers, and fruit in their favorite trees (often a giant ficus), in addition to the occasional insect and bird. They can be distinguished by their ridged backs, ranging in color from yellow-brown to muted gray, and (among males) reddish throat sacs. Local people love to eat the raw eggs of the basilisk, and the creatures are becoming scarce in areas where pesticides are used. Predatory birds are another enemy. The dominant males are quite territorial and can be seen perched on high tree limbs, surveying their domains along inland waterways.

Two iguanid species also live in Belize: the green iguana, also called the "bush-chicken," and the black or land iguana, locally called a "wish-willy." These creatures spend most of the day sunbathing on

Kevin Schafer and Martha Hill

The iguana is a popular game animal for rural Belizeans.

high branches and are very territorial, responding to trespassers with repeated patterns of head-bobbing. Iguanas (and their eggs) are easy prey for hungry villagers, as well as for birds, snakes, and coati. Wish-willies are commonly encountered on the offshore cayes of Belize, where they frequent vegetation near beaches and mangrove forests. Because so many iguana are killed each year by Belizeans for food, several groups are now raising them in captivity and releasing them in the wild to restore depleted populations.

FER-DE-LANCE

Variously known as the yellow-jaw tommygoff, *barba amarilla,* and *tres minutos,* the fer-de-lance is a nocturnal pit viper related to the water moccasin and tropical rattlesnake. Because of its fast-acting venom, it is considered to be among the world's deadliest snakes. There are many reliable reports in Belize of individuals who have died soon after stumbling on the animal in the bush. However, unless it's provoked or you are very unlucky, the vipers will generally avoid you and stick to birds, rats, and other small mammals.

The fer-de-lance is at home in any part of Belize, including cities, and can be vicious if it does decide to attack. Adults can reach eight feet in length, enabling them to strike from a coiled position.

Their two retractable fangs are the largest of any snake, in proportion to size. Keen awareness of smell and temperature enables the fer-de-lance to accurately pinpoint warm bodies in the dark, when it is most likely to be active. It is easily identified by its arrow-shaped head, diamond-patterned back, and thick-set body. If you are bitten, seek medical help at once. The best prevention is wearing boots, since most fer-de-lance bites are in the feet and ankles.

If you hear a rattle as you approach an unfamiliar snake, it is probably not a fer-de-lance but a tropical rattlesnake (or *cascabel*), the only rattlesnake species in Belize. It is the most poisonous of all rattlers and can grow up to seven feet in length.

FISH

Squirrel-fish are among the most numerous of fishes in the dimly lit recesses of the coral reef and their distinctive large eyes provide exceptional visual acuity in the dark. Nocturnal feeders, these fish sometimes leave their daytime shelters to forage for small crustaceans.

The four-eyed butterfly fish, another common reef species, is so named for the false eyespots on either side of its tail. These markings are designed to confuse predators.

Among the coral you will also frequently see the queen angelfish, easy to identify with its brilliant yellow, blue, and violet colors. Crawling and feeding on coral branches are such sea snails as the flamingo tongue, identified by its black-bordered, leopard-like spots. The scarlet-colored fire sponge is another interesting reef resident; it is harmful to touch but has yielded eight antibiotics for the biomedical industry.

TREES

PALMS

The cohune palm, widespread throughout Belize, is one of the forest community's most useful members. Its fronds are used as thatch in roofs, and a valuable oil can be extracted from its fruit. Husks from the tree's palm nuts make excellent fuel, and the nut meat can be pounded into a flour. The nuts are very hard and can be carved into clothing buttons and even jewelry. The cohune was highly regarded by the ancient Maya, who considered it a symbol of fertility. Because

Belize guide standing before a mahogany, the country's national tree and symbol.

of the palm's many practical uses, it is almost always spared when forests are cut down for subsistence agriculture.

Dominant in low-lying marshes and along riverbanks are palmetto palms, which can grow to great heights and provide fronds used in traditional house construction.

Coconut palms are not native to the region but were introduced on the cayes and coastal strip in the late 18th and early 19th centuries as a commercial crop. A few coconuts are still harvested for their oil, meat, and husks (an excellent fuel for making charcoal), but the industry has pretty much died out in Belize.

MANGROVES

Almost the entire coastline of Belize, including the fringes of its many cayes, are covered by dense stands of black, white, and red mangrove, with the latter species dominating. Different types of mangroves are adapted to varying degrees of salinity, and you will notice them changing as you go away from sources of saltwater. While 90 percent of the world's original mangrove forests have been destroyed, Belize can boast that 90 percent of its mangrove habitat remains intact.

The ancient Maya made extensive use of the mangrove wetlands, as evidenced by the use of crocodile and manatee images in their artwork. Mangroves as tall as 100 feet or more can be seen along some waterways, such as the Toledo District's Temash River within the Temash/Sarstoon Nature Reserve. A more accessible protected area in which to celebrate and visit mangroves is the Burdon Canal Nature Reserve, just west of Belize City.

Although these tangled saltwater thickets have traditionally been despised by settlers, who often cleared them as quickly as possible, they protect shorelines from erosion during storms and provide an irreplaceable nursery for small fish and crustaceans. Snorkeling near mangrove roots often is more rewarding, in terms of marine life, than swimming in open water or near coral reefs. Above the waterline, visitors can see egrets, herons, ibises, roseate spoonbills, pelicans, frigate birds, raptors, and boobies amid the tangled roots and branches. Coatimundis, crocodiles, anteaters, tapirs, jaguars, raccoons, and boa constrictors are also found in these wetland areas.

MAHOGANY

The national tree of Belize has never been very common and, after centuries of logging, it is even more rare. Its beautiful dark wood has long been prized for use in fine furniture and cabinetry. This tropical hardwood tree—more properly referred to as the Honduran or bigleaf mahogany—is what attracted some of the first European settlers to Belize, and it is displayed prominently on the country's coat of arms. It has a reddish-brown bark and can grow to over 100 feet tall (although this takes at least 70 years). A mature mahogany will be supported at its base by great buttresses that spread up to 20 feet across the forest floor. Look for its pear-shaped seed pods and small whitish flowers.

Very little mahogany is exported from Belize these days, although some entrepreneurs are cultivating the trees commercially. Several have been planted in front of the visitors center at Guanacaste National Park, near Belmopan. Another good place to see a mahogany is in the Río Bravo Conservation and Management Area, northwest of Belmopan, where tropical forest ecologist Nick Brokaw supervises research on harvesting methods that allow the tree to replace itself. Brokaw's methods, controversial among some environmentalists, include removing trees that compete with the native mahogany for sunlight, a practice that attempts to duplicate the natural thinning process ordinarily carried out by hurricanes.

A kayaker takes on a jungle river.

SPECIAL INTERESTS & ACTIVITIES

4

For enthusiasts of diving, snorkeling, fishing, natural history, archaeology, or simply taking it easy, a trip to Belize presents almost unlimited opportunities. For the most part, Belize *is* the outdoors. Those expecting lively nightclubs, gourmet restaurants, and sophisticated shopping will probably be disappointed by what they find. The mind-boggling variety and seemingly endless cycles of nature are the main event here, although the human domains of the ancient Maya and modern Belizeans are definitely worth seeing.

Although Belize is best known for water-based sports such as fishing and diving, the range of activities is continually expanding, with an emphasis on outdoor pursuits that take full advantage of the country's tremendous natural resources, such as hiking, birding, caving, and mountain biking.

For specific details on experienced guides and professional services catering to these specialized interests, please review the outfitter names, addresses, and phone numbers listed at the end of each section. In our special interest listings, note that some businesses offer a service in more than one category. All seven-digit and 800 numbers are in the United States and all six-digit numbers are in Belize, unless otherwise indicated.

DIVING AND SNORKELING

In 1989, *Skin Diver* magazine described Belize as "one of the western Caribbean's premier dive destinations," praising its unspoiled tropical waters, diversity of marine life, and easy access. Today, many of the publication's readers might argue that Belize has since become the most highly regarded diving spot in all the Caribbean, and certainly one of the top five scuba destinations in the Western Hemisphere.

With all those coastal waterways to choose from—along with literally thousands of little-known reefs, sand bores, islands, and marine formations—there is something here for every special interest and level of ability. Belize's offshore waters are consistently calm, warm (averaging 80 degrees Fahrenheit), shallow enough to make long dives pleasurable, and amazingly clear—up to 150 feet visibility is common in outlying waters. Closer to shore, visibilities usually range from 50 to 150 feet.

Water temperatures range from about 74 degrees Fahrenheit in winter to 86 degrees Fahrenheit in summer. A bodysuit is adequate much of the year, and you never need more than a warm-water wet suit for thermal insulation. Your body temperature is 98.6 degrees Fahrenheit, however, and low-grade hypothermia can set in if you stay in the water long enough without a break or some kind of protection.

In order to fully experience the best of what Belize has to offer—such as viewing deep-water gorgonians, black-coral forests, and the most exotic tropical fish—underwater explorers have three basic options. First, they may head for one of the more remote island hotels or resorts. Good choices include one of the several tourist operations on the Turneffe Islands, Glover's Reef, Lighthouse Reef, Spanish Lookout Caye, Placencia, or South Water Caye. Second, they may sign on with one of the several live-aboard dive boats shuttling among Belize's many uninhabited islands and isolated reef structures. And third, they may charter a boat, individually or as part of a larger group, so as to have maximum flexibility in destination and schedule. Any of these choices can be easily accomplished with the help of a local travel agent, dive shop, or large hotel.

Obviously, trade-offs are inherent in each selection. The less-accessible lodges are relatively expensive and usually require a minimum stay of six nights. Live-aboard dive boats are also somewhat costly, with fixed schedules and routes that generally exclude the Belize interior. The expenses involved in chartering a private boat can also add up quickly, and the trip may be limited by the abilities of craft and crew.

Klaus Eiberle

Snorkeling amid brain coral off the barrier reef

At the end of this section you'll find a comprehensive list of specialists involved in the three types of diving vacations just described. For further details, we suggest you contact these sources directly for advice on the most appropriate option. Keep in mind that many dive resorts also cater to anglers, so it is feasible to combine both pleasures in a single Belizean vacation. Examples include Maya Landings, Blue Marlin Lodge, Ramon's Village, Blackbird Caye Resort, Wippari Caye Lodge, Ranguana Reef Lodge, and Manta Reef Resort. Such operators usually have special rates for nondiving and nonfishing travelers as well as off-season visitors.

Diving for All Levels of Experience

For those with little or no open water experience, diving around Ambergris Caye, Caye Caulker, Placencia, and the Hol Chan Marine Reserve will likely provide more than enough variation in underwater scenery and marine life. These areas are usually calm and well-patrolled, with an abundance of marine life.

Although there is much to see close to Ambergris and Caulker, the experienced diver or snorkeler will probably want to go even farther afield, exploring areas of the barrier reef that have not suffered as much habitat damage at the hands of commercial fishermen and tourists. Many small species of fish, crustacean, sponge, fan, and coral inhabit the more well-traveled areas, but such larger and more timid creatures as turtles and grouper are notably absent. Among the walls, spur-and-groove canyons, and reef systems of more distant destinations you'll see eagle rays, barracuda, jewfish, groupers, turnicates, sponges, and several species of shark. Schools of amberjacks and sergeant majors are common. Overall, it's not unusual to count 50 or 60 fish species on a single dive, along with dozens of species of hard and soft coral, sea whips, anemones, urchins, fans, sponges, and gorgonia.

Among the many other favored dive spots are Socorrito Point and Mexico Rocks, both near Ambergris Caye, and The Elbow, off the southern tip of the Turneffe Islands. Glover's Reef and Lighthouse Reef also are full of excellent dive spots, especially in waters where the current stirs up plenty of oxygen and food sources for fish. There are a number of shipwrecks suited for diving at these outer atolls as well. Some of the better diving locations in southern Belize include North Spot (outside the Silk Cayes), Southern Moho Caye, and Laughingbird Caye.

If you're headed for the three atolls beyond the barrier reef you'll see even more variety of marine flora and fauna. Fortunately the circular structure of the atolls makes it possible to always find refuge on a leeward side or amid interior patch reefs when winds and seas kick up.

What to Bring

Be sure to bring your NAUI or PADI scuba certification card; reputable operators will not accommodate your scuba requests without it. While you can rent any necessary gear in Belize, it's always better to bring your own masks, wet suits, and other items that you've been fitted for and are used to. Some resorts only supply weights and tanks in their packages; ask what's provided before you leave home. TACA airlines is especially good about stowing diving equipment.

Where to Arrange a Dive Trip

Most of the major hotels, especially those on Ambergris Caye, offer one or more of these dive activities, plus whatever related equipment may be required. The Fiesta Hotel (formerly Ramada Royal Reef) and Belize Dive Connection in Belize City, Belize Yacht Club and Ramon's Village on Ambergris Caye, Maya Landings on Moho Caye, Rum Point Inn in Placencia, Turneffe Island Lodge on Caye Bokel, St. George's Lodge on St. George's Caye, and Blue Marlin Lodge on South Water Caye are also good places to inquire about diving trips and other water-related sports.

Telephone service to the Belize mainland and the developed areas of Ambergris Caye and Caye Caulker is good, and you can dial dive resorts directly from the United States and Canada. Most of the outlying islands can be reached only by VHF marine-band radio. As in the United States, Channels 16 and 68 are the standard hailing frequencies. Live-aboard boats and charter craft also stand by on Channel 78. Many resorts now have two-way radio telephones.

Where to Arrange a Snorkel Trip

Although most dive boats and diving resorts happily accommodate snorkelers and can easily supply any necessary equipment, it may be both easier and cheaper to arrange personalized day trips and hire your own boat operator. This is most easily done at hotels that have their own marinas, such as the Ft. George, Bellevue, Fiesta Hotel, and Sea Breeze (Ambergris Caye). Local fishermen and guides are often willing to drop off snorkelers and swimmers in good locations, then pick them up a few hours later. Small sandy cayes—notably Congrejo, Goff's, Rosario, Montego, English, and Rendezvous—are especially recommended. Even on the more active islands of Ambergris, Caulker, and St. George's, plenty of nearby reef—away from populated areas and traffic lanes—offers an astonishing array of marine life.

The 45-foot catamaran *Stingray*, based in Belize City, is recommended by experienced snorkelers. Contact owner/operators Michael and Donna Hill through the Fiesta Hotel. Another snorkel-only boat is operated by Ecosummer Expeditions.

Where to Learn to Dive

Some of the better places to receive scuba instruction are Coral Beach Hotel & Dive Club and Amigos del Mar in Ambergris Caye; Second Nature Divers on Tobacco Caye; Frenchie's Dive Service and Belize Diving Service in Caye Caulker; and Manta Reef, Glover's Reef, and Hugh Parkey's Belize Dive Connection in Belize City. We have also heard excellent reports about the Living Reef Dive Center on South Water Caye and Glover's Reef. It usually takes at least four days to complete a PADI or NAUI certification course, with prices ranging from $225 to $400 per person.

Specialty Diving

Night diving and cave diving are popular in Belize, and the major dive specialists can provide necessary guides and maps, along with lights

Diving the Blue Hole

One of the most famous and popular dive spots in Belize is the Blue Hole (not to be confused with an inland and very different Blue Hole that's the focus of a national park). Located about 3 hours from the Ambergris Caye at Lighthouse Reef, this Blue Hole is an enormous limestone sinkhole, some 412 feet deep and 300 feet wide, and surrounded by a shallow coral crust. This monstrous depression—and the flooded caverns that extend from its sides—was the subject of a Jacques Cousteau documentary some years ago and reportedly remained one of Cousteau's favorite dive spots. The walls are vertical for the first 125 feet, then widen into stalactite-adorned passages. This is a fairly challenging dive because of its depth, but the rewards are a chance to see some of the larger sea creatures that cruise the Blue Hole's cobalt blue waters.

Day trips to the Blue Hole can be arranged through, among others, Out Island Divers and Fantasea Watersports on Ambergris Caye, or from the nearby Lighthouse Reef Resort on Northern Two Caye.

and other gear. Night dives at Hol Chan are a treat, often including glimpses of black-tip shark, lemon shark, squid, eels, and octopus.

You also may want to explore the marine caverns here, some of the largest in the world. Frenchie's and Belize Diving Services on Caye Caulker; Bottom Time Dive Shop, Amigos del Mar, and Reef Divers Limited on Ambergris Caye; Turneffe Lodge on Caye Bokel; and Kitty's Place or the Rum Point Inn in Placencia are all highly recommended.

Live-Aboard Dive Boats

From Caye Caulker, an outfit called Sea-Ing Is Belizing offers excursions that last up to eight days and include the outer atolls and reef-structures. Your live-aboard vessel is a 28-foot sailboat. Nearby

Richard Mahler

A Belizean guide hands out snorkeling equipment off South Water Caye.

Ambergris Caye boasts a number of well-equipped, diesel-powered dive boats, as does Placencia. Popular live-aboards based in Belize City include the 36-passenger *Rembrandt van Rijn,* 20-passenger *Wave Rider,* and 14- to 18-passenger *Belize Aggressor I* (and *II*). All of these vessels are equipped with diving platforms, tank racks, freshwater rinses, and other services.

Photo Processing
For underwater color photo processing, try Wade Bevier at Placencia's Rum Point Inn (which also operates the 42-foot, 12-passenger *Auriga* custom dive cruiser). James Beveridge on Caye Caulker and Joe Miller on Ambergris Caye also provide processing and underwater camera rental.

Equipment and Boat Rental
Rental of a full complement of scuba gear generally starts at about $45 for a single-tank day, with an additional $75 and up for two tanks worth of diving around the barrier reef. Dive trips to Lighthouse Reef and other popular atoll dive sites start at about $200 per day per person. For day trips to Lighthouse, Ambergris-

Diving Safety

*Once in Belize, divers and snorkelers should not enter the
water before identifying its possible hazards. Besides ever-
fragile, living coral polyps, which should not be touched or
stepped on for reasons of ecology as well as health, there
are the usual urchins, anemones, jellyfish, and stingrays to
look out for. Fire worms (also called bristle worms) and certain types of sponges can cause a burning sensation if
brushed against, and the aptly named scorpion fish will
sting if stepped on. The sinister-looking barracuda and nurse
shark cruise Belize's reefs by the hundreds, but will not
attack unless deliberately provoked or drawn by the scent of
fresh food or blood (i.e., from spearfishing). Definitely don't
pull the nurse shark's tail. Dolphins, also, generally prefer
not to be touched, especially on certain sensitive spots. In
general, it is best not to feed fish underwater. Every species
is hungry, and some, such as the moray eel, have teeth
sharp enough to remove a finger or two. A good pair of
booties, fins, or Patagonia Reef Walkers will help reduce the
risk of foot injuries. As a rule, it's not a good idea to dive or
snorkel alone, or to dive or snorkel after drinking alcohol.*

*Snorkelers must remember that the sun is beating
down on them despite the fact that they're in the water.*

based **Out Island Divers,** has been particularly recommended by experienced divers.

Overnight trips on snorkel-only boats start at about $125 per person, with charters about $20 higher, based on a two-person minimum. Day trips start at around $40.

It's a good idea to thoroughly examine any rental equipment before heading offshore. You should also ask around before hiring a

Those without a tan will want to apply (and reapply!) waterproof sunblock and perhaps wear a T-shirt. Check the location of your boat and companions frequently, and if you're traveling with your own kayak make sure you are tied off to dead coral or tie a lead rope to your wrist.

Medical experts recommend that beginning or infrequent divers over age 35 get a physical exam before diving, preferably from a physician who is familiar with the sport. Among older divers, one out of every four fatalities involves cardiovascular problems. Other conditions that should preclude diving, at any age, are severe asthma, seizure disorders, insulin-dependent diabetes, and any disease that could result in a loss of consciousness.

Divers should always be aware of the risks of decompression sickness, or "the bends," caused by entrapment of nitrogen bubbles in the bloodstream. It is treatable by oxygen therapy or by spending time in a decompression chamber, but decompression chamber treatments typically run $400 an hour, and only one unit is available in Belize (on Ambergris Caye, funded by a tax on tank refills). Because aircraft cabins are pressurized to the equivalent of about 8,000 feet, it is strongly recommended that scuba divers not fly for at least 12 hours, preferably 24 hours, after a dive.

diving instructor, since the level of expertise varies considerably. And do not let anyone try to rent you a surfboard in Belize: except during hurricanes, surf is nonexistent here.

Advance Reading

Before departure, we also recommend that serious water sports enthusiasts check one or more of the specialty magazines and guidebooks that profile Belize on a regular basis. These are often available at large dive shops, sporting goods stores, or newsstands. There are several good guidebooks specializing in underwater sports off the coast of Belize, among them *Diving Belize*, by Neal Middleton, Aqua Quest Publishing and the *Diving and Snorkeling Guide to Belize*, by Franz O. Meyer, Pisces Publications.

Diving and Snorkeling Outfitters

Amigos del Mar Dive Shop, Box 53, San Pedro, Ambergris Caye; 26-2706, fax 26-2648. Complete dive shop.

Barbachano Tours, 9500 S. Dadeland Blvd., #71, Miami, FL 33156; (800) 327-2254. Dive packages from the United States.

Belize Dive Center, San Pedro, Ambergris Caye, 26-2797, U.S.; (305) 938-0860. Dive packages, instruction; located at Belize Yacht Club.

Belize Dive Connection, Box 1818, Belize City; 2-34526 or (888) 223-5403, e-mail *fortst@btl.net*. Dive packages and PADI instruction, marine ecology tours.

Belize Diving Service, Caye Caulker; 22-2217, or marine VHF Channel 68. Complete dive shop, rental and instruction.

Blackline Marine Service, Box 332, Mile 2 Northern Highway, Belize City; 2-44155, fax 2-31975, marine VHF Channel 70. Complete dive shop, hull and engine repairs, fishing/diving and sight-seeing charters, marina with fuel, water, and ice.

Blue Marlin Lodge, South Water Caye, P.O. Box 21, Dangriga; 5-22296, fax 5-22296. Full-service diving and fishing resort.

Bottom Time Dive Shop, San Pedro, Ambergris Caye; 26-2348, fax 26-2821. Dive shop, scuba instruction, night diving, sailing charters, equipment rental; located in Sun Breeze Hotel.

Caribbean Charter Services, Mile 5 Northern Highway, Belize City; 2-45814. Offering boat charters, car rental, diving and fishing tours.

Coral Beach Hotel and Dive Club, San Pedro, Ambergris Caye; 2-62013 or 2-62001. Packages for snorkelers, divers, fishermen, beachcombers.

Frenchie's Diving Services, Caye Caulker; 22-2111 or 22-2234. Fishing and diving guides, PADI instruction.

Harrison Cadle, Caye Caulker; 22-2263. Guided snorkeling and manatee trips.

Lighthouse Reef Resort, Northern Two Caye, Lighthouse Reef, Box 26, Belize City. Complete fishing and diving services.

The Living Reef Diving Center, 8 Magoon St., Dangriga; 5-22214, (800) 548-5843, e-mail tread@btl.net. Low-cost dive packages off Long Caye (Glovers Reef); also from South Water Caye.

Manta Resort, Glover's Reef, Box 215, 3 Eyre St., Belize City; 2-31895 or (800) 342-0053, marine VHF Channel 70. Dive and fishing resort on 12-acre island.

Maya Landings, Box 459, Belize City; 25-2002, fax 025-2298. Complete dive shop and diving resort on Moho Caye.

Out Island Divers, Box 7, San Pedro, Ambergris Caye; 2-62151, (800) BLUE-HOLE. Dive boat specialists.

Pisces Dive Service, Mike and Beverly McCarty, Placencia; 6-23183. Certified NAUI and NASDS scuba instruction, photography services.

Placencia Dive Shop, Ran Villanueva, Placencia; 6-22027. Complete dive shop, transportation to reef and atolls; also bicycle rentals, river trips, kayaking.

Reef Divers Ltd., Ramon's Reef Resort, San Pedro, Ambergris Caye; 2-62371, fax 26-2028. Complete dive shop.

Ricardo's Adventure Tours, Caye Caulker; 2-22087. River trips, island hopping, fishing, diving, snorkeling.

Robert Blease, Caye Caulker; 22-2154. Guided snorkeling and manatee trips.

Rothschild Travel Consultants, 900 West End Ave., Suite 1B, New York, NY 10025; (800) 359-0747. Diving and fishing packages, adventure trips.

Scuba Tours, 5 Paterson Ave., Little Falls, NJ 07424; (800) 526-1394, fax (201) 256-0591. Dive trips, live-aboard packages.

Sea & Explore, 1809 Carol Sue Ave., Suite E, Gretna, LA 70056; (800) 345-9786, fax (504) 366-9986. Diving and fishing trips; represents several live-aboard dive boats.

Sea Masters Company, Ltd., Ambergris Caye, Box 59, Belize City; 26-2173, fax 26-2028. Fishing and diving services.

Sea Safaris, 3770 Highland Ave., Suite 102, Manhattan Beach, CA 90266; (800) 821-6670 or (213) 546-2464. Dive trips, live-aboard diving packages.

Second Nature Divers, Dangriga; 5-37038 or 2-72109, e-mail divers@btl.net. PADI "Discover Scuba" and open-water courses off Columbus and Tobacco Cayes, special trips to Shark's Cave/the Black Hole. Accommodations with Island Camps, Tobacco Caye.

Sun Breeze Beach Hotel, San Pedro, Ambergris Caye; 2-62347, fax 2-62346. Dive shop, fishing trips, windsurfing, hotel, restaurant.

Travel Belize Ltd., 637-B S. Broadway, Boulder, CO 80303; (800) 626-3483. Dive packages, tours, air connections.

Tropical Adventures Travel, 11 Second Ave., Seattle, WA 98109; (800) 247-3483 or (206) 441-3483. Scuba specialists.

Turneffe Flats, Blackbird Caye, Turneffe Islands; 2-45634 or (605) 578-1304, fax (605) 578-7540. Sportfishing and diving specialists.

Turneffe Islands Lodge, Caye Bokel, Turneffe Islands, Box 480, Belize City; (800) 338-8149, fax 3-0276. Dive and fishing specialists.

Dive Boat Services
Belize Aggressor I, II, and **III,** based at Ft. George Pier, Belize City, and Drawer K, Morgan City, LA 70381; (800) 348-2628. 100-foot dive boats.

Coral Bay and Offshore Express, Coral Beach Hotel, San Pedro, Ambergris Caye; 26-2001 or (800) 433-7262 or (305) 563-1711. 62-foot dive boat.

Hotel Fiesta, formerly Ramada Royal Reef Hotel, Barracks Road, Belize City; (800) 228-9898. Berth for various dive boats.

La Strega, Box 673, Belize City; 2-3108 or (800) 433-DIVE. 85-foot dive boat.

M.V. Greet Reef, Box 214A, Corpus Christi, TX 78415; (800) 255-8503 or (512) 854-0247; 65-foot dive boat.

M.V. Manta IV, Box 13, San Pedro, Ambergris Caye; 2-62371 or (800) 473-1956, fax 2-62028. Overnight dive trips to Turneffe and Lighthouse atolls; interior tours.

M.Y. Gallic, 2-31351 or (800) 468-0123. 52-foot dive boat, specializing in Glover's and Lighthouse Reefs.

Out Island Divers, Box 7, San Pedro, Ambergris Caye; 2-62151, or (800) BLUE-HOLE. Operators of *Reef Roamer I, II,* and *III.*

Wave Dancer, based at Ft. George Pier, Belize City, and **Peter Hughes Diving,** 6851 Yumuri St., Suite 10, Coral Gables, FL 33146; (800) 932-6237.

SPORTFISHING
All the joys of the ocean are found in the waters of Belize. Great fishing—spin, fly, or troll—can be enjoyed year-round, and the abundance of species guarantees excellent sport. Some anglers insist that it is virtually impossible to go fishing in Belize and not catch something. A distinct advantage here for non-Spanish-speaking fishermen (and women) is that virtually all guides and boatmen speak

English. The estuaries and mouths of jungle rivers of Belize are best known for their tarpon, black snapper, jack-revalle, cubera, and snook; lagoons and coral flats for their bonefish, permit, triggerfish, and barracuda; reef formations for their king mackerel, kingfish, jackfish, grouper, barracuda, and snapper; and the deeper waters off the outer reefs and atolls for amberjack, sailfish, shark, wahoo, pompano, blackfin tuna, yellowfin tuna, bonito, dolphin-fish, mahi-mahi, and marlin.

A proud fisherman displays his catch.

Kevin Schafer

Species availability varies considerably, depending on the depth and clarity of water, proximity to reefs and rivers, and time of year.

Where to Fish

If fishing is the primary purpose of your trip, you'll want to spend little or no time in Belize City. There is no beach here, and the waters are foul. Luckily, with some advance planning, you can easily transfer to a better base of operations on the day you arrive. Many fishing lodges have airport pickup service and often arrange overnight accommodations in Belize City, departing the next morning on chartered boats. Scheduled domestic airline service is also easily arranged from Belize City to Ambergris Caye and Caye Caulker, as well as the outlying coastal towns of Placencia, Dangriga, Corozal, and Punta Gorda, all located near rich fishing sites. The only other island with an operating airstrip is privately owned Northern Two Caye, at Lighthouse Reef. There are a few seaplanes in Belize, but they are expensive to charter and seem to get little use.

Fishing the Interior

Because of the unique conditions and high quality of the country's offshore waters, freshwater fishing in the interior receives scant attention from visitors. Conditions are excellent in many streams, however; you should inquire locally about when and where to go. Take a spinning rod up a jungle river and you're liable to hook a tarpon, snook, jack, or snapper. River fish are easiest to snag when the water is clear and low, from February through May. Some of the better inland waterways for fishing are the Sittee, Monkey, Belize, and New Rivers.

Coral Flat Fishing

Many saltwater fly-fishers come to Belize to stalk the elusive bonefish, an almost transparent fish known for its feisty spirit and crafty ways. As the name implies, the creature is too bony to make a decent meal. Although the bonefish is relatively small—averaging 2 to 6 pounds—ounce for ounce it is considered the toughest fighter in the sea. This predator is often found in knee-deep, crystal-clear coral flats, particularly from September through January, where it attacks smaller fish with lightning speed. The bonefish is taken on both fly and lure. Fishing resorts that specialize in guided bonefish excursions include Turneffe Flats, Turneffe Island Lodge, Maya Landings, and Wippari Caye Lodge. The shallow, grassy, hard-sand coral flats of the Turneffe Islands are a particularly fine habitat for bonefish—bring your waders!

The same marine habitats also teem with permit, especially on coral flats at incoming tides. Many fishing lodges claim Belize is the "permit capital of the world," with specimens weighing in at 30 or more pounds. The largest concentrations of this wily species are in the southern coastal waters of Belize. For those determined to snag a permit, we recommend the outfitters listed above for bonefishing, along with the Blue Marlin Lodge on South Water Caye and Pow Cabral in Placencia. The coastal lagoons and coral flats of southern Belize are especially good places to find permit, often at the end of an incoming tide. Permit fishing is best from August through October and again from March through June.

Reef Fishing

Tarpon, barracuda, and cubera snapper are equally plentiful near Belizean reefs. Forty-pound or larger tarpon are fairly common from February through June, sometimes in the same coral flats where you'll find permit and bonefish. Although they are not considered good eating, a large tarpon can easily take 90 minutes to subdue with a 10-weight fly rod. Tarpon can be fished year-round, but are most plentiful from October through mid-December and again in June and July.

Good-size snook are reported all winter, both in rivers and estuaries. These species can be found around reefs, flats, and mangrove cayes the rest of the year. The aggressive barracuda are notorious for breaking leaders in the water or, once landed, snapping at fishermen's feet. Mutton snapper, ladyfish, and crevalle jack also frequent the coral flats, along with the occasional grouper and red snapper. Fishing outfitters specializing in snook and tarpon include Maya Landings on Moho Caye, Blackline Marine Service in Belize City, and El Pescador, on Ambergris Caye. Trolling and bottom fishing along the reef can yield grouper, king mackerel, jack, cobia, kingfish, snapper, wahoo, bonito, and tuna, depending on the season and water depth.

Deep Water Fishing

The much deeper, ocean side of the barrier reef often serves up king and Spanish mackerel, grouper, snapper (several varieties), bonito, blackfin tuna, and wahoo, along with sailfish and marlin. You will also encounter many shark, porpoise, and dolphin. The warmest months often offer the best chance to hook grouper, mutton snapper, tarpon, sailfish, and mangrove snapper. For a sight not soon forgotten, go to Glory Caye during the night of January's full moon and watch the spawning of thousands of Nassau grouper. Deep-sea fishing is not particularly popular in Belize, although spring and fall are good times to catch marlin and sailfish.

Lobster Fishing

Lobster season is March 15 to July 14, but most of these spiny crustaceans (lacking the large claws of the cold-water species off the Maine coast) are taken by local fishermen, who also commercially harvest conch, shrimp, snapper, and other species. You won't see many Maine-size lobster here due to many past years of over-harvesting.

Saltwater Flyfishing

Saltwater flyfishing is best in the southern part of Belize, where the presence of divers, snorkelers, and Belizean fishers has been felt the least. Anything south of Dangriga is likely to be especially promising. It's not unusual to go for days at a time without seeing another rod or line.

How to Arrange a Fishing Trip

Many resorts, boat operators, lodges, and guides serve the needs of sportfishers (see the end of this section for a complete list of names and addresses). Almost any hotel near the water can easily provide you with a fishing guide, a boat, and tackle—for rent by the hour, day, or week. Flies, as well as extra tackle items, are available for sale to guests who need them, although it's better to bring your own favorite tackle. Many dive shops, dive resorts, and dive boats also welcome fishing enthusiasts. Fishing instruction is widely available and no licenses are required.

Hiring a Fishing Guide or Outfitter

Because of their years of experience, many private fishing boat operators are also excellent guides. Some resorts hire locals whose only job is to help you find and catch the fish of your choice. With hundreds of varieties to choose from, simply making a selection may be a daunting task. Native Belizean "consultants" are sometimes included in the price of package tours, especially the week-long excursions to outer islands.

The services of such guides can also be engaged for about $200 a day, including boat, tackle, and fuel. Week-long fishing packages begin at around $1,100 for six days of actual fishing. These Belize-born experts are considered some of the best fly-fishers in the world.

Local guides, such as Charles Leslie of Placencia's Kingfisher Belize Adventures, specialize in fly-fishing guiding, spin fishing, and offshore fishing. Other recommended guides include Richard Young Jr. of Belize City; Casey Eiley, Eddie Leslie, Pow Cabral, and Kevin Madera of Placencia; Raul Young and Porfilio "Piggy" Guzman of Caye Caulker; and the Cabral family at Wippari Caye Guiding on Wippari Caye (10 miles east of Placencia). On Calabash Caye in the Turneffe Islands, David Young has an excellent reputation as a fishing guide.

The investment in a good "consultant" is worth it: during guided visits to nearly virgin Belizean waters, anglers regularly complete a "grand slam" by landing at least one tarpon, snook, bonefish, and permit within a 24-hour period.

On Ambergris Caye, the El Pescador Lodge is recommended as a well-equipped base of operations for saltwater anglers. The resort, which has its own sportfishing boats, guides, and marina, was built by a German-American couple with the help of local Mennonite carpenters.

The flats between here and the Belizean mainland are renowned for their tarpon (also called silver kings locally), recorded at up to about 100 pounds. We've also heard consistently positive reports about the Blue Marlin Lodge on South Water Caye, Pegasus Boat Service on Caye Caulker, and Ranguana Lodge in Placencia and Ranguana Caye. Another good choice is Angler Adventures, a Connecticut-based outfitter that represents a number of Belize fishing lodges and specializes in all-inclusive fishing packages.

One final word of caution about operators promoting offshore "fishing trips." Some are merely snorkeling trips where the guide fishes for you, then grills and serves his catch as a "shore lunch." When hiring a guide, make it clear that you want to fish.

What to Bring or Rent

Some fishing equipment can be rented from local hotels and outfitters in Belize, but the selection is rather limited (though improving over time). Live bait, for example, is sometimes hard to come by. Fortunately, you can usually make do with frozen shrimp or wriggling fingerlings plucked from the sea.

Indispensable for Inner Channel fishing (in the relatively shallow waters between the barrier reef and the mainland) are a good 9-foot fly rod, a sturdy reel, and an 8-weight floating saltwater tapered fly line. Experienced fishers often bring along one each of a light and medium spinning or fly rod, along with a heavier fly, spinning, or bait-casting rod and a deep-running lure.

Major resorts that specialize in sportfishing, such as the Paradise Hotel or Victoria House on Ambergris Caye, can make exact recommendations on tackle, line strength, lures, rods, and reels, depending on what the angler is after and the time of the year. In general, equipment will vary considerably for the following conditions: coral flats, mainland shoreline, mangrove lagoons, river-mouth casting, and deep-water jigging or trolling.

Belize Sportfishing

When fishing in tropical Belize, remember that reels in particular need daily cleaning in fresh water and regular lubrication. Other accessories often useful here include tennis shoes or Patagonia Reef Walkers for wading in coral flats and shoals, lightweight ripstop nylon pants, and polarized sunglasses with side shields. The sun is so intense at these latitudes that a severe burn can occur after less than an hour of exposure. For that reason, we recommend that you bring long-sleeved shirts, cotton pants, wide-brimmed hats, bandanas, lip balm, and, of course, waterproof sunscreen (SPF 15 or higher).

What to Do with Your Catch

Although foreigners are allowed to take as much as 20 pounds of freshly caught fish with them when they leave Belize, the more common practice is to measure the creature and throw it back for the next customer. An alternative is to share the game fish with your guide, boatman, and fellow fisherfolk as a supper entrée. Some fishing lodges, such as Blackbird Caye Resort, require catch-and-release for ecological reasons.

Advance Reading

Those with a serious interest in fishing (and boating) will be well served by Freya Rauscher and Julius M. Wilensky's 288-page *Cruising Guide to Belize and Mexico's Caribbean Coast* (Westcott Cove, 1991).

Sportfishing Outfitters

Angler Adventures, Box 872, Old Lyme, CT 06371; (800) 628-8605 or (203) 434-9624, fax (203) 434-8605. Represents many fishing lodges in Belize, specialist in all-inclusive fishing packages.

Blue Runner Guiding, Kenny Villanueva, Placencia Village; 6-23153 or 6-23130. Heavy and light tackle or trolling sportfishing trips; snorkeling; reef, river, and coast.

Francis "Billy" Leslie, Ambergris Caye; 26-2128. Fishing guide.

Kingfisher Belize Adventures, Stanley Winborne and Charles Leslie, Placencia; 6-23104 or (800) 403-9995, fax (919) 676-9910. Bar, flycast/spincast, inshore, offshore.

Lillpat River Fishing, Sam Dawson, Hopkins; (805) 963-2501; e-mail *lillpat@aol.com*. Bonefishing specialists.

Manatee Lodge, Gales Point, Box 170, Belmopan; 8-23321, fax 8-23334. Sportfishing specialists.

Melanie Paz, Ambergris Caye; 26-2437. Fishing guide.

Melvin Bandillo Jr., Caye Caulker; 22-2111. Fishing guide.

Nolan Jackson, Tobacco Caye, Box 10, Dangriga. Fishing guide.

Pegasus Boat Services, Caye Caulker; 22-2223. Guides and charters.

Pow Cabral Flyfishing, Placencia; 22-2234 or (800) 333-5691. Sport- and fly-fishing.

Raul Young, Caye Caulker; 22-2133. Fishing guide.

Richard Young Jr., Belize City; 2-74385. Light tackle fishing guide specializing in tarpon, snook, and bonefish on flats or rivers.

Roberto Bradley Jr., Ambergris Caye; 26-2116. Fishing guide.

Romel Gomez/Luz Guerrero, Ambergris Caye; 26-2034. Fishing guides.

Roque Badillo's Fishing Tours, Caye Caulker; 22-2014. Fishing guides.

Wippari Caye Guiding, Wippari Caye; 6-23130. Cabral family fly-fishing guides, specializing in bonefish, permit, and tarpon; lodging.

CRUISE SHIPS

Unlike a number of ports in Mexico and the Caribbean, Belize does not show up on many cruise ship itineraries. There are several good reasons for this, including the lack of deep-water anchorages, limited onshore infrastructure (i.e. duty-free shopping malls), and the fact that the Belize government has taken a go-slow approach to cruise ship tourism, fearing that their presence could have a negative impact on the country's fragile marine ecosystem. Many in the domestic tourism industry are also fearful that cruise ships could drain precious dollars away from local enterprises.

Nonetheless, there are a handful of operators who offer specialized cruises along the barrier reef. Temptress Voyages, (800) 336-8423, for example, schedules cruises in Belize that feature nature and hiking activities for children (4 through 17) when the 65-passenger *Temptress* ship is in port. Adults will have their own adventures both on and offshore, including snorkeling trips and excursions to Mayan ruins. Other cruise ship operators that occasionally make stops in Belize include American-Canadian Caribbean Lines, (800) 556-7450 and OdessAmerica, (800) 221-3254.

Ecosummer Expeditions ($1,250 and up, meals included, 800-465-8884) has a live-aboard sailing vessel that makes snorkeling, kayaking, and natural history trips along the cayes and east to Lighthouse Reef. Ecosummer's 48-foot Belizean sandlighter *Excellence* departs Belize City about once each week from January through April, stopping at Lighthouse Reef, Glover's Reef, Placencia, and the barrier reef. There is a guide familiar with the region and its natural history onboard; special discounts are available for children and families. The offshore cruises are combined with extensions inland to Crooked Tree, Bermudian Landing, and the Cayo district that involve horseback riding, tubing, birding, and interpretive hiking.

Wilderness Travel ($1,100 and up, meals included, 800-368-2794 or 447-2931, e-mail *info@wildernesstravel.com*) operates the *Rembrandt van Rijn*, a three-masted gaff topsail schooner as a sail/dive alternative in Belize. This elegant craft was built as a Dutch "herring lugger" in the early 1900s and completely upgraded in 1993. It makes year-round, week-long trips from Belize City with intermediate- to advanced-ability dive stops off the Turneffe Islands, Lighthouse Reef, Glover's Reef, and Laughingbird Caye. Besides divemasters and a full onboard dive shop, the *Rembrandt van Rijn* carries water skis, Zodiacs, and a windsurfer.

Cruise Ships that Visit Belize

Ecosummer Expeditions & Tours, 1516 Duranleau St., Vancouver, BC V6H 3S4, Canada; (604) 669-7741, fax (604) 669-3244, U.S., (800) 465-8884. Sea kayaking, river running, caving, Mayan ruins, horseback riding, nature tours.

Wilderness Travel/Oceanwide Sail Expeditions, 801 Allston Way, Berkeley, CA 94710; (800) 368-2794 or (510) 548-0420, e-mail *info@wildernesstravel.com*. Seven-day, live-aboard sail/dive tours aboard the *Rembrandt van Rijn*.

RIVER TRIPS, KAYAKING, AND SAILING

Whitewater Adventures

Although Belize is a relatively small and low-lying country, it gets plenty of rainfall and boasts 20 major river systems, plus innumerable perennial streams. These sources supply the nation's domestic water needs and the demands of local agriculture, but they are also a potential source of outdoor adventure.

Some rivers in the upland areas (especially of the Cayo District) have navigable whitewater, but it is best to check with tour operators for expert advice on where and when to go. The Mopan and the Macal, along with their tributaries, are your best bet. The upper Macal River was dammed in the early 1990s for a hydroelectric project and its flow is now carefully controlled, which makes whitewater floats possible downstream as far as Chaa Creek—even farther during wet months.

Slickrock Adventures of Moab, Utah, offers a paddle-boat day trip (with mountain bike and cave-float extensions) through Class IV rapids on the upper Macal that floats from the hydroelectric dam to Black Rock or Chaa Creek, past tall limestone canyons and thick jungle. Flows must be 90-cfs to make this trip, however, and discharge rates vary. Among local operators in San Ignacio, we recommend Remo Montgomery of Float Belize (he also owns the Sandcastle Restaurant), and in nearby Cristo Rey, Victor or Jeronie Tut of Crystal Palace Resort.

Raft, Canoe, and Kayak Adventures

Historically, rafts and canoes have always been common modes of transportation on Belizean waterways, and such vessels can be rented through most major hotels and travel agencies. The cottage resorts of the Cayo District, for example, often supply rafts, canoes, and occasional kayaks to their guests or even casual visitors. The area's Macal, Mopan, and Belize Rivers are particularly well suited to these craft during the drier months, beginning in about January, or you may try Monkey, Sittee, and Temash Rivers farther south. Small boats can be rented for as little as one-half hour or as long as two weeks. Some operators arrange trips by raft, kayak, or canoe all the way from the Guatemalan border to Belize City.

This sort of journey is an excellent way to observe birds, plants, animals, and people along the riverbanks. Such travel is problematic during the rainy season, for obvious reasons. Lowland river trips by canoe (or kayak) can be arranged at Banana Bank Lodge, Chaa Creek Cottages, duPlooy's, Caesar's Place/Black Rock, Warrie Head Ranch, the Toledo Adventure Club, Paradise Inn, and Jungle Drift Lodge, among others. In the Cayo District, outfitters renting canoes include Float Belize, Toni's Canoes, and Windy Hill Cottage Tours.

Powerboat Adventures

Popular destinations by guided powerboat include the offshore islands, Crooked Tree Wildlife Sanctuary, Community Baboon Sanctuary, and the Mayan ruins of Cerros, Lamanai, and Xunantunich (see other chapters of this book for complete coverage). A trip up the New River from Orange Walk to Lamanai is a must for bird-watchers, and the New River Lagoon is arguably the loveliest body of freshwater in the country. Boat trips are also recommended to the Northern and Southern Lagoons, Gales Point, Placencia, Sittee River, Monkey River Town, and the Temash River.

Sea Kayak, Sailboat, Waterskiing, and Windsurfing

Sea kayaking and windsurfing are rapidly increasing in popularity along the coast of Belize. The calm and relatively shallow waters of the Inner Channel (that portion of the Caribbean between the barrier reef and the mainland) are ideal locations for enjoying these activities, and the islands' larger resorts can arrange equipment rental and instruction. Some of these hotels also rent small sailboats on a daily or weekly basis. Areas favored by sea kayakers include the waters of Chetumal Bay, Ambergris Caye, Caye Caulker, the Hol Chan Channel, and offshore atolls. Experienced kayakers can also follow the entire length of the barrier reef, camping along the way on such small islands as Bluefield Range, Spanish Bay, Colson Caye, Half Moon Caye, and Northeast Caye. Windsurfers report the best conditions are on the leeward sides of the cayes, especially in the shallow waters west and east of Ambergris Caye and Caye Caulker.

Windsurfers, Sunfish, and Hobie Cats are available for rent at some of the hotels on Ambergris Caye and Caye Caulker. More sailing equipment is being added at outlying resorts, so be sure to inquire in advance if this is a pastime of interest. Some of the larger resorts now offer complimentary windsurfing, Sunfish sailing, and pier fishing in their vacation packages. Even small guest houses often have dories and canoes available for use by visitors. Be aware that currents and winds on the reef can be tricky, especially in the afternoon.

Waterskiing and windsurfing are particularly popular off the waters of Ambergris Caye. Check with Amigo Travel, 26-2180, for suggestions. The Sunbreeze Hotel, Ramon's Village, and Journey's End Caribbean Club on Ambergris all rent waterskiing and windsurfing equipment, as do the larger hotels on Caye Caulker.

Slickrock Adventures offers sea kayaking trips in the waters off Glover's Reef from December through April, and Ecosummer

Expeditions runs kayaking trips during the same period around Lighthouse Reef. Canada-based Island Expeditions offers sea kayak excursions offshore from Dangriga as far as Glover's Reef, and into the interior via the Manatee River. The company has extensions to Tikal, Caracol, the Toledo District, and other inland destinations. Monkey River Expeditions has guided kayak trips around Placencia and up the Monkey River. Laughingbird Adventures runs sea kayaking expeditions from Placencia as far as Honduras. Kayaking equipment is also available in Placencia and on Ranguana Caye from the Ranguana Reef Lodge & Resort through their association with Reef-Link Kayaking, a recommended outfitter, particularly for the serious kayaker. On Ambergris Caye you can rent kayaks by the hour or day from Travel & Tour Belize, as well as from some of the larger hotels.

Advance Reading

The best book by far on the region's kayaking is the very detailed *Belize by Kayak*, self-published by Kirk Barrett. To buy a copy, call him at (515) 279-6699, or write to 3806 Cottage Grove, Des Moines, IA 50311.

Those with their own sail or powerboats are well served by Capt. Freya Rauscher's *Cruising Guide to Belize and Mexico's Caribbean Coast* (Wescott Cove Press), which features 119 charts (including a foldout cruising chart for offshore Belize) as well as diagrams, maps, and sailing itineraries.

River Trips, Kayaking, and Sailing Outfitters

Adios Charters, Placencia; 6-23154. 36-foot trimaran for day charters to area cayes for snorkeling.

Baboon River Canoe Rentals, Burrell Boom, Belize; 28-2101. Boat trips on Belize River and Mussel Creek.

Belize Land and Sea Tours (BLAST), 58 King St., Belize City; tel/fax 2-73897. Wide range of services, including bus excursions, two-man submarine, 34-foot cabin cruiser, and customized tours.

Caye Caulker Sailboats, The Reef Hotel, Caye Caulker; 22-2196. Sailboat rentals.

Fanta-Sea Charters, Box 768, Belize City; 2-33033, fax 2-3712, or (303) 226-1193. Day and overnight snorkel trips on 45-foot catamaran *Stingray*, based in Belize City at Fiesta Hotel (Ramada Reef) marina.

Heritage Navigation, Paradise Hotel Dock, San Pedro, Ambergris Caye; 26-2394. Recommended island and reef cruises on 66-foot sailboat *Winnie Estelle*.

Hinterland Tours, 3 Eve St., San Ignacio; 92-2475. River, ruin, and jungle trips.

Island Expeditions, 368-916 West Broadway, Vancouver, BC V5Z 1K7, Canada; (800) 667-1630 or (604) 452-3212, fax (604) 452-3433, e-mail *island@whistler.net*. Sea kayaking, snorkeling, fishing, windsurfing, river floating, camping, photography, birding, caving, archaeology, ecology, Garifuna drumming and culture, diving.

Journeys of Discovery, 1516 Duranleau St., Vancouver, BC V6H 354 Canada; (800) 688-8605, Canada (800) 465-8884. Sea kayaking and rain forest expeditions.

Laughing Heart Adventures, P.O. Box 669, Willow Creek, CA 95573; (800) 541-1256 or (916) 629-3516. Nature-oriented river and reef trips.

Monkey River Expeditions, 1731 44th Ave., S.W., Suite 100, Seattle, WA 98116; (206) 660-7777, fax (206) 938-0978; e-mail *mre@halcyon.com*. Monkey River tour by sea kayak, Mayan ruins, visits to cayes.

Pegasus Boat Charter, Box 743; 2-31138. Boat charter for reef, river, and caye trips.

Reef-Link Kayaking, Ranguana Lodge and Reef Resort, Placencia and Ranguana Caye; 6-22027 or (515) 279-6699. Sea kayak rentals and tours; manages bungalows and campground for kayakers on Ranguana Caye.

Sailing Fantasy, Ramon's Reef Resort, San Pedro, Ambergris Caye; 2-62439. Catamaran trips and rental, operators of *El Tigre*.

Slickrock Adventures, Box 1400, Moab, UT 84532; (800) 390-5715 or (801) 259-6996, e-mail *slickrock@slickrock.com* or *slickrock@btl.net.* Sea kayaking, windsurfing, white-water rafting; week-long trips to Glover's Reef.

Sunrise Boat Tours and Charters, Caye Caulker; 2-22195. Trips to cayes near and far, including weekly excursion to Half Moon Caye.

Timeless Tours, 2304 Massachusetts Ave., Cambridge, MA 02140; 27-2119, or (800) 370-0142. Seven to 12-day sailing/camping excursions with 38-foot schooner based in Punta Gorda, overnight on cayes and jungle rivers.

Toni Canoes, 22 Burns Ave., San Ignacio; 92-2267. River and canoe trips.

Wilderness Alaska/Mexico, 1231 Sundance Loop, Fairbanks, AK 99709; (907) 479-8203. Sea kayaking.

BIRDING, CAMPING, AND WILDLIFE EXCURSIONS

Largely because of its small population and lack of industry (including a limited amount of agriculture), Belize is blessed with hundreds of square miles of virtually undisturbed animal habitat. Roughly 70 percent of the country is still covered with forest. Birders, in particular, are blessed with the opportunity to see hundreds of species in a wide variety of ecosystems. Many of these creatures are still thriving in Belize after becoming locally extinct or endangered in neighboring countries. It's not uncommon to observe 50 or more bird species during a single walk, out of the more than 500 species of residents and migrants that have been recorded here.

Birding

A growing number of hotels and tour companies in Belize are catering to the special needs and interests of birders, and a few (notably Chan Chich near Gallon Jug, Caribbean Villas in San Pedro, and Chau Hiix near Crooked Tree) are targeting birders specifically. You'll find nature trails, recorded species lists, and viewing platforms at many locations throughout the country, but particularly among the jungle lodges of the Cayo District.

Birding tours of Belize are offered by several U.S.-based outfitters, including Victor Emanuel Tours, Massachusetts Audubon Society, and Field Guides. In Belize City, the Belize Audubon

Society (originally an overseas chapter of the South Florida Audubon Society) is a terrific resource for birders and can provide several books and bird lists tailored to Belize. We particularly like Dennis Rogers' *La Ruta Maya: A Guide to the Best Birding Locations in the Yucatán, Belize, Guatemala, Honduras, and El Salvador* (Site Guides, 1994). Other recommended guides for the area include Roger Tory Peterson's *Field Guide to Mexican Birds*; *A Guide to the Birds of Mexico and Northern Central America* (Steve N.G. Howell and Sophie Webb; and *A Field Guide to the Birds of Mexico* (Ernest P. Edwards).

Camping

Camping throughout Belize is restricted by government regulation. Unless otherwise posted or granted, prior permission must be obtained from private owners before camping on deeded land or, on government land, by writing the Ministry of Natural Resources, Attention: Permanent Secretary, Belmopan, Belize, C.A.; 8-22630. Camping is still something of a novelty in Belize, although a growing number of tourism operators cater to campers, and camping is now permitted at many national parks and archaeological sites, with prior permission. Personal items on any camping trip in Belize should include a flashlight, insect repellent, rain gear, sun protection, first aid kit, and waterproof shoes or boots. A set of warm clothes is a good idea, too, since it can get chilly at night.

Throughout this book we've mentioned campsites (and camping fees) wherever we've encountered them. If you're interested in roughing it outdoors, you'll have the greatest odds of success at the government protected areas, such as Cockscomb Basin Wildlife Sanctuary, Mountain Pine Ridge Forest Reserve, and Monkey Bay National Park.

Nature Tours

More generic wildlife tours are coming into their own and many hotels can arrange excursions to suit your particular interest. Many lodges maintain extensive, well-interpreted nature trails and at least one, Chan Chich, publishes an extensive guidebook to the region's natural habitats (*Exploring the Rainforest*). Another resort, the Hidden Valley Inn, has established a carefully mapped trail network that would take days to navigate. In addition, the national parks, sanctuaries, and nature reserves of Belize are all well served by local guides and, in many cases, knowledgeable resident caretakers.

For more than a dozen years, Colorado-based Natural Habitat

Adventures, (800) 543-8917, (303) 449-3711, has taken travelers to remote areas of Belize for up close encounters with wildlife in their natural environments. The company's Belize Explorer trips also highlight the country's rich cultural history. The 10-day trips are limited to 10 travelers and cost about $2,700 each. Destinations include Crooked Tree Lagoon, Lamanai, Hopkins, Gallows Point, Cayo, Cockscomb, and the barrier reef. The trips are guided bybiologist Ron LeValley and Hugo Panti, grand-nephew of the late Mayan shaman Eligio Panti and a past guide for England's Queen Elizabeth II.

The Central American Institute of Prehistoric and Traditional Cultures, (CAIPTC), offers a field school and seminar program that includes natural healing and alternative medicine instruction based on medicinal plants found in the forests of Belize. Additional courses are presented on tropical resources and wildlife ecology, with a focus on the relationship between traditional Mayan and Garifuna cultures and their environment. CAIPTC maintains a World Wide Web site at *http://world.std.com.*

Recommended Belize-based companies offering guided nature hikes include the Pelican Beach Resort, Jaguar Reef Lodge, Jungle River Tours, Melmish Mayan Ecotours, Mountain Equestrian Trails/The Divide Ltd., Chaa Creek Inland Expeditions, Placencia Tours, and Native Guide Systems.

Birding, Camping, and Wildlife Outfitters

Above The Clouds Trekking, Box 398, Worchester, MA 01062; (800) 233-4499. Nature treks.

Big Five Expeditions Ltd., 2151 E. Dublin-Granville Road, Columbus, OH 43229; (800) 541-2790. Nature and photography tours.

Chaa Creek Inland Expeditions, Box 53, San Ignacio; 9-22037, fax 9-22501. Guided expeditions to Mayan ruins, Mountain Pine Ridge, Vaca Plateau, Macal River, Tikal; horseback riding, nature trails, canoeing, trained mules for extended jungle trips.

The Divide Ltd., Nord Farm, Mile 63 Western Highway, Central Farm, Cayo; 8-22149, fax 8-23235. Natural history tours, rafting, horseback trips, caving, waterfalls, Mayan ruins, wilderness camping.

Eco Adventures, 632 Emerson St., Palo Alto, CA 94301; (415) 321-1113. Customized nature-oriented itineraries for independent travelers.

Environmental Journeys/Earth Island Institute, 300 Broadway, Suite 28, San Francisco, CA 94133-3312; (510) 655-4526, fax (510) 547-2881. Dolphin research, snorkeling, diving on Blackbird Caye through Oceanic Society Expeditions.

Field Guides, Box 160723, Austin, TX 78716; (800) 728-4953 or (512) 327-4953. Birding tours.

Great Trips, P.O. Box 1320, Detroit Lakes, MN 56501; (800) 552-3419 or (218) 847-4441, fax (218) 847-4442, e-mail *belizejq@ Tekstar.com*. Interior, reef, and sportfishing trips; wide range of destinations including nature reserves, Mayan ruins, and tropical forests.

Imagine Travel Alternatives, Box 27023, Seattle, WA 98125; (206) 624-7112. "Soft adventure" tours of Belize, with extensions to Costa Rica and Guatemala; hiking, canoeing, Mayan village tours.

International Expeditions, One Environs Park, Helena, AL 35080; (800) 633-4734 or (205) 428-1700, fax (205) 428-1714, e-mail *intlex@aol.com*. Archaeological, birding, barrier reef, and natural history tours; family trips; ecology workshops; rain forest pharmacology workshops; extensions to Tikal; co-sponsor of Crooked Tree Cashew Festival.

International Zoological Expeditions, 210 Washington St., Sherborn, MA 01770; (800) 548-5843 or (508) 655-1461, fax (508) 655-4445. Marine and rainforest ecology seminars and excursions in Toledo District and on barrier reef and Glover's Reef.

Journeys, 3516 NE 155th, Suite B-2, Seattle, WA 98155; (800) 345-4453. Conservation-oriented tours.

Manomet Bird Observatory, Box 1770, Manomet, MA 02345; (508) 224-6521. Birding tours.

Mark Smith Nature Tours/Full Circle Tours, 2421 Quimy NW, Portland, OR 97210; (503) 223-7716. Natural history and birding tour specialist.

Massachusetts Audubon Society, 208 South Great Rd., Lincoln, MA 01773; (800) 289-9504. Birding and natural history tours.

Maya Mountain Lodge, Box 46, San Ignacio; 9-22164, fax 92-2029. Excursions to Caracol, Cockscomb Basin Wildlife Sanctuary, and barrier reef; specialists in educational seminars and family-oriented nature travel.

Mountain/Sobek Travel, 6420 Fairmount Ave., El Cerrito, CA 94530; (510) 527-8100. Conservation-oriented expeditions.

Natural Habitat Adventures, 2945 Center Green Court So., Boulder, CO 80301; (303) 449-3711. Expeditions focusing on exotic animal life in natural habitats.

Oceanic Society Expeditions, Ft. Mason Center, Bldg. E, San Francisco, CA 94123; (800) 326-7491, fax (415) 474-3395. Dolphin research trips to Blackbird Caye, with extensions to Half Moon Caye, Tikal, and interior Belize; manatee and turtle research trips to Gales Point; bird and howler monkey research trips to Lamanai; tropical marine biology workshops for teachers.

Preferred Adventures, One West Water St., Suite 300, St. Paul, MN 55107; (612) 222-8131, fax (612) 222-4221. Conservation-oriented nature trips, birding tours.

Remarkable Journeys, Box 31855, Houston, TX 77231-1855; (800) 856-1993, fax (713) 728-8334, e-mail *cooltrips@ remjourneys.com*. Natural history-oriented interior, reef, and sailing trips with Tikal option, also adventure trips to Mexico and Honduras; occasional yoga retreats in Belize.

River Travel Center, P.O. Box 6-B, Pt. Arena, CA 95468; (800) 882-7238. Emphasis on natural history.

School for Field Studies, 16 Broadway, Beverly, MA 01952; (508) 927-7777, fax (508) 927-5127. Offers month-long tropical ecology course on Sittee River, with trips to Cockscomb Basin and Wee Wee Caye.

Tread Lightly, One Titus Road, Washington Depot, CT 06794; (800) 627-8227. Rainforest ecology, conservation; contributes to local environmental projects.

University Research Expeditions Program, University of California at Berkeley, Berkeley, CA 94720; (510) 642-6586. Research in environmental studies, archaeology, humanities, paleontology.

Victor Emanuel Nature Tours, Box 33008, Austin, TX 78764; (800) 328-8368 or (512) 328-5221. Birding and other nature-oriented tours.

Voyagers International, Box 915, Ithaca, NY 14851; (607) 257-3091. Natural history, ornithology, photography.

Winter Escapes, Daniel Weedon, P.O. Box 429, Erickson, MB R0J 0P0, Canada; (204) 636-2968, fax (204) 636-2202. Birding, nature tours.

BICYCLING

Bicycling opportunities in Belize are limited, and until recently the sport of mountain biking was virtually unknown. Nevertheless, a growing number of tour operators, resorts, and lodges are now catering to the needs of bicycle enthusiasts, and an infrastructure is gradually developing. Three of the best are Bike Belize in Belize City, Chaa Creek Cottages in the Cayo District, and Jungle Reef Lodge in Hopkins. Several lodges, including a couple in the Cayo, now have bicycles available for free or low-cost use by their guests.

The biggest problem bikers will encounter in Belize is the limited network of roads in the country and an even smaller number of trails suitable for bicycle transportation. Belizean roads are notoriously bad, characterized by an unusual number of potholes, mud bogs, sharp rocks, and sand traps. Even the best thoroughfares, such as the Western Highway from Belize City to Benque Viejo, typically have narrow traffic lanes, few service stations, and virtually no shoulders. The quality of bicycles available for rental is also highly variable; avid cyclists should bring their own bicycles for the best experience.

Where to Ride

Currently the most accessible and rewarding area of Belize for bicyclists is the Cayo District, especially the Mountain Pine Ridge forest reserve. Mountain biking is increasingly popular, and a few lodges now have bikes to rent. Try Chaa Creek Cottages near San Ignacio, Pine Ridge Lodge on the Chiquibul Road, or Pacz Hotel in San Ignacio. Most of the region's many attractions are easily reached from any of the Cayo's lodges or campgrounds, and there are a number of destinations worth visiting. The main routes are well-maintained dirt roads, and they are relatively uncrowded. This area's primary advantages are slightly cooler temperatures and lower humidity than the coast, with relatively few biting insects. Watch for rain, however, as these mostly dirt roads become mud in a hurry.

Side trips from either the Cayo or Belize District include the Belize Zoo, Guanacaste National Park, Community Baboon Sanctuary, Blue Hole National Park, St. Herman's Cave, Five Blues Lake National Park, Crooked Tree Wildlife Sanctuary, Gales Point Manatee Sanctuary, and the Mayan ruins of Altun Ha. Because Belize is a narrow country (about 70 miles wide), an ambitious cyclist can make it all the way from Belize City to Guatemala in a single day. A good midpoint is Monkey Bay Wildlife Sanctuary, which welcomes cyclists and provides food, drink, and lodging. Another popular one-day excursion is from Dangriga to the Cockscomb Basin Wildlife Sanctuary, with interesting rest stops en route at Hopkins and Maya Center.

Bicycling Hazards

Due to the rainy climate and lush vegetation, trails are often difficult to negotiate, even for those on foot. Bicyclists should be aware that unstable, slick, and mucky surfaces and narrow passageways are the norm off-road, not the exception. Trails are frequently blocked by fallen trees and branches, including those of many plants whose burrs, thorns, and nettles can lead to painful rashes and puncture wounds. Some very common varieties, such as the aptly named "give-and-take" palm and "sticky" bamboo, cause cuts that can easily become infected.

A different set of obstacles confronts bikers setting out on the crowded streets of Belize City and other big towns. Roads are sometimes very narrow and congested, crammed with jostling people, cars, trucks, and other bicycles. In addition, your bike may be much coveted by an impoverished Belizean, so make sure it is secured when unattended. Better yet, bring it indoors whenever possible.

On the cayes, the hard-packed sandy lanes that pass for modest thoroughfares are fine for wide-tired bicycles, but watch those potholes! Ambergris Caye has the most navigable trails, and both Amigo Travel and Travel & Tour Belize in San Pedro (among others) rent bikes for a reasonable fee. The proprietors can direct visitors to scenic areas north and south of the town. On Caye Caulker, the Island Sun Guest House rents bicycles. For those who want to peddle around Corozal, a flat and pretty area, try Stephan Moerman's rental agency at 37 First Avenue.

Bringing Your Bicycle
Customs officials at the international airport and land border crossings are now accustomed to seeing tourists bring bicycles into Belize, but it is a good idea to carry proof of ownership or have your passport stamped with the bike specifically listed. This is a precaution against having to pay import duty on the item, since authorities may assume the bicycle will be sold in Belize, where they are very expensive. In traveling to the cayes, remember that domestic airplanes are small, propeller-driven craft that may be unable to accommodate large bicycles unless they are disassembled. Most passenger boats and buses, however, can easily store such cargo.

Bicycling Outfitters
Amigo Travel, San Pedro, Ambergris Caye; 26-2180. Scooter and bicycle rental, sailing, other services.

Bike Belize, 104 New Road, Belize City; 2-33855. Moped, minibike, scooter, and bicycle rental; camping, guided tours throughout Belize.

Pacz Hotel, 2 Far West St., San Ignacio; tel./fax 92-2110. Rents mount bikes suitable for on-road/around-town use.

HORSEBACK RIDING
One of the best ways to see Belize is from the back of a horse. This is especially true in jungle areas where the terrain is often muddy and steep. In these situations a sure-footed horse can get you more places—faster—than you're likely to go on your own two legs.

Cayo District horseback riding specialists include Mountain Equestrian Trails, Windy Hill Cottages, Chaa Creek, Parrot's Perch, Ek'Tun, Banana Bank Ranch, and duPlooy's. Easy Rider offers guided trips along the Macal River and through the Mountain Pine Ridge (half and full-day trips available). Our favorite among these is Mountain Equestrian Trails, 8 miles south of the Western Highway on the Mountain Pine Ridge Road. MET's owners, Jim and Marguerite Bevis, run good, well-trained horses on more than 60 miles of back-country trails, many of them former logging roads. You can ride to remote Mayan ruins, caves, waterfalls, and nature reserves—overnight if you'd like.

There are a few outfitters and private individuals who rent horses on Ambergris Caye and in other districts: inquire locally at hotels and travel agencies to contact those currently involved.

Horseback Riding Outfitters

Easy Rider, Box 70, San Ignacio; 9-23310. Guided horseback tours, free pick-up and return.

Guacamallo Treks, c/o S& L Travel, Box 700, Belize City; 2-77593, fax 2-77594. Horseback trips throughout the Cayo.

Mountain Equestrian Trails, Central Farm, P.O. Cayo; 9-23310, fax 8-23505, e-mail *met@bcsl.com.bz*. Horseback riding on 60 miles of trails, also caving and nature tours.

CAVING

Thanks to its porous limestone topography and moist climate, Belize is an ideal place for the formation of caves. Dozens of cave systems have been discovered and explored here, with new passages discovered every year. Experts believe that one of these underground networks, called the Chiquibul, may be the most extensive in Central America and, when fully surveyed, could rank as one of the longest caverns in the world. One of its chambers is said to be the fourth-largest in the Western Hemisphere.

Caving Hazards

Caving is a sport with considerable risks, and you're advised to check with knowledgeable locals before attempting any cave adventure. For experienced cavers, Belize can be a dream come true. Underlying most of the country are the kinds of limestone platforms and uplifts that almost guarantee the formation of extensive cavern networks. Unlike the western rim of the Americas, which is part of the so-called

Ring of Fire circling the Pacific Ocean, there is almost no volcanic activity in Belize.

Because of their isolation, some Belizean caves have not been fully explored. It is likely that many entrances have not even been discovered.

According to Logan McNatt, a former Department of Archaeology employee who spent many years exploring Belizean caves, most of these sites are and should remain closed to the general public. "There are three main problems," McNatt told us. "First, most of the caves are important archaeological sites that have not yet been evaluated or protected. Second, many cave systems of Belize are subject to sudden, unexpected flooding that can make them very dangerous. Finally, few maps of the inner passageways exist."

Cave Geology

McNatt pointed out that many of the caves are part of underground river courses that form massive aquifers beneath Belize. A caver may descend under a clear blue sky, only to find a rapid surge in water elevation caused by a far-off thunderstorm. For these reasons, only experienced and well-equipped cavers should attempt to explore the wilder, lesser-known caves of Belize. Knowledgeable and experienced guides should also be engaged for every journey, except for the small and well-traveled caves.

These caves have an eerie kind of beauty, punctuated as they often are by occasional streams of light from ceiling cracks and side entrances. Some of the underground chambers are 100 or more feet high, adorned with majestic stalactites and stalagmites. They provide an unusual habitat favored by bats, sightless fish, spiders, and other small creatures.

Cave Archaeology

Many of the caves show clear evidence of ceremonial usage by the ancient Maya, who considered such places to be sacred passages to the underworld and the domain of the gods—this realm's Mayan name is Xibalba. Ceremonial fire pits with undisturbed ancient ash and charcoal, utility and ceremonial pottery, obsidian knife blades, jade beads, and other artifacts are often found in dusty yet pristine condition.

For those with a keen interest in archaeology and a tour that includes the Caves Branch area, we recommend Far Horizons Archaeological & Discovery Trips, (800) 552-4575 or (505) 822-9100. In the past Far Horizons has offered a package trip called "The Ceremonial Underworld of Belize"—using a Caves Branch Lodge guide—that brings participants face-to-face with remnants of Maya pitch pine torches, an ancient altar table used in blood-letting and rain-making rites, and an intact human skeleton. The itinerary also includes parts of St. Herman's Cave, the Che Chem Ha Cave, Xunantunich, and the possibility of a Tikal extension.

Where to Go

The easiest caves to visit are Che Chem Ha, Río Frío, St. Herman's, Caves Branch, and Barton Creek in the Cayo District; Blue Creek in the Toledo District; and Blue Hole (a collapsed underwater cave) at Lighthouse Reef. Exploration of any of these—with the exception of Río Frío and St. Herman's—should not be undertaken without an experienced and responsible guide.

In recent years "float trips," on the inflated inner tubes of truck tires, have become popular and we highly recommend trying one. The best of the lot is the Caves Branch tour offered by Ian Anderson's Adventure Company through his Caves Branch jungle lodge, which—among several unique itineraries—explores a sacred Mayan cave along the Caves Branch of the Sibun River. The Jaguar Paw jungle lodge offers similar floats on a separate set of Caves Branch passages. In the Cayo, Mountain Equestrian Trails arranges float trips through Barton Creek Cave. For a high-quality guided tour of an awesome archaeological prize, we recommend the Che Chem Ha Cave, near the Guatemala border. Owner William Morales and members of his family do the guiding. Fees for each of these trips varies, but you should expect to pay $20 and up. Bring your own flashlight or dive lights if you have them.

Caving Outfitters

Ian Anderson's Cave's Branch Adventure Company and Jungle Camp, Belmopan; tel/fax 8-22800, e-mail *caves@pobox.com*. Expeditions by inner tube through cave river systems, jungle expeditions, and dry land cave trips.

Tessa Fairweather, 24 Santa María, Belmopan; 8-22412 or 8-23234. Specializing in caving, nature tours, and Mayan archaeology.

ARCHAEOLOGY TRIPS

There are a handful of outfitters catering specifically to those with an interest in Mayan archaeology. Our favorite is Far Horizons

Expeditions, which is closely involved with on-site archaeologists and offers tours that are usually led by professional archaeologists. Another interesting option is an archaeo-astronomy tour offered by Pennsylvania's Steppingstone Environmental Education Tours, and the focus on shamanism, rainforest medicine, and natural healing (among many other topics) presented in the field schools and seminars of the Central American Institute of Prehistoric and Traditional Cultures (based in Florida and Belize). Various universities in the United States also arrange fieldwork expeditions that "amateurs" can join as short-term volunteers. For an update on who's doing what in Belizean archaeology, contact the government's Department of Archaeology in Belmopan at 8-22106.

Archaeology Outfitters

Central American Institute of Prehistoric and Traditional Cultures, 777 E. Atlantic Ave., Suite Z-376, Delray Beach, FL 33483; (561) 279-2262, fax 279-0518, e-mail *hacmol@world.std.com*. Field school and seminar programs in shamanism, ethnobotany, tropical ecology, and other subjects related to Mayan and Garifuna cultures; Belize office in San Ignacio.

Earthwatch, 680 Mt. Auburn St., Watertown, MA 02272; (800) 776-0188, *http://www.earthwatch.org*. Work-study archaeological tours.

Far Horizons Archaeological and Discovery Trips, P.O. Box 91900, Albuquerque, NM 87199-1900; tel, (800) 552-4575 or (505) 822-9100, e-mail *journey@farhorizon.com*. Web site *http://www.farhorizon.com*. "Cultural discovery" trips to Mayan villages and ruins, led by archaeologists trained in Belize; can arrange canoeing, horseback riding, fishing, and boat trips. The owner is an archaeologist; highly recommended.

Institute of Mayan Antiquities, 6828 Wofford Drive, Dallas, TX 75227; (214) 381-2311. Remote-sensing research trips to Mayan ruins in Belize and Guatemala.

Maya Research Program, St. Mary's University, Box 15376, San Antonio, TX 78212; (512) 826-1672. Fieldwork at Blue Creek site in Orange Walk District; contact Thomas H. Guderjan.

Oceanic Society Expeditions, Ft. Mason Center, Bldg. E, San

Francisco, CA 94123; (800) 326-7491. Fieldwork involving manatees, howler monkeys, dolphins, and sea turtles.

Smithsonian Odyssey Tours & Research Expeditions, 1100
Jefferson Drive S.W., Washington, DC 20560; (800) 524-4125 or
(202) 357-4700. Study tours and research expeditions.

Steppingstone Environmental Education Tours, P.O. Box 373,
Narberth, PA 19072; (800) 874-8784, fax (610) 649-3428. Vacation
and educational tours for school groups, nature and archaeology
enthusiasts, birders, snorkeling, diving, botanical artists workshops;
supports conservation.

University Research Expeditions Program, University of
California at Berkeley, Berkeley, CA 94720; (510) 642-6586,
fax (510) 642-6791. Research expeditions in archaeology, including
Río Hondo sites; develops cooperative projects with scientists from
developing nations.

Vincent Gillett, Department of Archaeology, Belmopan; 8-22106.
Archaeology tours.

Wildland Adventures, 3516 NE 155th St., Seattle, WA 98155;
(800) 345-4453. Tours specializing in Mayan archaeology, cultural
diversity, tropical nature, and the barrier reef; hires local guides and
contributes to conservation and community projects through the
Earth Preservation Fund.

VOLUNTEER OPPORTUNITIES

There are many ways you can do volunteer work in Belize, whether
it's sifting through Mayan ruins, counting howler monkeys, or
observing dolphin behavior. These opportunities are often offered by
specialized outfitters based in the United States and Canada. We've
listed a number of them in the section that follows. Other excellent
resources include the specialized magazines and newsletters catering
to specific interest groups. *Archaeology* magazine, for instance, publishes an ongoing roster of volunteer fieldwork opportunities in its
"Travel Guide" section. Some organizations distribute catalogues
that describe their trips in detail. The catalogue of *Oceanic Society*

Expeditions, for example, lists volunteer research trips involving dolphins, manatees, howler monkeys, and sea turtles.

Even though you're volunteering your time and labor, you'll likely pay for your own trip, including airfare, food, and lodging, although you may get discount rates. Because the Belize government is essentially broke and its business community is small, we encourage you to consider these travel options, which can be very rewarding.

Volunteer Opportunities

Earthwatch, Watertown, Massachusetts; (800) 776-0188, *http://www.earthwatch.org.* Volunteers drive research in sea grass ecology and other marine habitats.

Global Citizens Network, St. Paul, MN; (800) 644-9292. Past projects include renovating schools and installing water systems in Mayan villages.

Institute for Central American Development Studies, P.O. Box 025216, Department 826, Miami, FL 33102-5216. Internships dealing with social justice, agriculture, and immigration.

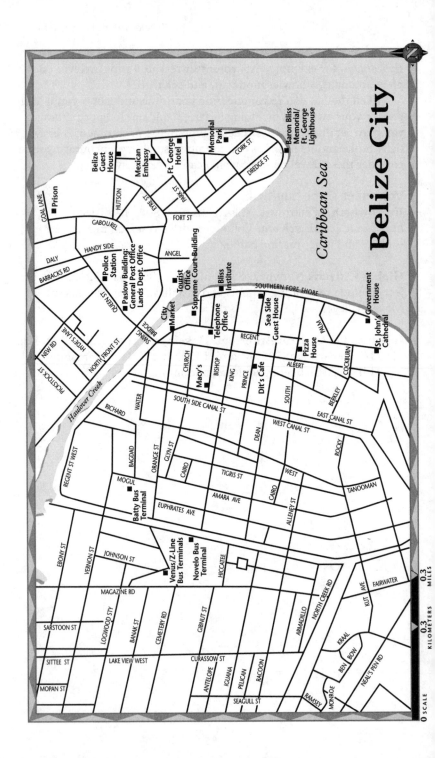

Belize City

Caribbean Sea

Baron Bliss Memorial/ Ft. George Lighthouse

Memorial Park

CORK ST

DREDGE ST

Belize Guest House

Prison

COAL LANE

Mexican Embassy

Ft. George Hotel

HUTSON

DYKE ST

PARK ST

FORT ST

GABOUREL

HANDY SIDE

Police Station

Paslow Building: General Post Office Lands Dept. Office

ANGEL

DALY

BARRACKS RD

QUEEN ST

Supreme Court Building

Tourist Office

Bliss Institute

SOUTHERN FORE SHORE

Government House

St. John's Cathedral

NEW RD

HYDE'S LANE

NORTH FRONT ST

SWING BRIDGE

City Market

Telephone Office

Sea Side Guest House

REGENT

PALM

COCKBURN

PICSTOCK ST

Hanover Creek

CHURCH

Macy's

BISHOP

KING

PRINCE

Dit's Cafe

SOUTH

Pizza House

ALBERT

BERKLEY

EAST CANAL ST

RICHARD

WATER

SOUTH SIDE CANAL ST

DEAN

WEST CANAL ST

ROCKY

REGENT ST WEST

BAGDAD

ORANGE ST

GLYN ST

CAIRO

TIGRIS ST

WEST

CAIRO

ALLENEY ST

TANOOMAN

MOGUL

Batty Bus Terminal

EUPHRATES AVE

AMARA AVE

EBONY ST

VERNON ST

JOHNSON ST

Venus/Z-Line Bus Terminals

Novelo Bus Terminal

HICCATEE

MAGAZINE RD

NORTH CREEK RD

KUT AVE

FAIRWATER

SARSTOON ST

LOGWOOD STY

BANAK ST

CEMETERY RD

GIBNUT ST

ARMADILLO

KRAAL

BEN BOW

NEAL'S PEN RD

SITTEE ST

LAKE VIEW WEST

CURASSOW ST

ANTELOPE

IGUANA

PELICAN

RACOON

RAMSEY

MONROE

MOPAN ST

SEAGULL ST

0 SCALE

0.3 KILOMETERS

0.3 MILES

BELIZE CITY

5

Characterizing Belize City as the nation's hub is an understatement. For many, this community of about 70,000 residents *is* Belize. Located on the Caribbean Sea at the mouth of Haulover Creek (a name given to the last few miles of the Belize River), this port town is the country's largest urban center. Belize City supports a growing tourism infrastructure, as well as other services, industries, and retail businesses. Despite this relative hustle and bustle, it still manages to retain a decidedly laid-back atmosphere. This may be the busiest place in Belize, but don't expect anything to get done in a hurry.

Sadly, the reputation of Belize City has gone from bad to worse in recent years, fueled by well-publicized accounts of street crime, drug trafficking, and panhandling. There seems to be no end to the number of horror stories visitors tell about their unfortunate adventures in this ramshackle, slightly seedy community. It's our opinion that Belize City is not as dangerous as many people make it out to be, although reasonable precautions should be taken when going from one place to another, especially on foot.

The authors have found that here, as elsewhere in the country, 99 percent of Belizeans are helpful, courteous, and genuinely happy to welcome visitors. In our view, Belize City's smiling residents and relaxed pace are among its greatest attractions. From hotel employees to restaurant workers, bank tellers to conservation leaders, almost everyone is eager to share information and exchange pleasantries.

This laid-back, tolerant attitude is perhaps a tribute to Belize City's colorful history and multicultural traditions.

HISTORY

The first full-time residents of what is now Belize City are believed to have been Mayan Indians, who maintained a busy fishing camp on nearby Moho Caye (now a private diving resort) for several centuries. Bones and other artifacts excavated at this site suggest there was abundant marine life, including large numbers of turtles and manatees. In the late 1600s, after the area had been mostly abandoned by the Maya, pirates from Scotland, England, and France began to spend time during the annual rainy season at the mouth of the Belize River. Over the years, these buccaneers and their African slaves harvested tropical hardwoods in the interior and used the broad, slow-moving waterway to float the precious timber to ocean-going vessels anchored offshore.

By the 18th century, the settlement of Belize Town had been solidly established by members of what the British referred to as their Bay Settlement (named after the nearby Bay of Honduras). Historians say the city is built on a foundation of loose coral, logwood chips, and

British Caribbean style guest house in Ft. George district of Belize City

Richard Mahler

rum bottles. Whatever its exact composition, this pile of debris seems to be sinking, as much of the urban area is now barely above sea level. Despite this swampy environment, the climate is fairly pleasant, owing to near-constant trade winds and an aggressive, ongoing government campaign against mosquito larvae.

Several violent hurricanes and accompanying surges have battered Belize City over the years. These storms occur primarily in autumn, as evidenced by Hurricane Hattie's destructive visit on October 31, 1961, which took hundreds of lives and nearly leveled the town. This was the prime motivation for Belizeans to move their capital some 45 miles inland to Belmopan, even though most residents have chosen to take their chances by staying in Belize City. (Only about 6,000 people reside permanently in Belmopan and a large percentage of government workers commute every day.) In spite of Mother Nature's unpredictable and sometimes destructive forces, Belize City remains home to about one-third of the country's population.

GETTING AROUND BELIZE CITY

Walking alone in certain areas—ask at your hotel or travel agency for a detailed description of trouble spots—is not recommended because a small but aggressive contingent of Belizeans is persistent in demanding money or selling drugs. At night, a single person on foot may encounter even more significant trouble; the dangers of being attacked and robbed are very real here. Taxis within Belize City's limits are inexpensive (about $2.50 or less for any destination) and readily available. We advise you to use them, and to avoid carrying unnecessary valuables on your person.

Although Belize City does have a local bus system, we hesitate to recommend it because routes are confusing and not well posted. Watch for the radio-equipped Tourism Police (identified by special uniforms and caps), who patrol heavily-touristed areas on foot and are trained to answer visitors' questions as well as to keep the peace.

Taxis

Within Belize City itself, taxis—any vehicles with green license plates—are generally the best way to travel, unless you have your own car or have arranged transportation in advance. In 1997, standard fare was about $2.50 for most in-city destinations. Remember, tipping of taxi drivers is not customary in Belize.

From the Airport

From **Phillip Goldson International Airport**, the 15-minute taxi ride into Belize City cost $15 in 1997. Rates are fixed by an informal cabdrivers' union—which squeezed out a hotel shuttle service a few years ago—so it does no good to bargain or shop around.

Visitor Information

The main office of the **Belize Tourist Board** is at 83 N. Front Street. Go up two flights and the friendly staff will answer your questions and give you informative brochures about the country. Guidebooks, maps, T-shirts, and other items are on sale. (Like most businesses, the Tourist Board is closed from noon to 1 p.m.)

SHOPPING

Romac's Supermarket, at 27 Albert Street, and **Brodie's,** directly across the street at the corner of Albert and Regent, come in handy for all those provisions you need for exploring the barrier reef or tropical forest. Brodie's has a pharmacy, a produce section, and an exceptionally good selection of Belizean books and magazines. You can stock up on even cheaper fruits and vegetables at the public market, in the **New Custom's House** about three blocks north on Regent Street.

Among the best places to buy Belizean souvenirs are the **National Handicraft Centre**, on Fort Street in the old TACA warehouse, 2-33636, and **Go Tees & Graphics**, 23 Regent Street, 2-74082. The **Belize Audubon Society**, 12 N. Front Street, 2-34987, sells T-shirts, hats, nature books, and other gift items. Belize isn't particularly known for its arts and crafts, but some carvings, baskets, and weavings are good buys. We urge you to avoid buying products made of endangered wildlife, such as turtles, shells, black coral, big cats, or crocodiles.

TRAVEL AGENCIES

Belize City is an ideal place to finalize travel arrangements and pick up lots of insider tips on things to do. We recommend, particularly for the ecology-minded visitor, **Jal's Travel**, 148 N. Front Street, 2-45407, and **Tubroos Tree Adventures**, 146 Barracks Road, 2-33398. **Belize Land Air Sea Tours**, 27 Dean Street, 2-73897, provides daily Belize City tours as well as customized, nature-oriented excursions.

For day trips to the howler monkey sanctuary, Altun Ha, and other northern destinations, we particularly recommend tour guide

Winston Seawell, 2-31979, manager of the **G & W Holiday** travel agency, 2-52461 at the International Airport and 14-8756 on his mobile phone. Expect to pay $50 and up for such day trips. Make sure your guide is knowledgeable before you leave.

THINGS TO SEE AND DO

Several landmarks have withstood the various hurricanes and can be seen during even a brief walking or taxi tour of Belize City. Another good way to see the city is via guided tour buses, such as those operated by **Belize Land and Sea Tours**, 27-3897.

Belize schoolgirls find their books make effective sun shades.

Belize Tourist Board

At the gateway to Belize Harbor is **Fort George Lighthouse**, dominating a finger of land that was originally the easternmost point on what once was **Fort George Island**. The channel separating the island and mainland was filled in during the 1920s, long after Fort George had fulfilled its function as an army base. Views of nearby cayes covered in mangroves now await visitors to the site, and brown pelicans often fish in small groups near the shore.

Next to the lighthouse is a small park and the **Baron Bliss Memorial**, a tribute to the "Fourth Baron Bliss of the former Kingdom of Portugal," Henry Edward Ernest Victor Bliss. An Englishman by birth, this eccentric adventurer sailed to Belize in 1926 and fell in love with its soothing climate, unspoiled waters, and palm-studded islands. As a result of food poisoning Bliss suffered in Trinidad, the baron was too ill to come ashore. He spent several months aboard his yacht, the *Sea King*, fishing in the harbor as he tried to recover his health. Bliss was impressed by the kindness and respect fellow sportfishermen and colonial officials showed him. Before Bliss died aboard his boat, he specified in his will that a trust fund of almost $2 million be established for the sole benefit of Belizeans.

The interest generated from the Bliss Fund has been used to help build clinics, water systems, and libraries. The baron stipulated that a portion of the trust funds be used to stage an annual yacht regatta in

Belizean waters. This is the focal event of the national holiday on March 9, which honors his contributions.

In the heart of Belize City, at the corner of Front and Queen Streets, is a wooden colonial-style building that houses the main post office. Here in the **Paslow Building** you may purchase the colorful Belizean stamps, among the most beautiful in the world. They depict brocket deer, storks, marine life, tapir, jaguar, macaws, and many other native animals. Postage rates are one of the few bargains in Belize: in 1997 you could still airmail a postcard to the United States or Europe for 15¢! A special sales counter for stamp collectors is on the Queen Street side of the post office. Upstairs, some of the best maps of Belize (divided into north and south sections) are available from a government office for about $10 each.

Facing the main post office is the **Swing Bridge**, reportedly the only such manually-operated bridge still in service. It was constructed in Liverpool, England, and has been cranked open for Haulover Creek's high-masted boat traffic since 1923. When the bridge is working, at about 6 a.m. and 5:30 p.m., police officers stop pedestrians and vehicles on either side of the bridge while men insert long poles into a capstan and gradually open a passageway that allows tall-masted vessels to pass upriver or out to sea. Sadly, the swing mechanism hasn't functioned well in recent years, and there is talk of replacing the bridge entirely.

Next to the bridge, in the renovated historic fire station, is the **Maritime Museum and Boat Terminal**, with scheduled water taxi service to Caye Caulker and Ambergris Caye. Several gift shops and cafés are under the roof of this large building, along with restrooms and a pay telephone. The terminal opens at 7 a.m. and closes at 6 p.m. The museum, which describes Belize's maritime history and marine ecology, is open from 8 a.m. to 5 p.m. daily.

South of the Swing Bridge, facing Battlefield Park on Regent Street, is the imposing **Supreme Court Building**. Built in 1923 in classic British Colonial-style (complete with dome-topped clock tower), it stands on the site of the original settlement courthouse built in 1818. The courthouse has been rebuilt twice: it was demolished in 1878 and destroyed again in a 1918 fire that took the life of then-governor **William Hart Bennett**. For a slice-of-life experience, step into a courtroom and watch the Belizean justice system in action. (The clock tower was being renovated in 1997 and may again give the correct time by the time you read this.)

Near the courthouse on Bliss Promenade (also called the

Southern Foreshore) is the **Baron Bliss Institute**, which, with its modern-looking circular second floor, seems out of place amid the Victorian gingerbread of Belize City's oldest neighborhood. The institute displays (poorly) some ancient Mayan artifacts from Caracol and other Belizean archaeological sites. It also houses a modest public library, auditorium, and art gallery, as well as the **National Arts Council**. Slide shows and lectures on science, history, conservation, and culture are held here. If you go, take a taxi; this has become a tough neighborhood in recent years.

Supreme Court building, Belize City, built in 1923

Belize Tourist Board

Headquartered on the south side of the Swing Bridge, near the busy intersection of Regent and Albert Streets, is Belize City's main public market, housed in a modern three-story building called the **New Customs House**. Another public market has operated from an old warehouse on North Front Street, a few blocks west of the Fort George Lighthouse. Although it is scheduled to be torn down, as of mid-1997 this informal market was still the best place to buy herbs from vendors whose wares include the negrito tree bark, used in the treatment of dysentery, and copal, a tree resin used for incense.

At the south end of Regent Street is a venerable mansion called **Government House**, a historic British Colonial landmark that is now a museum (open weekdays 8:30 a.m. to noon and 1 p.m. to 4:30 p.m.). In this former residence of the colony's governors, you'll see archival records and artifacts in addition to well-curated exhibits documenting the history of British Honduras. Take a few minutes to stroll the beautiful grounds and imagine the grand receptions once held here. There's even a tiny swimming pool—the first ever in Belize!

Across the street is **St. John's Anglican Cathedral**, the first Protestant church in Central America and one of the oldest buildings in Belize. Built in 1812 by slaves using bricks brought over as ballast in the hulls of ships from Europe, the church was the site of three coronation ceremonies for Indian "kings" of the Mosquito Coast, held between 1816 and 1845. These self-styled kings were members of an indigenous ruling class that once presided over the native tribes that lived along what is now the Caribbean coast of Honduras and Nicaragua. Inside the church are dozens of plaques commemorating prominent Anglican colonists, and you're welcome to wander around.

BUS SERVICE TO OTHER PARTS OF BELIZE

There are several bus stations in Belize City, each corresponding to the several competing companies that serve outlying areas. Because these terminals are in questionable neighborhoods, we recommend taking a taxi rather than walking to them. Buses to most large towns depart hourly throughout the morning, less often in the afternoon and evening. One-way bus fares average about $1.50 for each hour of travel. While several smaller bus companies serving specific villages depart from other locations (inquire locally for details), here are the major bus companies and bus terminals:

Batty—for travel to points north and west, 54 E. Collet Canal, 2-74924

James—for travel to points south, Pound Yard Bridge

Novelo's—for travel to points west, 19 W. Collet Canal, 2-71160

Venus—for travel to points north, Magazine Road, 2-73354

Z-Line —for travel to points south, Magazine Road, 2-73937

CAR RENTAL

For those who want to rent a car for their visit, we recommend **Crystal** at 1.5 Mile Northern Highway, 2-31600 or 2-30921. The American owner offers a wide variety of slightly used cars, vans, and even motor homes at reasonable prices (all major credit cards accepted). The four-wheel-drive specialist we recommend is **Safari**, which rents only well-maintained Isuzu Troopers, 2-35395, e-mail *safari@btl.ne,* International Airport and Ft. George Hotel.

Other vehicles are available at the offices of **Avis**, Ft. George Hotel, 2-78637; **Budget**, 771 Bella Vista, 2-32435; and **National**, 126 Freetown Road and at the international airport, 2-31586. Inquire about road conditions before you select your car; some destinations require four-wheel-drive.

Rates for car rentals are surprisingly high, starting at about $65 a day, plus $15 per day for insurance. Comprehensive insurance is not generally available in Belize and, unless stated otherwise, the person renting the car may be held responsible for any and all damage, including flat tires. The best insurance terms are offered by **Budget**. Gasoline prices are about double what you'd pay in the United States or Canada.

GETTING TO THE ISLANDS FROM BELIZE CITY

The **Marine Transportation Terminal** on N. Front Street (immediately east of the Swing Bridge) coordinates water taxi service to Caye Caulker and Ambergris Caye. An 11:50 a.m. express boat takes passengers to Chetumal, Mexico, where bus connections are easily made to Cancún and Merida.

Allow about 45 minutes for the trip to Caulker ($7.50 one-way, $12.50 round-trip), a little over an hour to Ambergris ($15 one-way, $25 round-trip), and roughly 2 hours to Chetumal (prices start at $30, one-way). Note that round-trip fares to the islands are for *same day* return only. Departure times and rates are posted inside the Terminal, which has food vendors, gift shops, and a maritime museum. In 1997 there were five daily water taxi departures for Caulker but only one (at 9 a.m.) for San Pedro.

There is a scheduled daily departure for Ambergris Caye by the *Andrea* from the Bellevue pier, in front of the Bellevue Hotel on Marine Parade. Prices are similar to those charged at the Marine Transportation Terminal. You can bargain among independent boat operators moored along Haulover Creek for trips to other islands.

WHERE TO STAY IN BELIZE CITY

Bellevue Hotel, 5 Southern Foreshore; $60; 2-77051. On the waterfront, with modern rooms and a lively upstairs bar decorated like an old ocean liner. Boat service to Ambergris Caye and Caye Caulker.

Best Western Biltmore Plaza, Mile 3, Northern Highway; $100 and up; 2-32302 and (800) 528-1234. A luxury hotel near the airport, with a consistently bad reputation.

Chateau Caribbean Hotel, 6 Marine Parade; $85; 2-30800. Comfortably upscale, with an ocean view and sea breeze (if you ask for a waterfront room). The restaurant and bar, which also feature a Caribbean view, are fairly good. The Chateau has been a consistent supporter of natural history tourism in Belize.

Colton House, 9 Cork St.; $45; 2-44666, fax 2-30451, e-mail *coltonhse@btl.com*. A five-room, 1928 colonial-style wooden house with high ceilings and paddle fans. The spacious "garden room" apartment ($60) is equipped with TV, fridge, coffeemaker, and air-conditioning. The Belizeans who run the place are happy to answer any and all questions about what to see and do hereabouts. This is our favorite guest house in the breeze-cooled Ft. George neighborhood.

Fiesta (formerly Ramada Royal Reef) Hotel & Marina, Newtown Barracks Road; $100 and up; 2-32670 or (800) 228-9898. Belize City's biggest hotel, boasting all the goodies one would expect with a high-rise price tag. Several decent restaurants lie within.

Fort Street Guest House, 4 Fort St.; $65, breakfast included; 2-30116 or (800) 240-FORT. This classy B&B occupies six rooms above a co-owned first-rate restaurant and gift shop. A long-time favorite of conservationists (although the shared bath may give some folks pause). American owners Hugh and Teresa Parkey are experts on things to do in Belize, and Hugh runs a full-service dive shop.

Hotel Mopan, 55 Regent St.; $35; 2-77351. A clean but rather shabby establishment with a modest restaurant and bar. The Mopan is run by Jean and Tom Shaw, longtime environmentalists who can answer questions about any of Belize's "natural destinations."

Radisson Ft. George Hotel, 2 Marine Parade; $120 and up; (800) 333-3333 or 2-33333, e-mail *rdfgh@btl.net*. This modern, upmarket hotel has a well-stocked gift shop, very good restaurant, swimming pool, and bar. You can rent Avis cars here, and the hotel maintains a full-service marina across the street. It also owns the **Villa Belize**, 2-77400, across the street, which offers similar rooms and amenities.

Seaside Guest House, 3 Prince St.; $5 dorm, $14 private; 2-78339. Basic but clean lodging for those on a budget. Shared bath; Quaker run.

WHERE TO EAT IN BELIZE CITY

Dit's, 50 King St. The best pastries and Creole cowfoot soup in town.

El Centro Hotel, 4 Bishop St. Excellent, reasonably-priced pizza and authentic Creole cuisine. Air-conditioned.

Fort Street Restaurant, 4 Fort St. One of the best places to eat in Belize City period, serving excellent and imaginatively prepared dishes (albeit at a borderline-exorbitant price).

G G's Café and Patio, 2B King St. A pleasant courtyard atmosphere, efficient service, and good food; try the Creole-style grilled chicken.

Goofy's, 6 Douglas Jones St. Terrific Jamaican food.

The Gourmet, 13 Prince St. Good pizza, with delicious *licuados* (blended fruit drinks) as accompaniments.

The Grill, near the Fiesta Hotel on Newtown Barracks Road. Very good seafood dinners.

Macy's Café, 18 Bishop St. Serves Belize's inexpensive and ubiquitous main dish of rice 'n' beans, with extras ranging from stewed chicken to freshly squeezed lemonade. Actor Harrison Ford ate here during the filming of *Mosquito Coast* some years back and proclaimed Macy's his favorite restaurant anywhere. But not even a movie star's presence affects the casual atmosphere, friendly staff, and humble furnishings. Do the natural world a favor, though, and resist the temptation to order wild game, which appears occasionally on the menu here and at a number of other Belizean restaurants.

The Marlin, 11 Regent St., West. Very good Belizean cuisine.

New Chon Saan Palace, 1 Kelly St. Some of the biggest portions of the best Chinese food in town. Air-conditioned.

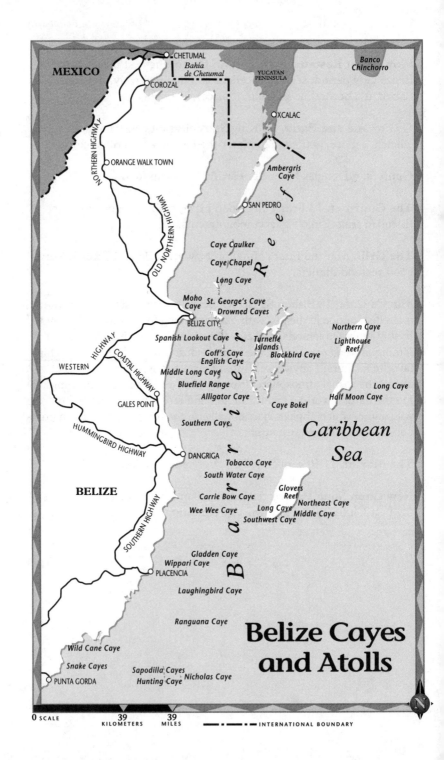

Belize Cayes and Atolls

MEXICO

CHETUMAL
Bahía de Chetumal
COROZAL

YUCATAN PENINSULA

Banco Chinchorro

XCALAC

NORTHERN HIGHWAY

ORANGE WALK TOWN

OLD NORTHERN HIGHWAY

Ambergris Caye

SAN PEDRO

Barrier Reef

Caye Caulker

Caye Chapel

Long Caye

Moho Caye

St. George's Caye

Drowned Cayes

BELIZE CITY

Spanish Lookout Caye

HIGHWAY

Goff's Caye
English Caye

Turneffe Islands

Blackbird Caye

Northern Caye

Lighthouse Reef

WESTERN

COASTAL HIGHWAY

Middle Long Caye

Bluefield Range

GALES POINT

Alligator Caye

Caye Bokel

Long Caye

Half Moon Caye

HUMMINGBIRD HIGHWAY

Southern Caye

Caribbean Sea

DANGRIGA

Tobacco Caye

South Water Caye

BELIZE

Carrie Bow Caye

Wee Wee Caye

Glovers Reef

Long Caye

Northeast Caye

Middle Caye

Southwest Caye

SOUTHERN HIGHWAY

Gladden Caye

Wippari Caye

PLACENCIA

Laughingbird Caye

Ranguana Caye

Wild Cane Caye

Snake Cayes

PUNTA GORDA

Sapodilla Cayes

Hunting Caye

Nicholas Caye

0 SCALE

39 KILOMETERS

39 MILES

INTERNATIONAL BOUNDARY

N

THE CAYES AND THE ATOLLS

6

The main—and often the only—attraction of interest to many first-time visitors to Belize is the country's barrier reef, a spectacular coral-based formation that runs almost the entire 185-mile length of the east coast and swings from within 10 to 40 miles of the mainland. In sheer size, this magnificent natural wonder is surpassed only by Australia's Great Barrier Reef and a couple of others in the South Pacific. It is by far the largest barrier reef in the Western Hemisphere.

One of the richest ecosystems on the planet, Belize's reef is punctuated by scores of beautiful tiny cayes (pronounced "keys"), sand bores, patch reefs, canyons, and various underwater structures that are home to hundreds of species, including 220 species of fish and untold hundreds of varieties of invertebrates—all thriving in clear, unpolluted, 78- to 86-degree water.

So exquisite is this habitat that the United Nations has named the reef as a World Heritage Site, arguing that its deterioration or disappearance would result in "a harmful impoverishment of the heritage of all nations of the world." One writer has equated the experience of snorkeling here to "sipping a fine glass of wine and soaking in a Jacuzzi at the same time, the water teeming with a mirage of color."

Belize finds itself engaged in a delicate balancing act. It vigorously promotes tourism, diving, snorkeling, and fishing on its barrier reef, while at the same time struggles to protect this exceedingly fragile environment from harmful human influence. Certain commercial species, such as lobster, conch, and shrimp, are already severely depleted, and some irreversible damage has been done to the reef by careless fishermen and visitors. It's important to realize that the reef is a living entity, dependent for its very existence on the health of living coral polyps and other reef-building organisms.

The government is involved in an aggressive public education and environmental protection campaign to preserve and protect its marine resources. Among other things, this involves shifting some foreign visitors away from high-impact areas—namely the Ambergris-Caulker-Chapel Caye corridor—toward lesser-known destinations that can more easily absorb the impact of newcomers. Impending development on Ambergris Caye prompted the government to declare the northern two-thirds of the island off-limits to further exploitation, but not before one last major project broke ground.

Despite this trend, there are still dozens of islands along the southern half of the reef that are completely uninhabited and have much to offer visitors, including first-rate scuba diving, snorkeling, sailing, kayaking, windsurfing, and fishing. Also overlooked in most discussions of Belize's coastal waters are the several atolls, banks, and offshore reefs that exist beyond the barrier strip. As a whole, Belize has an estimated 350 miles of coral reef line and 280 square miles of island land mass.

The atolls and southernmost cayes are not as accessible and have more limited accommodations than the northern barrier reef islands, but they do offer some very unusual and rewarding experiences. For serious anglers and divers, these sites provide the chance to fish and dive in little-disturbed natural environments that teem with marine life.

Since many outer destinations are an easy day trip from the hotels on Ambergris Caye and Caye Caulker, it is arguably more efficient to use those islands (or Belize City) as a base for exploring such remote offshore locations as Lighthouse Reef and the Turneffe Islands (or Glover's Reef from Dangriga). Although there are places to stay and eat on these atolls, cost and access may be a problem for travelers with tight budgets or time constraints. Those fortunate enough to have their own kayaks and sail or powerboats will be pleased to know that the barrier reef provides innumerable safe anchorages and some of the finest paddling and sailing conditions anywhere.

THE BARRIER REEF AND CAYES

Most of the 200-odd cayes of Belize lie in relatively shallow water along the barrier reef itself. The long, narrow stretch of water between the reef and the mainland—known as the Inner Channel—is also dotted with small islands, as are some of the country's inland lagoons.

The word *caye* is testimony to the varied history of the islands. It is a corruption of the Spanish cayo, translated as "small island."

Early Spanish explorers were the first Europeans to set foot on the barrier chain, and they apparently stopped regularly to obtain fresh water and repair their ships. The Spaniards no doubt encountered the Maya, who established many fishing and trading outposts here over a period of centuries.

English, French, and Scottish pirates, along with Puritan traders, were next to arrive. They found the cayes ideally suited for their respective sea-based livelihoods, and old coins, bottles, and tools are sometimes still found on the sandy beaches, along with ancient Mayan pottery and other artifacts. Europeans also settled here as fishermen, whalers, and plantation owners. They were joined in the late 1800s by a wave of Mexican immigrants eager to escape the brutal Yucatán Caste Wars.

Laughingbird Caye is an Inner Channel faro southeast of Placencia.

Dan Dancer/Lighthawk

AMBERGRIS CAYE

Getting There: *From Belize City, 20 minutes by plane or 1¼ hours by boat.*

Main Activities: *Diving, snorkeling, fishing, windsurfing, kayaking, birding.*

Visitor Information: *Ambergris Caye's Internet Web site* http://www.ambergriscaye.com *provides access to home pages of hotels,* *dive shops, and other tourist-related businesses. The Belize Tourist Board and Belize Tourism Industry Association's Belize Visitor & Tours, on Middle Sreet, north of the airstrip; 26-2728, fax 26-2402.*

The largest and best known of the cayes, Ambergris is part of a wide limestone peninsula dangling south from the Yucatán coast of the Mexican state of Quintana Roo.

Most Ambergris residents are of Mexican ancestry and speak Spanish among themselves. Early in Belize's history, its northern neighbor even laid claim to the island. Ambergris Caye has about the same land area as the Caribbean island of Barbados, although much of Ambergis is uninhabitable mangrove swamp.

The island's name is a holdover from colonial days and refers to a waxy substance, believed to originate in sperm whale intestines, that was once used in making perfume. Some say that ambergris washed up here regularly during the colony's early history, but marine biologists are skeptical. They maintain that whales have never been common in this part of the Caribbean and argue that sightings of ambergris have always been very rare.

Most visitors reach the island by taking a boat or airplane across lower Chetumal Bay from Belize City, 35 miles to the southwest. Locals refer to passenger boats as "skiffs" and their smaller canoe-like vessels as "dories." The crossing takes about 1¼ hours by skiff and less than 20 minutes by plane.

Fishing was once the caye's principal industry, but within the last 20 years tourism has taken over. Many fishers now use their boats exclusively to cater to visitor needs: snorkeling, sportfishing, diving, and manatee watching. **San Pedro**, the island's only town, offers a wide choice of hotels, restaurants, bars, gift shops, and travel agencies to suit every recreational interest and pocketbook, although food and services are relatively expensive here.

While San Pedro in some ways seems to be suffering under the strain of rapid growth, Ambergris Caye still has much to offer. People are friendly, accommodations are comfortable, and there's plenty to do. Resorts on the outskirts of San Pedro are noticeably more expensive, but tend to be more tranquil and luxurious than hotels in town. Hikers and bicyclists will find that much of the island is covered with a high broadleaf forest interspersed with freshwater sinks that attract lots of wildlife, including an abundance of birds.

Birders can spot warblers, egrets, herons, pelicans, and frigate birds. **Bird Caye**, located on the bay (leeward) side of Ambergris,

Kevin Schafer

San Pedro is the largest town along the barrier reef.

shelters rookeries for 30 species, including the reddish egret, greater egret, and cormorant. Spoonbills, avocets, and ducks also congregate here. Turtles nest on certain yet-undeveloped beaches, and even large cats prowl through the mangroves. Thousands of shells litter the beaches. (The coral reef is less than a mile offshore.)

Ambergris has the largest single concentration of tourist services in Belize yet still manages to retain a laid-back atmosphere. The streets are sandy and belong to slow-paced strollers. Vehicles (mostly electric golf carts) are few and far between. The water is iridescent blue and immediately accessible. A cooling trade wind sweeps in from the northeast much of the time, keeping insect pests at bay. A variety of food and drink is available, and some of the country's best cooks are happy to prepare fresh seafood exactly the way you like it.

The vast majority of San Pedro's residents are good-humored and tolerant, their lifestyle casual and simple. The tin-roofed, color-fully painted wooden houses are cheerfully dilapidated, giving the distinct impression that you can relax all day if that's your choice.

For all these reasons, Ambergris Caye makes a fine base for excur-sions to nearby attractions and the more distant islands. Experienced guides are easy to find and some of the best outfitters for fishing, snor-keling, windsurfing, sailing, kayaking, and diving are based here. There

Downtown San Pedro along
Front Street

Richard Mahler

are massive coral canyons full of caves and tunnels near San Pedro, and snorkelers report aquarium-like conditions. Within the confines of the reef itself, the Mexico Rocks area on the windward side is highly recommended. Conditions are ideal here and among the island's 13 lagoons for sailing, windsurfing, and kayaking.

Travel Tips

A few words of caution are in order. Some of the more than 700 hotel rooms on Ambergris Caye are very basic by American or European standards. Furnishings and other physical amenities are usually minimal, so what you're paying for is location and service, not luxury. For most visitors this is no problem, because they spend so much time outdoors. The more elegant resorts are located north and south of the village; many of these have freshwater swimming pools, satellite TV, and hot tubs. Don't expect broad beaches, however: Ambergris Caye isn't made that way.

San Pedro has only a half-dozen streets, and staying in town puts you close to the action—or noise, depending on your point of view. Keep in mind that some rooms are less than 100 yards from the airport, and takeoffs go right over the town. If you stay outside the town, transportation to and from San Pedro is usually provided by your hotel. Bicycles, golf carts, and motor scooters are available for rent or you can simply walk or take a taxi. The northern part of the island is accessible by bicycle or car via a hand-pulled "Huck Finn" ferry that runs until 6 p.m. daily (5 p.m. Sundays). The fare starts at 50¢ for pedestrians.

In general, the more sociable visitors will be happier in San Pedro, while those in search of a more rustic, inexpensive setting would do well to investigate on Caye Caulker and other islands.

Diving

If you wish to scuba-dive during your visit, there are many half-day, all-day, and overnight excursions available. It pays to ask around for suggestions, since some operators are definitely better than others. We've

A villa-style resort on the south end of Ambergris Caye

heard the most positive comments about the **Amigos del Mar** dive shop, 26-2706, based on one of the in-town piers; **Blue Hole Dive Centre**, 26-2982, which operates **Blue Hole Express**; and **Undersea Adventures**, which offers half-day, full-day, and night-dive trips. The latter also books overnight passage on its 55-foot *Manta IV* dive boat for wall dives at the famous Blue Hole on Lighthouse Reef.

Snorkeling

For snorkeling, **Ramon Badillo** is well-liked for his glass-bottom boat tours and gentle way with first-time snorkelers. **"Lil Alfonse" Graniel** and **Tulu Villanueva** also have good reputations. **David Nuñez**, 26-2314, and **Amigos del Mar**, 26-2706, are recommended for both snorkeling and fishing trips. Expect to pay about $15 per person for a half-day of snorkeling, $35 for a full day (ask if the fare includes the Hol Chan entrance fee). Most snorkel and dive trips leave at about 8:30 a.m. and again at 1:30 p.m. Besides **Hol Chan**, the best snorkeling locations are **Punta Azul**, **Mexico Rocks**, **Coral Gardens**, and **Los Cocos**.

We recommend day-long, three-stop snorkel trips on Roberto Smith's beautifully restored island trader *Winnie Estelle*, which include a stopover on Caye Caulker. The trip happens three times a week and costs about $45, including lunch. The catamaran *Me Too* has a similar snorkel-sail package trip to Caulker for around $40.

Fishing and Diving

Fishing is still a way of life for many San Pedranos, and there are dozens of guides to choose from. You should inquire locally for current recommendations, but we've heard good comments about **Pete Graniel**, **Ramon Guerrero**, and **Severro Guerrero**. **"Lil Alfonse" Graniel**, 26-2584, and **Tacio Badillo** are particularly recommended. Tacio also arranges windsurfing and sailing adventures, and his brother Geraldo specializes in moonlight sailboat rides. Prices start at around $20 per person. Guided fishing trips run from about $100 for a half-day to $150 for a full day ($125 for night fishing). Deep-sea rates are higher, from $250 to $350 per day. Lunches are sometimes extra. If you're learning to become a NAUI or PADI certified diver, expect to pay $350 or more for a four-day course.

Other Things to See and Do in Ambergris Caye

Besides the usual water sports, volleyball, and birding, Ambergris tour options include a turtle-nesting beach on the northeast corner of the island, offshore bird rookeries, and several unrestored but difficult-to-reach ancient Mayan sites. Visitors can fill their days with outdoor recreational activities and their nights with wining, dining, and dancing.

We also recommend spending at least part of one day simply walking around town, seeing how San Pedranos live, work, and play. There's a pleasant path along the beach south of San Pedro, which takes you past several luxury resorts and an octagonal building that is the home of **Barry Bowen**, Belize's most successful entrepreneur and the owner of Belikin beer (that's why his house is painted "Belikin green"). Next to Bowen's house is a private school that he built for his children and other island residents on San Pedro's last empty stretch of beachfront. On beaches like these, you can step outside at night and see a glittering array of constellations, including (in winter) the majestic Southern Cross. You can warm up at one of the bars along the waterfront, including the popular **Fido's** (pronounced FEE-do's) **Courtyard** and the nearby **Tackle Box** (home of the famous "chicken drop" contest).

Inland Day Trips

A number of local travel agencies arrange day trips up jungle rivers to the Altun Ha and Lamanai Mayan ruins on the mainland, as well as the Community Baboon [Howler Monkey] Sanctuary. Expect to pay $50 to $120 per person for these outings. Our favorite guides for these trips are **Daniel Nuñez** and **Carlos Alejos**. Day trips are easily arranged to Tikal (and other Mayan sites) from San Pedro. Inquire among the local airlines for scheduled flights to Flores/Santa Elena (the Tikal airport), which cost about $250 round-trip, including a guided tour of the ruins.

Shopping and Services

San Pedro services include a bank, several pharmacies, a post office, a BTL (phone company) office, and a public library. One source of general information is the well-written weekly newspaper, the *San Pedro Sun*, e-mail *sanpdrosun@btl.net*. The best book about the island is *The Field Guide to Ambergris Caye*, locally published by co-authors R.L. Wood, S.T. Reid, and A.M. Reid. Its chapters are packed with information on the history, biology, archaeology, and geology of the caye.

There are plenty of souvenir shops in San Pedro, offering everything from T-shirts to wood carvings. Black coral jewelry is sometimes offered. Locals can get permits to collect this rare coral by free-diving, but we discourage its purchase on environmental grounds.

Visitors recommend both **Amigo Travel**, 26-2180, and **Travel & Tour Belize** in San Pedro, 26-2031, fax 26-2185, for arranging excursions throughout Belize and for information on Ambergris Caye, including how to arrange long-term house or condo rentals. Amigo also rents scooters and bicycles.

The **Ambergris Caye Museum** in the Island Shopping Center was scheduled to open in late 1997.

At least one local entrepreneur, **Island Equestrian Trails**, offers horseback riding, and sailing can be arranged through Islands & Reef Cruise at the Paradise Hotel pier. You can rent golf carts for about $5 an hour and bicycles for around $1.50 an hour. Inquire at Ramon's Wheel Rental, at the airport. Underwater cameras and video recorders are also widely available for hire, as are windsurfers and Hobie-cat sailboats.

Festivals

Annual events include the **San Pedro Carnival**, February 10–12, **Festival of St. Peter**, June 29 (which includes the blessing of the fishing fleet), and the **Air & Sea Show**, a community-wide July celebration of San Pedro's diverse cultures and traditions. Note that a

Manatee Watching

*Many guides take visitors in search of the West Indian mana-
tee, an endangered marine mammal that's holding its own in
Belize. This huge, placid animal—sometimes called a sea
cow—looks like a cross between a walrus, elephant, and
whale. Please don't try to swim with manatees: they are
timid creatures and the presence of humans in the water dis-
rupts their natural eating and breeding patterns. The Belize
government has issued guidelines about how close you can
get to a manatee, how you should act around juveniles, and
when your boat's speed should be reduced to avoid propeller
damage. Motors should be cut entirely in the vicinity of manatees and a pole used to get around. Because of their shy-
ness, you'll be lucky to see a manatee for longer than a*

new marina is being developed on the southwest side of the island, an
area of increasing tourist activity.

Getting There

Tropic, **Maya**, and **Island Airlines** have as many as nine daily flights
each to Ambergris from Belize City'sairports. The flight from Belize
City lasts about 15 minutes and costs about $43 each way. Maya and
Island fly daily to Caulker for about $20 one-way (7 minutes).

Connecting flights are easily arranged to other Belize cities, Mexico,
and Tikal. If you're coming from the Yucatán, it's an easy hop from
Corozal to San Pedro, and Tropic has five flights daily ($30 one-way). In
1997 there was talk of direct flights between San Pedro and Mexico;
these may have started by the time of your visit. (If you are nervous
about single-engine flying, the Tropic Air twin-engine aircraft are considered more stable than the single-engine planes used by Island and
Maya.) Ambergris Caye can also be reached by private or chartered aircraft. San Pedro's airport is within walking distance of town and taxis
await every flight. A taxi union rotates drivers at pick-up points and
there's little fare-gouging; expect to pay $2.50 for most destinations.

fleeting instant, although sometimes a dozen or more will hang around and stare at the humans.

Costs for manatee watching trips, which usually include snorkeling, vary from about $30 to $65 per person. On these and other excursions you may see Atlantic bottlenose dolphins, which are fairly common in Belize waters and will sometimes let humans swim with them—permissible if one doesn't get too close.

If you want to help preserve and protect the manatees for future generations, make a donation to the Manatee Foundation of Belize, P.O. Box 986, Belize City, which has been fighting to establish a government-sanctioned marine reserve on their behalf in the area of Drowned and Swallow Cayes.

Boats regularly ply the channel between Ambergris and the mainland, departing from several locations in Belize City. The main Belize City departure point is the Front Street Marine Terminal, east of the Swing Bridge. The trip takes about 1 hour and 15 minutes each way and cost about $7.50 in 1997.

The *Andrea* (about $12 one-way) leaves Belize City's Bellevue dock (5 Southern Foreshore) weekdays at 4 p.m. and Saturday at 1 p.m., returning at 7 a.m. Private boats can also be chartered, or you can hop a ride from Belize City with a supply or fishing vessel (try the customs wharf on N. Front Street near the Fort George lighthouse).

Once on Ambergris, there are regular boats to Caye Caulker, plus charters to virtually any scrap of reef or atoll you care to visit. Most boats leave for Caulker at about 7 a.m. and charge about $6 for the 20-minute trip. You can also look around the public docks for a boat marked "CC" and ask if you can pay for a lift to Caye Caulker.

Where to Stay on Ambergris Caye
Barrier Reef Hotel, in town; $80; 26-2075. Another long-lived institution with Caribbean ambiance.

Small cayes are popular diving and snorkeling sites.

Kevin Schafer

Belize Yacht Club, next door to Ramon's, on the beach; $150; 26-2777 or (800) 688-1767. Upscale restaurant and meeting facilities were added in 1996. Dive shop has the largest boat on the caye.

Captain Morgan's Retreat, 3.5 miles north of San Pedro; $140 and up; (800) 447-2931 or 26-2567, e-mail *captmorgan@btl.net*. Freshwater pool, restaurant, bar, 21 beachfront casitas, excursion options. Meal plan available.

Caribbean Villas, south of town, on the beach; $175 and up; 26-2715, e-mail *c-v-hotel@btl.net*. Operated by San Pedro's only dentist, American expatriate Wil Lala, and his wife, Susan. Condo-style accommodations and "barefoot luxury." All rooms have full kitchens and are steps away from a well-groomed beach. Amenities include two outdoor hot tubs, a five-level "people perch" for bird (and sunset) watching, and an offshore swimming hole. Nature lovers will appreciate the artificial reef Wil and Susan have built off their boat dock, and the fact that they've maintained a rare vestige of native forest as a bird sanctuary in their backyard. The couple give free golf-cart tours of San Pedro to every arriving guest and are full of expert advice on what to see and do. Tours and day trips are booked easily from here.

Changes in Latitudes, on the southern edge of San Pedro; $80; 26-2986. A clean, friendly, Canadian-owned bed-and-breakfast. Recommended. Lower off-season rates.

Coconut's Bed-and-Breakfast, about 5 minutes from San Pedro; $85; 26-3500, e-mail *coconuts@btl.net*. With refrigerator and bicycles for guests at no charge. All 12 rooms are air-conditioned and some have a TV. Recommended.

Conch Shell Hotel, north of San Pedro; $90; 26-2062. A few kitchenettes available; some rooms can be rented by the week or month.

Green Parrot, 6 miles north of San Pedro; $90; 21-2096. A beach-front bungalow complex with restaurant and bar.

Hideaway Lodge, southern edge of town; $40 and up; 26-2141; e-mail *hideaway@btl.net*. Canadian-owned with large rooms, a pool, and the friendly Crazy Canuck Restaurant, meal plan available.

Hotel del Río, in town; rates start at $24 (with shared bath), with the fanciest rooms going for $85 a night (air-conditioned cabaña); 26-2286. Our favorite budget place.

Journey's End, accessible only by boat at the northern tip of the island; $90 and up; 26-2173. A family-oriented luxury resort. Free transport from San Pedro.

Laidy's Apartments, $85; 26-2682. A four-unit, north-side place specifically designed for long-term visitors.

Ramon's Village, south side; $130 and up; 26-2071 or (800) 624-4215, e-mail *ramons@btl.net*. One of the island's biggest resort hotels—and with a consistently positive reputation—it also has the highly-regarded Parrot's bar and a Cajun-style restaurant. The hotel is immediately south of town and is particularly popular with families, catering to virtually every need and whim. There's a fully equipped dive and snorkel shop onsite. Best beach on the island.

Rocks Inn, on the north end of San Pedro; $95; 26-2326, (800) 331-2458. Kitchens and air-conditioning. A good value for groups.

San Pedrano, in the middle of San Pedro; a good value at $35; 26-2054. Restaurant and simple rooms, very clean.

San Pedro Holiday, in town; $84; 26-2014. The island's first hotel, owned by San Pedro native Celi McCorkle. Close to the action.

Sunbreeze Resort, within walking distance of the airport; $100; 26-219. Well-appointed poolside rooms, 100-foot pier.

Victoria House, a 10-minute bike ride or courtesy shuttle drive south of San Pedro, on the beach; $120; 26-2067 or (800) 247-5139. Good restaurant and full-service dive shop.

Where to Eat on Ambergris Caye

Big Daddy's, seafront, south end of town. Where else can you get "lobster peanut butter"?

The Bun Man, will deliver fresh coffee, juice, and cinnamon buns to your hotel room if you call the night before.

Capricorn, a romantic spot north of "the river" (a narrow waterway dividing Ambergris Caye) and just south of Capt. Morgan's Retreat. The food is superb and there are three cabañas and rooms for rent if you decide to spend the night (rooms $75 and up, 26-2809). Because the ferry stops at 6 p.m., one can arrange a moonlight boat ride from San Pedro—we recommend Skipper George's *Rum Punch II*.

Drive-up Daiquiri, in downtown San Pedro. Don't miss this place, where you can order a daiquiri or piña colada without leaving your golf cart. (San Pedro's post office has drive-up P.O. boxes, too!)

Duke's Place, south end, across from Ramon's. Try the Mayan eggs and shrimp fajitas.

El Patio, in Rock's Grocery. Try the excellent tropical chicken.

Jade Garden, half-mile south of the airstrip. A long-time Chinese cuisine favorite with a large menu.

La Margarita, south of town. Mexican food and sunset views.

The Lagoon, Pescador Drive near the middle of town. New York-style and prices.

Mary Ellen's Little Italy, Barrier Reef Drive. San Pedro's best Italian food.

Mickey's, at the Hotel Payador. Best burritos on the caye.

Patty's Fruit Stand, on Middle Street. The best tropical fruits and veggies in the village.

Rasta Pasta/Pizza Amor, upstairs in the Playador Hotel. Particularly recommended for those on a budget (try the homemade ginger beer and wine, which go well with Albert and Marilyn's inventive seafood and veggie dishes).

Sweet Basil's, a fancy deli just south of Capricorn. Delicious lunches and stocks imported cheeses, patés, wines, and picnic supplies.

Other Options
The Reef, Lily's, or **Celi's**, all in town, are all known for well-prepared fish and Belizean cuisine. Many San Pedro restaurants have barbecue or buffet specials once or twice a week that are an excellent value, and the weekly **Lion's Club Barbecue** (a fundraiser for its Ambergris Caye clinic) is not to be missed. Also recommended is the Sunday beach barbeque at **Charlene's**.

HOL CHAN MARINE RESERVE
Location: Less than 5 miles southeast of San Pedro, along the barrier reef.
Size: About 6 square miles.
Hours: Dawn to dusk.
Visitor Information: The Hol Chan Visitor Center in San Pedro, Caribena Street; 26-2420. Open daily from 9 a.m. to 5 p.m. Well stocked with brochures and information about the underwater flora and fauna encountered in Belizean waters.

About 4½ miles southeast of San Pedro, off the tip of Ambergris Caye, is a natural break in the barrier reef called **Hol Chan**, Mayan for "little

Kevin Schafer

The Hol Chan Marine Reserve protects a natural break in the barrier reef.

channel." The cut is around 30 feet deep, has been protected since 1987 as a national marine reserve, and has become a major spawning ground that is strengthening underwater plant and animal populations.

Hol Chan's Ecological Zones

The reserve is divided into three distinct ecological zones, marked on the water's surface by anchored buoys. **Zone A** is the reef channel itself, where swimmers should be mindful of strong tidal currents while diving or snorkeling. **Zone B** encompasses broad beds of sea grasses as well as the Boca Ciega. The sea and turtle grass serve as an important feeding and breeding ground; visitors will see hundreds of tiny fish here. **Zone C** encompasses several mangrove cayes, a source of important nutrients and a critical habitat for the youngest sea creatures, who subsequently migrate into the sea grass beds and finally the outer waters. Above the surface, the mangrove islands provide a nesting area for several large bird species, such as herons, egrets, pelicans, rails, frigate birds, and ospreys. The mangrove ecosystem is also home to sponges, anemones, sea urchins, crabs, jellyfish, mollusks, sea squirts, and young lobsters.

Hol Chan Marine Reserve is the first park of its kind in Central America, and donations are welcome. Your contribution will encourage Belize and neighboring countries to expand such worthy ventures.

Exploring Hol Chan

As you explore Hol Chan, remember that all flora and fauna are protected. Feeding the fish is discouraged, since it upsets the balance of nature, promotes dependence on humans, and can lead to some potentially dangerous encounters with certain sharp-toothed animals.

The **Belize Audubon Society** advises visitors to any coral habitat in the country that collecting these tiny organisms is prohibited, and that overturning or disturbing any live coral will eventually kill them. Always be very careful when stepping or dropping anchor on the ocean floor, and try to avoid touching live coral at all costs. Even a vigorous kick by a swimmer can stir up enough sand to clog their orifices. Contact with fire (also called red) coral can be especially painful. Here, as in other areas with busy marine traffic, be careful of speeding powerboats that may be unable to see you bobbing in the water: an encounter can be deadly.

Radio-equipped patrol boats regularly visit the area, on the lookout for anyone in trouble—or anyone who is at odds with the law. Throughout Belize, mooring buoys should always be used when available.

Shark/Ray Alley

The newest addition to Hol Chan is an area known as Shark/Ray Alley, where visitors often see good-sized sharks, barracudas, and rays. They've been drawn to this area for years because fisherman traditionally clean their fish here. Today guides throw scraps (chum) into the water to keep them coming. They'll encourage you to scratch a nurse shark's belly and use an eagle ray for a hat. Biologists discourage this sort of thing and there is some danger—animals in a feeding frenzy are unpredictable—but Belize authorities seem oblivious. Meanwhile, the show is pretty amazing.

Snorkeling

Snorkelers will find that Hol Chan is unusually rich in marine life, including hundreds of fish species and a variety of living corals (including elkhorn, starlet, brain, and sheet). You may also come across colorful sea fans, sponges, sea whips, gorgonians, crabs, rays, and eels. (Don't get too close to the nearsighted green moray eel, which can chomp off a finger in an eye-blink.)

The sides of the channel, lined with both living and dead coral, are interrupted from time to time by small limestone caves and sink-holes, including the spectacular **Boca Ciega**, a collapsed cave with underwater freshwater springs that teem with tropical fish. Swimming inside the Boca Ciega should be explored only by experienced divers. Advance permission must be obtained from Hol Chan headquarters.) Humans share the clear waters here with everything from nervous squirrelfish to curious grey angels, from jaunty sea horses to parading parrot fish. Large schools of yellowtail snapper, horse-eye jacks, and blue-striped grunts cruise by, along with spotted eagle rays and purple cleaner shrimp.

If you have small children who wish to snorkel, it's wise to hire an experienced guide who can help keep an eye on them in the water. They—and their parents—should wear water-repelling sunscreen and consider wearing T-shirts to avoid burning. If you've just arrived in Belize—without a tan—it's prudent not to snorkel any more than an hour on the first day.

Diving

Divers can take advantage of Hol Chan's relatively shallow depth and stay down for an hour or more, drifting among the lovely spotted drum, hatfish, damsel, and butterfly fish. If a diver remains station-ary, the shy hermit crab may make an appearance. Night diving can also be very rewarding, providing a rare chance to glimpse flaming scallops, octopus, spider crabs, lobsters, and other nocturnal species. Eerie bioluminescent ostracods (tiny shrimp-like creatures) shimmer like tiny fireflies atop the water's surface, becoming especially notice-able in the wake of passing boats.

Getting There

Because of its close proximity to San Pedro, Hol Chan can easily be visited for a half-day (or even an hour) by booking a boat through a hotel, or simply showing up on any of the east-side piers in San Pedro. Dive and snorkel boats usually head out about 9 a.m. and again at 2 p.m. each day, returning about 3 hours after departure. Expect to pay at least $20 and up for a round-trip, with two snorkel or dive stops. Several glass-bottom touring craft follow a similar schedule. Guards on powerboats collect the reserve's $2.50 entrance fee and monitor anchoring activities.

The Marine Maya

*Beyond the border of the reserve, at the swampy southern extremity of Ambergris Caye, is the **Marco Gonzalez** archaeological site. This small and badly eroded Mayan ruin, named after the young boy who found it, was once part of a large trade network linking inland Indians with settlements along the Mexican and Central American coast. Trade items originating as far away as present-day Peru and New Mexico made their way along this route.*

Occupied between 200 B.C. and A.D. 1500, Marco Gonzalez has been excavated since 1986 by Canadian archaeologists, who confirm that some structures are built entirely from conch shells. The location is not well marked and is best approached with the help of a knowledgeable guide. Bring mosquito repellent!

BACALAR CHICO NATIONAL PARK AND MARINE RESERVE

Location: At the northern tip of Ambergris Caye, about 20 miles from San Pedro.
Size: About 20 square miles.
Hours: Dawn to dusk.
Visitor Information: Inquire at the Hol Chan Marine Reserve office in San Pedro for the latest information about Bacalar Chico.

One of Belize's newest protected areas, the 28,000-acre Bacalar Chico comprises the northernmost part of Ambergris Caye and its surrounding waters. Until a few years ago much of this area was private land slated for development as a golf course and luxury resort.

The name refers to the narrow channel that separates the island from mainland Mexico. This canal was supposedly excavated by ancient Maya around A.D. 500 so that their trade boats would have a shortcut into Chetumal Bay. The park's ranger station and visitor center are, in fact, at the badly eroded **San Juan** archaeological site, under excavation by a Texas university. Another ancient Mayan trading camp in the area, **Chac Balam**, is being studied by a Canadian team, and five other sites have been located within the park.

Birders will find much to see on a boat trip to Bacalar Chico, since more than 200 species have been identified in the area. Less visible are the mammals recorded here, including ocelots, deer, raccoons, peccaries, and boa constrictors. Evidence of pumas and jaguars has even been reported. Green sea turtles and loggerhead sometimes come ashore near **Rocky Point**, where the barrier reef actually touches the shoreline. (Except for a few other cayes and Manatee Bar beach on the mainland, this is the only known turtle-nesting site in Belize.) The offshore marine habitat was once known as a breeding area for Queen conch (now in decline due to overfishing) as well as a seasonal spawning bank for Nassau and yellowfin groupers. Rangers can advise about closed fishing areas.

The best birding is in mangrove lagoons along the coast, and in the high-ridge (littoral) forest that runs parallel to the beach along the east side of Ambergris Caye. Bring binoculars!

Offshore buoys and anchor sites are being installed by Bacalar Chico's management, which allows camping on the park's limited dry land. Be sure to bring whatever water, food, and supplies you'll need. The best snorkel sites are off the caye's northeast shoreline. Much of the area around Ambergris has been badly overfished, however, to feed the thousands of tourists who come expecting to find fresh fish listed on their restaurant menus.

Outfitters

The tourism infrastructure of Bacalar Chico is still being developed, but most San Pedro guides will take you there if asked. Expect to pay a bit more, $30 and up, than you would for a Hol Chan trip because of the cost of fuel. Another option is to stay at one of the few north-island lodges and start your excursion from there. Bacalar Chico has a $2.50 admission charge. The mainland communities of **Sarteneja** and **Corozal** are also involved in Bacalar Chico's development, and boat operators there can whisk you across Chetumal Bay for a reasonable fee.

CAYE CAULKER

Location: About 12 miles south of San Pedro and 18 miles northeast of Belize City, just west of the barrier reef.

Visitor Information: No formal tourist information center, but good *sources of information are the various gift shop and hotel operators. Best all-around visitor resource: **Dolphin Bay Travel Agency**, middle of town on Front Street, 22-2214. They can arrange lodging, day trips, and airplane tickets and can change money when the Atlantic Bank is closed.*

Lying directly south of Ambergris, Caye Caulker (sometimes spelled Corker) is a popular destination among many visitors who want an experience more akin to the laid-back San Pedro town of the 1970s, before the latter was "discovered."

Caulker is "less" of many things San Pedro has become: less expensive, less crowded, and less noisy. However, it also has fewer hotels, restaurants, and services than its northern neighbor. The beach isn't raked and manicured here as it is on Ambergris Caye, and you'll share the street with lots of flea-bitten dogs (and the occasional great blue heron). It's okay on Caulker to live in a rotting shack or a rusty camper shell—and even the best hotel in town couldn't compete with Motel 6. Some visitors absorb the "action" of Ambergris for a while and then slow the pace down on funky Caye Caulker.

The island was dubbed *Hicaco* by the Spanish, their name for the many coco-plum palms found here. Over the years, the English pirates who settled here apparently began pronouncing it "Corker," and, with their British accents, the word finally evolved into "Caulker." The British are mostly gone now, replaced by Mexican immigrants in the 19th century. Unlike their Ambergris neighbors, the Mestizos of Caulker have given up Spanish and now speak Creole English.

The caye is fairly small, and the inhabited portion covers a few sandy blocks. There are only two main north/south streets: Front (east, along the beach) and Back (west). Like Ambergris, a good portion of Caulker is bug-infested mangrove swamp, and the northern half of the island has only a handful of residents. Visitors walk everywhere, since nothing is far away, and vehicles are almost nonexistent. A golf cart is the only airport taxi. (Note the huge osprey nest on the telephone pole next to the runway.)

About 800 people live on Caye Caulker year-round, and, within a few days' time, it seems a traveler has waved to or chatted with them all. This friendliness, coupled with comparatively modest prices and a full range of services, has enticed many first-timers to extend their stay on Caulker. A few foreigners—budget-minded regulars on the "gringo trail"—have stayed for years and intermarried with the locals.

An airport opened in 1991 and the island's tempo has speeded up somewhat, but by keeping a measure of control over Caulker's pace of progress, residents have been able to remain owners and operators of most of the rustic guest houses, home-style restaurants, and simple shops that cater to visitors. Don't expect a lot of action on Caye Caulker; there isn't any. Most visitors schedule snorkeling or sightseeing day trips, then mosey out in the evening to shop, eat, and drink. The island offers many of the same attractions as Ambergris, including snorkeling, diving, sailing, windsurfing, kayaking, sunbathing, hiking, and fishing.

Travel Tips

Among the few persistent annoyances on Caye Caulker are sand flies and mosquitoes, which can make hikes very uncomfortable in calm or rainy weather. Since most buildings are on tall stilts, these biting insects are less of a nuisance indoors.

Vagrants and street hustlers have been a problem in the past, but a recent crackdown has brought things under control. There's a highly visible police station in the center of Caulker that's put the word out that drug abuse won't be tolerated. If you find yourself being hassled, our best advice is to ignore and avoid the offenders, then report any subsequent trouble to the police and/or your hotel owner.

Bob Mahler

On Caye Caulker, piers are locally known as "bridges."

Fishing, Snorkeling, and Manatee Watching

Caulker natives have long been known as fishing experts (lobster, conch, snapper) and skilled boatmen, so you are sure to find top-notch guides here for virtually any water-related activity.

San Pedro native **Lionel "Chocolate" Heredia**, 22-2151, is still the best boat captain for hire and these days he likes to take visitors to a manatee-watching area en route to superb snorkeling, fishing, and island camping sites. As many as 12 manatees at a time gather above what appears to be an underwater spring or collapsed cave (a location "Chocolate" doesn't wish to publicize for environmental reasons). The Belize government is in the process of extending official protection to manatee feeding areas and guides are already subject to a $250 fine if they violate rules designed to protect this shy beast. Remember, don't get into the water with the manatees!)

Other recommended snorkeling guides include **Robert Blease**, 22-2154, and **Harrison Cadle**, 22-2263, in particular. Harrison makes excursions almost daily to Hol Chan and Goff's Caye. The going rate for all-day snorkling was about $35 in 1997, or $30 without a "shore lunch" of fresh fish and picnic items. Most trips depart with a minimum of 5 passengers (and a maximum of 12). Also recommended is Rogue's (22-2014).

Vega's Inn, on the beach, 22-2142, arranges snorkeling or fishing trips. It also rents snorkeling gear and small (Sunfish) sailboats.

For fishing trips, we recommend **Porfilio "Piggy" Guzman** (especially for bonefish) and **Raul Young**, 22-2133, available through **Tom's Hotel**; the owner is his brother. If neither is available try **Rally Badillo** or **Roly Rosado**. **Frenchie's Services** and **Pegasus Boat Service** also provide fish-finding expertise. **Ricardo's Adventure Tours**, 22-2087, will organize river trips, island hopping, fishing, snorkeling, and even beach barbecues. You name it, and Ricardo Aloala will try to arrange it. Fishing excursions start at about $45 per day and dive trips slightly more, depending on equipment needed.

Diving

One of the better dive shops is **Frenchie's**, on the north end of the island (Frenchie's brother runs the Caye Caulker School of Scuba). Also recommended is **Belize Diving Services**, next to the soccer field on Back Street. You can arrange for Ambergris Caye dive operators to pick you up on Caulker for their offshore trips. Expect to pay about $45 for a local dive (add $10 if you need to rent equipment), and $130 for an off-the-reef dive to such destinations as the Blue

Hole. Typical marine life seen on a barrier reef dive off Caulker might include spotted eagle rays, nurse sharks, lobsters, and moray eels. A special attraction for experienced divers is a large underground cave system that lies between Caulker and Ambergris—said to be one of the biggest in the world.

Swimming

The best swimming (the offshore water is otherwise very shallow) is in a 100-foot channel called **The Split**, which bisects the island at the north end of the village. It was formed in 1961 by powerful Hurricane Hattie, the same storm that leveled Belize City. The water here is clear and relatively clean, but beware of currents and near-constant boat traffic. There's no beach, but the wooden dock and tiki bar are comfortable places to hang out.

In 1997 there were a handful of modest bungalows for rent at this site but construction was underway on a monstrous (and environmentally unwise) condominium complex called **Emerald Pointe**. This 60-unit, three-level, luxury development, a target of intense debate and protest, will probably be soliciting tenants by the time of your visit. As this book went to press, questions about sewage disposal and erosion control had not been fully addressed.

Hiking and Birding

Its idyllic tropical scenery makes Caulker a nice place to hike. A sandy path to the southeast part of the island brings visitors to a quieter, less developed side of Caulker (punctuated by the roar of an aircraft taking off or landing at Caulker's airstrip). On this path you're treated to fine views of the Caribbean through the mangrove, and you may glimpse iguanas, ospreys, or perhaps a roseate spoonbill. Migrant birds are biannual visitors, most prevalent from early November through mid-December and again in March and April.

Other Things to See and Do in Caye Caulker

Windsurfers, **kayaks**, and **Hobie-cat sailboats** can be rented from several outfits on Caye Caulker; inquire locally or watch for signs. Expect to pay about $15 for half-day use, or rent by the hour.

One recommended nighttime diversion is the slide show and lecture given at **Seeing Is Belizing**, 22-2189, a Front Street bookstore and gift shop operated by Dorothy Beveridge and her photographer husband, James, an expert on the area's natural history and ecology. For about $2.50 you can see Beveridge's excellent photos of Belizean flora and fauna, with accompanying expert commentary. Typical topics include "the birds of Caye Caulker" and "the Belize rainforest." The slides are for sale at about $1.50 each.

Ellen McRae's **Galeria Hicaco**, 2-22178, on Front Street is a must-see attraction: a combination gift shop and natural history museum. Married to a Belizean, Ellen is a well-informed expatriate, marine biologist who has lived here for many years. She conducts highly recommended ecology-oriented tours of the island and barrier reef through her company, **Cari Search**.

Nightlife

Most restaurants close by 9 p.m. and bars a few hours later. Nightlife on the island consists of dancing, drinking, and hanging out at the Rastafarian-style **I & I** reggae club (where they have swings and hammocks instead of chairs!) or **Reef Bar** (open 'til 4 a.m. on weekends). And, of course, there's always television. (Yes, even Caye Caulker has satellite dishes.)

Getting There

Members of the **Caye Caulker Water Taxi Association (CCWTA)**, 22-2992, will whisk you between Belize City, Caye Caulker, and Ambergris Caye at regularly scheduled times (at least five each day). In 1997 the fare was about $7.50 for the one-way, 45-minute trip between Caulker and Belize City; $6 to or from San Pedro. Advance purchase at the CCWTA office (near the main dock) or **Belize City Marine Terminal** (next to the Swing Bridge) is recommended because boats sometimes fill up and a second craft is not always available. In 1997, water taxis left the main dock in Caulker in the morning at 6:45, 8:00, and 10:00 as well as 3:00 in the afternoon.

Island and **Tropic** airlines make a total of 15 or more daily, 13-minute flights to Caye Caulker from Belize City's municipal airport. Some travelers fly to Ambergris Caye and later make the remaining short hop (7 minutes) to Caulker by water or air. Expect to pay about $20 for the one-way trip by air to or from Caulker, slightly more to or from Belize City.

Where to Stay in Caye Caulker

If you plan to be on Caye Caulker for a while, it pays to shop around for accommodations. Some of the guest houses and "cabins" are dirty and run-down. One option is to find something acceptable for the first night, then look for something better the next day. (Be advised that hotel owners here aren't usually up before 8 or 9 a.m.) The least friendly accommodations on the island are the dilapidated Ignacio's Cabins, surrounded by ominous signs that threaten all trespassers.

The Anchorage, a bit south of town on the beach; $50; 22-2002. Half-price in summer. Decent lodging in a pleasant location.

Barbara's Guest House, on the northern edge of the village; $15; 22-2025. Basic, friendly. Excellent fish, veggie, and chicken burritos.

Castaways, south of the village; $16; 22-2294. Restaurant and bar.

Chocolate's Guest Room, on the north end of Front Street; $60; 22-2151. The nicest place to stay (for non-smokers only). The Guest Room is a large, lovely roof-top annex to the home of Belizean boatman, "Chocolate" Heredia and his American wife, Annie Seashore. Amenities include a huge mahogany bed, fresh Guatemalan coffee, and a mini-refrigerator. A breezy balcony overlooks the human parade. Advance reservations are advised.

Heredia's House Rental, on Front Street. Houses typically rent for between $200 and $450 a month; 22-2132. Houses can be rented for stays of two days or more.

Island Sun Guest House, on the north end near The Split; $20; 22-2215. Clean, friendly, low-cost accommodations include a café that offers the best fruit and yogurt in town—and packed lunches for day trips.

Rainbow Hotel, Front Street in the middle of town; $25; 22-2123. Basic rooms with TVs but not much atmosphere.

Sea Beezzz, on the beach at the south end; $40; 22-2176. A laid-back hangout with a popular restaurant and bar.

Seaview Hotel, on the water at the southern edge of the village. Built in 1996, at $40 (and up) this is a good value, with attractive rooms and nice furnishings.

Shirley's Guest House, on the far south side of the village, set back from its own beach; $55; 22-2145. Rather expensive for what you get.

Tom's Hotel, on Back Street; $20; 22-2102. A modest place.

Tropical Paradise, on Front Street, next to the graveyard; $45; 22-2063. Offering hot water, fans, TV, and a choice of ten main building rooms or five beachfront cabañas. This large hotel is rather run-down and some guests have complained about fumigation odors, yet its restaurant is one of the best on Caulker.

Other Options

Camping on Caulker is available from **Vega's Inn,** $6 a night; 22-2142; which also rents rooms.

Where to Eat in Caye Caulker

It should be noted that, like everything else on Caye Caulker, restaurant service is on the slow side. Remember that you're on vacation; what's the hurry?

Glenda's, on Back Street near the soccer field. Prepares Caulker's best Belizean food, specializing in Creole-style breakfast and lunch.

The Sand Box, next to the water taxi pier. Provides a volleyball court for its patrons to use while their food is being cooked. This is also one of the best restaurants (and bars) on the island, though somewhat overpriced.

Sea Beezzz, on the beach. Tasty margaritas and Margaritaville ambiance.

Sobre de Olas, on the beach. Mouth-watering barbecue.

Syd's, near Glenda's on Back Street. Slightly fancier than Glenda's; a good choice for fresh fish.

Tropical Paradise, at the hotel of the same name. The food is good and the place even has tablecloths!

Other Options

Some of Caulker's eateries are simply open-air kitchens operated by local women outside their homes. Children sometimes hawk home-baked coconut bread. A friendly woman named Cordelia sells delicious fish, chicken, and veggie burritos at **Barbara's Guest House.**

You can stock up on supplies at **Chan's**, on Back Street; **Jan's Deli**, on Front Street; and other small groceries. The **Princesa del Mar** tortilla factory is on Back Street across from Marin's Restaurant. You can sometimes buy the fruit picked from large breadfruit and citrus trees near the center of the village.

SIWA-BAN NATURE PRESERVE

Location: The northern tip of Caye Caulker, beyond The Split, about a mile or two from the village.
Size: 150 acres.
Hours: Any time.
Visitor Information: Contact marine biologist (and former Californian) Ellen McRae at Galería Hicaco in the village, 2-22178, or write the Siwa-Ban Foundation, 143 Anderson Street, San Francisco, CA 94110 (tax-deductible donations gladly accepted).

A small yet important reserve being established at the north end of Caye Caulker, Siwa-Ban (the local name for the island's endemic—and increasingly rare—black catbird), is dedicated to protecting critical mangrove habitat, littoral (seaside) forest, sea grass beds, and offshore coral reef. The reserve, formed in cooperation with the Belize Coastal Zone Management Unit, is an important habitat and food source for birds, fish, and reptiles, including crocodiles.

Local conservationists—with support from their U.S. counterparts—established Siwa-Ban in the mid-1990s and access is by private boat. Well over 100 species of birds have been confirmed in the area, including many winter migrants who thrive on the fruits and berries found in the island's dense forest.

Siwa-Ban is not to be confused with a tiny "mini-reserve" next to the Caye Caulker airport that advertises itself as a conservation project of the Belize Tourism Industry Association. A posted sign calls for $1 admission, but as of mid-1997 there was no one there to collect it. Besides an overgrown nature trail and locked meetinghouse, there is not much to see at this "mini-reserve."

Getting There/Outfitters

A guided boat tour can be arranged among any of the outfitters in the village for about $20. If you wish, they will deposit you at the reserve and return to pick you up at a designated time. There is also a kayak available for rent ($15 and up) at **Galería Hicaco**, the park's current headquarters. Pack mosquito repellent for any visit!

CAYE CHAPEL AND LONG CAYE
Location: 15 miles northeast of Belize City.
Size: 1 mile by 3 miles.
Visitor Information: Belize Tourist Board, (800)624-0686.

Heading southeast from Caye Caulker, the next island in the barrier reef chain is Chapel, distinguished by its long sandy beaches and large groves of coconut palms. Because it rises to about 10 feet above sea level, the caye has been spared the terrible hurricane damage its neighbors have sometimes suffered. Easily visible across the horizon from Caulker, it's about 15 miles northeast of Belize City.

Only about 1 mile by 3 miles in size and privately owned, Caye Chapel is blessed with some of Belize's best scenery and the nation's second-longest airstrip. The latter is a paved runway built to serve the now-defunct **Pyramid Island Resort**, which owns all of Chapel and until a few years ago provided upscale accommodations and services. It's not known when the resort might reopen; inquire locally. When the resort is operating, you can fly here from Ambergris Caye or Belize City for about $20 one-way.

Warships of the Spanish Armada stopped at Caye Chapel after the decisive 1798 battle that effectively ended Spain's claim on Belize. Some of the fleet's soldiers were buried here, and there are also graves of English colonials who came to fish and grow coconuts. Mayan artifacts have been found at the site of a large vegetable garden planted by the resort's owners.

A small lodge has operated in past years on nearby mangrove-studded Long Caye, (also called Northern Long Caye) but it has been closed for some time. Inquire locally about its current status. Both Long and Chapel Cayes provide good diving, snorkeling, swimming, sailing, windsurfing, and fishing in their offshore waters.

ST. GEORGE'S CAYE
Location: About 9 miles northeast of Belize City.
Size: Less than 1 square mile.
Visitor Information: Belize Tourist Board, (800) 624-0686.

During Belize's early years as a haven for British pirates and traders, its largest settlement was on St. George's Caye. It served as the Bay Settlement's informal capital for nearly two centuries, starting in the mid-1600s. Manatees and turtles were slaughtered here by the thousands, their smoked meat later sold to the crews of oceangoing vessels, thus the island's old name: Kitchen Caye.

This small island is best known as the focal point of a great sea battle between a ragged band of Baymen, a single British schooner, and seasoned Spanish naval forces (in 32 warships). Despite the overwhelming odds against them, the Belizeans prevailed. Thus, the anniversary of the day Spain was defeated, September 10, 1798, is a national holiday (St. George's Caye Day). On the island's southern tip is a small cemetery where some of the early soldiers and settlers were buried. Tropical storms have washed away most of the grave markers (along with dozens of houses and much of the island), but old coins, bottles, and other artifacts are still occasionally found.

There are a number of piers (called "bridges") on St. George's where day-trippers can tie up for an hour or so. A footpath runs the length of the island and the snorkeling offshore is rated excellent (there's even an underwater cave that you can swim through). St. George's Caye is home to a few lobster fishermen and has several retreats that belong to wealthy Belizeans. Old maps will show nearby Sergeant's Caye, a once-inhabited island that was reduced by

A Belizean tour guide prepares a "shore lunch" for kayakers at Glover's Reef.

Hurricane Hattie to little more than a three-palm sandbar—a great place for a picnic and a day of snorkeling.

Getting There

There is no regular public transportation to St. George's Caye (transportation is prearranged for guests), but private boats can be hired for the 20-minute crossing from Belize City. En route, visitors will pass a number of uninhabited mangrove cayes that have little or no dry land, including **Mapp's**, **Swallow**, and **Riders Cayes**. Keep the binoculars handy, since this dense foliage harbors plenty of birds and manatees often cruise nearby. This trip provides a good chance to observe the wooden, sail-driven cargo ships, known locally as "island traders" or "sand lighters," which ply the waters from Mexico to Honduras.

Where to Stay and Eat in St. George's Caye

St. George's Lodge, highly regarded but questionably expensive at $140, meals included; 2-12121 or (800) 678-6871, and co-owned **Island Cottages**, 2-44190. St. George's Lodge and the Island Cottages cater almost exclusively to avid scuba divers (certification available), although fishing enthusiasts and snorkelers are welcome. The two-part resort is supplied with electricity by windmills and solar collectors. Some of the ten cabañas are built on stilts right over the waters of the Caribbean; others are on the island's sandy soil. The food served here (family style) is first-rate. Bring your own liquor if you wish to drink. Unlike many diving lodges, the atmosphere is very relaxed. You may be tempted to curl up in a hammock all day and do nothing but watch the diving pelicans.

The Cottage Colony, at the oppostie end of the island. A cluster of five charming bungalows called The Cottage Colony was out of business and seeking a new operator in 1997. This upmarket resort may have reopened by the time of your visit. Inquire at the Bellevue Hotel, 2-77051, in Belize City, its most recent owner.

MOHO AND DROWNED CAYES

Location: One-half mile off the coast, opposite St. John's College on north side of Belize City.
Size: These cayes are each less than an acre in size.
Visitor Information: Belize Tourist Board, (800) 624-0686

The Life of a Lobsterman

Staying with Ricardo Castillo offers visitors the unusual opportunity of observing traditional Belizean lobster fishing firsthand. Ricardo is a lifelong fisher and free diver, originally from the boat-building village of Sarteneja. He will take you along as he checks traps over a meandering route above sea grass beds. Lobsters are still plentiful enough in these waters that they can be enticed into bait-free traps—such as wooden cages equipped with trapdoors and anchored with stones—that rely entirely on the animal's natural inclination to seek refuge during the day in dark places. Ricardo is a by-the-book member of Belize's large fishing cooperative and immediately throws back any undersized lobster, along with the occasional crab or fish that wanders into his traps. Later, you will dine on fresh lobster cooked to perfection. Boats hail Castillo via marine-band radio from as far away as Guatemala to make dinner reservations in the tiny restaurant.

Moho Caye is a very small island with a big past. It's the site of an ancient Mayan fishing camp where thousands of pounds of old manatee bones have been found. The mammals were apparently butchered in great numbers here, and the meat then prepared for transport to other Mayan communities. Fortunately, manatees can still be found in these waters, especially around the Drowned Cays, east of Moho. While they hold almost no dry land, these swampy mangrove cayes provide excellent anchorage during storms and are an important manatee habitat. Local outfitters can arrange excursions to the area.

Whiskered manatee noses also can be seen popping up in breathing holes near the Municipal Airport, where the Belize River enters the sea. The docile creatures have become rare in much of their range, which extends as far as south Florida, but are holding their own in Belize, thanks to government protection.

Richard Mahler

*Lobsterman and fisherman Ricardo Castillo throws
undersized lobsters from his trap.*

During colonial times, Moho was used as a quarantine area for
those suffering from smallpox and other contagious diseases. A small
graveyard marks the final resting place of many victims. The privately owned caye is now home to a yachting and diving resort, **Maya
Landings,** 2-45798, which offers week-long dive/sail trips as far as
Lighthouse Reef's Blue Hole and Guatemala's Río Dulce.

CENTRAL BARRIER REEF CAYES
Location: 7–10 miles southeast of Belize City
Size: These tiny cayes vary in size.
Visitor Information: Belize Tourist Board, (800) 624-0686

Each of these tiny cayes retains the kind of charm visitors typically
associate with exotic tropical islets. They are only a few acres in
size, consisting of little more than a mound of sandy beach and a
dozen or so coconut palms. Even native Belizeans like to visit for an
afternoon or weekend of snorkeling, diving, fishing, and picnicking.

No regularly scheduled transportation serves them, but day trips can easily be arranged through larger hotels, local guides, and travel agencies.

As you approach the islands from Belize City or points farther north, you may pass flat-bottom sugar barges taking their loads out to oceangoing cargo ships that cannot anchor any closer because of the shallow water. Within the Inner Channel depths range up to 150 feet; they quickly plunge to 2,000 feet or more beyond the barrier reef.

Gallow's Point Caye, about 7 miles southeast of Belize City, derives its name from the (now gone) hangman's gallows used here many years ago for the execution of convicted criminals. Today the island is home to **The Wave: Gallows Point Resort**, $100 and up, meals included, 2-73054, a six-room fishing and diving facility (in a large house) that offers a variety of services, including yacht anchorages at its **Weir Dow Marina**. Transportation is arranged from Belize City, and the resort also provides day trips and weekend excursions from the mainland.

English Caye, a few miles south of the swampy Gallows Point Reef, has been an important navigational aid for hundreds of years. It marks the entrance of the deep English Caye Channel that large commercial ships follow into the Belize City harbor. The tiny island is dominated by a brick lighthouse, where oceangoing ships stop to pick up one of the two pilots who navigate them through the Inner Channel. The lighthouse keeper has a small home where overnight stays can be arranged with special permission. Day-trippers are welcome to stop and visit the historic lighthouse at any time.

Goff's and **Rendezvous Cayes** are mere specks of palm-shaded sand off the major shipping lanes that make excellent stopovers for snorkeling (especially by beginners), fishing, swimming, and diving. Both islands are perched right on the edge of the barrier reef, which allows visitors to swim in either deep or shallow water. Overnight camping and anchorage is allowed, but please be careful about damaging the ecosystem.

Local fishers frequently visit Goff's and Rendezvous Cayes in their shallow-draft dories, mostly to find lobster and conch that will be sold to restaurants in Belize City and San Pedro. Not far from Goff's Caye is an area where manatees can almost always be found. Consult local guides for details.

Spanish Lookout Caye is 10 miles southeast of Belize City and 2 miles west of the main barrier reef. Once used by British pirates to spy on Spanish galleons, it now holds a 10-unit, bungalow-style lodge,

Richard Mahler

Rendezvous Caye is one of dozens of uninhabited islands along the barrier reef.

Spanish Bay Resort, $100 and up, meals included; 2-77288 or (800) 359-0747, with over-the-water lodging and an accompanying restaurant, bar, dive shop, and experienced fishing guides. Dive packages (with instruction) can be arranged. We recommend this Belizean-owned facility, which caters to nature lovers, fishing enthusiasts, divers, and snorkelers. It is well positioned for those who wish to patrol the outer reef or atolls, and you can arrange to be dropped off on a remote island for a day on your own. A powerful dive barge—complete with compressors and other necessary paraphernalia—can take visitors to uncharted waters. The atmosphere is casual and friendly.

Oceanic Society Expeditions uses Spanish Bay as its headquarters for manatee research trips to nearby cayes as well as a NAUI specialty course in research diving certification (dive sites are less than 30 minutes from the lodge). Transportation is provided from Belize City (20 minutes away) for guests.

BLUEFIELD RANGE, ALLIGATOR CAYE, AND MIDDLE LONG CAYE

Location: *Approximately 20 miles southeast of Belize City.*
Size: *Each of these cayes comprise less than an acre of dry land.*
Visitor Information: *Belize Tourist Board, (800) 624-0686*

How to Help Study the Reef

From an Island Camps base on Tobacco Caye, various squir-relfish species have had some very dedicated scientists and volunteers following them around Tobacco Reef for the past 7 years. (The squirrelfish is a reddish, largely nocturnal fish with a prominent, spiny dorsal fin and large, squirrel-like eyes.) In 1997, Dr. Susan Hammen-Winn of the University of Rhode Island was completing the fieldwork on an intensive squirrelfish study with the help of Earthwatch volunteers. This study focused on habitat mapping, a squirrelfish census, and recording fish behaviors of these sometimes elusive species that feed on small crustaceans. Scientists attach small glow-ing lights to individual squirrelfish and rotating teams of volunteers help record their movements throughout the night for a foraging segment of this study.

*Other teams from the nonprofit **Earthwatch** organiza-tion, (800) 776-0188, http://www.earthwatch.org., are*

Along Belize's barrier reef, the word "range" refers to the marshy clusters of mangroves that seem to be half land and half water. At least part of every caye seems to fit this description; therefore, we do not mention here the scores of islands on which it is virtually impos-sible to set foot. (The Belize government has imposed a ban on the purchase of unoccupied islands in the hope that many, if not most, can someday be included in an offshore national park system.)

Bluefield Range is unusual in that it supports several habitats. A couple of its mangrove cayes are permanently soggy, while the largest has a thin strip of high ground that accommodates **Ricardo Castillo's Beach Huts**, 2-31609. Ricardo and his family have built (very rustic) guest cabañas and a restaurant on stilts right over the water. Several tent sites on a pleasant stretch of sand are also avail-able at about $5 per person per day (this is a favorite stopping point *needed to participate in what scientists hope will be ongoing research on the ecology of nearby sea grass beds and other marine habitats. This study is uncovering new information about habitats around Tobacco Caye, building an important long-term database that will enable scientists to assess damage and changes in the reef community over time. When we last visited Tobacco Caye, Island Camps was hosting groups of up to 10 Earthwatch volunteers who stay for about two weeks to participate in this research. According to the late Dr. Howard Winn, who pioneered the Tobacco Caye project, "the reef's biodiversity and wealth of complex interactions provide a unique and outstanding laboratory for studying the theoretical aspects of community ecology, the mechanisms of evolution and speciation, and the relative benefits of various social behaviors. Such information will benefit Belize in efforts to manage coastal zone planning, establish parks, and address fishery problems."*

for southbound sea kayakers). Cabañas are about $85 a night, including meals. The owner will pick you up in Belize City.

Excursions from Bluefield Range

Bluefield Range is a good base for excursions to other nearby cayes and reefs, plus the many fine diving and fishing sites hereabouts. Ricardo Castillo serves as an experienced guide to little-known underwater limestone caves, coral canyons, and unoccupied cayes. Snorkelers and nature buffs can easily arrange trips to remote islands where exotic birds and other creatures make their homes.

Recommended nearby destinations include **Columbus Caye**, which has an underwater sinkhole more than 140 feet deep where large jewfish and sharks are often sighted, and **Caye Glory**, a submerged coral formation off Southern Long Caye, which is an important breeding ground for grouper and other fish. Snorkelers and divers in this area will see black coral and, occasionally, sea turtles.

Saltwater crocodiles and waterfowl are plentiful on **Middle Long Caye** (also called Alligator Caye), a few miles north of Bluefield Range. This large, swampy island has been the site of a small lodge in the past (inquire locally about its present status), and for many years local fishermen have used Middle Long's tiny beaches as camp-grounds—you can too!

TOBACCO CAYE

Location: *12 miles southeast of Dangriga, on the barrier reef.*
Size: *About 5 acres.*
Visitor Information: *Belize Tourist Board, (800) 624-0686*

Farther south from Belize City, east of the town of Dangriga, several little-known cayes offer attractions and services to visitors eager to explore the reef in relative solitude.

The islands of the Tobacco Range have been heavily used over the centuries for fishing camps, trading centers, and coconut plantations. In fact, Puritans set up a post here more than 350 years ago from which goods (including tobacco) were exchanged with visiting mariners.

On 5-acre Tobacco Caye, the largest island in the complex, travelers have several choices of modest accommodations. Local fishermen and their spouses operate most of the friendly rustic resorts and restaurants here as a supplement to their income during months when sea creatures are breeding or when the weather is too foul to venture out in boats.

Snorkeling and Diving in Tobacco Caye

Excellent snorkeling begins as soon as you enter the water on the windward (reef side) of Tobacco Caye. Snorkelers can either swim around the southern end of the caye to explore the reef near the **Reef End Lodge** or wade across a shallow lagoon from in front of **Ocean's Edge Lodge** to a break in the reef. (We strongly recommend wearing Reefwalkers or old tennis shoes that you don't mind sacrificing to saltwater.) If larger waves are breaking, either wait for calmer water (when the water visibility is better anyway) or swim around the reef from the south end.

During a 1997 visit to Tobacco Caye we saw an interesting brown, algae-like plant with disk-like "leaves" attached to the reef.

Turbinaria turbinata is an edible marine plant—eaten raw or pickled—that has also been used as fertilizer on coconut plantations throughout the Caribbean.

In deeper water, we were amazed by the pristine "forests" of many-branched elkhorn coral alongside common sea fans interspersed with brain and scores of other coral species. Among countless other reef dwellers, we identified the bluehead, a very colorful fish with a blue head, white stripe, and emerald-green tail; the hogfish, with its distinctive flattened face; and several species of colorful parrotfish, munching away at the coral.

PADI instructors Martin Spragg and Jeanette Melvin of **Second Nature Divers**, 5-37038 or 2-72109, e-mail *divers@btl.net,* offer a half-day **"Discover Scuba"** diving course, a four-day PADI open water certification, a dive shop, and excellent diving at nearby Columbus and Tobacco reefs. **Island Camps** has a partnership with Second Nature for the lodge's guests. Trips for experienced divers can be made 8 miles north to **Shark's Cave**—also called **The Black Hole**, where underwater enthusiasts will occasionally see a reef shark—as well as to Glover's Reef and Turneffe atoll.

Getting There/Outfitters

Contact Raymond Stephen at **Ocean's Edge Lodge**, 14-9633, to arrange a boat transfer to Tobacco Caye from Dangriga, or ask Jim at Dangriga's **New River Café**, 5-39908, about transportation to Tobacco. **Shipmate's Restaurant** is also a good place to make arrangements. Several reputable boatmen depart regularly from the **Stann Creek River** dock near the New River Café; expect to pay at least $15 one-way. We particularly recommend the experienced boatman, **Buck**, for the 1-hour crossing from Dangriga to Tobacco.

If you want to visit the caye directly from Belize City, contact Mark Bradley at **Island Camps**, 2-72109 or 14-7160, who makes a weekly run (usually Fridays) to the **Fiesta Hotel Marina** (formerly Ramada Royal Reef) in Belize City, charging about $20 per passenger. Be prepared for a sometimes rough ride and, if necessary, take Dramamine in advance or use sea-bands around your wrists to help ward off seasickness.

Where to Stay and Eat in Tobacco Caye

Gaviota Coral Reef Resort, in the center of the caye; $25–55, with meals; 14-9763 or 5-22085. Bert and Marie Swasey offer home-cooked meals and a comfortable bed in a relaxing, quiet setting.

Island Camps, north end of the island; $50–65, with meals; 2-72109 or 5-23433. Mark Bradley at Island Camps offers private, well-spaced cabañas, a fine restaurant, and bar. All electrical systems on Bradley's compound are solar operated.

Ocean's Edge Lodge, $53, with meals; 14-9633. Operated by friendly, helpful Raymond and Brenda Lee Stephen. Comfortable accommodations with private bath and hot water, a restaurant with great family-style Belizean meals, and a pleasant bar. Ocean's Edge also arranges saltwater fly-fishing or casting trips as well as half- or full-day sailing trips. The lodge arranges airport pickup on request.

Reef End Lodge, $70, with meals; 5-22419. The name speaks for itself; lodge, restaurant, and bar are at far south end of caye next to a shallow lagoon—an easy swim to the reef.

SOUTH WATER CAYE
Location: About 12 miles southeast of Dangriga.
Size: About 14 acres.
Visitor Information: Belize Tourist Board, (800) 624-0686

A wide range of services are available on South Water Caye, a picturesque palm-covered island a few miles south of Tobacco Range. An unusual aspect of this privately owned caye is the fact that it is located directly atop the barrier reef, next to one of the deepest channels through that reef. As a result, South Water enjoys some of the best and most easily accessible snorkeling and diving in Belize. The island is clean and quiet, home to many birds, including ospreys, royal terns, green herons, pelicans, and kingfishers.

Like the Tobacco Range cluster, South Water Caye sits on the outer edge of the barrier reef. Because the island is also next to a relatively deep cut through the reef, marine life is particularly abundant. There's talk about turning the offshore area into a national marine reserv, and the government of Belize may have taken this action by the time you visit.

Outfitters
At a separate 2.5-acre, solar-powered facility on South Water, marine ecology workshops are offered to the general public by **International Zoological Expeditions (IZE)**, $80 and up; phone (508) 655-1461,

e-mail *ize2belize@aol.com,* Web site *http://www.ize2belize.com* at its bio-logical research station. With more than 25 years experience in Belize, this Massachusetts-based outfitter is known for the quality of its instruction and accommodations (all meals included). Day trips are made to nearby cayes and reef formations to study birds and marine life.

A full-service, affordable dive operation, the **Living Reef Dive Centre**, 5-22214, e-mail *tread@btl.net,* is affiliated with IZE and has all necessary dive and snorkeling gear available for rent, plus PADI-certified scuba instructors and a marine lab. Day trips can be arranged for divers interested in exploring dive sites off Hunting Caye, Glover's Reef, and other locations. Living Reef's divemasters and instructors are also trained in marine biology and focus on education in marine ecology including fish identification, coral identification, reef ecology, and study of mangrove systems for both certified and novice divers alike. Living Reef—which also operates from Long Caye at Glover's Reef—has many options for divers including a half-day "Discover Scuba" resort-type course to get beginners the basic training they need to begin diving as soon as possible, while also providing a great foundation for those participants who want to go ahead with full PADI certification.

IZE's guests stay in a 15-bed "marine lodge" dorm or at **Leslie Cottages & Cabañas**, a comfortable five-unit complex operated by members of an extended Belizean family. Snorkeling and fishing trips can easily be arranged here. Cottage guests have free use of kayaks, a Sunfish sailboat, and windsurfer. IZE maintains separate research stations on Long Caye (Glover's Reef) and at Blue Creek in the Toledo District rainforest. Some IZE workshops can be taken for college credit.

Getting There
Guests of the lodges on South Water will be given transport to the island as part of their package; others can arrange to hire a private boat from Dangriga for $20 and up. Allow about 45 minutes to an hour for the crossing.

Where to Stay and Eat in South Water Caye
Blue Marlin Lodge, at the north end of South Water; $120 and up, including meals, four-night minimum; (800) 798-1558 or 5-22243. Fourteen double rooms and six bungalows, plus a restaurant, bar, volleyball pit, billiard table, and complete dive and fishing shops. Boats, guides, and a divemaster are also available for the eager anglers and scuba enthusiasts drawn to this sandy, flat island. Game

fish found near South Water Caye include tarpon, snook, grouper, bonefish, permit, marlin, sailfish, tuna, and wahoo. Blue Marlin is a PADI dive-training facility praised for the quality of its instruction. A seven-night dive package starts at about $1,300.

Dangriga's Pelican Beach Resort, at the south end of South Water Caye; $60 and up; 5-22044. Maintains two sets of accommodations, both made environment-friendly through the use of solar power, composting toilets, and rainwater collection. On the grounds of a renovated Catholic convent are two cottages, the **Heron's Hideaway**, a three-bedroom house, the **Osprey's Nest**, and a five-room main building, the **Pelican's Pouch**. The second set of rooms is at Pelican's University, a five-bedroom building near the center of the island that caters to student and educational groups. There are kitchen facilities for guest use, and the hotel will send over a resident cook to prepare meals on request (for a fee). Dive packages can be arranged with the island's dive shops, and fabulous snorkeling is as near as the water.

CARRIE BOW, MAN-O'-WAR, AND WEE WEE CAYES

Location: See text below.
Size: Wee Wee Caye is seven acres in size; Carrie Bow and Man-o'-War are each less than one acre.
Visitor Information: Belize Tourist Board, (800) 624-0686

Carrie Bow Caye is only about an acre in size—it was twice as big before the mangroves were chopped down and several devastating storms struck. The Smithsonian Institution leases it from the Bowman family, which also owns part of South Water Caye. Scientists from all over the world come to Carrie Bow to study the hundreds of species of underwater plants and animals, including mangrove and other important flora and fauna. As many as five scientists at a time are working on the island, whose waters provide some of the Caribbean's best snorkeling. Over the years, these experts have set up a baseline of valuable data that are being used to track the impact of agriculture, fishing, storm systems, pollution, and other influences on the fragile coral reef ecosystem.

Visitors are welcome at the research center by prior appointment, which can be arranged (along with transportation) through Tony Rath or Therese Bowman Rath at their **Pelican Beach Resort** in

Dangriga. Overnight accommodations in the house and dormitory are limited to Smithsonian personnel. The underwater marine area surrounding Carrie Bow teems with many varieties of multicolored fish, sponges, and coral and is easily accessible from the island's concrete pier. Again, beware of strong currents through the reef cut.

The Smithsonian, active in the area since 1977, also conducts research on **Twin Cayes**, several miles northwest of Carrie Bow. Studies in this area, which is not permanently occupied, concentrate on the mangrove ecosystem flora and fauna. In one curious (and unsuccessful) experiment, scientists attempted to rebuild nearby Curlew Caye by planting mangrove at the site of the island, which became submerged some years ago by a series of hurricanes.

Man-O'-War Caye, a few miles to the northwest, is an important rookery for several species of large water birds, including the magnificent frigate bird (also called the man-o'-war bird). If you pass by during mating season, you'll see the male puffing out his immense red, throat balloon. Boobies and terns can also be seen on this mangrove-dominated island. Man-O'-War Caye is federally protected, and you should not attempt to land here. A short distance west is a former pirate hang-out called **Coco Plum Caye**, a crescent-shaped island with a fine beach and secluded picnicking spot.

A small, privately operated marine research station is based on **Wee Wee Caye**, about 8 miles farther south, run by Paul and Mary Shave of **Possum Point Biological Research Station** on the Sittee River. Overnight accommodations at Wee Wee Caye are limited and should be arranged well in advance. The name, by the way, derives from the local name for leaf-cutter ants: wee wees.

THE SOUTHERNMOST CAYES
Location: *Remote locations; see text for details.*
Size: *Varies.*
Visitor Information: *Belize Tourist Board, (800) 624-0686*

As visitors head farther south in Belizean waters, the barrier reef gradually swings away from the mainland. These cayes are remote and, for the most part, uninhabited. Aside from fishing shanties, rustic cabins, and sandy campgrounds, there are only a few overnight accommodations. This situation is changing; inquire locally about any new lodges that have opened since this book's publication.

In large measure because they are so inaccessible, these islands and the marine life surrounding them are almost exactly as they were centuries ago, when the Maya paddled among them in dugout canoes.

Birders can expect to log dozens of species here, including many varieties of tern, gull, pelican, booby, heron, and egret. Grackles, vireos, hummingbirds, cuckoos, and pigeons also breed on the cayes. During the winter, many migratory birds visit these cayes on their way to and from North and Central America.

Some of the cayes also shelter a surprising number of land-based animals—lizards, frogs, crabs, snakes, and even large mammals, including opossums, raccoons, pacas, and armadillos. Apparently some of these creatures were swept out to sea on log rafts and washed up on beaches, then managed to sustain themselves and procreate.

Several of the southern cayes, including Laughingbird, Bugle, Colson, and Lark, are popular destinations for day trips out of Placencia, where the services of boats and guides are easily arranged. Other than group excursions out of Placencia, Punta Gorda, and Dangriga, the best way to visit these pristine areas is by chartered boat.

Wippari Caye

Divers, snorkelers, and fishing enthusiasts eager for a taste of Creole life in a seldom-visited part of the reef are encouraged to visit Wippari Caye (sometimes spelled Whiprey), where friendly George and Hortense Cabral operate the six-cabin **Wippari Caye Lodge**, $20 and up, 6-23130, that provides excellent meals and first-class guide service. George is a former Placencia storekeeper who moved his family to Wippari—the local word for eagle ray—about 15 years ago. They've planted trees, established an extensive garden, and discovered one of the country's best bonefish flats on the perimeter of their tiny island, located about 9 miles east of Placencia. Two of the couple's sons—Pow and Breeze—are among the best fishing guides in Belize. Contact the Cabrals by VHF radio, or through either the **Rum Point Inn** or **Kitty's Place** in Placencia.

Little Water Caye

On Little Water Caye, about 12 miles southeast of Placencia, is the small, exclusive **The Little Water Caye Resort** ($100 and up, 2-31237 or 6-22267).The lodge reopened in 1995 under new ownership (after being shot down in its first incarnation as a nudist colony). It offers full scuba services, snorkeling, fishing, sailing, and a full-service restaurant.

Ranguana Caye

Rustic but comfortable bungalow accommodations are available on Ranguana Caye, about 20 miles southeast of Placencia, at **Eddie Leslie's Ranguana Reef Resort**, $50, no phone. Visitors are reminded to bring their own food, and bathrooms are shared. Fishing and diving trips are a specialty here, but you'll need to bring your own equipment. Ranguana is one of the few places in Belize where sea kayaks can be rented, from **Reef-Link Kayaking**, (515) 279-6699. Paddling conditions are excellent, and camping is also available for a modest fee.

Other Southern Cayes

Lodges on nearby **Nicholas Caye** and **Lime Caye** have been in the planning stages for several years; check locally on their status, facilities, and access to these privately-owned islands. **Mosquito, Hatchet,** and **Pompion Cayes** are also privately owned.

Island-hoppers heading south will find a campground on **Rendezvous Caye**, directly east of Placencia (not to be confused with the island of the same name near Bluefield Range) and nearby Colson Caye. Overnight visits are now discouraged at **Laughingbird Caye**, a national park, in order to encourage the return of the nesting gulls for which the island is named.

By the time you reach the **Toledo District**, the barrier reef is out of sight across the northeastern horizon. Because the archipelago is a considerable distance from the mainland, travelers should expect to stay overnight and pay a hefty price for the trip. A campground, a picnic area, and sparsely furnished cabins are available for general use on Hunting Caye; a diving/fishing lodge there is under development. The caye also hosts a small outpost of the Belize Defense Forces, charged with interdicting smugglers and other lawbreakers.

SAPODILLA CAYES

The waters of the Sapodilla island complex remain almost completely unexplored by anyone except local fishermen and Guatemalan vacationers. The coral walls that plunge steeply into the ocean's depths offer spectacular viewing opportunities for experienced divers and snorkelers. The islands have secluded, shaded beaches that make idyllic camping and picnicking spots. British scientists began a long-term ecological study of the Sapodilla Cayes in 1992.

SNAKE CAYES

From Punta Gorda, excursions can also be arranged to the Snake Cayes, small islands hugging the coastline a few miles northeast of town. Many of these are swampy mangrove ranges, but a few have enough high ground to support significant numbers of coconut palms, wild figs, buttonwoods, and other native trees. These cayes are not a part of the barrier reef system, but instead lie on their own coral reefs emerging from a limestone ledge that extends several miles into the Caribbean Sea. One small island near the mainland, **Wild Cane Caye**, is the site of an important ancient Mayan ceremonial center that is now being excavated. The area's sportfishing is rated excellent (especially around river mouths), and several hotels and guest houses in Punta Gorda make a good base of operations. The town is also a jumping-off point for trips to Guatemala and, from there, Honduras and the Bay Islands. In recent years, several resorts specializing in sportfishing and diving have operated north and south of Punta Gorda, around Punta Negra and Punta Ycacos. Contact **Kingfisher Sports** in Placencia or **Nature's Way Guest House** in Punta Gorda for details. (See Chapter 9: Southern Belize.)

THE ATOLLS

An atoll is a ring-shaped coral island and associated reef that fringe an enclosed, relatively shallow lagoon. While such formations are common in the South Pacific and other tropical oceans of the world, only four of any size exist in the Caribbean. Three of the four atolls are located off the barrier reef of Belize (the other is near Trinidad). Because of their isolation from the mainland, atolls are often home to species of flora and fauna rarely seen anywhere else. Their waters tend to be exceptionally clear, calm, and unpolluted, which makes them ideal for diving, fishing, snorkeling, windsurfing, sailing, and kayaking.

The islands themselves are frequently used as breeding sites by birds and other animals that prefer undisturbed habitats for raising their young. Belize has moved swiftly to preserve the relatively pristine quality of its offshore atolls. Day trips can be made to **Lighthouse Reef** for birding and snorkeling, and to the **Lamanai ruins** for Mayan archaeology and howler monkey study. At Lighthouse Reef you may encounter Pita, a very friendly female dolphin who often plays in the bow waves and wakes of passing boats.

A trip to one or more of these destinations takes extra effort (and money), but the rewards are unmatched.

TURNEFFE ISLANDS
Location: *About 25 miles east of Belize City.*
Size: *The archipelago measures a maximum of 30 miles long and 10 miles wide, covering a surface area of 205 square miles.*
Visitor Information: *The Belize Tourist Board (800) 624-0686, and the Belize Tourism Industry Association.*

The Turneffe Islands comprise the largest of the country's three atolls and is also the atoll nearest the mainland, separated from the barrier reef by a 6- to 10-mile channel that plunges to a depth of 1,000 feet or more. Like its companion atolls, Glover's Reef and Lighthouse Reef, Turneffe has been given a deceptive name. Instead of "islands," the archipelago is actually a cluster of about 35 tiny coral islets and swampy mangrove ranges (also known as "wet cayes") encircling a shallow lagoon punctuated by seaward channels.

Most of the cayes at Turneffe are covered with thick forests of red and black mangrove that form a rich and vital breeding ground for conch, lobster, and fish, as well as waterbirds. Close inspection reveals many of the islands on the west (leeward) side to be little more than dense masses of mangroves clutching at shallow sandbeds. On the east (or windward) side a few acres of land rise high enough to support human habitation, and several of these sites (easily identi-fied by coconut palm clusters) are occupied by either sportfishing/diving lodges or the informal "fish camps" of Belizeans. Openings between the mangrove thickets are called "bogues," and they connect the shallow interior lagoons with the open Caribbean.

During the Classic and Late Classic Maya periods, fishers and traders established small outposts here as well as at **Glover's Reef**. Later, pirates set up camps on the Turneffe Islands (bringing Mayan slaves with them) and preyed on passing Spanish trade ships. In the early 20th century the Turneffes were well-known for their sponges and coconuts, largely wiped out by diseases and hurricanes in recent decades. Only a few lobster and coconut collectors, along with a handful of resort operators, now call the islands home.

Things to See and Do
The snorkeling and diving here are excellent. The water is more

crystalline here than on reefs closer to the mainland, where some turbidity is caused by the muddy runoff from mountain-draining rivers. Visibility in the warm water (74- to 84-degrees Fahrenheit) is often more than 150 feet in any direction.

The waters around the Turneffe atoll, especially the wadeable coral-debris "flats," are teeming with permit, barracuda, and bonefish. Tarpon are plentiful from March through June around Turneffe's channels and inlets. Larger, deeper-water species include mackerel, bonito, marlin, blackfin tuna, grouper, sailfish, and wahoo. Billfish are most common here from January through April.

Divers and snorklers are especially fond of the atoll's steep drop-offs and tall coral heads adorned with colorful tube sponges, fan coral, sea fans, and gorgonians among the natural crags and occasional shipwrecks. Black coral and sponges are especially evident in the inland waters of Vincent's Lagoon. **Black Beauty** is a favored dive spot where black coral covers a small reef. **Mauger Caye**, at the atoll's north end, is another popular location among divers, who find a wide variety of sharks there. The island is identified by its lighthouse, in place since 1821.

On the east side of the atoll, **Soldier's Caye** is a sanctuary for nesting roseate terns and white crowned pigeons, both rare in Belize. Animals native to the Turneffe archipelago include boa constrictors, raccoons, lizards, and land crabs.

Research at the Turneffe Islands

A Texas A&M University research station at Blackbird Caye studies the behavior of bottlenose dolphins, which frequent nearby lagoons. This is said to be the first such research undertaken in a diverse environment where mangrove islands, coral reefs, and sea grass beds form a delicately balanced ecosystem.

In a program modeled after a similar project in the Bahamas, San Francisco-based **Oceanic Society Expeditions**, (800) 326-7491, conducts excursions here that allow visitors to participate in A&M's surface and underwater studies of bottlenose behavior and distribution. Visitors swim with the dolphins or observe them from boats, plotting locations and collecting other data. Area manatees are also under study. The Oceanic Society offers some of these options in cooperation with the Elderhostel program, catering to older travelers.

On **Calabash Caye**, immediately south of Blackbird, the **Planetary Coral Reef Foundation (PCRF)** has a research station where coral reef ecology is being studied. Visitors must have permission from PCRF to visit. Calabash and the other islands south to the tip of Turneffe have been declared a national marine reserve by the Belize government. An important part of the scientific analysis is comparing reef response to Blackbird's ecotourism and Calabash's restricted visitation.

Two areas in the Turneffe Islands group have been recommended by the Belize Center for Environmental Studies for establishment as government reserves. **Vincent's Lagoon** (also known as **Northern Lagoon**) is a breeding ground for the Morelet's crocodile and Caribbean manatee, both endangered. **Soldier's Caye**, mentioned above, is the nesting site of several important bird species. Increased human activity could have a negative effect on both areas.

Getting There/Outfitters

There is no regular public transportation to the Turneffe Islands. The vast majority of visitors arrive as part of sportfishing or diving packages offered by the handful of resorts based on the islands (transportation from Belize City is prearranged by private skiff). Because it is close to the mainland in comparison to the other two atolls, Turneffe can be reached fairly easily through arrangements with local charter or live-aboard boat operators, either as a final destination or a stopping point en route to the Lighthouse Reef and/or Glover's Reef atolls. Expect to pay at least $85 per person for the 1½- to 2-hour trip from Belize City.

Where to Stay and Eat in Turneffe

Blackbird Caye Resort on Blackbird Caye; $100 and up, meals included; 2-32772. A most unusual resort complex, occupying a stretch of east-facing beach on 4,000-acre Blackbird Caye, both a living marine/land resource management community and an environmentally sensitive resort. (The caye takes its name from the local term for the great-tailed grackles found here in abundance.) This recommended, nature-oriented resort provides a little-disturbed setting for visits to the nearby coral reef, turtle nesting beaches, saltwater crocodile habitat, manatee breathing holes, and bird rookeries. Blackbird's cabaña-style lodge is used by nature-oriented tour groups and scientific research teams that arrive by boat from the mainland. Besides marine ecology studies, activities include diving, snorkeling, fishing, hiking, and beachcombing. The resort accommodates as many as 16 visitors with a full-service kitchen, electricity, hot water, and fishing guides. A certified dive instructor is based here and 7-night dive packages begin at around $1150.

Turneffe Island Lodge, on 12-acre Caye Bokel at the southern tip of the atoll; $140 and up; 1-49564 or (800) 338-8149. Nine rooms, plus a dining hall and bar. Several boats are outfitted for diving and fishing. The lodge caters primarily to experienced divers, who explore such popular nearby underwater destinations as the Elbow, Myrtle's Turtle, and the shipwreck *Sayonara*. Wall diving off the reef is a favorite pastime here. The resort's 38-foot dive boat can take visitors to remote locations for up to three dives a day. Saltwater fly fishers are pleased to learn that bonefish and permit are found in large numbers near here. The lodge limits anglers to six per week.

Turneffe Flats Lodge, midway up the atoll's east side on the northeast tip of Blackbird Caye; $130 and up, one-week minimum; 2-30116 or (800) 815-1304. Built on the site of an old fishing camp that dates back to the Mayan era, the piles of weathered conch shells here are several feet high. The American-owned lodge can accommodate 12 guests among several bungalows. Beach camping is allowed by advance reservation. The facility specializes in saltwater fly-fishing, although divers, birders, and snorkelers are also welcome. Bonefish, permit, and tarpon are the most sought-after species here, and all are found in abundance. Guides, boats, equipment, and meals are provided.

LIGHTHOUSE REEF
Location: About 50 miles east of Belize City.
Size: 28 miles long; 2 to 6 miles wide (varies).
Visitor Information: Belize Tourist Board, (800) 624-0686

The center of this largely uninhabited offshore atoll is almost completely surrounded by coral formations, which form a solid ridge on its east side. Its six islands are widely separated and form a near-perfect semicircle.

Lighthouse is best known to most visitors as a **diver's paradise** (there are more than 40 popular dive sites) and as the home of **Half Moon Caye Natural Monument**.

Vegetation on the cayes is rich and varied, thanks in part to the natural fertilizer provided by thousands of birds and reptiles. Ficus (fig) trees, ziricote, gumbo-limbo, sea grape, spider lily, and coconut palm are all abundant here.

Half Moon Caye Natural Monument

Established as Belize's first protected area in 1981, Half Moon Caye Natural Monument comprises 10,000 acres of the atoll and more than 15 square miles of surrounding waters. The monument shelters a large nesting colony of rare red-footed boobies, an estimated 77 migratory bird species, and the magnificent frigate bird (an arch-enemy of the booby with up to an 8-foot wingspan). The 4,000-member booby colony is one of only two in the Caribbean (the other is on Tobago Island off Venezuela), and the nesting area can be observed from a special 15-foot viewing platform at the end of a half-mile trail. Along the way you may see male frigate birds in their mating display, which involves puffing their crimson throat pouches into giant balloons.

The slow-witted boobies are so named because they showed no fear of early sailors, who killed them easily and indiscriminately for food. Red-footed boobies are usually dull brown (with red feet), but most of the Half Moon Caye birds have white feathers accentuated by pale gold heads and long blue-gray beaks.

The Belize Audubon Society, caretaker of the sanctuary, has counted over 100 bird species on tiny Half Moon, among them the black-chinned hummingbird, white-crowned pigeon, and mangrove warbler. Several species of reptiles also live here, and both hawksbill and loggerhead turtles lay their eggs on the caye's beaches, where you may also encounter the largest species of land crab in Belize.

Hiking

Hiking is allowed on Half Moon Caye with consent of the resident warden, who can provide maps and information on sanitation facilities. Overnight camping has been suspended by Belize Audubon because of over-visitation. An historic lighthouse, first built in 1820 and now sun-powered, provides good views of the atoll and bird colonies. As you walk you'll probably see many iguanas scurrying about. German U-boats refueled here during World War II, but no physical evidence of their visits remains.

Diving, Snorkeling, and Marine Life

The underwater area immediately surrounding Half Moon Caye is also protected and is full of marine life—more than 220 species of reef fish have been identified. Conch, which has almost disappeared from local waters, is gradually being reintroduced. The underwater park surrounding Half Moon is easily accessible from a broad sandy beach and pier. Swimmers, divers, snorkelers, and kayakers are all welcome, provided they stay in designated areas and observe conservation rules.

Red-footed booby on Half Moon Caye.

Kevin Schafer

Some distance north of Half Moon is **Sandbore Caye**, which has an old lighthouse as well as excellent diving and snorkeling areas. Despite the presence of such stations, many ships have gone down in these waters. The Spanish trade ship *Juan Batista* sank about a mile offshore in 1822 and is said to have carried a cargo of still-unrecovered gold and silver bullion.

At popular dive sites in the area depths plunge dramatically from 30 feet to several thousand feet within a short distance. The range of marine life includes some deep-water species that seldom enter Belize's shallower reef areas. Also look for enormous sponges, grouper, hogfish, and snapper.

BLUE HOLE NATURAL MONUMENT

Location: *About 50 miles east of Belize City.*
Size: *Lighthouse Reef is 28 miles long and from 2 to 6 miles wide.*
Visitor Information: *The Belize Tourist Board and the Belize Tourism Industry Association.*

Eight miles north of Half Moon Caye and roughly in the middle of Lighthouse Reef is the popular Blue Hole, an almost perfectly circular limestone sinkhole that is more than 300 feet across and 412 feet deep. Created by the collapse of an underwater cavern some 12,000 years ago, the Blue Hole was the subject of a documentary by underwater explorer Jacques Cousteau, who concluded that a network of caves and crevices extends far beneath the entire reef. The presence of stalagmites and stalactites supports the conclusion that offshore Belize was dry land during the last age, which ended about 11,000 years ago. In 1996 a 1,023-acre parcel that includes the Blue Hole was protected by the Belize government as a natural monument.

Sport divers (limited to a depth of 130 feet) can admire the Blue Hole's outstanding stalagmite and stalactite formations, while swimming in crystal-clear water that appears to be a peculiar shade of deep blue when seen from the surface. The Hole is a habitat for shrimp and jewfish, but you should not expect to see much besides an occasional shark or tuna if you dive here. Surrounding waters are only about 20 feet deep and big fish have trouble making their way to the Blue Hole.

Outfitters

Ecosummer Expeditions, (604) 669-7741, fax (604) 669-3244, e-mail *trips@ecosummer.com,* of Vancouver, BC, has offered week-long sea kayaking expeditions to Lighthouse Reef, including the Blue Hole, since 1982. Participants camp on Half Moon Caye and spend their days exploring the area. Instruction, equipment, meals, and transportation from Belize City are provided. Ecosummer also arranges one-week sailing trips to Lighthouse Reef from San Pedro aboard the 48-foot traditional Belizean lighter *Excellence*. Guests are taken to the best snorkeling and fishing spots, including the Turneffe and Glover's atolls. Meals and accommodations are provided, and trip extensions to the Belize interior can be arranged.

Getting There

Day trips to Half Moon Caye and the Blue Hole start at about $125 per person ($175 for divers) for groups of several individuals (the atoll is 3 to 4 hours from Belize City and about 2 or 3 hours from San Pedro). Some live-aboard dive boats based in Belize City, Ambergris Caye, and elsewhere make trips to Lighthouse, as well as the two other atolls. Try **Out Island Divers** and **Indigo Belize**, both in San Pedro, for information on their dive trips to Lighthouse. (Out Island also maintains a tent camp on Long Caye.) Expect to pay a minimum of $160 per day for live-aboard boats and ask around before making a commitment—some visitors have complained about poor conditions on some of the boats.

Because of its remote location, boat excursions to the atoll by individuals or couples are fairly costly; it is wise to make the trip with other passengers to reduce the per-person expenses. Boats are allowed to dock only at the pier on the leeward side of Half Moon Caye, and deep-draught vessels may anchor only in designated areas. Charter flights can be made to the Northern Two Caye strip with

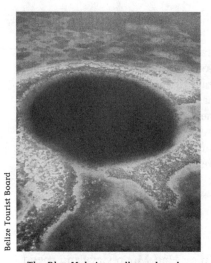

The Blue Hole is a collapsed underwater cave at Lighthouse Reef.

permission of the Lighthouse Reef Resort.

Where to Stay and Eat Near the Blue Hole

Lighthouse Reef Resort, on 16-acre Northern Two Caye (sometimes called Northern Caye), provides the atoll's only lodging; $200 and up, one-week minimum; 2-31205 or (800) 423-3114, e-mail: *lighthouse@btl.net.* A 20-unit full-service diving facility, with private paved airstrip for shuttling guests to and from Belize City. The lodge specializes in diving and fishing, seven-night packages start at about $1,350, with all meals, guides, and other services included. Registrants may use kayaks and windsurfers free of charge. Non-guests must bring their own food, drink, and fuel. Advance permission is required to land on the airstrip.

GLOVER'S REEF ATOLL

Location: About 20 miles east of the barrier reef, 30 miles from the mainland, and roughly 50 miles southeast of Belize City.
Size: The atoll encompasses roughly 100 square miles.
Visitor Information: The Belize Tourism Board and the Belize Tourism Industry Association.

Glover's is a splendid offshore atoll, the most remote island group in the country. Rising from an ocean depth of over 2,000 feet, Glover's Atoll consists of a well-defined, oval-shaped coral formation (19 miles long and 7 miles wide) that surrounds more than 700 patch reefs inside a 100-square-mile crystalline lagoon. A special area on the northeast side of Glover's Reef—closed seasonally by the Belize Fisheries Department—is an important breeding ground for grouper and snapper. Surrounding walls begin at about 30 feet and drop suddenly to well over 2,000 feet. Because of its unusual diversity, *Skin*

Diver magazine has proclaimed this reef one of the three best dive/snorkel sites in the world.

The atoll is named after 17th-century pirate **John Glover**, who used the remote islands as the base for his raids against Spanish galleons heading in and out of the Bay of Honduras. One of his ancestors lived on Northeast Caye well into the 20th century and several alleged pirate graves can be seen on that island. The ancient Maya had camps here long before Glover, however, and centuries-old artifacts still turn up.

During the early 1970s, a visiting team of international scientists pronounced Glover's the biologically richest atoll in the Caribbean Basin. It is one of the region's only nesting sites for the white-capped noddy, least tern, and marine turtles. In 1993 the entire Glover's Reef atoll was declared a marine reserve by the Belize government. All six of the atoll's islands except Northeast Caye are zoned as conservation areas and one, Middle Caye, is a designated wilderness. Seasonal closures and strictly enforced conservation and fishing restrictions allow the reserve to maintain its biological integrity for future generations and for species to recuperate.

In 1991, **Middle Caye** was purchased from its private owner by the Wildlife Conservation Society (formerly the New York Zoological Society), which now manages the 15-acre island. Middle Caye has been called the keystone to the long-term preservation of Glover's Reef, in that scientists and Belize Department of Fisheries employees can now use Middle as their base for monitoring activities around the atoll. In 1997 the Belize Fisheries Department had a manager and ranger stationed on the island. Marine ecologists study the area's rich flora and fauna, while government enforcement officers work to protect the remote area from such human disturbances as overfishing, garbage dumping, and careless diving. There is concern that unrestricted human activity in this fragile ecosystem could degrade what remains one of the world's most pristine marine environments.

During our 1997 visit to Middle Caye we met a researcher who was studying a group of small fish called triple-fin blennies, a possible "indicator species" that may help determine the overall health of a marine ecosystem. Other researchers have been studying a variety of fish species here, as well as conch and lobster. Recent results suggest that Glover's Reef remains an important breeding ground for marine creatures that have been over-harvested in other parts of Belize.

A visit to **Middle Caye** is by permission only, although those

Steele Wotkyns

Sunset is a quiet time on Glover's Reef.

staying on nearby islands are routinely welcomed for guided tours. The island has a small freshwater lagoon and a surprising variety of animals and plants. Facilities include a small museum, a wet lab, and a marine research aquarium. The research center is a model of self-sufficiency: producing its electricity from the sun and wind, obtaining water from a reverse-osmosis desalinization plant, and disposing of its human waste in composting toilets.

Two commercial lodges operate on Glover's Reef atoll and for part of each year a sea kayaking outfitter (**Slickrock Adventures**) operates on Long Caye, which is also used by an adventure travel company (**International Zoological Expeditions**).

Sea Kayaking

Sea kayaking off Glover's Reef is exceptional, and the atoll works well for both experienced and novice paddlers. Outfitters provide expert guides for boat-handling instruction and safety briefings. Kayaks are used to visit other islands as well as for snorkeling adventures to patch reefs and the outer reef.

Snorkeling and Diving

The snorkeling here is truly world-class. The perimeter of the atoll is lined with awesome elkhorn coral forests that are filled with dozens of fish species. A deeper sandy zone is home to bigger fish, and visitors finally reach a "wall" that eventually drops off some 2,600 feet to the ocean floor about a mile east of Glover's. The diversity of sea creatures within these environments is staggering.

The atoll is usually deserted, except for resort folks, Long Caye's full-time resident caretaker and his family, a few visiting fishermen (from as far away as Honduras), researchers and Belize Department of Fisheries staff on Middle Caye, and a lighthouse-keeper on Southwest Caye. Conditions for snorkeling and diving are superb everywhere, and several interesting shipwrecks lie in relatively shallow water at the atoll's north and south ends.

Outfitters
International Zoological Expeditions, 5-22119 or (800) 548-5843, e-mail *travel@ize2belize.com*. Arranges visits to Long Caye, which the outfitter now owns. IZE maintains services here primarily as an annex for participants in its marine ecology seminars, based on South Water Caye. We recommend visitors try IZE's affordable, well-maintained camping facilities on Long Caye's south end. When we visited in 1997, IZE was planning to add a new main lodge with a kitchen/dining room and a few cabañas. Similar to IZE's arrangement with the **Living Reef Dive Center** on South Water Caye, Living Reef and IZE are cooperating to stress marine conservation principles and marine ecology education for student groups and other visiting drivers on Long Caye. Living Reef's knowledgeable Long Caye manager is **Tony Read**, 5-22214, e-mail *tread@btl.net*. See the previous section about South Water Caye for a description of his company's services.

The northern portion of Long Caye is used from November to May by **Slickrock Adventures**, (800) 390-5715, e-mail *slickrock@slickrock.com*, Web site *http://www.slickrock.com.*, which offers recommended 6- and 10-day package trips featuring kayaking, windsurfing (short and long boards), snorkeling, fishing, and diving. Guests spend part of each day paddling among the islands, observing underwater flora and fauna in remote parts of the atoll. Instruction, most equipment, meals, and rustic accommodations (as well as tent sites) are provided, along with transportation by boat to and from Belize City or Dangriga. Visitors bring their own snorkeling masks, fishing gear, and sleeping bags. Slickrock offers trip extensions to the Belize interior as well as Honduras. Diving instruction, short courses, certification courses and a variety of world-class, open-water dives can be arranged through the above-mentioned Living Reef Dive Center.

Slickrock's unobtrusive facilities on the island include passive-solar showers, pit toilets, rainwater collection systems, volleyball court, sun deck, dining pavillion, and a special nesting platform for a resident osprey family.

Getting There
Lomont's Reef Resort, Manta Reef Resort, International Zoological Expeditions, and **Slickrock Adventures** each provide transportation to and from the atoll as part of their packages, which usually last from one to two weeks. Because of the distance from the mainland, expect to pay a minimum of $150 for a charter boat to Glover's Reef, probably departing from Dangriga, Placencia, or Big Creek. An alternative is to sign onto one of the several live-aboard dive boats that regularly anchor off the atoll. **Glover's Reef Resort** guests are picked up every Sunday morning at the dorm-style Glover's Guest House ($5–$8), on the Sittee River south of Dangriga, for the 5- to 6-hour voyage to Northeast Caye. The boat returns the following Saturday afternoon, and both trips are included in the price of lodging. The resort prefers advance reservations and reduces rates for second-week stays. (Closed September–November.)

Where to Stay and Eat on Glover's Reef
Manta Reef Resort, on privately owned Southwest Caye on the archipelago's southern tip; $140 and up; 2-32767 or (800) 326-1724. Caters to serious divers and fishers (one-week minimum) eager to explore the underwater world or to hook bonefish, permit, and barracuda, which are abundant on the atoll's coral flats. Conditions are also excellent for tarpon, snapper, grouper, marlin, jack, tuna, bonito, wahoo, sailfish, and other billfish (plus the huge manta rays that give the resort its name). Manta provides lodging on the 12-acre island in thatched-roof cabañas and transportation for divers in small V-hull boats. Forested with coconut palms, like all of this atoll's islands, Southwest Caye is bisected by a hurricane-created cut and dominated at its southernmost end by a government-operated lighthouse. Transportation to Manta Reef Resort is by boat (included in the price) from Belize City. The entire operation was for sale in 1997, and its name may have changed by the time you read this.

Glover's Reef Resort, on Northeast Caye; $100/week cabin, $80/week camping, meals not included; 1-48351 or 5-23048. This rustic camping/cabaña facility specializes in diving, snorkeling, and fishing trips for individuals and small groups. Members of the French-American Lomont family, who manage the property, live nearby on a tiny sandbar off of neighboring Long Caye. Attractions on 12-acre Northeast Caye include an old and massive gumbo-limbo tree, which shelters the alleged graves of pirates who lived here over two centuries ago. Turtles nest on the island's beaches and ospreys are common. Canoes, power-boats, guides, air compressors, and water recreation gear are usually available, but remember that there is no electricity or indoor plumbing: conditions are primitive. Meals (expensive) can sometimes be purchased at the resort's headquarters, but visitors are strongly encouraged to provide their own food (cooking gear and water are provided for a fee, as is camping equipment). Be advised that the owners have been involved in contentious property rights disputes, and some travelers have reported very negative experiences here.

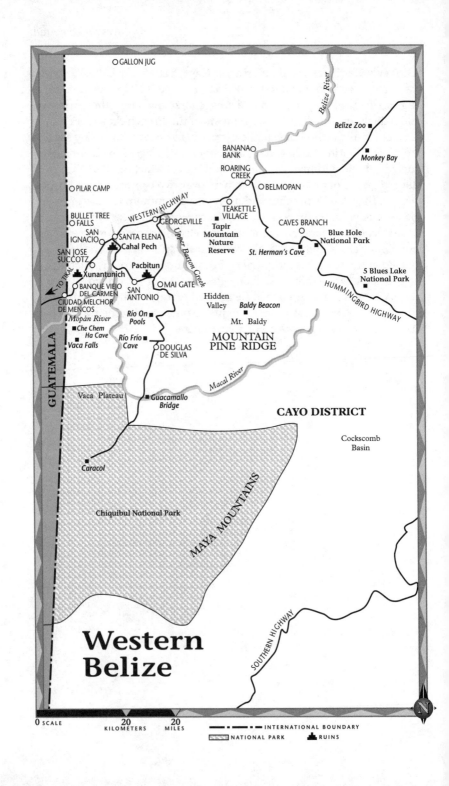

Western Belize

○ GALLON JUG

Belize River

Belize Zoo ■

■ Monkey Bay

BANANA BANK ○

ROARING CREEK ○

BELMOPAN ○

○ PILAR CAMP

WESTERN HIGHWAY

GEORGEVILLE ○

TEAKETTLE VILLAGE ○

CAVES BRANCH ○

Blue Hole National Park ■

BULLET TREE FALLS ○

SAN IGNACIO ○

SANTA ELENA ○
Cahal Pech

Tapir Mountain Nature Reserve ■

St. Herman's Cave ■

SAN JOSE SUCCOTZ ○

Pacbitun

Upper Barton Creek

5 Blues Lake National Park ■

Xunantunich ■

MAI GATE ○

BANQUE VIEJO DEL CARMEN ○

CIUDAD MELCHOR DE MENCOS

SAN ANTONIO

Hidden Valley

Baldy Beacon ■

HUMMINGBIRD HIGHWAY

-TO TIKAL-

Mopán River

■ Che Chem Ha Cave

■ Vaca Falls

Río On Pools

Río Frío Cave ○

DOUGLAS DE SILVA ○

Mt. Baldy

MOUNTAIN PINE RIDGE

Macal River

CAYO DISTRICT

GUATEMALA

Vaca Plateau

Guacamallo Bridge ■

Cockscomb Basin

■ Caracol

Chiquibul National Park

MAYA MOUNTAINS

SOUTHERN HIGHWAY

0 SCALE   20 KILOMETERS   20 MILES   —··—··— INTERNATIONAL BOUNDARY
░░ NATIONAL PARK   ♣ RUINS

N

WESTERN BELIZE

CAYO DISTRICT

Until the late 1980s, few visitors ventured west of the Belize Zoo unless they were heading across the Guatemalan border to the ancient city of Tikal. The conventional wisdom was that, except for the capital of Belmopan and the Mayan ruins of Xunantunich, there was not much to see in the country's interior. We have talked to some travelers whose only memory along the Western Highway is of the roadside Belize City cemetery and an unsightly municipal garbage dump, since closed down.

Fortunately, the interior's infrastructure has improved to the point where many rewarding destinations can (and should) be added to any visitor's itinerary. Besides the country's most extensive Mayan ruins and a growing number of comfortable lodges, Belize's interior offers the best opportunity to encounter the marvelous flora and fauna of a relatively undisturbed subtropical forest. Although some of the nation's newest nature sanctuaries and wilderness preserves offer virtually no access to the casual visitor, others provide an "up close and personal" experience you are not likely to forget. In addition, there are caves, rivers, horse paths, waterfalls, foot trails, mountain bike tracks, butterfly farms, museums, whitewater rapids, campsites, and flora and fauna galore, just waiting to be discovered—in some cases quite literally, since much of the interior remains virtually untouched by humans.

159

Canoeing on the Macal River of the Cayo District

Richard Mahler

Cayo (Spanish for "small island") is the second-largest district in Belize. The district begins about 35 miles south and west of Belize City and encompasses roughly 1,500 square miles, including much of the Macal River watershed and Maya Mountains. In 1997, the population in Cayo was estimated to be about 44,000.

The capital city of **Belmopan** lies at the district's eastern border and its western edge is the Guatemalan frontier. In between, besides thick forests and wild rivers, visitors find some of the nation's richest farmland, at times so carefully manicured by Mennonites that it looks more like rural Pennsylvania than Central America. Besides cattle, poultry, and pigs, Cayo farmers raise corn, sorghum, beans, fruit, and various vegetables for both domestic consumption and export. Significant amounts of pine, rosewood, Santa María, cedar, and mahogany are harvested by timber interests.

San Ignacio, on the Macal River, is the hub of commerce and tourism for western Belize. Other Cayo District towns include **Santa Elena**, San Ignacio's sister city across the suspension bridge, and **Benque Viejo**, which practically straddles the border. Both of the latter communities are largely Spanish-speaking, and you are likely to encounter marimbas, fiestas, and colorful social customs

160

centered around Catholic holidays and the rituals of baptism, confirmation, and marriage. Many inhabitants are descended from Mayan and Guest house Guatemalan immigrants who crossed the border into Belize to escape political persecution and economic exploitation.

The Cayo District and western Belize are easily reached by private or rental car by way of the Western Highway, or by the same route via the low-cost **Batty**, **Novelo**, **Piache**, and **Shaw** bus lines. Check with local agents or innkeepers for schedules and fares. The drive from Belize City to San Ignacio takes just under 2 hours by car, the bus trip somewhat longer (cost is $3). There are taxi stands at Columbus Park (the traffic circle on the west side of the suspension bridge) in San Ignacio and Market Plaza in downtown Belmopan. Most resorts can arrange a pickup at Belize's international airport for a fee of between $85 and $125. Except for **Gallon Jug** (on Programme for Belize lands), there is no scheduled air service to the Cayo District, although charters fly to airstrips at Blancaneaux Lodge and Central Farm.

SAN IGNACIO AND VICINITY

SAN IGNACIO
Location: *Roughly 22 miles west of Belmopan and 9 miles from the Guatemala border.*
Population: *About 8,000 (1997 estimate).*
Visitor Information: *local travel agencies; the Belize Tourism Industry Association, 2-75717, or their Cayo representative, Windy Hill's Robert Hales, 92-2017; the Belize Tourist Board, 2-77213 or (800) 624-0686. The tourists' social hub is Eva's Bar & Restaurant (see* "Where to Eat in San Ignacio"*).*

San Ignacio is the largest town in the Cayo District, and its many services make this a fine place to have a meal, mail a postcard, arrange a tour, fill the gas tank, fix a flat tire, exchange currency, and load up on supplies. There are many pleasant hotels in San Ignacio, although most visitors prefer to find accommodations in the surrounding countryside.

The town is laid out on a series of bluffs alongside the Macal River, at an elevation high enough to be noticeably cooler and less

humid than the coastal plain. The people are friendly and happy-go-
lucky, pointing with pride at their Hawkesworth Bridge, a scaled-
down version of the Brooklyn Bridge, erected in the late 1940s and
still the only suspension span in Belize.

Things to See and Do
Locals will also steer you to the partially restored Mayan ruin of
Cahal Pech, just past Main Street at the crest of a hill, and **Arts &
Crafts of Central America**, a well-stocked souvenir and bookstore
next to Eva's Restaurant.

Day trips throughout Cayo and to Tikal can be arranged through
Yute Expeditions, 92-2979, fax 92-2076, run by reputable tour
operator Sergio Paiz. Also recommended is Collego Tours (92-2483).

About 6 miles west of San Ignacio, near the Xunantunich site
and along the Mopan River, is a stretch of surging white-water rapids
that some travelers enjoy running in canoes, kayaks, rubber rafts, or
inner tubes. There are fine swimming holes in the area and birding
is excellent. Several area operators arrange excursions down the
Mopan and other nearby rivers. Check with Remo Montgomery at
the **Sandcastle Bar & Grill** in San Ignacio for suggestions.

Where to Stay in San Ignacio
Cahal Pech Village, near the ruins; $40; 92-3203. Excellent value.

Clarrisa Farms, on the Macal River; $40; 92-3916. Well-run cabin
and camping facility with a restaurant/bar, also offering tours.

Mida's Eco-Resort, on the Macal, near downtown; $50; 92-3845.
Thatch-roofed cabins rented by a Belizean-English couple who
arrange canoeing, sight-seeing, and nature treks, as well as inexpensive camping. A full complement of meals available.

New Belmoral Hotel, 17 Burns Avenue; $20; 92-2024. Clean
rooms and helpful staff. Owner Godsman Ellis provides excellent
guided tours on local rivers, roads, and jungle pathways.

Pacz Hotel, Far West St., San Ignacio; $20; 92-2110, e-mail
pacz@btl.net. Clean, basic, inexpensive rooms. Airport shuttle, mountain bike rentals, and local sight-seeing (including day trips to caves).

Piache Hotel, 22 Buena Vista St.; $25; 92-2032, e-mail
piache.hot@btl.net.

San Ignacio Hotel, 18 Buena Vista St.; $50; 92-2034, e-mail *sanighot@btl.net.* Fine restaurant, spacious rooms, satellite TV, basketball court, and the best swimming pool in town. A nature trail and iguana hatchery are extra added attractions. Recommended.

Note: We have heard the most consistently negative comments about the Venus Hotel, and you should be advised that downtown San Ignacio often rocks to the music of loud discos on weekend nights, often as late as 3 a.m.

Where to Eat in San Ignacio

Eva's Restaurant, 22 Burns; 92-2267, e-mail *evas@btl.net.* American-style hamburgers, Belizean rice 'n' beans, plus several veggie dishes. A convivial meeting place, with cold beer and CNN, too. Run by English expatriate Bob Jones and his Belizean wife, Nestora. Open 7 a.m. to 11 p.m. daily, 'til midnight Friday through Saturday. Eva's is the unofficial nerve center of the district, its walls adorned with local travel literature and its tables crowded with bonafide Cayo characters. Bob Jones is a walking encyclopedia of what to see and do here, and will cheerfully dispense suggestions suited to any budget and interest.

Maya Café, on Burns Avenue. The best coffee, pastries, and reading material in town. The owners provide information on mountain bike and canoe rentals.

Mystic Moon Country Kitchen, 5 Mossiah St. A friendly, moderately priced restaurant specializing in Italian and vegetarian dishes, along with fresh fruit, shakes, and coffee. A couple of former New York City artists run the place.

Palpito's Upstairs, on Mission St. Good meals, friendly service, and budget prices. Top choices: Mexican dishes and tropical cocktails.

Sandcastle Bar & Grill, next to the bus stop. Some of the best food and drink in town (plus open-air blues, jazz, and reggae music). Try the delicious algae drink!

Serendib, on Burns Avenue. This Sri Lankan is justifiably revered for its spicy curry. Prices are moderate and the service at Serendib is friendly.

RESORTS NEAR SAN IGNACIO

Tucked into the folds of the lush green hills are a dozen or more "cottage" resorts ranging from rustic to elegant, each catering to the visitor who wants to get away from urban distractions in a wooden bungalow, stilt-supported tree house, or palm-thatched cabaña. Some of these charming retreats are located on working farms or ranches, while others are luxury lodges exclusively dedicated to a kind of gracious, low-key, tropical tourism that brings to mind images of the African veldt or Costa Rican jungle.

Each set of accommodations is slightly different in style and character, with its own specialization. Some focus on horseback riding or canoeing; others cater to forest trekkers and birders. Still others can arrange mountain biking tours, white-water rafting, kayaking, strenuous camping trips in the unexplored wilderness, or investigations of little-known caverns. All, however, supply meals and other basic amenities to their guests, and most can set up tours of the nearby Mayan ruins at Xunantunich, Caracol, Cahal Pech, and Tikal. A few even have reciprocal agreements with resorts on the coast or cayes that allow visitors to package a "surf and turf" holiday. Rates and accommodations vary widely, from budget dorms to comfortable tent-camping to five-star villas, depending on such variables as location, meals, services, and transportation costs. (Don't expect telephones, e-mail, or TV; most resorts don't have them—and some have no electricity.)

Most Cayo resort operators take individual preferences into account, making breakfast at 5 a.m. for birders, for example, or eliminating the meal entirely for late-risers who wish to sleep in. If you want to be chauffeured, they will pick you up at the Belize City airport or San Ignacio bus stop, for example. If you have private transportation, operators will be happy to give you detailed instructions and maps to whatever destination pleases you. The least expensive rooms in Cayo are generally found within the town limits of San Ignacio, although there are a growing number of budget and moderately priced options in the countryside. All of the luxury resorts are in rural areas of the Cayo.

Black Rock River Lodge; $65, meals included; 92-2341, fax 92-3449. A short distance upriver from Ek' Tun, this 250-acre bungalow compound along the Macal offers simple accommodations, but the lodge is surrounded by thick forests and towering limestone cliffs. You can make arrangements through the co-owned Caesar's Place, between Belmopan and San Ignacio on the Western Highway.

Chaa Creek Cottages/Macal River Camp, 7 miles upstream from San Ignacio, offering Mayan-style cabañas $125, including meals, and safari-style camping on a bluff above the Macal River for $90, including meals; 92-2037, fax 92-2501, e-mail *chaacreek@btl.net.* Established in 1981 by British expatriate Mick Fleming and his American wife, Lucy. Tents boast comfortable cots and open-hearth cooking, while the spacious cottages have thatched palapa roofs and mahogany furniture. Visitors are serenaded by exotic birds every morning. There is no glass in the windows because this area, like much of Cayo, has almost no biting insects. Nature-oriented tour operators regularly bring their clients here because of the resort's high standards, diversity of activities, and commitment to environmental education. The adjacent **Butterfly House** ($115) is a perfect getaway for vacationing couples, with a kitchen and solar electricity. Make arrangements here for one of the smoothest day trips available to Tikal, as well as to many Cayo sites, including the little-known Chumpiate Maya Cave. Highly recommended.

Crystal Paradise Resort, 4 miles upriver from San Ignacio; $55 and up; 92-2823 or (800) 552-3419, e-mail *evas@btl.net.*This 100-

Typical cabaña bungalow of the Cayo District

acre farm, operated by a Mayan-Creole family, offers birding (binoculars provided), horseback riding, and boat trips. Manager Jeronie Tut and his staff go out of their way to please guests and know the Cayo as only lifelong residents can. Extensive natural history library and impressive historic artifacts. The homegrown coffee and Teresa Tut's Creole cooking are delicious. Free pickup by boat or van from San Ignacio. More unusual activities include stargazing (with a powerful telescope), nighttime horseback rides, Mayan ruin tours, guided exploration of nearby caves, and trips to Laguna Aguacate (a jungle lake near a Mennonite settlement).

duPlooy's Resort, is just up the river from Chaa Creek; $95 and up; 92-3101, fax 92-3301, or (803) 722-1513, e-mail *judy@bcsl.com.biz*. Developed by an American-Zimbabwean couple, this lodge is also an active member of the Belize EcoTourism Association. Known for its lush tropical garden. Besides the usual day trips and meals, duPlooy's offers bungalow, guest house, and family-style accommodations. About 4 miles west of the Western Highway.

Ek'Tun, Macal River about 12 miles southwest of San Ignacio; $160; 93-2536 or (303) 442-6150, fax 93-2446. American expatriates Ken and Phyllis Dart have created a lovely and luxurious two-cottage retreat on their 200 acres of pristine jungle. It is worth the extra effort (four-wheel-drive Land Rover and boat) to get to this compound, built on the grounds of an ancient Mayan village. The Darts love to pamper their guests with personal, customized service, ranging from gourmet meals (extra charge) to canoe trips down the Macal and guided tours of unexcavated ruins. Committed environmentalists, the Darts are growing mahogany, teak, and other valued trees that have become scarce through exploitation. Check out the Ek' Tun Web site at *http://www.ektunbelize.com*.

Maya Mountain Lodge & Tours, 1/2 mile south of Santa Elena on the Cristo Rey Road; $40 room, $60 cottage; 92-2164, fax 92-2029, e-mail *mml@btl.net*. Emphasizes cultural tourism, encompasses a forest preserve and Mayan ruin on the slopes of Maya Mountain. Owners Bart (a prime mover in the Belize EcoTourism Association) and Suzi Mickler have helped develop a ceramic handicrafts industry using local artisans, teachers, and materials. As a result, many residents of nearby San José Succotz are now making and selling Mayan-style art objects. Besides sight-seeing trips, Maya Mountain offers guided horseback trips, canoe rides, birding walks, archaeological tours (destinations include Che Chem Ha Cave and Tikal), and nature treks (with accompanying guidebooks prepared by biologist Bruce Miller and Suzi Mickler, who holds a master of science degree in education). The facility maintains an educational field station and reference library for cultural, archaeological, and wildlife studies. One of the few Belize lodges that actively *encourages* families to visit, providing a growing number of activities for parents and their children. Family or group experiences include sharing Belize an folklore and rainforest stories, demonstrating Mayan handicrafts, cooking local and international foods, and providing a unique culture exchange through overnight "home visits" (booked in advance) with participating families in the immediate area and other parts of Belize.

Special summer workshops are available for interest groups, including artists, families interested in ecology or multiculturalism, and teachers studying tropical ecology or Mayan culture. **Luis Godoy**, one of the top guides in Belize, works with Maya Mountain and is delighted to show off his country to visitors. Accommodations range from comfortable cottages to a bunkhouse for budget student groups. Free e-mail service for guests.

Mountain Equestrian Trails, Mile 8 on the Chiquibul Road (turn off at Georgeville) and one mile north of the Mountain Pine Ridge boundary; 92-3310 or (800) 838-3918, e-mail *met@bcsl.com.bz*. Stay at the safari-style tent camp ($50) or in beautiful bungalows ($100 and up); all meals available. A 150-acre, 20-horse ranch adjacent to the private Slate Creek Nature Preserve, MET offers several options for an authentic horseback riding experience (tailored for equestrians of all abilities, including novices). Also available are vehicle-based tours of Xunantunich, Pacbitun, San Antonio, the Mountain Pine Ridge, Caracol, and El Pilar. Adventurous travelers can choose from 4- or 5-day Chiclero Trails Base Camp adventures or MET's 6-day Wildlife Encounter/Kayak Expedition. A Belizean of American descent, owner Jim Bevis and his well-informed local guides lead visitors on horseback to remote area caves, waterfalls, the Mountain Pine Ridge, and a large sinkhole called **The Vega**. Resident guide **Francisco Rash**, the apprentice of a Mayan bush doctor, shares information during scheduled presentations on Mayan culture and points out medicinal plants during his nature tours. **Jan Meerman**—one of the most experienced conservation scientists in Central America—conducts ecology and conservation workshops.

Nabintunich, west along the Mopan River near Xunantunich; $40, meals available; 93-2096. This 400-acre working ranch has 11 cabins and lots of horses. Bridle trails extend through miles of dense bush.

Parrot Nest, on a bend in the Belize River near the Maya/Mestizo village of Bullet Tree Falls; $20 with shared bath; 9-37008, e-mail *parrot@btl.net*. Features low-key adventure and fine food (for a fee). Up to eight visitors at a time are accommodated in rustic, stilt-supported, thatch-roof tree houses. German-born owner Fred Prost has vowed to keep his lodge affordable for backpackers. Swimming and birding are excellent, and Prost can arrange all sorts of sight-seeing and adventure tours. $5 to $8 taxi ride from San Ignacio (7 miles away). Recommended.

Windy Hill Resort, a few miles west of San Ignacio on the Western Highway; $70, fine food, satellite TV, and a swimming pool; 92-2017, fax 92-3080, (800) 946-3995. Yet another cattle ranch with luxurious private cottages. Arranges local tours, including daily departures to Tikal priced in 1997 at $75 per person (a good value).

IX CHEL TROPICAL RESEARCH CENTER AND RAINFOREST MEDICINE TRAIL
Location: *About 7 miles southwest of San Ignacio, at the end of Chaa Creek Road.*
Hours: *Daily 8 a.m. to 12 noon and 1 p.m. to 5 p.m.*
Fees: *A self-guided tour of the mile-long Rainforest Medicine Trail is $5.75 per person. A guided tour and lecture by an Ix Chel staffer is $17.25, if arranged in advance.*
Visitor Information: *Ix Chel Tropical Research Center, 9-23870.*

Ix Chel Tropical Research Center is a pioneering medicinal research facility specializing in the healing properties of plants. It is nestled on a hill above the Macal River and is surrounded by thick second-growth subtropical vegetation. A maze of pathways snakes through this foliage, and among these is the remarkable **Rainforest Medicine Trail.**

The Rainforest Medicine Trail winds through a living display of arboreal and herbal remedies making it an essential component to Ix Chel's success. Signs describe the plants, many bearing unusually descriptive names. The tres puntas plant—distinguished by its large three-pointed leaves and also known as "jackass bitters"—is used to treat and prevent such ailments as salmonella, intestinal parasites, and skin infections. A few steps farther is skunk root, effective in treating pain and ulcers, and wild grapevine, filled with an antiseptic used to wash newborn infants. Nearby grows the fiddlewood tree; its bark in an herbal bath kills the parasite known to cause a painful condition called leishmaniasis. Also present is the wild yam, a popular Belizean household remedy for urinary tract ailments and arthritis pain.

One section of the trail, **Granny's Garden**, displays about 50 useful common plants from various parts of the world. These include amaranth, basil, rue, marigold, lemon grass, and hibiscus. All are marked and correspond to descriptions found on laminated sheets used in a self-guided tour.

Yet another Ix Chel endeavor is the cultivation and marketing of plants for production of herbal formulae used in cosmetics. Besides its own production of these items, the Ix Chel team is helping local farmers rejuvenate their degraded lands by cultivating medicinal cash crops that can be an effective alternative to slash-and-burn agriculture. The program thus provides a new, health-oriented alternative to traditional practices that deplete soils (in return for short-term subsistence crops) while destroying thousands of valuable native plants and their habitat.

Ix Chel sells many herbal elixirs and potions—with names like Belly Be Good and Female Tonic—as well as fresh allspice berries (used in cooking and for the relief of fever, toothache, and stomach ache). Prices for such items start around $10. Some of these products are also available in gift shops and groceries in other parts of the country; look for the Rainforest Remedies label, which is also marketed in the U.S. by Lotus Light. A percentage of sales goes to traditional healers and educational programs in Belize. Owners Rosita Arvigo and Greg Shropshire welcome donations to support their work, either sent directly to Ix Chel or the Traditional Healers' Foundation, General Delivery, San Ignacio, Belize.

Ix Chel's Rosita Arvigo

During the summer rainy season, when visitors from other parts of Belize complain about bug bites, Ix Chel founder Rosita Arvigo walks out the back door of her farmhouse and snaps a small branch off a red gumbo-limbo tree. The bark, she informs them, produces a natural insect repellent. It can also be made into a tonic for treating urinary tract infections and provides an antidote to the itchy rashes caused by contact with the poisonwood tree, which invariably grows nearby. (When nature creates a problem in tropic environments, it often provides its own solution.)

A dedicated herbalist and botanical field practitioner from Chicago, Arvigo is in a race against time. She and her family, staff, and volunteers are scouring the Central American forests in search of tropical plants that may help win the war against a number of deadly diseases. With her husband, Greg Shropshire, Arvigo works at the place where the timeless wisdom of venerable native healers intersects with the theories of Western medicine.

"Much of what I have learned was from Don Elijio Panti," she explains, referring to the late Mayan healer who began—albeit reluctantly at first—sharing his secrets (beginning at age 86) with Arvigo. Over 106 years old when he passed away in 1996, Panti's legacy survives in a new generation of healers through the Belize Association of Traditional Healers (referred to locally as BATH).

Arvigo has accomplished one important goal: to preserve the encyclopedic herbal lore that Panti memorized during his lifetime.

Rosita Arvigo displays dried leaves of the tres puntos plant.

Richard Mahler

Major progress has also been made in determining the healing properties of hundreds of native plants that may never have been ingested
by humans and thus have unknown biochemical effects.

"In 1987 the U.S. government's National Cancer Institute
awarded a contract to the New York Botanical Garden's Institute of
Economic Botany to survey the flowering and cone-bearing plants in
the New World tropics for chemical compounds that could be used
to treat diseases such as cancer and AIDS," explains Dr. Michael
Balick, a director of New York's Institute of Economic Botany, who
has co-authored a book with Arvigo (*Rainforest Remedies: 100 Healing
Herbs of Belize*). "Ix Chel Tropical Research Foundation is the collab-
orating center for this work in Belize." Drs. Balick, Arvigo, and
Shropshire have—along with numerous Belizean traditional healers—
collected hundreds of plants in support of the project. The effort
underscores a deepening alliance between native healers and modern
scientists in a bid to study potentially useful plants before they are
wiped out by deforestation and industrialization.

The work under way at Ix Chel and elsewhere in Belize by members of BATH is spurred by the knowledge that the world's forests
have already yielded such medicines as quinine (an antimalarial), vin-
blastine (used to treat Hodgkin's disease), and taxol (a treatment for
ovarian cancer). Many so-called miracle drugs are plant-derived
compounds from tropical forests. Examples include tubocurarine
(curare), used in operating rooms to relax muscles and prevent
spasm, and pilocarpine, used for the treatment of glaucoma.

"We're teaching healthcare workers in village clinics how to use
medicinal plants," said Arvigo, who welcomes thousands of visitors
each year to Ix Chel and sees patients privately for specialized health
treatments. Her husband is a homeopathic doctor with his own practice as well. Every year Arvigo teaches a course in medicinal plants at
the Belize College of Agriculture, and the couple have mounted an
annual "useful plant" exhibition that has been viewed by hundreds of
Belizeans. These educational outreach efforts include an "Adopt a
Healer" program whereby classrooms ask a local healer to share
information with sponsoring schoolchildren about the many uses of
the country's medicinal plants.

Arvigo and Shropshire regularly conduct medicinal plant seminars at nearby Chaa Creek Cottages, and the couple sell a variety
of materials directly to the public at their gift shop. Since 1993, Ix
hel has collaborated with BATH in the protection of a tract of forest
in western Belize for the specific purpose of growing and harvesting

medicinal plants. The resulting 6,000-acre medicinal plant reserve, **Terra Nova,** is now managed by the Belize Enterprise for Sustainable Technology and is not currently accessible to tourists. One of the innovative projects at Terra Nova recruits and trains Belizean youths to help rescue young native medicinal plants that are in areas scheduled for development.

Getting There
Follow the Western Highway west of San Ignacio and exit left (south) on the Chaa Creek Road. About 4 miles from the Western Highway, the road splits, with a right fork heading toward duPlooy's Resort and the other to Chaa Creek Cottages. Immediately before reaching the lodge, a well-marked left fork leads down a steep hill to Ix Chel Tropical Research Center, 9-23870.

CHAA CREEK NATURAL HISTORY CENTRE AND BUTTERFLY FARM
Location: About 7 miles from San Ignacio, on the Macal River.
Size: 330 acres.
Hours: 9 a.m. to 5 p.m. daily.
Fees: $6 covers admission to both Butterfly Farm and Natural History Centre.
For Information: 92-2037, fax 92-2051, or Box 53, San Ignacio.

About 7 miles southwest of San Ignacio is a compound near the confluence of the Macal River and one of its small tributaries, Chaa Creek. What started many years ago as a small farm has been transformed by Mick Fleming, an expatriate of Britain, and his American wife, Lucy, into a haven for nature lovers (as well as one of the country's finest jungle lodges).

Blue Morpho Butterfly Breeding Centre
A short nature trail leads up the hill from Chaa Creek's office to the Blue Morpho Butterfly Breeding Centre, open to the public for a $6 fee. Here your guide points out the four distinct changes the brilliant neon-blue morpho undergoes during metamorphosis from a pale green egg to a striking, indigo-colored butterfly. The guide explains the butterfly's eating habits as it progresses through the caterpillar stage. If your timing is right, you'll witness the miracle of a blue mor-

The Howler Monkey Reintroduction Program

In the last couple of years, Mick and Lucy Fleming have demonstrated their active conservation leadership through a black howler monkey reintroduction program operated in conjunction with the villages of Cristo Rey, Scotland Half-moon, and Monkey River Town. Sponsored by Chaa Creek and the Foundation for Wildlife Conservation with involve-ment by the Yerkes Regional Primate Center, a successful first stage of the program was completed with the release of eight black howlers (captured at the Community Baboon Sanctu-ary in north-central Belize) at Chaa Creek's Macal River Camp. The program is designed to help ensure the long-term survival of these monkeys in Belize and to promote reforesta-tion of the lower Macal River—enhancing a key portion of a wildlife corridor that stretches over 60 miles across the Maya Mountain divide. After monitoring the movements of the original group—reported to be doing well as this edition went to press—the plan was to capture another eight to 12 individuals from the Monkey River area in southern Belize and release them along the Macal.

pho's emergence from its strange brown pupa. The center releases into the wild about 45 percent of the some 200 butterflies it breeds each day; the rest are exported to help keep this educational enter-prise operating.

Natural History Centre

As part of the same admission, visitors may explore Chaa Creek's exceptional Natural History Centre, situated near the blue morpho flight cage. This is probably the most comprehensive such facility in Belize. Its research room includes a rarely found archive of scientific studies carried out over the years in Belize, as well as a complete collection of books and field guides to help you answer those nagging questions about an exotic animal or plant you may have seen.

Designed to stimulate awareness and understanding of the local environment for both Belizeans and visitors, the Centre features a **Cayo Room**, introducing visitors to the biological and archaeological diversity of the immediate area. There is an exhibit on birds and mammals, including a display about bats (featuring the amazing fishing bat of Belize). High on one wall is a time-line of the Mayan civilization along with a special exhibit on local archaeology. You'll also find a butterfly exhibit, reptiles and amphibians display, gift shop, and yet another research room containing topographic maps, books, and a variety of color slides.

Other Activities

The Flemings have developed a wide array of on-site activities on their property, gearing them toward couples and individuals, family visitation and groups. Visitors can go horseback riding, canoe on or swim in the Macal, tour the river by motorized dugout, arrange a guided nature walk, hike to three recently discovered Mayan ruins (currently under excavation by UCLA archaeologists), or rent well-maintained, front-suspension Trek mountain bikes here.

Another on-site attraction at Chaa Creek is Chef Bill Altman's week-long "eco-sensitive cookery" courses featuring cuisines of Belize, the Yucatán, the Caribbean, and Central America. "Each of our dishes represents local foods from one of Belize's different cultures," said Lucy Fleming, noting Chaa Creek's growing interest in cultural tourism. Guests may be served such delicious regional specialties as Garifuna *sere* (a coconut-milk fish stew) or Mestizo-derived *mole poblano*.

Getting There

Guests can arrange for pickup in San Ignacio or Belize City, nonguests will need transportation via taxi, private car, or boat.

SLATE CREEK PRESERVE

Location: About 15 miles southeast of San Ignacio, in the foothills of the Mountain Pine Ridge.
Size: Around 4,000 acres.
Hours: Variable.

Visitor Information: *Mountain Equestrian Trails, 92-3310, or write c/o Central Farm Post Office.*

Several of the Cayo's resorts, outfitters, and tour guides have become actively involved in projects that combine conservation and sustainable economic development. This private-sector leadership is a growing trend that should make a big difference in long-term protection of Belize's natural areas.

Owners Jim and Marguerite Bevis of Mountain Equestrian Trails (MET), collaborate with 15 neighboring private landowners in managing Slate Creek Preserve, a hilly area an hour drive southeast of San Ignacio that is covered with moist broadleaf forest and home to such rare or endangered fauna as the keel-billed motmot, Baird's tapir, and jaguarundi.

MET and a community-based nonprofit organization involve residents of the nearby villages of San Antonio and Siete Millas in handicraft production, nature-oriented tourism, and environmentally sound farming as an alternative to slash-and-burn subsistence agriculture (also called *milpa* farming), which threatens the Slate Creek watershed and other unspoiled wilderness.

"I really see education as an important focus," reflected Marguerite Bevis, on her family's efforts to show the importance of watershed protection, the dangers of deforestation, and the value of low-impact farming techniques. She stresses the importance of helping villagers supplement their incomes by creating and selling arts and crafts. "We can be the medium here to help," she told us. In the process, this also enriches the experiences of visitors interested in cultural tourism.

The great variety of trails that wind through Slate Creek Preserve's unique biological corridor (connecting the Mountain Pine Ridge and its limestone karst foothills east to the Tapir Mountain Nature Reserve) make this an ideal place for visitors to encounter flora and fauna on foot as well as on horseback. The birding, in particular, is excellent. In all, more than 240 bird species have been identified here.

BARTON CREEK CAVE

This small but interesting cave is accessible only by water and only via a prearranged 4- to 5-hour tour. For your trouble you'll see a sacred Mayan burial chamber, where a few of the ancient Maya were laid to rest alongside large pottery vessels. A natural bridge used by

Other Slate Creek Area Attractions

*We recommend that visitors stop in directly across the Chiquibul Road from MET to meet Jan Meerman and Tineke Boomsma, who can provide a tour of their national passionflower (Passiflora) collection and recently-completed **Papillon: The Belize Butterfly House**. As part of their non-profit organization, Belize Tropical Forest Studies, the couple has opened a new research facility with low-cost lodging for research groups, a 1,000-square-foot butterfly flight area and a butterfly rearing facility. Although they plan to be open during regular morning to afternoon hours from Christmas through Easter, we suggest you contact them before you visit, 92-3310 or e-mail tfs@pobox.com.*

*Another good option for visitors to the Slate Creek Preserve area is the moderately priced, **Huru Kaan Lodge**, 92-2755, at mile 8.5 on the Chiquibul Road. Like their neighbors at MET and Papillon, Huru Kaan proprietor Ben Butenschoen is a Slate Creek Preserve member. His resort is located in part of a 1,600-acre, family-owned valley protected by the family since 1972. Huru Kaan offers rainforest treks, mountain stream swimming, and inexpensive half- and full-day jungle safaris, to name a few outdoor adventures. Accommodations in Huru Kaan's thatch-roofed pavilions are by reservation only.*

early visitors is adorned with a carefully placed skull. Because this is a registered archaeological site, nothing may be touched or removed. Tours are by canoe along the slow-moving river that flows through the cave, then exits into Upper Barton Creek. Nearby is a village of the same name, inhabited by traditional Mennonites (please do not photograph them without their permission). The cave itself has miles of passages and rooms with ceilings reported to be as much as 300 feet high. Expect to pay about $25 for a guided tour, arranged through nearby Mountain Equestrian Trails.

THE MOUNTAIN PINE RIDGE

Location: About 10 miles southeast of San Ignacio, extending for about 20 miles south toward the Maya Mountains.
Size: Nearly 300 square miles.
Hours: 24 hours, 7 days a week.
Fees: There is no entrance fee to the reserve.
Visitor Information: Inquire at local travel agencies and lodges, or the Belize Tourism Board, (800) 624-0686.

A peculiar sight for many travelers is their first glimpse of stately pine forests carpeting the steep hillsides of the Cayo District's subtropical Maya Mountains. After winding through moist broadleaf jungle en route to this highland ecosystem, you are suddenly confronted with a landscape straight out of red-dirt Georgia. As far as the eye can see, tall, skinny pine trees reach to the deep blue sky. The sandy terrain is covered with rust-colored pine needles interspersed by tiger bush ferns, a sparse grass called dumbcane, and delicate wildflowers. In some areas, clusters of oaks, miconias, and other hardwoods grip the thin topsoil. Gymnosperms, cycads, and palms crowd the boggy banks of surface streams.

The Mountain Pine Ridge—in Belize, the term "ridge" refers to a forest type and not a geographic formation—is an unusual natural phenomenon covering nearly 300 square miles.

The ancient Maya chose not to settle here, apparently concluding that seasonal droughts and shallow soils made the area unsuitable for farming. They did, however, extensively use the many caves along its limestone perimeter. Unpaved but well-maintained logging roads and nature trails cross the forest reserve, and the terrain is especially suited for hiking, mountain biking, and horseback riding. Birds and butterflies are as vivid as they are numerous. Travelers will spy many unusual varieties of colorful bromeliads, orchids, and other air plants among the boulders and branches.

Along the edges of the pine ridge are waterfalls, white-water rivers, and sharp escarpments that offer sweeping views. The almost total lack of human habitation means that much of this wilderness is virgin, although hurricanes and selective logging have occurred in some areas.

A few San Ignacio-area operators rent mountain bikes that can be used to tour the dirt roads and trails of the Mountain Pine Ridge (see Special Interests chapter for details). This can be a great way to see the area for experienced bikers who don't mind getting hot and sweaty in the near-constant warm and humid weather.

Primitive camping is allowed in certain areas with permission from the Department of Forestry (check with officials at the main entrance or at the Douglas De Silva forest station). Rustic cabins can also sometimes be rented by the forest station for a modest fee.

Hidden Valley Falls

Hidden Valley Falls, also known as Thousand-Foot Falls, is one of the Mountain Pine Ridge's primary attractions. This is believed to be the tallest waterfall in Central America, plunging almost ¼ mile over a granite precipice into a deep jungle canyon. The distance is so great that the bottom of the waterfall becomes lost in mist and green foliage.

To see the falls, follow Baldy Beacon Road east of the forest reserve's main entrance for about 5 miles. Then proceed as directed by the well-marked signs for a couple of miles to an overlook area. This is a good place to take photographs, savor a picnic, and observe bird life. The king vulture and rare orange-breasted falcon are sometimes seen riding the thermal air currents here—the latter nests near the waterfall. On a clear day, the capital buildings of Belmopan shimmer on the horizon.

Across from the caretaker's cabin is the **Hidden Valley Institute for Environmental Studies,** a private research facility that conducts fieldwork and develops much-needed conservation education materials for local schools. Bungalows accommodate visiting naturalists, and there is a small natural history museum. Immediately below the institute is a rugged 4-mile trail to the base of the waterfall. The trail is not well maintained and should not be attempted without a guide. A round-trip hike may take all day.

Guests of the nearby Hidden Valley Lodge have access to three other waterfalls: **King Vulture**, **Tiger Creek**, and **Butterfly**. Inquire at the resort about permission to visit them on your own.

Río On Pools

About 10 miles southwest of the Hidden Valley Falls overlook, the forest reserve's main road crosses the Río On, a cascading upland tributary of the Macal River. As it makes its way down from the Mountain Pine Ridge, the Río On swirls and splashes through a maze of granite boulders. The warm pools formed by these enormous rocks are as much as 15 feet deep and make delightful swimming holes, especially after a long day of hiking, biking, or horseback riding. The smooth stones make natural water slides, and many visitors like to stretch out and sunbathe on them in the tropical sun. There are out-

*The Río On is a popular swimmers' destination
in the Mountain Pine Ridge.*

houses (doubling as changing rooms) and picnic tables nearby, plus a freshwater tap. The parking lot accommodates a growing number of visitors, which may swell to several dozen on weekends and holidays, when Belizeans like to picnic here.

Río Frío Cave and Nature Trail

Not much farther south, a few miles past the village of Douglas De Silva and the forest reserve headquarters, visitors descend into subtropical vegetation and one of Belize's best-known cave districts. Look for a sign indicating the start of the Río Frío Nature Trail, which makes its way through dense forest to the largest and most spectacular cave in the group. (Río Frío Cave can also be easily reached by driving a mile or so down the same road to a picnic area outside the cavern's entrance.)

The nature trail takes about 45 minutes to negotiate and displays a wide variety of trees, each carefully labeled. There are even naturally occurring rubber, mahogany, and sapodilla trees (the latter is the source of chicle, a natural chewing gum base). Birds and other wildlife are abundant.

179

The Río Frío Cave extends about 300 yards through a solid limestone mountain. Centuries ago the tunnel was used as a ceremonial center by the ancient Maya, but all artifacts have long since been removed or washed away. There are enormous arched entryways at either end of the cave, which narrows midway to a height and width of about 40 feet.

Because the Río Frío cuts a broad channel through the passage, the cave is sometimes difficult to traverse during rainy months. Even in the dry season, visitors will probably find it necessary to get at least their feet wet. The interior of the cave is musty and cool but not entirely dark. Enough daylight filters through from either end to make flashlights unnecessary. Footholds can be slippery, however, and some rock climbing is required.

The other caves in the region—including the **Domingo Ruíz, Blancaneaux, Skeleton Head, Barton Creek**, and **Chiquibul** caves—should not be visited without an experienced, knowledgeable guide. Information can be obtained through hotels, travel agencies, or conservation organizations. Recommended local guides include Richard, at **Pine Ridge Lodge**, and Mr. Bol, at **Bol's Guiding Service**, near the forest reserve's main gate.

Río Frío cave interior

▲ A horse-drawn Mennonite buggy in the Cayo District (Steele Wotkyns)

▼ Conservation education at the Belize Zoo

Maya children

Wilderness rainforest areas and pristine rivers are protected in the Bladen Nature Reserve. (Dan Dancer/Lighthawk)

Belize River boatman
(Steele Wotkyns)

Painted cement Mayan head in San Pedro (Richard Mahler)

▲ Black howler monkey

▲ Scarlet macaw

▼ Baird's tapir

▼ Jaguar

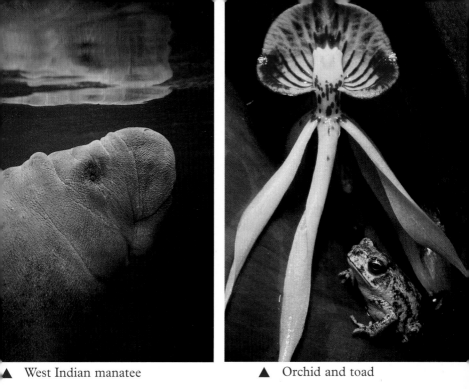

▲ West Indian manatee

▲ Orchid and toad

▼ Calliandra flower

Iguana hunters with their catch of "bamboo chicken" (Kevin Schafer)

▲ Keel-billed toucan

▲ Jaguarundi

▼ Creole children along the Northern Highway

▲ The Blue Hole, Lighthouse Reef

▼ Snorkeling at Lighthouse Reef

Douglas De Silva Village and Beyond

The headquarters for the Mountain Pine Ridge Forest Reserve is in a large wooden building in the settlement of Douglas De Silva (renamed from Augustine in 1990 after a politician's grandfather). Only about 100 people—all forestry employees—live here, and the place has the look and feel of a run-down summer camp. Many of the houses are in disrepair and others are being used to store pine seeds for reforestation projects. Worth visiting are the self-guided nature trail on the headquarters grounds and the small store (the only source of supplies for many miles around).

Swimming in the Río On

Thatch-shaded picnic tables are available, but there is no restaurant or gas station. Inquire at the headquarters about camping and overnight rental of government-owned guest houses.

If you are continuing on to the Mayan ruin at Caracol (see chapter 10, Archaeological Sites) you may want to check with the Forestry Department officer on duty in Douglas De Silva. Access to Caracol is not granted when the road is judged to be in such poor condition that travel will be hazardous (both to visitors and the road surface itself). When the surface is dry, it takes about 45 minutes to reach Caracol from here. Heading in the other direction, Georgeville and San Ignacio on the Western Highway are 90 minutes and two hours away, respectively. It may be possible by the time you read this to pay your $5 Caracol entry fee at the forestry office here.

San Antonio Village

The more westerly of the two routes leading into the Mountain Pine Ridge—the Cristo Rey Road—passes through the small and mostly Yucatec/Mopan Maya farming village of San Antonio. (Note that there is another San Antonio, populated by Kekchí-speaking Maya, in the Toledo District near Punta Gorda.)

The Cayo's San Antonio village is situated in a lush valley where terraced fields of beans and corn have been carved out of the leafy jungle. Agriculture has persisted here for thousands of years. Recently, a few small shops, restaurants, and museums have been opened in an attempt to diversify the local economy. Among the several attractions that are worth visiting in the San Antonio area is the Pacbitun archaeological site (described in chapter 10, Archaeological Sites).

San Antonio Museums

Immediately north of the village on the main road to Cristo Rey and Santa Elena is the **García Sisters Museum**—a combination crafts shop, herbal medicine pharmacy, and Mayan shrine. At least one of the five García sisters is always on hand, making and selling black-slate carvings that depict Maya-related masks, gods, and historic figures. Be advised that the museum has a steep $5 admission charge and that the García sisters are aggressive salespersons.

Another family of local artisans, the Magañas, also operates an art gallery, "Mayan culture preservation outpost," and gift shop. Javier, José, and Carmelita produce and sell wood and stone carvings that incorporate traditional Mayan themes. Glyphs from the Mayan calendar are also hand-painted by family members on the same type of cloth supposedly used by ancient royalty. Their **Itzamna' (Magaña Family) Gallery & Gift Shop** is a few miles north of San Antonio on the Cristo Rey Road at a small Mayan site called **Sac'Tunich**.

Getting There

The easiest way to see the Mountain Pine Ridge is by signing up for a minivan tour through a hotel or travel agency. This can be done easily through one of the lodges within the forest reserve or those located in the rest of the Cayo District. During the dry season, several vehicles a day explore the area, and overnight camping and equestrian trips can be arranged. There is no public transportation into the Mountain Pine Ridge except for taxis and rental cars. Drivers of private vehicles are advised that the region's dirt roads are sometimes a challenge during rainy periods—four-wheel-drive is advised.

Where to Stay in the Mountain Pine Ridge

Blancaneaux Lodge, about an hour south of San Ignacio on Five Sisters Falls Road; $150; 92-3878, fax 92-3919. Owned by movie director Francis Ford Coppola, set in a lush, 50-acre, pine-forested area crisscrossed by white-water rivers and nature trails. For those who can afford it, accommodations and meals are first-rate. Tours are arranged to destinations throughout the area (including nearby caves and the spectacular Five Sisters Falls). Guests arrive either via Blancaneaux's private airstrip—visitors can arrange to be flown in by the staff pilot—or 16 miles of dirt road from San Ignacio. Coppola has supervised the construction and furnishing of beautifully appointed Mayan-style, thatch-roof cabañas and two-bedroom villas, set in garden-like surroundings beneath tall pines. Each room overlooks the Privassión River, where a large pool (suitable for swimming) is used to generate electricity through a hydroelectric turbine. Coppola imported a wood-burning oven from Rome to make pizza at Blancaneaux, and his dining room—open to the general public—also features wines from his own Napa Valley winery, as well as the Coppola family's imaginative pasta and seafood recipes. Produce and coffee is grown in an organic garden adjacent to the lodge. (Don't expect to meet Coppola; he spends only a few weeks here each year.) Recommended.

Five Sisters Lodge, perched on a high ledge above a beautiful series of cascades on the Privassión River, about 2 miles off Mountain Pine Ridge Road; $95; 92-2985. Day-trippers are welcome to make their way down a steep stairway to the base of the falls, where the resort has an outdoor bar. There are cabaña-style rooms as well as a restaurant—with a fine overview of the Five Sisters Waterfall.

Hidden Valley Inn, a few miles away from the Pine Ridge Lodge on the Cooma Cairn Road, which continues to **Thousand-Foot Falls** (also on the Inn's property); $180, includes meals; (800) 334-7942 or 8-23320. Maintained by the Georgia timber-cutting family that owns 18,000 acres of the adjacent pine forest and jungle, visitors can either stay in comfortable cottages or camp under the stars and pine boughs. Easy-to-follow trails lead to Central America's highest waterfall, several caves, and a small lake. A large section of the property constitutes the **Hidden Valley Reserve**, where biologists have found a new toad species and a rare nesting pair of orange-breasted falcons. Tours—including river rafting and photo safaris—are arranged to **Caracol**, the Chiquibul subtropical forest, **Tikal**, and other area attractions. Hidden Valley's bungalows are plush, complete with fireplaces and bathtubs (both hard to find in Belize).

Pine Ridge Lodge, about a mile from Blancaneaux on Mountain Pine Ridge Road; $50 and up; 92-3310, e-mail *prlodge@mindspring.com*.

Friendly and comfortable, offers caving, hiking, river trips, birding, mountain biking, and both equestrian and archaeological explorations. This recommended, bungalow-style hotel also operates a small restaurant that serves excellent meals. Pains have been taken to make this lodge environment-friendly, and there are many trails to follow through the nearby pine forest and jungle, where you'll see orchids, possibly deer, and maybe even a jaguar. A nice feature is the "hammock room," a screened-in, high-ceiling shelter where you can curl up with a glass of fresh, cold limeade and read a book or take a snooze. Ask about off-season (summer) rates.

Where to Eat in the Mountain Pine Ridge
There are no restaurants in the Mountain Pine Ridge except for those that are part of the few lodges in the area (see above). Most of these are not open to the public without prior reservations.

THE UPPER MACAL REGION AND CHE CHEM HA CAVE
The mountainous stretches of the Macal River extend into a remote and seldom-seen area that drains the Vaca Plateau watershed and much of Chiquibul National Park. Access has improved in recent years through grading of a new road used in the construction of a Taiwanese-funded dam and hydroelectric plant, which flooded part of the upper Macal basin above the confluence of the Mollejon River in 1995.

Floating the Upper Macal
White-water raft and kayak trips are available from several operators on the scenic upper reaches of the Macal River gorge. One-day trips usually begin below the hydroelectric dam (accessible by Negroman Falls Road) and end either near the **Black Rock Jungle Lodge** or **Chaa Creek Cottages** (depending on water levels). The Class III and IV float takes you through a remote tropical forest dominated by limestone walls that tower as high as 1,500 feet above the river. Several easy portages are required during this 7-mile run. The area abounds in wildlife and the steep-sided canyon is covered with broad-leaf tropical forest.

We recommend **Slickrock Adventures**, 2-34129 or (800) 390-5715, e-mail *slickrock@slickrock.com*. It originates its day trips at 7:30 a.m. from the San Ignacio bus depot and returns about 6 p.m.

Expect to pay about $100 for a one-day, whitewater trip, which includes transport from San Ignacio, guide fees, equipment, and lunch. Guests of Chaa Creek Cottages (which books its visitors on Slickrock trips and is an occasional pull-out point) can be dropped off there on their return. You can make a two-day itinerary by combining with Slickrock's Class I "river of caves" float on the Caves Branch of the Sibun River.

Another rivertrip outfitter in the area is **Juan Marcos Parras** (c/o Island Air, San Pedro, Ambergris Caye), a Guatemalan who was raised in Arkansas. Parras also provides guided tours of Tikal and other destinations in the Cayo and Petén.

Che Chem Ha Cave

The privately owned Che Chem Ha Cave (sometimes called Vaca Cave), located near Vaca Falls, a scenic and rocky plunge on the Macal River, is a recommended destination in the Upper Macal Region.

This extensive, important Mayan ceremonial site, discovered in the early 1990s by farmer William Morales, is well worth seeing. It contains many pristine ancient artifacts, including over 60 ancient pottery vessels, paintings, incense burners, and a circle of special carved stones where animals were sacrificed and prayers spoken to underworld gods. These items have been left undisturbed for at least 1,000 years, and iron grates now protect them from looters and vandals. The interior of these caves is dark, wet, and slippery. Visitors should wear grip-tread shoes and bring a flashlight or diving light. Some fairly strenuous climbing is involved but the effort is well worth it.

The **Antonio Morales family** provides rustic, bungalow-style accommodations and meals as well as guided tours of Che Chem Ha, which means "poison vine water." The Morales compound may be reached by local VHF radio (try Bob Jones at Eva's Restaurant in San Ignacio) or through Maya Mountain Lodge, Ek'Tun, or Chaa Creek Cottages, all of which arrange tours. Visitors are asked not to enter Che Chem Ha Cave without a member of the Morales family. This is not only for safety, but also to protect the integrity of the cave's fragile artifacts, which have been left exactly where they were placed many centuries ago.

The guided visit lasts roughly 90 minutes and costs about $15, with a minimum of three people on each tour. If you arrive in the late morning and place your order, the Moraleses will have lunch ready when you finish your cave tour and make the 30-minute hike back to the compound. Lunch costs about $6 and overnight lodging around $80 (double occupancy, including all meals).

From the Morales home you can hike to the Macal River's spectacular **Vaca Falls** in about an hour, then trek onward to the previously described **Ek'Tun resort**, located a few miles downstream from the waterfall. Ek'Tun and Che Chem Ha Lodge have a reciprocal agreement for those who wish to overnight in both places. Horses can be obtained at either location for rides into the jungle. Trails lead from here as far as San Antonio and Caracol.

Getting There
Note that the road to Che Chem Ha can be treacherous when wet; it's not unusual for cars to get stuck in the last 100 yards of steep road, just below the Morales residence. The turnoff to Che Chem Ha is 6 miles south on the Negroman Falls Road from Benque Viejo, about 7 miles west of San Ignacio. Watch for the signs.

CHIQUIBUL NATIONAL PARK
Rather than loop through the Mountain Pine Ridge in only a day or two, some travelers continue south beyond the Río Frío Cave into some of the wildest areas of Belize. Only a handful of people live fulltime in this area, mostly chicle tappers, illegal Guatemalan immigrants, poachers, and looters. In 1991 the government of Belize established more than 200,000 acres of this former forest reserve as a national park, now accessible by crude road.

Inside the Chiquibul National Park is the enormous Mayan ruin of **Caracol**, currently under excavation (see Chapter 10, Archaeological Sites), located about 30 miles southwest of Douglas De Silva. Caracol is protected under a separate designation because of its archaeological significance. Chiquibul's broad tableland consists of hundreds of square miles of intact forest, the last stronghold of many wildlife and plant species that are rarely seen elsewhere in Central America and southern Mexico, such as the keel-billed motmot. During the rigorous Maya Mountain Traverse Expedition of 1995 an unusual species of "hairy palm" was found to be abundant here, even though this plant was not known to exist in Belize as recently as 1987.

The national park also protects the **Chiquibul cave system**, about 8 miles south of Caracol, with more than 20 miles of explored passages and no end in sight. No systematic scientific exploration occurred until the late 1970s and since then, in some of the caves, researchers have found ancient fossilized insects and crustaceans that have been extinct for centuries. The complex which cannot be entered without government permission, has yielded several previously unknown animal species, Mayan artifacts, and one of the world's largest underground chambers.

The plateau is crisscrossed by old logging and chiclero trails, but many have been reclaimed by the jungle. A detailed map may suggest that there are a number of villages in the area, but in reality these are abandoned lumbering camps established long ago, when hardwoods were being selectively harvested and skidded, then floated, downriver to Belize City. Travel in this area is now limited to horseback and high-clearance, four-wheel-drive vehicles. Overnight and day trips can be arranged to Mayan ruins, caves, waterfalls, jungle rivers, and chiclero camps, as well as **Puente Natural**, a high-arch cave similar to Río Frío, through which a small river flows. Recommended for such rugged adventures is **Mountain Equestrian Trails**; contact Jim Bevis for details. Because of the rough terrain and the absence of freshwater streams during the dry season, overland trips to the area are recommended only for travelers who are healthy and adventurous. The scenery and birding, however, is some of the finest in Central America.

BELMOPAN AND VICINITY

BELMOPAN
Location: *About 40 miles west of Belize City via the Western Highway.*
Population: *Roughly 6,000 (1997 estimate).*
Visitor Information: *Belize Tourist Board, (800) 624-0686; Belize Tourism Industry Association, 2-75717; and local hotels or travel agencies.*

The capital city of Belize, on the eastern edge of the Cayo District, has yet to find its way onto the itinerary of most foreign visitors. This is not surprising, considering the community's meager attractions. Looking more like a second-rate college campus than a national seat of government, Belmopan's concrete and stucco buildings are spread over a wide expanse of weedy lawns and empty lots. The main complex is clustered around a central plaza that features a lively open-air market, several unremarkable restaurants, and a noisy bus depot.

The architecture and layout are designed to evoke a Mayan ambiance. The name Belmopan combines the "Bel" of Belize with the name of one of the country's indigenous tribes, the Mopan Maya. Despite warnings that another big hurricane could level Belize City, as *Hattie* did in 1961, less than 6,000 Belizeans have heeded the call to relocate to Belmopan.

The main attraction for travelers in Belmopan is the national assembly (where you can watch politicians debate legislation) and the walk-in **Archaeology Vault** of the country's Department of Archaeology. While the vast majority of Belize's Mayan treasures have been hauled off to foreign museums and private collections, enough fine pieces remain to make a stop here worthwhile. Department staffers take reservations for tours (2 days' notice required) at 8-22106. The vault—which is exactly that—is open from 1:30 to 4 p.m. on Mondays, Wednesdays, and Fridays.

Permission from the Department of Archaeology is required to visit certain remote Mayan ruins. Serious students of the culture may wish to schedule a conversation with the Archaeology Commissioner.

The Belize government has long promised a national museum in Belmopan to house the Archaeology Vault collection, and many other historic and cultural artifacts. Projected to cost at least $3.5 million, the facility hadn't gone past the drawing board stage in 1997.

Services
Services in Belmopan include a bank and a post office. Free overnight parking is available to recreational vehicles at **The Oasis**, near Guanacaste Park, which also has an inexpensive restaurant, restrooms, and a water tap.

Getting There
The road (Western Highway) between Belize City and Belmopan is the best in the country and one can make the drive in under an hour; the turnoff to Belmopan is opposite Guanacaste National Park. Although Belmopan has a small airstrip, there is no scheduled commercial air service. Several bus companies (**Batty's**, **Z-Line**, **James**) run buses daily to Belmopan from Belize City, Dangriga, and San Ignacio (about $2 one-way from each). Buses run about once every hour between these communities from 8 a.m. to 5 p.m., less often on

Horseback riding in the Cayo District

weekends and holidays. Because there are no significant tourist attactions in Belmopan, there are no outfitters or tour companies serving the community as such.

Where to Stay and Eat in Belmopan
Note: Belmopan's restaurants are characterized by overpriced, undistinguished meals and slow service. The International Café and all Chinese restaurants here are best avoided.

Bull Frog Inn, 22 Halfmoon Avenue; rundown and overpriced at $75; 8-22111. Bar can be very noisy until the wee hours of the morning. Decent restaurant on the premises with a pleasant outdoor terrace.

Caladium, north end of the public market. Standard fare (in small portions), close to the bus terminal.

El Rey Inn, 23 Moho St.; $25; 8-23438. Recommended budget hotel (and café), located in a relatively quiet residential area. Spacious, clean rooms with private baths.

Yoli's Lounge, Constitution Drive. The best place in town for Belizean, Mexican, Italian, and American cuisine. A popular bar, too.

BELMOPAN AREA JUNGLE LODGES
In recent years the Belmopan area has become a kind of "mini-Cayo," offering travelers a growing number of worthy jungle lodge options. These have the advantage of being closer to the international airport and cayes, which can be an important consideration for those on a tight schedule. Other advantages include ready access to the region's many caves and several national parks.

Banana Bank Ranch, on the Belize River west of Belmopan (follow the signs at Mile 47); $80 and up, includes breakfast; 81-2020, fax 81-2026, e-mail *bbl@bcs.com*. Web site *www.belizenet.com/banana.html* Former Montana cowboy John Carr and his artist wife Carolyn operate this 4,000-acre working cattle ranch with five guest cabañas and four rooms in the ranch house (all meals available). About half of the Carr's property is undisturbed subtropical forest, with nearly 200 species of birds identified as well as many varieties of mammals, reptiles, and amphibians. The focus here is on horseback riding, and the Carrs have two dozen mounts to choose from. You can take a guided tour of their old-growth jungle, stopping occasionally at small Mayan ruins. River fishing and canoeing (both on the Belize River), in addition to stargazing (with an 8-inch Meade telescope) are offered. Unusual extras include Carolyn's fine oil paintings of Belize wildlife and the couple's private zoo, which includes monkeys, kinkajous, peccaries, and a jaguar. There is also a gift shop and natural history museum. New trails and a birding "observatory" were added by the Carrs in 1997.

Jaguar Paw Jungle Resort, at Franks Eddy, several miles east of Belmopan (at Mile 37) and accessible by a 7-mile private road; $155 with breakfast; (800) 335-8645 or 8-13024. On 215 acres along the Caves Branch of the Sibun River, a full-service luxury resort offering gourmet meals, air-conditioning, swimming pool, satellite TV, hiking (on 8 miles of nature trails), and inner tube rides through flooded caves ($60 per person). Each room is decorated in a different international motif. The owners will provide transportation from Belize City.

Steele Wotkyns

Traditional thatch-roof cabañas at Pook's Hill

Pook's Hill Lodge, on Roaring Creek, a few miles west of Belmopan; $95 and up, includes breakfast; 8-12017, fax: 8-23361, e-mail *pookshill@pobox.com.* Well-appointed facilities situated in a small Mayan plaza, includes eight screened cabañas with private bath (hot showers) and an elegant, diverse bar/restaurant. Horseback riding through a variety of habitats via 4 miles of well-maintained trails (superb for hiking, too). Swimming in a private Roaring Creek pool, refreshing inner tube floats down the same stream. Pook's Hill Lodge is raising (and reintroducing into the wild) green iguanas. Recommended.

Warrie Head Lodge, 137-acre ranch at Mile 56 on the Western Highway, about 15 miles west of Belmopan; $60; 2-77257. Caters primarily to groups, but will accommodate independent travelers. Besides a restaurant, this former colonial logging camp offers horseback riding, nature treks, canoeing, and swimming on the Belize River.

GUANACASTE NATIONAL PARK
Location: Less than 2 miles from Belmopan, at the intersection of the Hummingbird and Western Highways.
Size: 50 acres.
Hours: 8 a.m. to 5 p.m. daily

Fees: $3
Visitor Information: Contact Belize Audubon Society, 2-34987, or Guanacaste National Park, 8-22018.

On Earth Day (April 22) 1990, the Belizean government officially created Guanacaste National Park in a lush parcel of forest alongside the Belize River. The park is named after a huge guanacaste tree growing near the reserve's southwestern boundary. Also known as the tubroos or monkey's ear tree, the guanacaste is a highly prized hardwood known for its resistance to insects and decay. Guanacaste lumber is the material of choice for construction of dugout canoes, feeding troughs, and rice-hulling mortars. Cattle and monkeys love to nibble on the fruit of the guanacaste tree, which appears during the dry season as shiny brown pods after an explosion of small white flowers.

This particular giant (the species produces some of the largest trees in Central America) towers more than 120 feet above the forest floor and was spared the woodcutter's ax only because naturally occurring splits in its massive trunk make it unusable as timber (all other guanacaste trees in the park have been harvested). The tree's broad, sky-seeking branches support hundreds of epiphytes, including many brilliant species of orchid and bromeliad.

A short trail leads through the forest to the guanacaste tree from a visitors center operated by the Belize Audubon Society. Known as the Guanacaste Education Center, the facility was dedicated to the U.S. Peace Corps as Audubon's way of honoring the Corps' contributions to conservation and education in Belize.

Other large trees seen along the trail to the guanacaste tree include the mammee apple, bookut, ramon, quamwood, silk cotton, and raintree. Several mahogany trees have been planted near the park's visitor center as part of a reforestation program. You can hike a self-guided interpretive loop trail and view a display of native orchids at the visitors center.

Despite Guanacaste's diminutive size, it harbors abundant wildlife. Species observed here include jaguarundi, kinkajou, paca, armadillo, iguana, deer, and opossum. Resident birds include the blue-crowned motmot, black-faced ant thrush, smoky-brown woodpecker, red-lored parrot, black-headed trogon, and squirrel cuckoo, among more than 50 confirmed species.

Getting There

Accessible by bus, taxi, private car, or package tour. Restrooms, drinking water, and picnic facilities are available; cooking and camping are not permitted. The well-maintained trail network throughout the park follows a graceful curve of the Belize River at its confluence with Roaring Creek. Call ahead if you're interested in information on guided tours.

TAPIR MOUNTAIN NATURE RESERVE

Location: *Wedged between Roaring Creek and Upper Barton Creek in the northern foothills of the Mountain Pine Ridge, about 10 miles west of Belmopan.*
Size: *6,828 acres.*
Hours and Fees: *Not open to the general public. Qualified scientists and other researchers can make arrangements to visit by appointment with the Belize Audubon Society (see below).*
Visitor Information: *Belize Audubon Society, 2-34987, or Pook's Hill, 8-12017.*

Tapir Mountain (formerly Society Hall) Nature Reserve is an intact block of tropical forest, home to all manner of flora and fauna. It has been kept this way because of the determination and foresight of its conservation-minded landowner. **Svea Dietrich-Ward** had for many years sought a way to permanently save this area. Finally, in 1986, the German-born conservationist entered a long-term lease agreement with the Belize government on the condition that the property's natural resources be protected. Soon after, officials proclaimed it a "nature reserve." (In Belize, this designation is a subcategory of the National Parks System Act, specifying that such lands be preserved only for scientific research and education.)

The nature reserve label means that Tapir Mountain is not a destination for the casual tourist: the only legally allowed visitors are researchers with specific scientific objectives or groups of students with competent leaders, all with prior permission.

Perhaps the greatest threat to Tapir Mountain is illegal hunting within the reserve's boundaries by nearby residents. Another encroachment is by farmers engaged in slash-and-burn agriculture. This is compounded by the lack of access for land managers to monitor and prevent such deforestation.

In the last few years the reserve has benefited from the presence of Ray and Vicki Snaddon and family who established their jungle resort, **Pook's Hill**, on Tapir Mountain's northeast corner boundary.

What's Worth Saving?

In 1994 a preliminary biological survey carried out by Bruce and Carolyn Miller—working with the Wildlife Conservation Society—recorded a glimpse of Tapir Mountain's biological treasures. Among other findings, this "snapshot" survey confirmed the presence of numerous mammals, at least 129 bird species, and more than 15 tree species within the reserve's tropical moist forest. Notably, the team recorded the presence of several migrant birds—including the wood thrush and Kentucky warbler. The Millers concluded that such reserves play a key role in ensuring the future survival of neotropical migrant birds. Conservationists have focused much attention on these neotropical migrant bird species that spend summers in North America and winters in the tropics. Many species of these amazing songbirds have been declining as a result of habitat loss in both their winter and summer homes.

Bird life in the area is so rich that even casual visitors

The Snaddons have kept watchful eyes on this remote nature reserve while operating what is—in our estimation—one of Belize's best lodges for natural history tourism.

The Tapir Mountain area consists of undulating limestone karst dotted with sinkholes, exposed rock outcrops, small streams, and bubbling springs. Ancient Mayan garbage "middens," consisting mostly of shells, pot shards, and bones, are concealed by a dense forest of climbing vines, palms, and scores of other tree species. In some of the valleys and low-lying portions of this reserve, the forest canopy crests at nearly 100 feet.

Getting There/Outfitters

Because of its protected status, access to the Tapir Mountain Nature Reserve is limited to scientists and other researchers (contact the *not interested in birding take notice. In 1997 when we visited Pook's Hill Lodge adjacent to the reserve, the raucous calls of red-lored parrots filled the morning air. We witnessed the dipping flight and distinctive beak of Belize's national bird, the keel-billed toucan, and also saw the smaller toucan, the collared aracari. The lineated woodpecker greeted us next to the Pook's Hill dining hall, while the bat falcon ate breakfast in a tall snag nearby. A spectacled owl family lives close to one of the Pook's Hill nature trails, and at least 20 hummingbird species are found in the reserve area.*

Diverse wildlife populations are also encountered in the Tapir Mountain Nature Reserve and surrounding areas, including the Central American or Baird's tapir—Belize's national animal—for which the reserve is named. According to 1997 data from the World Conservation Monitoring Centre the species is listed as "vulnerable" throughout its range in Central and South America, meaning the tapir faces a high risk of extinction in the wild in the medium-term future.

Belize Audubon Society, which manages the reserve). Immediately adjacent to Tapir Mountain is the **Pook's Hill** 300-acre private nature reserve and jungle lodge, a recommended overnight destination.

THE CAVES BRANCH REGION

For those with a special interest in caves and in a unique outdoor experience, we recommend a visit to the Caves Branch area along tributaries of the Sibun River, about 45 minutes southeast of Belmopan. The limestone hills and valleys of the region are honeycombed with caves, a number of which were used for sacred rituals and burials by the ancient Maya.

Even for experienced travelers who have been to many of the great Mayan ruins, it's hard to imagine the deeply spiritual ceremonies held underground here by the priests of the Maya. Only until you stand quietly in an utterly dark cave, absorbing and processing the archaeological evidence of blood-letting ceremonies, animal sacrifices, and shamans, can you begin to appreciate the power of Xibalba, the sacred netherworld of Mayan gods.

The caves are found within of one of Belize's most ecologically diverse natural areas, punctuated by citrus orchards and small farms. Some visitors see jaguars in close proximity, and more often there are sightings of howler and spider monkeys, Baird's tapir, white-tailed deer, coatimundi, kinkajou, river otters, boa constrictors, and bats. Some 214 bird species have been identified locally. High tropical forest canopy, thicket areas, and marsh/riverine areas make up the three general habitat types found here, all excellent for birding.

Outfitters

Ian Anderson's Caves Branch Adventure Company, Box 356, Belmopan, 8-22800, e-mail *caves@pobox.com*, brings visitors directly inside the extensive below-ground realm of the Caves Branch region. Anderson and his guides were still discovering dryland crystal caves and new passages off of five extensive underground river caves systems when we last visited in 1997, the seventh year Anderson had explored and mapped caves in Belize. In all, there are at least 36 dry "crystal" caves in the area (guests of the Caves Branch Camp have a chance to enter five or six of these venues), known for their sparkling array of calcium carbonate crystals). Anderson's team takes visitors into all five of the region's underground river systems. Featured trips include a float through Belize's longest (over 7 miles) river cave system; a cave rafting trip in the security of large inflatable rafts; a "crystal cave" expedition, where visitors scramble for miles beneath the surface through narrow passageways that connect cathedral-sized caverns; overnight jungle treks; horseback excursions; and after-dark jungle and river safaris. All outings are reasonably priced (several are available without a minimum number of participants) and the groups are always kept small enough to give everyone the best experience. Also offered are day trips by vehicle to the Cahal Pech and Xunantunich ruins as well as to the Belize Zoo and the Community Baboon Sanctuary. Recommended.

Slickrock Adventures offers Caves Branch day trip cave floats using inflatable and hard-shell kayaks and riverboats (see Chapter 4, Special Interests). Tours of these and other caves are also available from **Pacz Hotel & Tours**, 2 Far West Street, San Ignacio, 92-2110, which can arrange area mountain bike trips, horseback riding, and jungle treks. On any cave trip, be sure to bring good hiking shoes, an extra pair of old tennis shoes for the mud and water, long pants, long-sleeved shirts, and insect repellent.

Getting There

The Caves Branch area is located from 10 to 20 miles south of Belmopan, along the Hummingbird Highway, near Blue Hole National Park.

There is frequent daily bus service from Belize City via Belmopan and from Dangriga. Contact the **Z-Line**, 2-73937 in Belize City and 5-22160 in Dangriga for information. Cars can be rented in Belmopan, Belize City, San Ignacio, and Dangriga.

Where to Stay and Eat in the Caves Branch Region

Caves Branch Jungle Lodge, at Mile 41.5 on the Hummingbird Highway, 300 yards northwest of the Blue Hole; $20 and up, food extra; 8-22800, e-mail *caves@pobox.com*. Camping, bunkhouses, private cabañas, and excellent family-style meals on a 58,000-acre estate, owned by Caribbean Investments Ltd. and managed by expatriate Ian Anderson. Visitors participate in the adventure of floating on inflated truck-tire inner tubes into and through an underground network, while Anderson and the other guides point out such natural cave features as stalactites, stalagmites, rimstone dams, flowstone, and calcite soda straws, as well as archaeological wonders. About 25 miles of birding and walking trails begin just outside the compound. Also on the estate there are five aboveground "blue holes" (collapsed cave formations filled with water). The area's flora is outstanding, including 160 varieties of epiphytes, bromeliads, and ferns (orchids grow in the enclosed outdoor showers!). Recommended.

ST. HERMAN'S CAVE AND BLUE HOLE NATIONAL PARK

Location: About 12 miles southeast of Belmopan on the Hummingbird Highway
Size: About 200 acres.
Hours: 8 a.m. to 4 p.m. daily.
Fees: $3
Visitor Information: A visitors center is a few hundred miles north of the

park on the Hummingbird Highway. The Belize Audubon Society, 2-34987, manages the park.

A well-marked sign guides visitors to the entrance trail of Blue Hole National Park, a federally protected area administered by the Belize Audubon Society. (This Blue Hole is not to be confused with the more famous offshore Blue Hole located near Half Moon Caye.)

The Belize Audubon Society maintains a visitors center just off the Hummingbird Highway for the Blue Hole National Park and St. Herman's Cave (both attractions are within the boundaries of the park, connected by an undisturbed stand of tropical forest and a short trail). All visitors must check in at the center, where a small admission fee is collected to cover management expenses.

The centerpiece of the park is an amazing sight: a deep pool of churning sapphire water formed by the collapse of an underground river channel. A **Caves Branch Creek** tributary wells up from an unseen source and travels for about 100 yards before plunging mysteriously down a siphon that carries it into yet another cave beneath the mountain. The dome-shaped chamber where the water is sucked underground creates an unusual echo-chamber effect as liquid swirls beneath it. This tranquil setting is a good spot for swimming, picnicking, and birding. The sparkling pool is about 25 feet deep and moves fast, so bathers should be careful. Some foreigners swim nude here, although this practice is actually illegal in Belize and it offends the large percentage of Belizeans. There are no overnight camping facilities here or anywhere in the park.

The same Caves Branch Creek travels through nearby **St. Herman's Cave** which is accessible from the Blue Hole via a well-maintained forest pathway called the **Nature Trail**. Fauna recorded in this area include jaguar, ocelot, jaguarundi, tapir, peccary, anteater, gibnut, coatimundi, deer, and kinkajou. Once you arrive at the cave, a flashlight is handy for exploration, along with a good pair of waterproof boots, such as Wellingtons, with a decent sole for traction.

The hike to St. Herman's Cave from the Blue Hole is about 1.5 miles and takes about 45 minutes along an interesting and moderately strenuous jungle trail that has many steps to carry walkers over the rugged topography. The most direct route, however, is from the **Blue Hole Visitors Center** located about 1 mile north along the Hummingbird Highway, from which it's an easy 15-minute walk from the St. Herman's entrance. The trail to St. Herman's begins immediately behind the center and curves to the right along a dirt road next to a citrus plantation.

St. Herman's was used by the Maya during the Classic period, A.D. 100 to 900, and the concrete steps leading into its mouth are laid over stone steps carved more than 1,000 years ago. Ancient pots used to collect "virgin water" from cave drippings, along with spears, torches, and other artifacts, have been removed by archaeologists for study.

OTHER CENTRAL BELIZE CAVES

A small cave a few miles southeast of Over-the-Top, off the Hummingbird Highway, is **Petroglyph Cave,** named for its ancient rock drawings left by indigenous people centuries ago. Permission from the Department of Archaeology, 8-22106, fax 8-23345, must be obtained to enter this cave. We suggest that you ask Archaeology officials to recommend an experienced local guide as well.

A fairly large cave that is open to the public but not as accessible as St. Herman's is **Ben Lomond Cave,** located in the limestone hills fringing Southern Lagoon, about 25 miles southwest of Belize City and not far from Five Blues Lake National Park (see below). Ben Lomond is full of Mayan artifacts (please don't disturb!), and its surroundings offer a perfect example of habitat transition from savanna to tropical forest. It can be reached only by taking a boat to the lagoon and then hiking through dense coastal bush. A stream flows from the cave's wide mouth. Not visited by the authors is **Manatee Cave,** located in the same area off the Coastal Highway west of Southern Lagoon. This is a difficult cave and definitely *not* for beginners.

We strongly recommend hiring a local guide with caving and wilderness evacuation/first-aid experience before entering either Ben Lomond or Manatee caves. Contact **Tony Rath** of **Naturalight/ Pelican Beach Resort,** 5-22004, or e-mail *trath@btl.net.,* for suggestions.

FIVE BLUES LAKE NATIONAL PARK

Location: About 32 miles south of Belmopan.
Hours: Dawn to dusk, daily.
Size: 4,050 acres.
Fees: Donation requested.
Visitor Information: 81-2005 (Over-the-Top community phone).

About 10 miles south of Caves Branch on the Hummingbird Highway is **St. Margaret's Village** and **Over-the-Top Camp,** near the crest of a ridge on the Belize and Stann Creek District borders. On the same side of the highway as the popular **Over-the-Top Restaurant** is a small sign marking the turnoff (at Mile 32) onto an unpaved road heading north 4 miles to Five Blues Lake National Park. The park's crown jewel is a small, 200-foot-deep lake surrounded by steep karst limestone hills. It's called Five Blues because of the various shades of blue reflected by the sky during the course of a day.

Five Blues Lake National Park is a remarkable testament to private-sector conservation efforts in Belize. It is one example of helpful local involvement in the management of protected areas by residents and business owners in nearby villages. Largely through the efforts of the Association of Friends of Five Blues, a grassroots community group, the original 885-acre park was expanded to include 4,050 acres of tropical forest and an extensive cave complex.

The park's trails—**Gibnut, Howler Monkey,** and **Jaguar**—wind through the jungle and along one side of the spectacular lake. One trail ends at an interesting cave with an unusual entrance in the side of a tall limestone cliff. At Five Blues Lake itself you can enjoy a picnic lunch, take a swim, or arrange for a serene boat ride across the water. With your local guide, we also recommend a short trek past the lake into a Mayan cave system located within the protected area. The ancient Maya reportedly used the deep pools of the lake as sacrificial wells.

During our 1997 visit, we learned of some frustrating setbacks here. In December 1996, unknown persons burned down the park's visitor center and stole several donated mountain bikes. Yet community residents are determined to make Five Blues a success and reiterated their open invitation for more visitors. Ideally, they'd prefer to see travelers spend a night or two in an area homestay or at least hire local guides. One of the current members of the Five Blues Association, **Francis Reid**, told us that villagers are eager to find ways that tourism can help them preserve their natural wonders, while providing some financial rewards as well.

One main goal of the Friends of Five Blues, according to Reid, is to establish enduring local participation in nature-oriented tourism, such as training residents of St. Margaret's Village in management and administrative duties related to the park. "But to succeed," he reiterated, "we need people to visit us!"

Where to Stay and Eat in Five Blues Lakes

Over-the-Top Restaurant, at mile 32 in Over-the-Top Village; 81-2005. We suggest you contact Francis and Gloria Reid at the Over-the-Top Restaurant to arrange lodging, meals, or accommodations. The telephone number listed here is also the village's one and only community phone. The Reids can coordinate with Barbara Borland and the **Woman Rising Bed & Breakfast Group** that works in association with the Friends of Five Blues. This group of about 10 local women provides basic rooms in their homes (or separate rustic guest facilities) on a rotating basis and at a modest cost. Meals are provided for a small fee.

Palacio's Resort, no phone, just outside St. Margaret's Village toward Dangriga. Offers a restaurant, lodging, swimming, and horseback riding.

Tamandua, on the Five Blues Lake Entrance Road, (Box 306, Belmopan); 8-23182. A private 170-acre wildlife sanctuary and fruit orchard; meals and tours available.

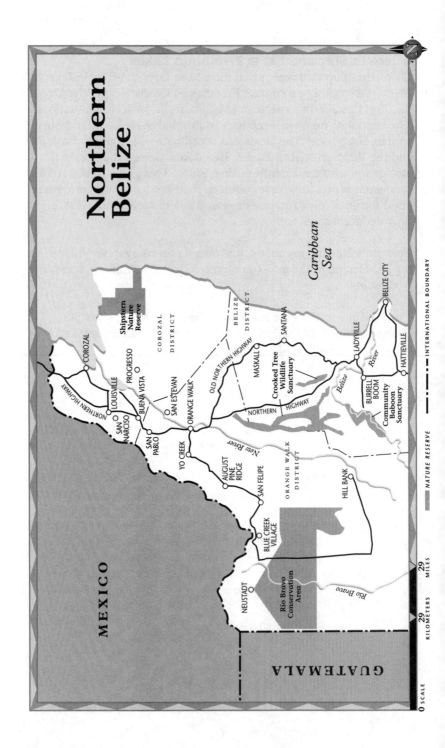

Northern Belize

MEXICO

GUATEMALA

Caribbean Sea

Shipstern Nature Reserve

COROZAL DISTRICT

BELIZE DISTRICT

ORANGE WALK DISTRICT

Río Bravo Conservation Area

Crooked Tree Wildlife Sanctuary

Community Baboon Sanctuary

COROZAL
LOUISVILLE
PROGRESSO
BUENA VISTA
SAN ESTEVAN
ORANGE WALK
SAN NARCISO
SAN PABLO
YO CREEK
AUGUST PINE RIDGE
SAN FELIPE
BLUE CREEK VILLAGE
NEUSTADT
HILL BANK
MASKALL
SANTANA
LADYVILLE
BURRELL BOOM
HATTIEVILLE
BELIZE CITY

NORTHERN HIGHWAY
OLD NORTHERN HIGHWAY
NORTHERN HIGHWAY

New River
Río Bravo
Belize River

0 SCALE   29 KILOMETERS   29 MILES

NATURE RESERVE   INTERNATIONAL BOUNDARY

NORTHERN BELIZE

8

COROZAL, ORANGE WALK, AND BELIZE DISTRICTS

Northern Belize is not a priority destination for most visitors, even though it has much to offer, including nature reserves, Mayan ruins, and jungle lodges, along with such outdoor recreation opportunities as sailing, birding, fishing, swimming, and windsurfing. And since you may very well begin and/or end your trip at Belize City's international airport, we urge you to spend at least one or two days exploring the attractions easily accessible to the north of that area.

The northern coastal strip of Belize has a distinctive cultural personality, since it was the first part of the country settled by Europeans. The vast majority of the nation's people live in the three districts of the north: Corozal, Orange Walk, and Belize. This includes most of the Creole, Mexican, and European-descended population.

The climate is warm and humid; much of the terrain is a swampy savanna that is crisscrossed by waterways. Geologically speaking, this coastal plain is fairly young, formed as a limestone seabed before the oceans receded and mainlands uplifted. A few karst formations and ridges provide texture, as well as thermal currents for hawks and other raptors. Nature lovers can find plenty of wading birds in the region's numerous wetlands, and anglers can hook a wide variety of fish in the broad, nutrient-rich rivers.

This area is the most cultivated in the country, particularly in the northeast, where sugarcane is king, and in the northwest, where

Mennonite farmers have recreated a landscape straight out of the American Midwest. True, northern Belize lacks the dramatic scenery and abundant wildlife of the offshore islands and interior mountains. Yet it also offers many unique and worthwhile natural and archaeological destinations, including the Shipstern Nature Reserve, Lamanai ruins, New River, Crooked Tree Wildlife Sanctuary, Belize Zoo, Río Bravo Conservation Area, Monkey Bay National Park, Altun Ha ruins, and the Community Baboon (Howler Monkey) Sanctuary. All are described in this chapter except the archaeological sites, which are found in a chapter of their own.

COROZAL DISTRICT

Today's bucolic Corozal District (which borders the Mexican state of Quintana Roo) masks a turbulent past. A series of massacres of Mestizos and whites by enslaved Mayans throughout the Yucatán peninsula led to a long, bloody retaliation in the mid-19th century known as The Caste Wars. Thousands of people, Mayans and Mestizos alike, fled to safety across the Río Hondo into British Honduras; today their Spanish-speaking descendants make up the majority of the population. Their farming expertise was welcomed by colonial authorities and, as a direct result, Corozal is today one of the country's most extensively cultivated areas (primarily sugarcane). The main city, Corozal Town, and surrounding areas are a good escape from the sometimes hectic pace of travel in other parts of Belize. Corozal is also the gateway to Belize for travelers coming from Cancún and other points in Mexico. Except for the sticky summer season, there are near-constant trade winds off the water, and extremes of precipitation and temperature are unusual.

The word *Corozal* is modified from the Spanish name for the cohune palm tree, which ancient Mayans considered to be a symbol of fertility. This area—along with most of northern Belize—has always been relatively prosperous because of its fertile soil and benign climate.

COROZAL TOWN
Location: *About 85 miles north of Belize City and less than 10 miles south of the Mexican border.*
Population: *About 13,000 (1997 estimate).*

Visitor Information*: Menzies Travel, Vince Murray, and Jal's Travel Agency (see below) in Corozal Town. Or try the Belize Tourist Board, (800) 624-0686, and Belize Tourism Industry Association, 2-77213.*

Corozal Town consists of a mixture of clapboard wooden houses and concrete block buildings. All are built on foundations of the Mayan ceremonial center of Santa Rita. In 1955, Hurricane Janet destroyed much of the town, which until then featured mostly adobe (mud-and-straw brick) buildings.

The Corozal District was originally settled in 1849 by refugees from an Indian massacre in Bacalar, Mexico. For a good visual description of this history, see the fine mural by Manuel Villamor Reyes in Corozal Town's municipal building. (If the town hall is closed, the Reyes mural can be seen through windows on the ground floor.) In 1986, the painting was restored and updated to show the economic exploitation of immigrant workers in the district during the 1850s and 1860s.

Surrounding Corozal Town's Central Park are a modern Catholic church, a library, the city hall, an Adventist church, and government offices. There are also several old brick "pillboxes," used as defensive fortifications by the British during the last century.

Although Corozal Town is built along the shoreline of Chetumal Bay, the water immediately adjacent to the city is polluted. There is a long stretch of beach here, called Miami Beach, linked by a clean, lawn-covered park that is landscaped with rain shelters, picnic tables, playgrounds for children, and sea grape and palm trees.

Corozal provides a good base for visitors for a couple of days because the town has the area's best accommodations and services. In addition, we recommend Corozal Town as a base of operations for sportfishing enthusiasts looking to hook a huge tarpon or other game fish without having to share the rich waters on the Belizean side of Chetumal Bay with many other fishers.

Check the calendar before you start your trip; Corozal Town comes alive at Lent, Mexican Independence Day, Columbus Day, and Christmas, turning each of these holidays into boisterous fiestas.

Things to See and Do

The economy of the entire Corozal District centers on the sugar indus-try. The old **Aventura Sugar Mill**, about 5 miles south of Corozal Town, started operation in the 1800s. Although the processing plant is no longer in use, its chimney stands as a symbol of an industry that generates an estimated 80 cents out of every dollar earned here. The foundation of an old Spanish colonial church is also on the site. Raw sugarcane is now processed at two other area mills: **La Libertad** and **Tower Hill**. Tours of the mills now operating are available by prior arrangement; the facilities usually shut down from July until December.

About 7 miles to the north of Corozal Town and less than 2 miles from the Mexican border (off the right side of the main road to Chetumal) is picturesque **Four Mile Lagoon**. Locals use this as a favorite picnicking spot and weekend hangout. It is recommended for foreign visitors, too, especially those interested in sailing, fishing, swimming, windsurfing, and kayaking, all well-suited to these calm waters.

Besides the small ruin of **Santa Rita**, now surrounded by the modern roads and buildings of Corozal Town, a small yet interesting coastal Mayan site known as **Cerros** is a quick boat ride across Corozal Bay. More fully described in Chapter 10, Archaeological Sites, Cerros is a late Pre-Classic trading center—reached after a short, pleasant walk on a trail cut through tropical forest—boasting tombs, ball courts, and a magnificent temple. The temple offers a fine view back across the bay to Corozal Town, Sarteneja, and Chetumal.

Guides

Skilled boatman **Manuel Hoare**, 4-22744, is recommended as an excellent area guide to Mayan ruins, Shipstern, and Chetumal. If you are coming from Sarteneja, on the tip of the Shipstern Peninsula, we recommend boatman and fishing guide **Fernando Alamilla**, 4-32085, who also gives a good tour of Cerros.

Getting There

From the United States, you may wish to consider flying to the Yucatán and taking a bus or shuttle flight to Chetumal, just north of Corozal, since commercial airfares from the U.S. to Cancún can be half the cost of airfares from the U.S. to Belize. Information on transportation options from Cancún is available from **Joan** and **Henry Menzies**, 4-22725, **Tony's Inn**, 4-22055, and **Vince Murray**, 4-22784, or e-mail *Vince@btl.net*. Good service is also reported by travelers using **Jal's Travel Agency** in Corozal Town (and Belize City), where tours and airplane tickets are available.

From within Belize, the **Venus**, 4-22132, and **Batty**, 4-23034, bus companies both run regularly between Corozal Town and Chetumal, 10 miles to the north. In 1997, Venus had early morning express buses to Belize City, as well as an hourly morning schedule

south from Corozal Town. Batty had afternoon express buses to
Belize City as well as regular, nearly hourly afternoon service to points
south. The express trip from Corozal to Chetumal takes about 20
minutes and to Belize City around 3 hours.

Tropic Air, 4-22725, e-mail *tropic@cybersim.com.*, offers twice
daily flights to San Pedro (on Ambergris Caye) from Corozal with
connecting flights to both the municipal and international airports in
Belize City. **Island Air**, 4-22874, also serves the San Pedro route with
several flights daily. Other airlines occasionally offer service here.

Where to Stay in Corozol Town

Caribbean Village Resort, south end of town; $20; 4-22725, fax 4-
23414. Proprietors Henry and Joan Menzies are local agents for
Tropic Air as well as a full-service tour/transportation company. They
offer thatched-roof cabañas (with private baths), full RV hookups,
and camping ($5). Recommended.

Corozal Central Guesthouse, 22 Sixth Avenue, one block south of
the Venus Bus Station; $20; 4-22784, e-mail *Vince@btl.net.* Owner
Vincent Murray is wired on the World Wide Web, offering free e-
mail and computer access for guests, along with kitchen facilities,
clean rooms, and a good deal of information about the Corozal area.

Hok'ol K'in, south of town, on the beach; $40; 4-23329; run by a
former Peace Corps worker. Recommended. Meals and well-priced
tours available.

Hotel Maya, on the Corozal-Orange Walk Highway; $30 (a bit over-
priced); 4-22082. Great view of the bay and good Mexican restaurant. An agent for Island Air, which flies daily to San Pedro.

Hotel Posada Mama, 77 G St. South; $20; 4-22107.

Nestor's Hotel, 123 Fifth Avenue; $15; 4-22354. Popular among
experienced, budget-minded travelers; has bar and restaurant.

Quality Hotel, 5th Avenue and 3rd Street; $20; 4-23324. Upstairs
from the Wonderful Chinese Restaurant.

The Santa Cruz Lodge, a few miles south of town in the village of
Santa Cruz; $90 and up; 4-22441. Offers tours of the Petrojam

Sugar Factory, as well as guided excursions to local ruins and nature destinations. An upscale resort on 35 acres that incorporates the renovated former homes of sugar industry executives. Besides 18 air-conditioned rooms, the lodge has two restaurants, a bar, swimming pool, and tennis court. Expansion plans call for a jogging track, golf course, and health spa.

Tony's Inn & Beach Resort, far south end of town; $65; 4-22055, fax 4-22829, Web site *http://www.belize.com/tonys.html.* The Tony Castillo family offers upscale, air-conditioned rooms, a private b each and marina, along with many tour and water sports options for guests There's a gift shop, bar, restaurant, and car rental service on the premises.

Where to Eat in Corozal Town

Crises Restaurant, north of town on the bay. Serves above average Belizean cuisine and is recommended for its home-style atmosphere.

Hailey's Restaurant and Bar, at the Caribbean Village Resort. Good food and friendly service. Recommended.

Jack and Fanny's Wonderful Chinese Restaurant, on the corner of 5th Avenue and 3rd Street. The best Asian food around. (In fact, we have heard uniformly negative comments about Corozal's other Chinese restaurants.)

Nestor's, at 123 Fifth Avenue. A varied menu of delicious items. A restaurant/bar downstairs and a nightclub upstairs.

Smugglers' Den, at nearby Consejo Shores, serves both drinks and food (the fare is Belizean, with an emphasis on such tasty local snacks as *garnachas* and *salbutes*). A nice place to picnic and swim on sunny days.

Tony's Inn, south of town, includes the recently remodeled Vista del Sol Restaurant (expensive), with a patio that overlooks Chetumal Bay. Tony's also features Corozal's only tiki bar on the beach, the Y-Not.

THE SHIPSTERN NATURE RESERVE
Location: 3 miles south of Sarteneja.
Size: Almost 24,000 acres.

Hours: *9 a.m. to 12 noon and from 1 p.m. to 4 daily, overnight camping allowed for registered visitors.*
Cost: *$5 entrance fee includes a tour of the visitors center, the butterfly center, and a guided walk on the Chiclero Botanical Trail. Other guide fees are $5 per hour and the transportation cost to Xo-pol Pond is $18.*
Visitor Information: *Belize Audubon Society, 2-34987, or write 12 Fort Street, Belize City.*

Sticking out like a hitchhiker's thumb into the northern end of Chetumal Bay, the Shipstern Peninsula is one of the least developed areas in all of Belize. Until relatively recently, it could only be reached by private boat (now there is an all-weather road). A few thousand, mostly Spanish-speaking people, live in this vast expanse of waterlogged jungle, savanna, and mangrove swamp. Most of the population is concentrated in the isolated fishing village of Sarteneja, which perches on a small patch of dry ground near the peninsula's northeastern tip.

San Estevan, Progresso, Chunox, and a few other small settlements—situated between huge sugarcane fields— punctuate the lush landscape en route to Sarteneja. However, the peninsula's main attraction is its large nature reserve, named after the abandoned village of Shipstern. This nature sanctuary is in the vicinity of the government's large Freshwater Creek Forest Reserve and its boundaries take in a large portion of the Shipstern Lagoon before sweeping west to the coast near Condemned Point. A wardens' quarters, guest house, visitors center, butterfly center, and the Chiclero botanical trail of the Shipstern Nature Reserve are 3 miles south of Sarteneja.

Shipstern Nature Reserve's boundaries encompass northern hardwood forests, saline lagoon systems, freshwater lagoons, and mangrove shorelines that are little-disturbed by humans. Shipstern is an infrequently visited showcase for four of Belize's ecosystem types: savanna, lagoons, river, and canopy forest.

The Belize Audubon Society assumed responsibility for Shipstern in 1994, and it is now overseen by Crooked Tree Wildlife Sanctuary manager Donald Tillett and four full-time wardens. While Tillett travels between the two protected areas, head Shipstern warden Juan Aldana lives at the Shipstern reserve compound year-round.

Shipstern Nature Reserve is considered an exceptional example of a heterogeneous forest regenerating from devastating tropical storm damage. (Most of the mature trees were destroyed by Hurricane Janet in 1955.) With assistance from one of Shipstern's wardens—who also serve as visitor guides—it is possible to see the transition from different forest types, particularly as you approach lagoon and savanna areas.

Flora and Fauna

The flora and fauna have made a remarkable recovery during the past four decades, and hundreds of plant and animal species have been recorded here, including scores of migratory birds from North America that winter in Shipstern. The moist forest of the Shipstern Peninsula, still largely untouched, is the only protected area in the country that includes the more seasonal hardwood trees, as well as vast saltwater estuaries that are an especially important habitat for many wading and fish-eating birds. Bird-watchers can expect to see several species of flycatcher, toucan, warbler, wading birds, ducks, and parrots. Among the birds recorded here are the Yucatán jay, reddish egret, wood stork, and black catbird (rarely recorded on the mainland). During our 1997 visit we also saw the American coot, great white egret, and roseate spoonbill. All five species of Belize's native cats, along with tapir, paca, coatimundi, white-tailed deer, peccary, and armadillo, roam the Shipstern forests and savanna. Jaguar sign and tracks are seen frequently.

The reserve's mascots include the feisty coatimundi, Martina. When not scratching to get through the screen of a building for a papaya feast, she's attracting wild coatimundis that are seen almost daily on the compound. Shipstern's other semi-tame mascot is Kiko the peccary, who is also sometimes allowed to roam the grounds.

Reserve Accommodations

Overnight accommodations originally built for scientists working at the Shipstern Nature Reserve are now being shared with visitors. Keep in mind that the focus here is on observing nature, not indulging in cozy amenities. The reserve features large, screen-sided observation towers on sturdy metal frames strategically placed for excellent wildlife observation. Simply called "tree tops" by the staff, one is located at the end of an access road (in early 1997 we saw two white-lipped peccaries here) where the dense forest gives way to a seasonally wet savanna fringed by buttonwood, black poisonwood, and other trees. Here Shipstern wardens are in the process of constructing a freshwater pond using rainwater collected from the observation platform's roof. This strategy has worked before at Shipstern as a magnet for fauna—affording excellent viewing at sunrise, at dusk, and during spotlight checks at night. Warden Aldana reports seeing white-tailed deer here frequently and the elusive Baird's mountain tapir has also been seen. Visitors can arrange with Shipstern wardens to camp here. See "Where to Stay in Shipstern," below, for more information.

Another "tree tops" observation tower is located on a bank of **Xo-pol Pond**, a prime place to watch birds. This is part of the most recent addition to the Shipstern Nature Reserve, the 660-acre Chacan Choc Mol.

Recommended Hikes

The nature trail around the banks of **Xo-pol Pond** is a haven for wood storks, roseate spoonbills, American coots, great white egrets, northern jacanas, and many other birds (as well as Morelet's crocodiles). Located about 11 miles west of Shipstern's main compound, a well-informed Shipsten warden will take you to Xo-pol for a modest guiding and transport fee.

Another recommended guided hike is along the **Chiclero Botanical Trail**, located in the forest near the headquarters building. A warden will explain the traditional medicinal and ceremonial uses of dozens of trees along the path. The excursion is included in the reserve's $5 entrance fee, along with a visit to Shipstern's visitors center and a complete tour of the butterfly breeding/education facility.

Butterfly Breeding Program

The reserve's butterfly breeding and education efforts remain a primary program at Shipstern. Its goals include visitor education, including a display of food plants required by specific species and of the different life stages of butterflies. Most of the latter are brilliantly-colored members of the order Lepidoptera, which are eventually reintroduced into the wild after getting a head start in the reserve's breeding and rearing enclosures. Visitors may see giant swallowtail, postman, and zebra, among other colorful varieties.

Getting There

Shipstern Nature Reserve can be reached by private car or take a taxi from Sarteneja (see below).

Where to Stay in Shipstern

Shipstern Nature Reserve Lodging—The only guaranteed lodging in the Shipstern/Sarteneja area as of 1997 was at the Shipstern

Saving the Wood Stork

Raising and showing butterflies to visitors is not the only work underway at Shipstern. An intensive, round-the-clock vigil near wood stork nests keeps the four wardens busy on rotating shifts from February through July every year!

"People from Sarteneja kill them to eat them, so we have to be there," Aldana explained. The program has been quite successful, too. From an estimated 60 breeding pairs in 1991, this astounding 24-hour "nesting watch" helped increase the population to some 300 breeding pairs in 1996. Visitors who visit the wood storks' nesting caye may stay overnight at the small observation outpost, with advance approval from Shipstern's wardens.

The Shipstern Nature Reserve is also an active and unique place for ecological research in Belize through an ongoing cooperative research agreement between the reserve and the University of Neuchâtel in Switzerland. During our last visit, one researcher was establishing permanent botanical transects in order to better track the evolution of the forest, while a colleague made an inventory of both fruit and insect-eating bats (10 species had been identified).

"The future for Shipstern looks very bright," declared manager, Donald Tillett, during our 1997 visit. He told us that the Belize Audubon Society would like to see more groups (as well as individuals) visit Shipstern. Another attractive incentive for groups is that, on request, Tillett gives a slideshow covering ecology and management at both Shipstern and Crooked Tree Wildlife Sanctuary.

Nature Reserve (see text above). Contact manager Donald Tillett at Belize Audubon headquarters in advance, Box 1001, Belize City; 2-34987 or 2-34988. It costs $10 per night to stay at Shipstern's guest house, any of the "treetops," or at the facility near the wood stork nesting site. The tent camping fee is $5 (bring your own tent). Modestly priced meals are also available at the Shipstern Nature Reserve. Because of the strong possibility of seeing wildlife and heavy concentrations of birds, we recommend guided visits to the Xo-pol Pond/Chacan Chac Mol Addition as well a trip on the main trail to the treetops overlooking savanna habitat.

SARTENEJA
Location: Northern tip of Shipstern Peninsula, on Chetumal Bay.
Population: About 400 (1997 estimate).
Visitor Information: Belize Tourist Board, (800) 624-0686.

The village of Sarteneja, northeast of the Shipstern reserve, was almost completely washed away in 1955 by Hurricane Janet. The tin-roofed, cinder-block settlement has been rebuilt several times in its history, always around a well located, massive piece of seemingly solid stone. Legend has it that this particular well, once used by sea-faring Maya, has never gone dry. *Sarteneja* is a Spanish word meaning "water between the rocks."

The Maya apparently abandoned the original village about 1700. During the mid-1800s, Yucatán settlers fleeing the Caste Wars reestablished Sarteneja, which became widely known for its skilled boatbuilders. To this day, Sarteneja's fishermen sail as far south as Guatemala and Honduras in the beautiful handcrafted sailing vessels they call "lighters." The fishers sell their catch in Belize City, San Pedro, or Chetumal on the way home, then turn around and start another fishing expedition a few days later. They often pick up sand and coconuts on the cayes they visit, which they sell on the mainland. Every Easter a huge, festive sailing regatta is held in Sarteneja harbor and prizes are awarded for the fastest and most elegant boats.

Although more than 400 Mayan sites have been pinpointed on the Shipstern peninsula, only one ancient structure has been excavated. Visitors reportedly can tour the small Mayan site near the village by asking the landowner's permission and paying a small entrance fee. While the world's archaeologists organize themselves, local residents continue to dismantle many of the old buildings to make modern houses of their own.

The native shrimp, lobster, and conch are fished during a careful-ly-controlled season by the more than 90 percent of Sarteneja residents who earn their living from commercial fishing. After the lobster and conch season, another controlled commercial season allows the harvest of snapper and grouper.

Things to See and Do
A couple of nearby cayes and reefs offer snorkeling possibilities here, but they are difficult to reach without a chartered boat. Birders are advised that the area's murky lagoons are important feeding grounds for such rare waterbirds as the flamingo and spoonbill, as well as manatees and crocodiles.

Outfitters
Fishing: A growing number of foreign sportfishers are now plying the waters off Shipstern in search of barracuda, grouper, snook, yellowtail, and particularly tarpon. We recommend Sarteneja-based fisherman, boatman, and guide, **Fernando Alamilla**, 4-32085, for a memorable and likely productive fishing trip in Chetumal Bay or nearby waters.

Tours: An adventurous option for visitors is a guided boat tour of the recently established **Bacalar Chico National Park and Marine Reserve** across the bay near Ambergris Caye. Local guide **Alamilla**—who is said to have come up with the idea for the park—can take you there. If he's unavailable, contact restaurant owner **Israel Cruz**, 4-32031 for other options. Tours to nearby areas, including night trips into the jungle to observe some of the forest's unusual nocturnal wildlife, can be arranged in Sarteneja by simply asking around town for a knowledgeable guide.

Getting There
An all-weather paved and gravel road to Sarteneja branches off the Northern Highway at a main bridge over the New River just north of the main market in Orange Walk Town. The trip by car takes about 1 hour from Orange Walk Town and around 2 hours from Belize City, in good weather. **Venus**, 2-73354, has an afternoon bus to Sarteneja from Belize City, with a stop in Orange Walk Town en route. A Sarteneja bus from Belize City's Magazine Road station runs several times in the afternoon with a 20-minute layover in Orange Walk.

As of 1997, the main difficulty with bus transportation to and from Sarteneja—besides the fact that frequent stops along the way make the trip rather long—is that all return buses from Sarteneja depart around 3:30 or 4 a.m. One option is to hire a boat (most operators charge $75 for the one-way transport) from Sarteneja to Corozal, thus avoiding the bleary-eyed Sarteneja bus departure.

Where to Stay and Eat in Sarteneja

Cruz's Restaurant, on the waterfront; 4-32031. Owner Israel Cruz has information on the village's (limited) lodging and boat charter options.

Diani's Hotel, on the main street; $15; 4-22154. Eleven simple rooms and a restaurant.

The Last Resort, in the seaside village of Copper Bank. Ten modest bungalows, a campground, and restaurant, accessible by boat or vehicle for $35 pickup charge. No phone.

ORANGE WALK DISTRICT

Slightly inland from Corozal but still influenced by the breezy, balmy coastal climate, Orange Walk District is one of the least-visited areas in Belize. This is because most accessible parts of Orange Walk are cultivated in the form of sugarcane and citrus plantations, as well as Mennonite farms of corn, sorghum, rice, and vegetables. The coast is swampy and much of the pristine wildlife habitat is either privately owned or inaccessible.

Worthy destinations here include the **Río Bravo Conservation Area**, Mayan ruins of **Lamanai** (described in Chapter 10, Archaeological Sites), and the **New River Lagoon** (Belize's largest lake). In the far northwest corner of the district is **Aguas Turbias National Park**, which has no services and limited access. For more information about this remote park, which borders wilderness areas in Guatemala and Mexico, contact the Belize Audubon Society.

A good base for visitors is Orange Walk Town, a bustling mercantile center on the banks of the New River. Major roads from here lead in four directions and link the more than 20 villages of the district, consisting mostly of Spanish-speaking Mestizo, English-speaking Creole, and German-speaking Mennonites.

215

ORANGE WALK TOWN

Location: *About 60 miles northwest of Belize City.*
Population: *16,000 (1997 estimate).*
Visitor Information: Try **Caribbean Holidays**, *3-22803, a travel*
agency on Beytias Lane, where you can also book international flights.
Also check with the **Belize Tourist Board**, *(800) 624-0686, and*
Belize Tourism Industry Association, *2-77213.*

Settled largely by refugees from the mid-19th-century Yucatán Caste
War, Orange Walk Town has the badly eroded ruins of two forts,
Mundy and Cairns, that recall the scene of bloody conflicts between
Belizean settlers and the district's earlier occupants, the Icaiche Maya.
These indigenous residents pressed an unsuccessful series of attacks in a
bid to rid the area of intruders. The final battle took place on September
1, 1872. One of the last remnants of this standoff is the old flagpole in
front of the Orange Walk City Hall, site of one of the old British forts.

Before settlement by Mexican Mestizos occurred in the late 1880s,
the Orange Walk District was dominated by loggers for more than a
century. During that time the timber taken from the region was floated
down the New River into Corozal Bay (also called Chetumal Bay).

Now agriculture reigns supreme. Sugar has been the most important crop for many decades (surpassing chicle and corn earlier this
century), and Belizean rum (distilled at the Cuello processing plant
under the "Caribbean" label) is a lucrative market for the cane that is
harvested here. Other cane is rendered into molasses and, of course,
processed sugar. The region is also an important producer of citrus,
papaya, and beef cattle.

The best gift shop in Orange Walk Town is **KU's**, 26 Liberty
Avenue, which sells ceramics, wind chimes, and cotton boxes.

Outfitters

Several local hotels and travel agencies arrange tours to Mayan sites
and boat trips along the district's inland waterways, which are home
to a wide variety of flora and fauna.

To Lamanai: For a recommended trip down the New River to
the Mayan ruin of Lamanai, contact **Jungle River Tours**, 20 Lover's
Lane, 3-22293, fax 3-22749. Brothers **Antonio** and **Herminio**
Novelo are among the best Belizean guides for archaeology as well as
natural history. The Novelos provide a superb day trip of birding on
the New River and sight-seeing at the ruins.

For larger groups interested in an excellent New River/Lamanai trip, we recommend contacting **Maya Mountain Lodge & Tours**, near San Ignacio, 92-2164, fax 92-2029, e-mail *Maya_Mt@btl.net*. Budget travelers may wish to try **Lamanai Maya Tours**, located next to the New River toll-bridge, 3-23839.

    Orchid Tours: If you are interested in seeing 75 of Belize's more than 300 native species of orchids, **Carlos Godoy** offers a tour that will bring you face to face with Belize's national flower, the black orchid—and much more. Godoy greets visitors at a small house on the east side of the northern highway in the village of **Trial Farm,** just north of Orange Walk, 4 Trial Farm Road, 3-22969, and guides them down the New River to see some of the exotic species that thrive in Belize. Operating under a government permit, he gathers and propagates orchids and bromeliads that would otherwise be destroyed by logging and farming. For the serious orchid enthusiast, Godoy can also facilitate the procedures involved in exporting these delicately beautiful flowers. He also runs recommended birding, botany, archaeology, and boat trips on the New River to Lamanai and other destinations.

Getting There

Buses from Belize City to Orange Walk Town run daily at about 1-hour intervals. Check with the **Venus** or **Batty Brothers** bus services for fares and schedules. A private car or express bus can make the trip from Belize City in roughly an hour; local buses take slightly longer. There is frequent service from Chetumal and Corozal Town, and much less frequent connections can be made for Sarteneja and villages en route to the Shipstern Peninsula. All through-buses stop for about 20 minutes in Orange Walk Town, where passengers can buy food and change money. There is no scheduled air service.

Where to Stay in Orange Walk Town

Some hotel locations are very noisy, and be advised that there are at least a dozen rowdy brothels in Orange Walk, fronting as hotels and/or restaurants. Cocaine and marijuana are sometimes sold openly here, despite severe government penalties. Unless you want to risk spending time in a Belize jail, resist the temptation to buy illegal drugs.

Chula Vista Hotel, in the adjacent village of Trial Farm; $20; 3-2365.

D'Victoria, south end of Belize-Corozal Road; $25 and up; 3-22518. Best hotel in town, with 31 rooms, a bar, swimming pool, disco, and other amenities.

Jane's Guest House, Baker at Riverside Streets; $8; 3-22473. Cheap!

Mi Amor, 19 Belize-Corozal Road; $25; 3-22031, fax 3-23462. Our favorite: clean rooms (with fans or air conditioning), private baths.

New River Park, near the New River toll-bridge south of town; $40 and up; 3-23987, with bar and restaurant. Only lodging for visitors at the put-in and take-out for the popular New River/Lamanai ruins trip.

Where to Eat in Orange Walk Town

*Orange Walk has many Chinese restaurants, but get a recommendation from a local before picking one, since Chinese food in Belize is of variable quality. At last report, **Lee's Restaurant**, west of the plaza, was a favorite. Many hotels also serve decent food, notably the **D'Victoria**.*

The Diner, on Clark Street, serves pretty good Belizean and international food at all three mealtimes.

HL's Burgers, downtown. A favorite among locals for American-style fast food.

INDIAN CHURCH

Indian Church is a small village immediately northwest of New River Lagoon and about a mile southwest of the ancient Mayan city of Lamanai (see Archaeological Sites chapter). Although there's not much to see in this impoverished community of mostly Spanish-speaking farmworkers (many of them Guatemalan refugees), there are several places to stay while touring the area.

Where to Stay in Indian Church

Lamanai Outpost Lodge, a 20-minute walk or 10-minute canoe ride from the Lamanai ruins; $100 and up; tel/fax 2-33578, e-mail *lamanai@btl.net*. Overlooking the 28-mile-long New River Lagoon, this impressively landscaped, cabaña-style retreat offers guided canoe tours, swimming, birding, a medicinal plant trail, massages, and even a spotlight "river safari."

Tours to the nearby **Lamanai ruins**, **Mennonite farms**, **Crabcatcher Lagoon**, **Colonial Sugar Mill**, and **Indian Church** are available as part of the lodge's packages. The facility was constructed using largely local materials and labor, in a manner that minimizes negative environmental impact. Among the amenities are a pontoon boat for cruises on the lagoon. A fine restaurant and bar are open to non-guests.

From Belize City the lodge may be reached in about 2.5 hours, by either auto or auto/boat combination. Driving from Orange Walk Town, take Yo Creek Road to San Felipe and turn left for the final 12 miles to Indian Creek.

Other Options

Not visited by the authors are two newer and more modest accommodations in Indian Church: **Doña Blanca's** and the **Gonzalez Guest House** (both 3-23369, community phone).

RÍO BRAVO CONSERVATION & MANAGEMENT AREA/PROGRAMME FOR BELIZE

Location: About 75 miles northwest of Belize City
Size: 229,000 acres
Hours: Open by appointment or prior arrangement only.
Cost: None
Visitor Information: 2-75635 or Box 749, Belize City

A nonprofit group called **Programme for Belize** has, since its formation in 1988, achieved remarkable success in protecting a major portion of the northwest corner of Belize as relatively pristine lowland jungle. Thanks to their intervention, this forest remains one of the largest tracts of undisturbed subtropical habitat in the region. From its inception, the sponsoring group's primary objectives have been to create a model of appropriate economic development and to provide funding for conservation, education, and scientific and management training throughout the country for the lasting preservation of Belize's natural heritage and biological diversity.

In the early 1990s, Programme for Belize acquired 26,892 acres in the Río Bravo area. This purchase connects two blocks of land that, together with other acquisitions, comprise the **Río Bravo Conservation and Management Area**. The Programme has thus converted 229,000 acres into a single unit that facilitates management; assures the future for an extensive, wildlife-rich tract of tropical forest; and secures a vital habitat corridor along Irish Creek. Programme for Belize has raised several million dollars from corporations, foundations, and individuals to purchase and administer these lands, which are surrounded by another 450,000 acres of largely intact forest and savanna.

The government-approved management plan for the Río Bravo Conservation Area allows for the development of low-impact agriculture, forest product propogation and harvesting, and tourism based on natural history and archaeology. (There are at least 60 ancient Mayan sites on Programme for Belize land, including **La Milpa,** third-largest in Belize, where a royal tomb was discovered in 1995.) A fundamental long-term goal for the Río Bravo area is to pay for its conservation through sales revenues derived from its renewable natural resources. Programme for Belize believes lessons learned at Río Bravo will serve as a model for the region.

Private contributors continue to be key to the success of this large-scale conservation project. Through the Massachusetts Audubon Society, contributors are invited to donate $50 to "adopt" an acre of tropical forest, something many schoolchildren have done as class projects throughout the United States and Europe. The Society sends a certificate to donors indicating how many acres the individual or group has helped protect.

Most of the Río Bravo area is a nearly untouched subtropical haven where howler monkeys, spider monkeys, king vultures, gray foxes, more than 80 species of bats, and 110 species of orchids now enjoy a permanent refuge. Some 200 species of trees have been identified here along with all five Belizean species of cat: margay, jaguarundi, jaguar, puma, and ocelot. At least 344 species of birds have been identified as either year-round residents or migrants that frequent the area (out of a total of about 540 species identified to date in Belize).

The Río Bravo Conservation and Management Area covers the northeastern part of the Petén wilderness, a large, biogeographically distinct expanse that extends into southeastern Mexico and northern Guatemala. Nick Brokaw and Elizabeth Mallory have identified more than a dozen floristically distinct vegetation types in Río Bravo, including upland forest, palm forest, swamp forest, riparian forest, and second-growth. A research facility has been strategically located for easy access to these distinct habitat types. It provides training in archaeology, forest management, and ecology while concurrently monitoring the reserve's biological diversity. Outreach to villages surrounding the Rio Bravo area has involved local residents in chicle harvesting, handicraft production (culminating in sales to foreign visitors), guide training, and environmental education.

Chan Chich Lodge

Visitors wishing to see Programme for Belize lands are best off staying in Chan Chich Lodge, near the settlement of Gallon Jug. This is a luxurious and expensive group of elegant cabañas set in the middle of a Classic-period Mayan ruin, which was being systematically looted before Chan Chich's construction. The accommodations were built for Belizean businessman Barry Bowen (the lodge's owner) by Tom and Josie Harding, who now manage Chan Chich. Ancient Mayan monuments border the resort's grounds on all sides, giving the impression that the cabañas are original Mayan homes. Their plush interiors, however, give a different impression. Polished and oiled woodwork, colorful drapes, a full bar, and gourmet dining combine to make Chan Chich one of Belize's finest lodges. Indeed, it has received a top ranking in at least one world survey of jungle accommodations.

By prior arrangement with Programme for Belize, 2-75616, tourists can visit the nearby La Milpa and Laguna Seca archaeological sites. Other activities include superb birding (Chan Chich means "little bird" in Mayan), jungle walks, canoeing, horseback riding, guided nature/archaeology tours, and simply relaxing. An escarpment west of Gallon Jug is a favorite of king vultures, white hawks, crested eagles, and other raptors.

Getting There

Unless the weather has been dry, it is best to fly to Gallon Jug rather than attempt the rough dirt roads into the area. **Javier's Flying Service**, 2-45332, flies here three times each week, charging around $100 round-trip from Belize City.

It is possible to drive to Gallon Jug by turning north at Orange Walk Village (not to be confused with Orange Walk Town) near Belmopan and following the Iguana Creek Bridge Road or by turning south from just west of Blue Creek Village near the Mexican border. The Blue Creek road is shorter (about 4 hours from Belize City) and better maintained than the Iguana Creek route. Be sure to inquire locally about road conditions, especially when the ground is wet. A four-wheel-drive vehicle is recommended during any season.

Where to Stay near Río Bravo

Chan Chich Lodge, near Gallon Jug; $140 and up; in Belize 2-75634 or fax 2-76961, in U.S. (800) 343-8009, e-mail *info@ chanchich.com*. Book well in advance, as rooms fill up quickly. (For more information, see text above)

Kevin Schafer

Chan Chich Lodge occupies the plaza of an ancient Mayan city.

Río Bravo Research Station, near Gallon Jug; $70 and up; 2-75616, fax 2-75635. Nature trails and tour guides, as well as educational facilities. Day visits cost about $20 and include a 2-hour tour.

BELIZE DISTRICT (NORTH)

The Belize District is located in the heart of the country, roughly midway between the northern and southern borders, along the Caribbean coast. Most of its population is concentrated in Belize City, with a few farming and fishing communities in the north and west. Most visitors pass through Belize City (covered in chapter 5) at some point during their stay, but many are oblivious to the district's outlying attractions, each an easy day trip from the country's biggest-ed population center. In contrast to the congestion of Belize City, there are virtually pristine nature reserves and protected areas less than an hour's drive away that teem with wildlife. For the traveler interested in an "up close and personal" look at Belize's exotic flora and fauna, the rural Belize District offers several must-see destinations. (For information on destinations in the southern portion of the Belize District, see chapter 9, Southern Belize.)

CROOKED TREE WILDLIFE SANCTUARY

Location: *33 miles northwest of Belize City and 3.5 miles west of the Northern Highway.*
Size: *3,000 acres.*
Hours: *Dawn to dusk daily.*
Fees: *$4*

Crooked Tree Wildlife Sanctuary, a wetlands area on the northern boundary of the Belize District, is one of Belize's prime destinations for nature-lovers. Visitors from temperate-zone countries can easily see more birds in a single day than they are likely to see back home in a year. Even before you cross the causeway that connects to the fresh-water island where Crooked Tree Village is located, you are liable to spot the American coot, northern jacana, snail kite, least grebe, white ibis, olivaceous cormorant, and rough-winged swallow. More than 200 different bird species have been recorded within the sanctuary, but the richness and variety of habitats here suggest that many more may be waiting to be "discovered." Mexico Lagoon, Spanish River, and Black Creek are some of the many excellent birding spots within the sanctuary's boundaries.

Not only is the variety of bird life tremendous at the Crooked Tree wetlands, especially later in the dry season (March through May), but the aggregate number of waterfowl is astonishing. Huge flocks of birds congregate here, taking advantage of the area's abundant food resources and safety as a resting spot on spring migration routes. The rare jabiru stork nests within the sanctuary, and the limpkin, with its black body and strange-looking neck, is another frequently observed inhabitant. You may delight in identifying an elegant green-backed heron, sleek blue-winged teal, multicolored black-bellied whistling duck, ungainly wood stork, or brilliant Yucatán jay.

For the best experience while visiting the Crooked Tree Sanctuary, we recommend contacting manager **Donald Tillett** through the **Belize Audubon Society** in Belize City, 2-35004. We also recommend that you allow at least a full day to visit Crooked Tree, and that you hire a local guide.

Conservation at Crooked Tree

Crooked Tree Wildlife Sanctuary was established voluntarily by the area's 750 residents in November 1984, with substantial financial assistance from the Wild Wings Foundation. But local residents and the Belize Audubon Society have made the most significant contributions to the success of Crooked Tree. During the early years, Audubon's management was accomplished exclusively by dedicated volunteers, mostly community residents.

"Crooked Tree Village has always been interested in conservation," village chairman Rudy Crawford pointed out in a 1997 interview. "When the Audubon Society came around, the idea of a wildlife sanctuary readily appealed to residents." Crawford believes that the subsequent sanctuary has succeeded because, first, the village is a family-oriented community with a long-standing conservation ethic, and second, Crooked Tree has responded to the demand for tourism-related businesses. While tourism is the village's fastest-growing industry, its mostly Creole residents still engage in subsistence farming, livestock raising, and fishing.

Visiting Crooked Tree by Land

The sanctuary's well-maintained visitors center and museum are situated at the beginning of the long causeway, which—together with the entrance road—runs between Crooked Tree Village and the paved Northern Highway linking Orange Walk and Belize City. You are required to check in at the visitors center before you explore the sanctuary ($4 entrance fee). If it is not open when you arrive or if the village bus fails to stop here, most Crooked Tree lodges will collect this fee and pass it on to the sanctuary. You may also pay on your way out.

The visitors center itself has informative displays that are designed to test your knowledge of the sanctuary's birds, as well as of the general natural history of the area. The sanctuary manager and wardens are happy to answer questions and assist in your explorations.

Several marked nature trails emanate from the village and, in fact, the majority begin simply as the meandering unpaved roads of Crooked Tree. One is appropriately named after the northern jacana, a delicate bird that flashes yellow wings when it flies and is light enough to tread confidently on water hyacinth as it forages for small fish and mollusks. Other trails bear the names of birds you may also see in the course of a half-day stroll through this tranquil village: **Trogon**, **Limpkin**, and **Kiskadee**. During our 1997 walk on these same trails we spotted a little blue heron, a blue-gray tanager, a vermillion flycatcher, several tropical mockingbirds, and a great kiskadee.

Crooked Tree's managers are planning to build a ¾-mile-long boardwalk connecting the sanctuary's Spanish Creek to the ancient Mayan ruin of Chau Hiix, which has been under excavation in recent

Crooked Tree Wildlife Sanctuary's visitors' center and museum

years. **Chau Hiix** is the Mayan name for one of Belize's lesser-known cats, the jaguarundi.

David W. Steadman of New York's State Museum in Albany has compiled an impressive list of birds seen near Chau Hiix, including the crested guan, great curassow, ocellated turkey, bare-throated tiger-heron, azure-crowned hummingbird, scissor-tailed flycatcher, white-crowned parrot, yellow-lored parrot and rufous-browed peppershrike. These are only a fraction of some 235 species he recorded in the Crooked Tree area.

Visiting Crooked Tree By Boat

We recommend hiring a boat and guide for a half-day trip south from Northern Lagoon, to Spanish Creek, up Black Creek, and to the Chau Hiix ruin. Fortunate visitors also have an opportunity to see black howler monkeys, iguanas, and Morelet's crocodiles, among other fauna. We also suggest that, if necessary, you remind your guide to periodically kill the engine and float quietly among the birds and other animals. Boat trips can be arranged through either the highly recommended **Paradise Inn** (see below) or **Jex Tours**, 21-2032. The latter is located on the main entrance road to Crooked Tree Village.

Your Donation at Work

Donations to Crooked Tree Wildlife Sanctuary are encouraged and graciously accepted. This financial assistance keeps both the sanctuary and the Belize Audubon Society going. The Crooked Tree Wildlife Sanctuary turns over 10 percent of its entrance fees to the community for local service projects.

By supporting the sanctuary through the Belize Audubon Society, visitors can be part of current management activities, such as an annual May census of jabiru storks—one of the world's largest birds—accomplished with the help of local guides who volunteer their time and expertise. Belize Audubon is also carrying out a study of jabiru nesting behavior, the fledglings' growth period, and preparations for leaving the nest of this flagship species at a couple of targeted nests within Crooked Tree.

The greatest concentration of wildlife can be seen during April and May, when the water level is lowest. Mornings and evenings are peak activity times year-round. As you travel along the shore of Crooked Tree Lagoon, you will see Belize's largest contiguous stand of remaining logwood. Crooked Tree, one of the first non-Mayan villages founded in Belize's interior, was established because of its accessibility to this commercially valuable timber, still exported in small amounts. On the way to **Spanish Creek** your guide can also point out distinctively shaped bullet trees. These trees are used to make boat gunwales; its wood is so hard that bullets cannot penetrate it. Along this portion of the shoreline, the master of hovering flight, the snail kite, searches for the abundant land snails that cling to logwood stems. The captured snails leave behind white, multichambered clusters of eggs, thus replenishing the food chain.

Calabash Pond, Revenge Lagoon, Western Lagoon, Southern

Lagoon, and **Jones Lagoon** are other wild places encompassed by the Crooked Tree Wildlife Sanctuary. Crocodiles and several turtle species can be found here, as well as howler monkeys and iguanas.

Outfitters
Visitors with a serious interest in birds should arrange their trips through **Rudy Crawford,** 2-12084, fax 2-32579, or **International Expeditions,** (800) 633-4734. Crawford arranges personalized birding trips as well as horseback and carriage rides; guided trips to the Altun Ha Maya Ruins, Lamanai, and the Community Baboon Sanctuary. Rudy's son Glen is an experienced naturalist who can help visitors add new species to their checklists. Most outfitters will charge $70 and up for a guided 4-hour boat excursion, conducted on horseback if the water is low.

Travel agencies and lodges in other parts of Belize also arrange sanctuary tours. For larger groups interested in an excellent tour of Crooked Tree—and/or the nearby New River/Lamanai trip—we recommend **Maya Mountain Tours,** 92-2164, fax 92-2029, e-mail *Maya_Mt@btl.net,* and **G&W Holiday Tours,** 25-2461 or 2-33417, e-mail *gholiday@btl.net.*

Getting There
Buses from Belize City run daily to Crooked Tree. Check with **Venus,** 2-73354, or **Batty Brothers,** 2-72025, for fares and schedules. A Crooked Tree community bus, 21-2032, also runs between the village and Belize City—the advantage is that it comes all the way into Crooked Tree Village instead of dropping you on the Northern Highway. Taxis can also be arranged from Belize City or Orange Walk Town during the dry season. Expect to pay $75 and up for a round-trip from Belize City, slightly less for a round-trip from Orange Walk.

Where to Stay and Eat near Crooked Tree
Bird's Eye View Lodge, on the water; $55, with breakfast; 2-32040 or fax 2-24869. Also has a dorm facility with shared bath ($10) and accommodates tent campers for $5 per night.

Chau Hiix Lodge, accessible by 40-minute boat ride up the Spanish River; rates start at $575 for three nights, including all meals and other services; 2-73787 or (800) 735-9520. Small and unique; operated by American expatriate Robert Brooks. Caters specifically to birders.

Cashew Festival

Since 1993, a Cashew Festival has been held at Crooked Tree during the first weekend each May. This celebration exemplifies community-driven conservation diversified through music, dancing, feasting, storytelling, demonstrations of cabaña thatching, folklore performances, and, of course, demonstrations of the harvesting and preparation of local cashew nuts. The festival affords a rare opportunity to learn first-hand about the variety of cultures in Belize: rich Creole, Garifuna, Maya, and Mestizo traditions. Crooked Tree residents even select a Cashew Queen.

"By harvesting, processing, and selling cashews, residents have established a livelihood that enhances their natural environment, an achievement which they feel is cause for celebration," explained Tom Grasse of International Expeditions, an Alabama-based tour company that helped start the successful festival. Cashew trees are native to the area, and their delicious fruits are used to make wine, jam, and sandwich spreads; they are sold in raw and roasted form as well. Mango products are also made and sold from the enormous, centuries-old trees that dominate the village. During the festival, birding trips often yield excellent results, since low water levels in the sanctuary's lagoons concentrate and draw in vast numbers of waterbirds.

Maruba Resort, outside the village of Maruba on the Old Northern Highway; $180, includes meals; 3-22199. This self-styled "spa" has drawn many complaints from travelers about alleged poor service, high prices, and substandard facilities.

Paradise Inn, on the main lagoon; $50; 2-12084, fax 2-32579. Comfortable bungalow accommodations and good restaurant, first-rate tours. Ideal for birders. Recommended.

Pretty See Jungle Ranch, at Mile 39 on the Western Highway; $85 including meals; 31-2005. Pretty See Jungle Ranch is a lush 1,360-acre property with a large, thatched cabaña equipped with a Jacuzzi bathtub and private deck. Besides the on-site restaurant/bar, amenities include river and lagoon fishing, horse and nature trails, birding, and even a crocodile pool! Regional day trips easily arranged.

A ripe nut dangles from a much-larger cashew fruit in Crooked Tree Village.

International Expeditions

Other Options

Other overnight accommodations are provided in homes of Crooked Tree Village residents. These are simple, inexpensive bed-and-breakfast arrangements in a rural atmosphere. Try **Rhaburn's Room**, **Molly's Room**, or **Mary Tillett** (each about $15). While none of these families had a private telephone as of early 1997, visitors can make advance arrangements by calling Crooked Tree Village's community phones, 2-44101 or 2-44333.

Where to Eat in Crooked Tree Village

Meals, which may include local fish, are available at local hotels and homestays, as well as the **Corner's Inn Restaurant**, in the center of the village.

THE COMMUNITY BABOON SANCTUARY

Location: *About 30 miles northwest of Belize City.*
Size: *18 square miles.*
Hours: *8 a.m. to 5 p.m. daily.*
Fees: *Visitors must check in first at the museum and pay a $5 registration fee, which supports management of the sanctuary.*
Visitor Information: *Community phone, 21-2001 or Jungle Drift Lodge 14-9578.*

The Community Baboon Sanctuary, an easy day trip from Belize City, is one of the best places in Central America to get a close-up view of a monkey in its natural habitat. In Belize, black howler monkeys are called baboons; therefore, the "baboons" being protected at this unusual private sanctuary have little in common with their African cousins of the same name. They are, in fact, an endangered species found only in a few lowland forests from southern Mexico to Honduras (most howlers in Central America are golden mantled, not black).

Howlers—so named because adults (mostly males) emit a distinctive raspy, guttural growl that can be heard for a mile or more—are threatened in much of their rapidly shrinking range. The protected colony that can be seen by visitors on an easy day trip from Belize City numbered about 1,500 monkeys in mid-1997, and these troops make up one of the few healthy-sized populations in the region. And thanks to an innovative management scheme, the size of this group is increasing all the time.

What is most unusual about the Community Baboon Sanctuary and its interpretive museum is the fact that the project is voluntary, entirely reliant on the goodwill of interested subsistence farmers who work the lands immediately adjacent to the broadleaf jungle the howlers prefer. Although the sanctuary is both praised and admired by government officials, it is completely dependent on private lands and funding for its survival. Since the sanctuary's creation in 1985, the area's mostly Creole landowners have responded generously to the international scientific community's concern about the primate's dwindling habitat.

The current situation is a dramatic change from only 15 years ago, when the howler monkeys were frequent targets of Mayan Indians and Guatemalan refugees (who killed them for meat), as well as unscrupulous poachers (who sold them as pets). Both practices are now against the law throughout Belize, where only licensed hunters are allowed to legally stalk wild game. The howlers have also been hard hit over the years by hurricanes, which destroy their treetop aeries, and by yellow fever, the same deadly disease that affects humans. But more significantly, they have been victims of deforestation. As arboreal vegetarians partial to wild fruits and flower blossoms, they need a thick forest canopy to survive.

In order to preserve this critical habitat along the Belize River, about 25 miles inland from the Caribbean, about 140 farmers have agreed to maintain corridors of tall broadleaf jungle along the borders of their fields, to refrain from cutting such favored food trees as strangler fig, breadnut, amate fig, trumpet, and hogplum, and to protect

Traditional Creole house, Crooked Tree Village

66-foot-wide strips of forest along the riverbank. These practices not only ensure that the monkeys will have a safe place to live, eat, and raise their families, but also help reduce erosion, minimize river siltation, and allow more rapid regeneration of the soil after slash-and-burn agricultural clearing. The smaller plots of cultivated land are now hedged in by thick vegetation that will quickly invade the area once it loses its productivity.

Organizers began asking their neighbors to sign conservation pledges in the mid-1980s, and so far very few farmers have refused or withdrawn from the sanctuary. Locals have found that visitors help them out financially by hiring guides, patronizing businesses, and overnighting at homestays. The women of the village often prepare hot meals for tourists, and the men take foreigners on leisurely walking or canoe trips to observe the flora and fauna along the meandering Belize River. Also, several small stores sell food and drinks.

Like Bermudian Landing, eight other villages within the sanctuary are gradually attracting tourism business. They bear the sort of colorful names encountered all over Belize, including **Double Head Cabbage, Scotland Halfmoon,** and **Flowers Bank**. The howler population has expanded vigorously within all nine participating communities.

"When I came here, I immediately noticed that the monkeys had a strong, viable community and the forest was relatively intact," recalls Robert Horwich, a zoologist from the University of Wisconsin who helped develop the plan for a voluntary wildlife sanctuary operated by local residents. "People seemed to genuinely like the howlers," notes Horwich, who still comes every spring to study the animals. "It struck me as logical to ask villagers to help preserve this habitat."

Backed by a coalition that includes the Zoological Society of Greater Milwaukee, World Wildlife Fund, Lincoln Park Zoological Society, International Primate Protection League, and Belize Audubon, the Community Baboon Sanctuary now embraces a 20-mile stretch of Belize River watershed. The Sanctuary has a full-time manager, and the helpful Iola Joseph keeps the museum and visitor registration center open daily. Many of the sanctuary's visitors are Belizean schoolchildren, most of whom had never seen a wild monkey before their visits. (Since almost all of the reserve is on private land, visitors are asked not to stray from designated trails without a guide.) The natural history museum here is one of the best in Belize.

Howler monkey troops, ranging from four to eight individuals, seem to appreciate the efforts being made to save them. "There isn't a competition between howlers and people," observed local guide Camille Young. He added that residents and area farmers on both sides of the Belize River accept and even embrace the presence of the monkeys, and this makes the sanctuary's villages some of Belize's best places to learn about Creole culture and to experience community-driven conservation firsthand.

Although the primates still spend most of their lives high in the tree boughs, they sometimes scamper closer to the ground within a few feet of lucky observers. The howlers' loud rasping call is used most often by dominant males to mark territorial boundaries between the troops they lead. The monkeys, including females, also howl when waking up in the morning and before going to sleep at night. Some locals swear that they also become vocal before the onset of big rainstorms. Howlers can reach up to four feet in length and weigh about 50 pounds when full-grown. Like other monkeys, they nurse their young, use their hands during feeding, and communicate by human-like facial expressions.

The black howler is one of only two species of primate found in Belize. Its primate cousin, the spider monkey, prefers wetter forests at higher elevations. In the entire world, there are only five other species of howler.

Starting in 1992, the monkey colony along the Belize River was

*The Dawsons are one of several Creole families that operate
homestays for visitors to the Community Baboon Sanctuary.*

strong enough to withstand the transfer of some of its members to the
Cockscomb Basin Wildlife Sanctuary, about 80 miles to the south. A
1996 reintroduction program was successful in transferring eight
howlers to the Macal River near San Ignacio. In these locations, a
combination of hurricane damage, hunting, and yellow fever had
wiped out indigenous troops during the past 30 years.

Another side benefit of the Community Baboon Sanctuary's success is the resurgence of other wildlife in the protected area, including
the much-hunted iguana. Nearly 200 bird species have been identified, along with dozens of different mammals, including jaguars,
ocelots, paca, and deer. Researchers are also coming here to study the
highly endangered Central American river turtle, which is now holding its own within the sanctuary's borders.

The sanctuary is the winter home of many migratory birds that
fly to Belize every year from as far away as Canada. Colorful year-
round residents include parakeets, parrots, toucans, and tanagers.
Though modified by centuries of selective logging and small-scale
farming, local forests still support about 100 tree species and scores
of varieties of vines, shrubs, flowers, and herbs. Many wild orchids
and bromeliads can be seen clinging to the trunks of tall trees.

Help Save the Howlers

Donations to the Community Baboon Sanctuary's tax-deductible endowment fund are welcome. Checks should be made payable to Howlers Forever, Inc. and sent to Robert "Baboon Man" Horwich, RD 1, Box 96, Gays Mills, WI 54631. Donors of $50 or more receive a sanctuary-theme poster by artist Caroline Beckett, along with a quarterly newsletter.

*The book **A Belizean Rain Forest: The Community Baboon Sanctuary** has been written by Robert Horwich and Jon Lyon for distribution to Belizean schools and interested individuals. It contains a wealth of information about Belize's flora and fauna, and can be ordered from the Howlers Forever address above for $12, plus $2 postage and handling. For more information, call **Community Conservation Consultants** at (608) 735-4717 or e-mail ccc@mwt.net.*

Outfitters

The sanctuary staff can direct you to reputable local guides. Fees vary and are sometimes negotiable, but expect to pay up to $25 an hour. Guided canoe trips are also available for up to $20 an hour. **Jungle Drift Lodge** offers an affordable, 15-mile Belize River canoe trip, among other excursions. Also try the **M&H Rivercamp** (see below). Because the jungle trails are often overgrown and muddy, rubber boots, long-sleeved shirts, trousers, hats, and insect repellent are advised. Always check with the headquarters and obtain a map before heading out.

Knowledgeable guides can be hired in Bermudian Landing and nearby Flowers Bank for a recommended canoe trip on nearby Mussel Creek. This river and wetland complex boasts a great diversity of waterbirds, flora, and reptiles. Our 1997 half-day guided Mussel Creek tour with Camille Young yielded close encounters with two troops of howler monkeys, a manatee, and over 18 bird species (including a hooded oriole and a pygmy kingfisher).

As of mid-1997, the only direct contact with sanctuary head-

quarters was by two-way radio, which is sometimes unreliable.
It is possible, however, to simply stop at the office, buy a field guide,
tour the sanctuary with one of the nature guides, and arrange a
homestay.

Getting There

The sanctuary can be reached by private car in about an hour from
Belize city via the Northern or Western Highway. From either direction, take the Burrell Boom cut-off and follow the signs to Bermudian
Landing. Taxi fare is about $40 one-way from the international air-
port or Belize City. Note that there are only a few stores and no gasoline stations within 20 miles of the reserve. Specific directions on getting to the sanctuary by car or bus are available from the sanctuary's
office, which can also make arrangements for groups interested in
touring the area, as well as for overnight accommodations.

As of early 1997, **Leonard Russell's orange bus** provided
scheduled service between Belize City and Bermudian Landing,
departing from Cairo Street, near the intersection of Euphrates
Avenue and Orange Street, in Belize City at 12:15 p.m., 4:15 p.m.,
and 4:50 p.m. on weekdays. The bus returns to Belize City around
6 a.m. (about $2 one way). **Jungle Drift Lodge** picks up visitors at
the International Airport for about $40.

Where to Stay and Eat near Community Baboon Sanctuary

Jungle Drift Lodge, only 400 yards from sanctuary headquarters;
$25 and up; 14-9578, fax 27-8160. Bungalows (with and without pri-
vate bath); a two-story family cabaña; and shower, kitchen, and
restroom facilities. Camping is allowed (for a small fee), and canoes
can be rented.

M & H Rivercamp & Ranch, in Scotland Halfmoon, just north of
Bermudian Landing, Box 961, Belize City; $20 for cabañas, $4 for
campsites. Meals, river tours, and horseback rides available at reasonable rates. No phone.

Russell's Place, a pleasant bar and restaurant on the riverbank in
Bermudian Landing.

Other Options

A few informal and decidedly rustic homestay bed-and-breakfasts
(about $15 a night) are available in the sanctuary and outlying vil-

lages. We suggest calling the Bermudian Landing community phone, 21-2001, and arranging your stay in advance. We particularly recommend the **Geraldine Joseph family, Alexandra Young,** or **Helen Herrera.** Meals usually cost about $5 each. Camping is available on the museum grounds (usually for a small fee) by arrangement with the sanctuary's staff. RVs are allowed to park overnight next to the museum, also for a fee.

BURDON CREEK NATURE RESERVE

This mangrove and wetland ecosystem west of Belize City was protected in 1992 primarily as buffer against flooding and water pollution in the country's largest city. Urban sprawl threatens the area and tourist services are minimal. Inquire locally about boat trips along the natural and man-made canals that transect the reserve, and offer wonderful birding opportunities.

Several local tour operators offer excursions through Burdon Creek as part of their package trips to the Northern and Southern Lagoons en route to Gales Point. Inquire at the Belize Audubon Society, 2-35004, for more information.

THE BELIZE ZOO

Location: About 30 miles west of Belize City and 14 miles east of Belmopan on the Western Highway.
Size: About 1,600 acres, with 28 acres devoted to animal exhibits.
Hours: Daily, except major holidays, from 9 a.m. to 4:30 p.m.
Fees: Admission to the zoo in 1997 was $7.50 for adults and $3.75 for kids. Zoo memberships (starting at $25 for individuals) are available by writing to Box 474, Belize City. Supporters receive a newsletter about the Belize Zoo's ongoing activities, and contributions are used for conservation education.

One place where you are guaranteed to see native animals in their natural surroundings is the Belize Zoo. Most of us regard zoos as anything but a natural setting; however, as you know by now, things are done a bit differently in Belize. Instead of placing its animals behind bars in severe-looking cages, the zoo's managers have created an intimate, cozy atmosphere by putting their creatures in chicken-wire enclosures beneath a shady forest canopy. Each of the animals is referred to by its own pet name—from Sugar, the purring ocelot, to Rambo, the keel-billed toucan—and all are well cared for.

The philosophy that permeates the zoo's exhibits is one of respect for all wildlife. Hand-lettered signs remind visitors that practices such as poaching and live capturing continue to threaten the survival of several unusual Belizean natives, including cats, macaws, and monkeys. In fact, many of the creatures held by the zoo are "pets" that were abandoned by their owners after they became too big, too wild, or too unwanted. Guides at the zoo are involved in a conservation outreach program designed to teach visiting Belizean schoolchildren (as many as 300 a day) about the natural wonders of their homeland.

At least 100 animals can be seen here, including the endangered scarlet macaw, jaguarundi, margay, jaguar, black howler monkey anteater, and great curassow. The assembly includes some 18 mammal species, 12 bird species, six reptile species, and several species of fish and insects. All live within areas that are as large and as close to their natural habitats as could be achieved by the zoo personnel.

Not long ago the zoo added two jabiru storks to its family. The jabiru is a flagship species for conservation in Belize. It has a huge slightly upturned bill, a bright red neck collar, stands up to five feet tall, and has up to a nine-foot wing span. While it is possible to see this magnificent bird in the wild in Belize, a visit to the zoo is worth it just to be sure you see a jabiru.

Such Belize-loving celebrities as actor Harrison Ford and musician/author Jimmy Buffett made donations that enabled the zoo to move to expanded quarters in late 1991. A large waterbird aviary was opened in 1993, and future plans include a butterfly exhibit, a freshwater aquarium (with advice from the famous Monterey Bay Aquarium), and a reptile center. A biologist by training, director Sharon Matola works constantly to improve the zoo and has taken advantage of Belize's thawed relations with Guatemala to acquire both a jaguarundi and a male spotted jaguar (named C.T. Katun) from that country. In 1996 a female black jaguar (Ellen) came to the zoo from Texas, where she was born in captivity.

The zoo is an easy day trip from Belize City, as well as a good diversion en route to the Cayo District, Caracol, or Tikal.

Visitor Information and Services

There is no restaurant but a vendor sells snacks. The zoo operates a Deluxe Guest House on its property, where you can arrange tours of both the zoo and the education center. To contact the zoo during business hours, call 8-13004.

How It All Started

The Belize Zoo was founded in 1983 by its director, Sharon Matola, after wildlife filmmaker Richard Foster's budget was cut and he was left with 17 animal "stars" that had no movies to appear in and no place to go. Matola, Foster's assistant, was told to disband the troupe of jaguars, coatimundis, peccaries, pumas, and other animals that had been trained to "act" in nature documentaries.

Instead of abandoning them, Matola boldly painted a description in front of each creature's enclosure and put a "Belize Zoo" sign in front of the compound. Success came only after she devoted thousands of hours to finding ways to feed and house the animals, while at the same time cultivating countrywide interest in their well being. Matola's credo is manifest in the way she has always run the zoo: public awareness and education are critical to wildlife conservation. Her nature-oriented storybooks have become favorites of Belizean children who, in turn, are convincing their parents to adopt lifestyles that protect the country's environment. The

There are many biting and stinging insects (uncaged) at the zoo and a good repellent is strongly advised. We recommend keeping your arms, legs, and ankles covered while observing the animals, since wildlife tends to attract flying creatures that pester humans.

Getting There

The Belize Zoo is clearly marked on the Western Highway at about Mile 29. Going west from Belize City, you will encounter the Tropical Education Center first on your left, then the old zoo site on your right, and finally the well-marked new zoo a little farther along, also on the right. The visitor center, which includes an excellent gift shop and playground, is about one-half mile off the highway on a dirt access road. Taxis are easy to arrange from either Belize City or Belmopan. Many package tours also stop at the site. Expect to pay $70 and up for *zoo's educational programs have made a noticeable impact on prevailing attitudes toward native flora and fauna.*

A particular favorite is April, the Baird's tapir, which thrives at the zoo. Throughout Central America, this large but shy creature is in trouble; its future survival as a species is threatened by habitat destruction and hunting. The tapir, a relative of the hippo, is the largest of all native Belizean land animals, and adults may weigh up to 650 pounds. The zoo's female tapir has endeared herself to thousands of Belizean children, who have watched her frolic in her jungle paddock. April's pairing with a new mate reflects one of the major goals of the zoo—to give every animal a partner and thus ensure that future visitors will always be able to view each species at close range. Captive breeding programs for creatures such as the citreoline trogon and iguana have also been carried out at the Belize Zoo. For iguanas, the Belize Zoo has collaborated and shared information with other captive rearing programs like the successful one at Pook's Hill Lodge adjacent to the Tapir Mountain Nature Reserve.

a round-trip. Buses from Belize City run virtually every hour throughout the day (less often on weekends and holidays). Check with **Venus**, 2-73354, or **Batty**, 2-72025, for current fares and schedules. Drivers will pick you up and drop you off on the highway.

BELIZE TROPICAL EDUCATION CENTER

Across the highway from the zoo is the Tropical Education Center, a sort of nature school for Belizeans operated by University College of Belize. The property was previously owned by Dora Weyer, one of the first conservation leaders in Belize and a founding member of the Belize Audubon Society. Weyer retired to the U.S. in 1989, and one of her conservation legacies is this 140-acre complex, with self-guided nature trails, visitors dormitory, lecture rooms, a library, and offices for its Belizean staff. Schoolchildren and college students who have never been in the bush come here to spend a few days surrounded by nature. Solar energy powers the entire compound. Visiting educators are welcome to visit.

MONKEY BAY WILDLIFE SANCTUARY AND NATIONAL PARK

Location: 31.5 miles west of Belize City on the Western Highway.
Size: 1,070 acres.
Visitor Information: Contact Monkey Bay Wildlife Sanctuary at P.O. Box 187, Belmopan; 23180, fax 8-23235, e-mail mbay@pobox.com.
Fees, Services, and Lodging: There is no admission fee to the sanctuary, and overnight visitors are welcome ($5–$8).

Located along the Western Highway about 2 miles west of the Belize Zoo is Monkey Bay Wildlife Sanctuary. Adjacent to the property, across the Sibun River, is Monkey Bay National Park. Monkey Bay Wildlife Sanctuary was established on Earth Day 1990 as a privately owned and operated protected area of mostly pine savanna, cohune palm, and tropical gallery forest, along with freshwater wetlands, lagoons, and river habitat. Monkey Bay National Park was legally established in May 1994 and, together with the Sanctuary, comprises a 3,300-acre wildlands corridor spanning the Sibun River watershed.

Among the sanctuary's attractions are rolling jungle ridges, two miles of nature trails, and Sibun River frontage that includes a secluded bathing beach. The field research station and other facilities—all open to visitors—are part of an evolving permaculture that integrates solar power systems, rainwater catchment, a biogas-generating latrine, reforestation, composting, and raised-bed organic gardens.

Observers at Monkey Bay have reported seeing at least 220 species of birds within the reserve's borders, including parrots, toucans, crakes, trogons, flycatchers, and cuckoos. Other wildlife sightings include jaguar, puma, deer, peccary, crocodile, iguana, tapir, and coatimundi.

Visitors might wonder why this particular name was chosen, since no monkey species are listed among the native denizens. Monkey Bay retains a name given to the property at a time when black howler and white-faced spider monkeys frequented this stretch of the Sibun River. A hurricane in 1978 destroyed the tall forest canopy habitat that these monkeys favor, forcing the remaining animals to retreat to the limestone karst hills visible on the southern

Richard Mahler

A tour guide displays a boa constrictor at the Belize Zoo.

horizon. However, on two occasions in 1993, monkeys were again observed near the sanctuary.

"We hope that with more recovery time, the forest here will again host these two endangered species," the sanctuary's co-founder, Matthew Miller, told us. "In order to enhance this recovery process and provide an attractive and well-protected habitat, the Monkey Bay staff has actively been planting tropical forest trees, including mahogany, sapodilla, balsam, baboon cap, and velvet apple."

Several North American high school and university groups participate in Monkey Bay's experiential-based learning programs, and visitation from Japan is also increasing. Belizean students visit Monkey Bay regularly for guided walking tours of the tropical forest. On neighboring lands, they learn about human impacts on the environment, including river mining and monoculture agribusiness.

A large wooden field research station at Monkey Bay (dubbed "The Barn") accommodates a classroom, library, and natural-history display room. It doubles as accommodations for visiting researchers and teachers. Monkey Bay is considered an ideal location for earth literacy and natural-history education programs, and offers homestay opportunities with families in rural villages for visitors with a thirst for cultural immersion.

A Mayan Presence

An archaeological team from Boston University has been investigating ancient Mayan cultural remains within the Middle Sibun watershed, which includes Monkey Bay. In 1997, experts found evidence of three main settlement areas along the Sibun River, including a site with a raised plaza and ceremonial stone structure that has been named **Pech Tun Ha.** *It's believed that the Maya who lived here were gathering cacao beans for export to offshore trade settlements via the Sibun River. Pech Tun Ha is a 1-hour hike from Monkey Bay's research station and local guides are available for walking tours. Of special interest in a nearby lagoon is a colony of boat-billed herons, a notoriously shy bird associated with coastal wetlands.*

Children of all ages are encouraged to visit, as well as education and/or research groups. The managers of this facility are in the process of establishing a school of sustainable living in the Ozark Mountains of Arkansas.

Camping and Nature Programs

Monkey Bay is one of the few places in Belize where visitors are not only allowed, but encouraged to camp. Tenters are offered one of several large, thatch-covered, raised camping platforms in the savanna. Nature hiking, photography, picnicking, swimming, canoeing, and self-directed study are also available.

Monkey Bay has an "open door" policy, but it's best to call or write ahead. There are campsites ($5) and basic rooms ($8), plus a kitchen where you can get an inexpensive meal.

Getting There

The well-marked dirt entrance road is about 45 minutes by car west of Belize City. Local buses will drop you off at the junction, and you can walk the short distance to the field station. A taxi from the international airport costs about $50.

Where to Stay and Eat in Monkey Bay

J.B.'s Kool Spot, within walking distance of Monkey Bay; 1-49311. This American-owned restaurant and bar (with live music on weekends) is popular with Belizeans and foreigners since it's founding years ago by a colorful (and since departed) expatriate named J.B. The current owners also rent basic cottages for about $13 a night.

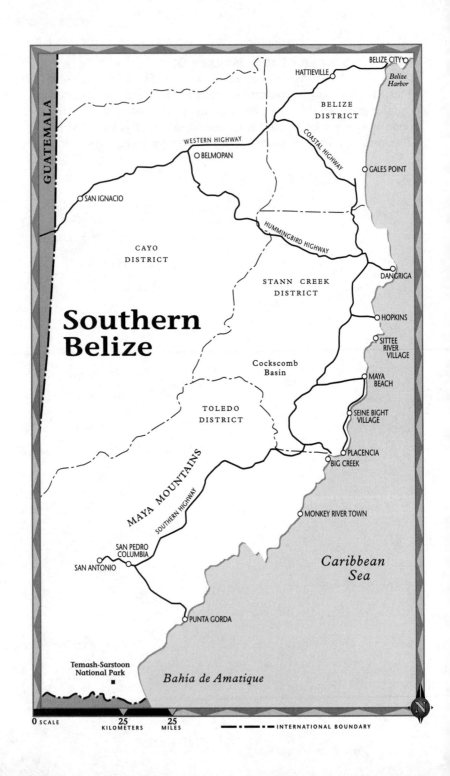

SOUTHERN BELIZE

9

BELIZE, STANN CREEK, AND TOLEDO DISTRICTS

Long neglected as a tourist destination, the south of Belize is coming into its own among visitors looking for smaller crowds and more pristine outdoor attractions. Not long ago this part of the country was difficult to travel in and offered few amenities or services for those passing through. Today it boasts a solid infrastructure of hotels, restaurants, tour companies, and related services. True, conditions are sometimes a bit rough, but the area's natural beauty more than compensates for an occasional dusty road or lumpy mattress.

Southern Belize has special appeal for those interested in natural history and indigenous cultures. Offshore are seldom-visited cayes and atolls, plus some of the country's best places to dive, snorkel, fish, sail, kayak, windsurf, and study marine life. We particularly recommend areas near South Water, Coco Plum, Stuart, and Curlew Cayes off Dangriga; Colson, Pompion, and Ranguana Cayes east of Placencia. For those who can make the distant trip, Glover's Reef is one of the finest sites in the entire Caribbean for snorkeling, diving, and sportfishing.

Birders will be rewarded with many opportunities in this ecologically diverse region. Our favorites include Man o' War Caye (a nesting area for the magnificent frigatebird) and both the Sittee and Monkey Rivers (wide jungle waterways with many side channels and lagoons). The Cockscomb Basin is an excellent place to see

245

flora and fauna of the tropical forest—including the occasional jaguar—as are the various protected areas of the Toledo District. In swampy areas and beaches along the coast, you may see such wildlife rarities as the Caribbean manatee, hawksbill turtle, and jabiru stork.

For those eager to learn more about the rich cultural mosaic of Belize, the southern districts are fascinating places to explore. As elsewhere in this tiny country, ancient Mayan ruins abound. At Lubaantun, for example, you can see how a mortarless building technique yielded temples more reminiscent of Peru's Machu Picchu than the Classic Maya. Near Dangriga, the Mayflower site is tucked amid thundering jungle waterfalls. Among and around all such ruins, the contemporary Kekchí and Mopan Maya live 20th-century lives amidst the ghosts of their ancestors.

Southern Belize is also the heartland of the Garinagu (Garifuna) culture, representing a unique blend of African, Caribbean Indian, and European traditions. Many of the region's Garifuna music, dance, and religious rituals are openly shared with outsiders—an experience not to be missed. Other communities are equally proud of their Creole, Guatemalan, East Indian, Chinese, and Lebanese ethnicities. At least one village boasts of its pirate origins, while another traces its roots to immigrant Confederates who sought refuge after the U.S. Civil War!

We're approaching the region from the north in this chapter, and heading sequentially toward the south.

BELIZE DISTRICT (SOUTH)

Much of the Belize District's southern area is uninhabitable swamp, with limited access and few attractions for the foreign visitor. One important exception is the village of Gales Point, and the brackish lagoons that lie between this Creole community and Belize City. (For more information on the Belize District, see chapter 8, The North.)

GALES POINT
Location: About 20 miles south of Belize City
Population: 350 (1997 estimate)
Visitor Information: Gales Point Bed & Breakfast Association, 5-22087

Gales Point offers visitors a refreshing dose of rural Creole hospitality, some unparalleled nature attractions, and a great example of community conservation. A limestone escarpment on the northwest bank of this lagoon is the site of several caves that can be explored as a guided side trip. We also recommend a boat ride up **Soldier Creek** (also called Plantation Creek), which has abundant orchids and other exotic plants.

The name Gales Point describes both a community and a narrow 2-mile finger of land jutting up from the south end of Southern Lagoon. The village was founded by logwood cutters many years before Belize became a British colony and is inhabited mostly by their descendants—Creole farmers and fishers.

The lagoons and estuaries near the village are full of marine life and represent the region's most important stronghold for the Caribbean manatee. This is, in fact, the species' largest breeding ground. The reticent mammal, which looks something like a tuskless walrus, feeds on the thick grasses and other vegetation found in the lagoons. Manatees are distant cousins of elephants and often weigh over 200 pounds. Local guides are happy to take tourists to feeding areas where the gentle beasts are seen most often. The nearest feeding ground is only a few hundred yards from the village.

Gales Point Manatee Community Sanctuary

In 1992, residents created the Gales Point Manatee Community Sanctuary to protect the manatee and develop conservation-oriented tourism. This cooperative venture pools local skills and resources to provide boat trips, wildlife observation, sportfishing, and cave exploration. About 15 residents provide boating and/or guiding services, while some 20 homes are open to overnight visitors. Other residents produce and sell handcrafted items such as tie-tie baskets and hats. Cashew and berry wines, as well as mango and cashew preserves, are made and sold locally. This visitor-related activity is designed to enhance Gales Point's base of subsistence agriculture without jeopardizing its rural character and beautiful environment.

Local conservation efforts have focused on protecting endangered hawksbill turtles, since nearby **Manatee Bar** is one of the few known nesting beaches for this endangered marine reptile. With assistance and training from Wisconsin-based Community Conservation Consultants, area residents have installed wire mesh to protect nesting hawksbill turtles from predation near Manatee

Bar. As a result of this community-driven work, as many as 12,000 turtle hatchlings make it into the Caribbean in a single year.

With the help of international organizations, residents have installed buoys and signs to help protect the manatee from power-boats, planted disease-resistant coconuts, and installed improved sanitation facilities to maintain water quality in the lagoon. These seemingly small efforts are critically important to the long-term viability of small communities like Gales Point, which have staked much of their future on the growth of natural-history tourism.

Gales Point Outfitters
Tour operators arranging trips to the area include the recommended **Jal's Travel** in Belize City, **Pelican Beach Resort** in Dangriga, and **Ricardo's Beach Huts** on Bluefield Range Caye. Scheduled boats from Belize City depart from **Blackline Marina**, on Haulover Creek, 2-44145. Competent local boatmen include **Allen "Passo" Andrewin** and his brother, **Mose**.

Getting There
Gales Point is at the culmination of a dead end, 15-mile dirt road that stretches through swampy terrain north of Dangriga. Although it is not difficult to reach by road, the village is more frequently approached from the north by boat via the Southern Lagoon. Small crafts can make an inland passage from Belize City via the Burdon Canal Nature Reserve and Boom's Creek in an hour or two, navigating a bewildering maze of waterways. An alternative is heading directly south along the Inner Channel in open water and then following a narrow estuary across Manatee Bar into Southern Lagoon, also called Manatee Lagoon.

Where to Stay and Eat in Gales Point
The Gales Point Bed and Breakfast Association, 5-22087 (community telephone). Offers simple homestays ($15 and up) and tent sites ($5), with no advance reservations required. There is one small store in the village for basic supplies.

Manatee Lodge, at the tip of Gales Point; $150, meals included; 2-12040 or (800) 334-7942. Co-owned by the Hidden Valley Inn and oriented toward sportfishing, the Manatee was remodeled in 1993. The 12-room facility offers boat tours to manatee breathing holes and a turtle nesting beach. Foreign anglers are attracted to the sever-

Learning Experiences

For an unusual cultural experience, visitors may wish to enroll in the recommended **Maroon Creole Drum School**, operated by Emmeth Young, one of the best drummers in Belize. Young offers camping on his land (meals included for a modest fee) and charges $5 an hour for expert instruction in making and playing the traditional Belizean drum. You'll learn a good deal about Creole history and culture in the process. Advance reservations are preferred, since Young performs in Belize and other countries from time to time. Write him c/o Gales Point Village, Belize District, Belize.

Oceanic Society Expeditions offers trips in which participants are asked to help researchers assess the distribution and habitat use of resident manatees, and to protect hawksbill turtle hatchlings (on Manatee Bar beach) from predators. Guests stay in village guest quarters and campsites, taking meals with local residents. The nine-day expedition includes a trip to nearby Ben Lomond Cave.

Boat excursions from Gales Point take visitors past small cayes in the various bodies of water—particularly **Bird Island** in Northern Lagoon—that are important breeding grounds for iguanas, crocodiles, and waterbirds, including the white ibis and boat-billed heron. Aquatic flora and fauna are abundant here, since a tremendous amount of nutrient-rich runoff flows through these passageways en route from the Maya Mountains to the Caribbean. The tangled mangrove forest along the shoreline is an important nursery for young shrimp, crabs, lobster, and fish. Wildlife in the area includes deer, peccary, armadillo, gibnut, and various cats.

al species of game fish that abound in these waters, notably tarpon, snook, and cubera.

STANN CREEK DISTRICT

Southern Belize has only two distinct political jurisdictions: the citrus-rich Stann Creek District immediately below Belize City and Belmopan, and the lightly-populated Toledo District south of the Cockscomb Basin and Monkey River.

The easiest ways to reach the region's far-flung communities are by air (fast but relatively expensive) or boat (slower but cheaper). Other alternatives are private car or scheduled bus service. Daily buses ply the bumpy Hummingbird Highway that links Belmopan with Dangriga, continuing from Dangriga to Hopkins, Placencia, and Punta Gorda via the mostly unpaved Southern Highway. (A gravel-surfaced shortcut, known variously as the Lagoon Road or the Manatee Cutoff, heads directly south from the Western Highway near Hattieville and rejoins the Hummingbird Highway a few miles west of Dangriga.)

Although paved, the 52-mile Hummingbird Highway is scenic and uncrowded, but notorious for its bone-jarring potholes and muddy bogs. Allow at least 2 hours for the drive from Belmopan to Dangriga. Along the way, you may wish to stop at Caves Branch, Blue Hole National Park, Five Blues Lake National Park, and/or St. Herman's Cave. There are also a couple of large citrus plantations where tours are available by appointment.

Midway along the Hummingbird Highway you enter the Stann Creek District, the more populous of Belize's two southern districts. Although Dangriga is Stann Creek's administrative center and largest town, several nearby communities are well worth a visit.

DANGRIGA
Location: 32 miles south of Belize City.
Population: 11,000 (1997 estimate).
*Visitor Information: Sight-seeing suggestions are cheerfully dispensed at **PJ's Gift Shop** and new **River Café** (which also has a pay telephone). Airplane tickets can be purchased at **The Treasure Chest**, which doubles as a souvenir store and travel agency, or at **Pelican Beach Resort**.*

The name of this busy port town was changed from Stann Creek to Dangriga some years ago to honor the proud Garifuna (also called

Garinagu) people who make up the majority of its residents. The name means "standing water" in the Garifuna language, a reference to the brackish pools that form when the rain-swollen Stann Creek overflows its banks on its way through town toward the Caribbean. Dangriga was settled by European traders and farmers in the late 17th century, then became an important shipping center during colonial times.

Services
In addition to a post office and BTL office, there are three banks, several gas stations, and many grocery stores.

Things to Do in Dangriga
Melinda's Historical Museum, next to PJ's Gift Shop at 21 St. Vincent, 5-22266, displays Garifuna artifacts such as mahogany *badaya* bowls used in making cassava flour. The museum is open ($1 admission) from 9 a.m. to noon and 2 to 5 p.m. daily except Thursday and Sunday.

Punta rock can be widely heard on holidays or at one of several nightclubs: the **Wrong House, Son-Flo Disco,** and **Dada's Disco.**

Richard Mahler

Main street in Dangriga, the largest town in the Stann Creek district

Outfitters

Because of its location and services, Dangriga is a good base for
excursions to the southern cayes and atolls or to the nearby Gales
Point Manatee Community Sanctuary, the Cockscomb Basin
Wildlife Sanctuary, the Garifuna village of Hopkins, the Mayflower
Mayan site, and the modern Mopan village of Maya Center. Most of
the hotels can arrange guided trips or you can contact **Rodney's
Tours**, 5-22294, at the airstrip. **Pelican Beach Resort** arranges
highly recommended day trips, that are open to non-guests. Expect
to pay $45 to $75 for most day trips. Be prepared to pay about $50
for a snorkel trip, slightly more for fishing or diving trips.

The Garifuna

The Garifuna (otherwise known as Black Caribs) are a distinct and
close-knit ethnic group of mixed West African and Caribbean Indian
ancestry who arrived here in great numbers beginning in 1823, after
civil unrest along the Honduran coast drove them north. The
Garifuna legacy begins many years earlier, when shipwrecked slaves
escaped to the British-controlled islands of Dominica and St. Vincent
in the West Indies. These West Africans (mostly males) intermingled
with aboriginal Red and Yellow Caribs (mostly females), sharing
many customs and rituals as the years progressed. Their mixed-blood
offspring developed impressive skills in fishing, farming, and hunting.
They also remained staunchly independent, refusing to bargain with
the Europeans who tried to subdue them and take over their lands.
For several decades they successfully resisted colonization.

Finally, in 1795, the Garifuna chief was killed by an English soldier's bullet. His conquered people were rounded up and shipped off
to the Bay Islands off Honduras, at that time a part of the British
empire. Over the next 25 years, small bands of restless Garifuna wan-
dered up and down the Central American coast, establishing settlements in what are now Belize, Guatemala, Costa Rica, and
Nicaragua, as well as mainland Honduras.

On November 19, 1823, a large group of Garifuna from the Bay
Islands joined about 200 others who had settled at the mouth of Stann
Creek some 20 years earlier. A Puritan trading post had been built on
this spot, and the traders called these structures "stands." Over time,
this term was locally corrupted into "stann," and the revised name
stuck. The date of the mass Garifuna landing, November 19, is still
celebrated loudly and enthusiastically each year on Settlement Day, a

Belizean national holiday. Because Dangriga is one of the largest Garifuna communities among the many now spread along the coastline of four Central American nations and the Windward Islands, a visit here provides an excellent opportunity to learn about a fascinating Afro-Indian subculture that is little known outside Belize.

Settlement Day

The ideal time to come is on Settlement Day and, if possible, the week leading up to the November 19 celebration. Hundreds of Garifuna from throughout Central America and the Caribbean flock to Dangriga for the festivities. The streets are alive with dancing, drumming, and impromptu music concerts. (At other times of the year, several nightclubs and hotels offer indigenous music and dancing.) Feasts and celebrations last far into the night.

Scheduled events include a reenactment of the arrival of Garifuna leader Alejo Beni and his boats from Honduras, plus a fascinating religious ceremony in the Catholic church which combines European, African, and Carib rituals. (Most Garifuna—like most Belizeans—now consider themselves at least nominally Roman Catholic.) The ceremonies are performed in the Garifuna language, a unique mixture of West Indian, West African, Spanish, English, and French words. Interestingly, there is a long-standing gender difference in grammar, with males following more of an African pattern and females following more of a Carib pattern.

On Settlement Day, Dangriga's main street (St. Vincent) is closed to traffic so that musicians, costumed dancers, and revelers can parade with abandon, carnival-style.

Garifuna Culture

It is in arts and crafts that the Garifuna particularly excel. Their drum-makers are revered for a perceived ability to induce the obeah magic through the music of their instruments. Dances are performed to the beat of three drums of varying sizes, traditionally made out of carved cedar trees or sea turtle shells. Some of the younger Garifuna have incorporated these ceremonial instruments into reggae and calypso musical stylings, giving birth to a distinctive style of music known as "punta rock," now popular throughout Belize. More traditional groups that perform in Dangriga include the Turtle Shell Band and Warribaggabagga Dancers. The chance to see a performance by these or any other Garifuna dance troupe should not be missed. Fortunately, many of the region's upscale hotels schedule visits by

The Garifuna Religion

Many outsiders, including Belize's early white colonists, have contended that the traditional spiritual beliefs of the Garifuna are akin to Haitian-style voodoo, which is only partially true. The central focus of Garifuna religion is the mysterious and magical practice of obeah, originating in West African traditions brought to the Americas during the 1600s. Through the use of fetishes, amulets, symbols, and rituals, followers believe spiritual energy—both positive and negative—can be directed to individuals. Indigo crosses on the foreheads of small children, for example, keep away bad spirits, and the blood of sacrificed animals (usually chickens or pigs) wards off evil. A small cloth doll stuffed with black feathers, called a puchinga, *may be buried under an enemy's doorstep to bring about tribulation, illness, or even death.*

At the opposite end of the spectrum, a kind of white-magic healing ceremony and feast of reconciliation known as the dugu *is also used to rid the community of evil spirits. This ritual, rarely observed by outsiders, takes place over the course of*

these dance groups once or twice each week. The local office of Island Expeditions (5-23328) presents free Garifuna drumming weekend nights at Len's Cool Spot in the Sabal Neighborhood.

In the weeks leading up to Christmas, garishly painted and masked John-Canoe (also spelled Yan-kunu) dancers perform in the streets for gifts of rum, money, and candy. The dance is performed only by men, who imitate the strident movements of a white slave master. At midnight on Christmas Eve, the town echoes with the deep blast of several hundred hollow conch shells blown simultaneously.

These vivid community rituals are favored subjects of several well-known Garifuna painters, residents of Dangriga, whose studios are open to visitors. Most have adopted a kind of folk-primitive realism recalling the simple artwork of Haiti. The paintings emphasize bright colors, flat perspective, and festive or rural themes.

a full week and is accompanied by animal sacrifices, hypnotic music, and nonstop dancing.

Through the intercession of a byei, *or shaman, the Garifuna believe they can communicate with the dead, thereby tapping into the power of their ancestors. Some expatriate Belizeans come from as far as the U.S. and Canada to attend special ceremonies, called* gubida, *whereby contact with the deceased is used to cure sick relatives or avenge evildoings.*

Practitioners of obeah believe they can make contact with the dead whenever certain ceremonies are performed with the accompaniment of monotonous, trance-like drumming, singing, and dancing. These performances may last all night, or even days on end, without a break. Ethnomusicologists have noted that the rhythms and call-and-response patterns of the Garifuna are very similar to those used in the religious and social rituals of West Africa, where they presumably originated. The practice of playing with sticks is also African. If you'd like to learn more, ask a Dangriga tour guide to show you around the city, which boasts a "Garifuna cathedral" among other culture-specific attractions.

Benjamin Nicholas—probably the most famous Belizean artist—welcomes visitors at his 27 Oak Street gallery, near the Bonefish Hotel. Nicholas' paintings are on display in public buildings and offices throughout Belize. Accomplished drum-maker **Austin Rodriguez** has a similar studio at 32 Tubroos Street, where he sells baskets, masks, and reed purses, as well as fine drums (priced from $50 and up). Next door to Rodriguez is a boatbuilder who carves dories out of a single tree trunk. **PJ's Gift Shop**, 21 St. Vincent, and **The Treasure Shop**, 64 Commerce Street, are recommended for smaller handicrafts.

Garifuna Cuisine
While visiting Dangriga, try to sample some traditional Garifuna cuisine, which vaguely resembles the "soul food" of the American South.

Home-brewed cashew wine and "local dynamite" (a mixture of raw coconut milk and Belizean rum) are popular lubricants, along with chicory-flavored coffee.

Endless varieties of cassava bread—all delicious—can be purchased from the smiling housewives who make them from scratch. The preparation of such breads, using a flour made from potato-like cassava roots that have been strained and ground by hand, is a time-honored Garifuna practice which takes at least two days to accomplish. The cassava's importance to local people cannot be overstated, and in fact the word "Garifuna" roughly translates as "the cassava-eating people." Other popular dishes are *hudut*, masked plantain (also called "plantain fu-fu"), and boiled fish in coconut sauce (known as *sere*). Not to be missed are the sweet oranges and grape-fruits grown on nearby citrus plantations and in backyard gardens.

Getting There

Several bus companies, notably the **Z-Line**, 5-22211, have daily departures to and from Dangriga via the Hummingbird and Southern highways. The Z-Line depot is at the south end of Dangriga, at the intersection of St. Vincent and Havana Streets. Other buses pick up passengers downtown near the Stann Creek Bridge. The 1997 fare from Belize City was about $5 (allow about 3 hours). Dangriga is

Richard Mahler

Dangriga schoolchildren listen attentively to their teacher.

about 35 miles by boat from Belize City, 105 miles via the Hummingbird Highway (through Belmopan), or 70 miles via the Lagoon Road Cutoff. (As of mid-1997, buses were operating irregularly on the latter route.)

Maya Airlines has scheduled flights several times daily to Dangriga from Belize City's international and municipal airports. In 1997 the fare was $41 from the former, $28 from the latter. The airstrip is at the northern end of Dangriga, next to the Pelican Beach Resort.

Where to Stay in Dangriga

Accommodations on Glover's Reef and Tobacco and South Water Cayes, along with the research stations on Carrie Bow and Wee Wee cayes, are easily reached by chartered boat from Dangriga. Inquire among the water taxi operators whose boats are docked near where North Stann Creek enters the sea.

The Hub Guest House, next to the bus stop at the river; $18; 5-23389, with restaurant and bar. Good source of travel information.

Jungle Huts Motel, on Ecumenical Drive next to North Stann Creek; $30-$48; 5-22142 or 5-23166. Cabaña-style, private baths (with hot water) and cable TV in some rooms. Recommended.

Pal's Guest House, south of the bridge near Havana Canal; $22 with bath, $16 without; 5-22095. Clean and comfortable seafront rooms with fans and cable TV.

Pelican Beach Resort, north end of town on Pelican Beach, next to airstrip; $80-$150; 5-22044, fax 5-22570, e-mail *pelicanbeach@alt.net,* Web site *http://www.belizenet.com/pelican.html.* Our favorite, this is the only full-service resort in town, with a fine restaurant and bar. A two-story wooden colonial building (renovated in 1996) with high ceilings and a wide veranda. Friendly, well-informed staff arranges trips to the **Cockscomb Basin, Mayan ruins, Gales Point, Sittee River, Hopkins,** and the barrier reef. Local tours of the town of Dangriga and nearby citrus plantations are also available.

Owned by members of the Bowman clan, a pioneering British colonial family that has contributed much to the Belize conservation movement. Your hosts are Belize Audubon board member Therese Bowman Rath and her American husband, nature photographer Tony Rath, whose photographs and videotapes are on sale here. Tony's slide shows at the Pelican are not to be missed.

Riverside Hotel, on St. Vincent Street at the river bridge; $20; 5-22168, shared baths, no hot water, clean rooms adjoining a large common area.

Other Options
A few campsites on the beach can be rented from Mr. Williams or Mr. Sue about a mile south of Dangriga in an area known as Commerce Bight.

Where to Eat in Dangriga
Bonefish Hotel, 15 Mahogany Road. A runner-up for best restaurant, with fresh seafood a specialty.

Burger King, at the Commerce/Street Vincent St. Bridge. No relation to the international franchise. Serves standard Belizean fare and OK breakfasts.

New River Café, on the riverfront downtown. Helpful tourist information center, a departure point for boat trips to the cayes, and a great place to meet local guides. Also known for its delicious daily specials. Serves vegetarian dishes.

Pelican Beach Resort, north of town. Has the best selection, though rather overpriced. Makes a point of including a Garifuna dish in each evening's meal.

Richie's Creole Diner, on Commerce near the police station. Giant, delicious, Belizean breakfasts served with born-again Christianity.

The Ship's Mate, on Stann Creek in the center of town, next to the bus terminal. A classic fisherman's diner and hangout.

Starlight, north end of Commerce Street. The best of a motley lot of Chinese cafés.

MELINDA FARM
Location: No. 1 Stann Creek Valley Farm Road, west of Dangriga.
Hours: Open to visitors by appointment.
Visitor Information: Call 5-22080, fax 5-22299, or arrange a tour

*through the **Pelican Beach Resort** in Dangriga. In the U.S., products can be ordered by calling (305) 477-2616. When ordering hot sauce, be sure to specify low, medium, or high "heat levels."*

A pleasant excursion from Dangriga is to the 400-acre Melinda Farm, located in the foothills of the Maya Mountains. This plantation is the home of Marie Sharp's (formerly Melinda's) Hot Pepper Sauce, a fiery condiment made from the habañero chili pepper. (Products sold under the Melinda's label are now manufactured and distributed by a Costa Rican competitor.) Praised by connoisseurs as nature's hottest pepper, the tiny habañero is native to the Yucatán peninsula, which technically includes Belize.

Marie and Jerry Sharp began making their pepper sauce atop a kitchen stove in 1983, and now it is one of Belize's most popular exports, gracing tables throughout the world. Their farm also produces oranges, Surinam cherries, papayas, mangos, guavas, pineapples, and passion fruit, most of which are used in the Sharps' extensive line of dried fruits, chutneys, jams, and jellies. The cottage-style factory relies on recipes personally developed by Marie and tested on discriminating Belizean palates.

HOPKINS
Location: *8 miles south of Dangriga.*
Population: *1,100 (1997 estimate).*
Visitor Information: *52-2033 (community phone).*

Situated on the sandy, palm-shaded inlet of a small bay south of Dangriga, Hopkins is a relaxed Garifuna fishing village. It can easily be reached by private boat or by following a 4-mile unpaved road from the Southern Highway. This route crosses a marshy landscape that is particularly rich in bird life. Even the majestic jabiru stork has been sighted here, so keep a sharp eye out as you head for the village.

In Hopkins, life is simple and unhurried. People walk everywhere, using sandy paths that parallel the beach. There was no electricity or TV here until 1992, and running water is a recent innovation. Most residents subsist on small-scale fishing and farming. Women still tend the family garden plots and sing together as they weave red baskets or grate cassava roots on wooden slats. The men hand-carve their dugout canoes and weave fishnets out of hemp cloth. Children chase each other on the broad beach and splash about in the aquamarine water.

At the end of each day, the fishers of Hopkins haul their brightly painted dories beneath the coconut palms and join their families for the evening meal inside one-room houses, many of traditional thatch-and-pole construction. Homes are clustered together, with marvelous views of a gently curving bay to the east and misty jungle mountains to the west. Happily, this is one of the few remaining Garifuna villages where the old customs and language not only survive, but are embraced daily.

At night, you may want to take in the Ayumahani Band, which performs often at the Laru Beya Bar. There are several grocery stores in Hopkins, a BTL office, and a post office.

Outfitters

The best all-around outfitter in the area is the recommended **Jaguar Reef Jungle Lodge** (see below). For diving trips, contact **Second Nature Divers**, next to Jaguar Reef. Two-tank dives cost about $65 in 1997.

Many tour operators will gladly make an excursion to the village when traveling to or from either the **Cockscomb Basin Wildlife Sanctuary** or the **Possum Point Biological Station** (both are easy day trips from Hopkins). Better yet, take the quick boat ride from Dangriga with one of the locals, setting out from the Stann Creek bridge. En route you can often arrange accommodations with the boatman, since everyone in Hopkins knows everyone else.

Getting There

Getting to Hopkins usually involves an inexpensive, 30-minute bus ride from Dangriga or Placencia via the **Z-Line**. If the daily schedule isn't convenient, try hopping aboard one of the daily supply trucks heading south from downtown Dangriga at 2 p.m. or arranging private transportation via the Southern Highway.

Where to Stay and Eat in Hopkins

Caribbean View Hotel, on the north beach; $30; 5-22033. Comfortable and clean.

Hopkins Guest House, on the beach; $25; no phone. Offers canoeing, camping, and rafting.

Hopkins Inn, in the heart of the village, near the school and church; $40; 5-22033. The beach cabañas have tiled bathrooms, private verandahs, refrigerators, and coffeemakers. Breakfast is included in the rate, and the American owners offer fishing, snorkeling, and sight-seeing trips. A catamaran and bicycles are available for rent. Recommended.

Jaguar Reef Jungle Lodge, a few miles south of the village near False Sittee River Point; $120; 92-3452 or (800) 447-2931. By far the most upscale place to stay. This cabaña-style resort sits on one of the finest beaches in Belize and offers such amenities as a gourmet restaurant, well-stocked bar, and daily excursions. The latter include Belizean-guided snorkeling and sailing trips as well as jungle river tours, Mayan ruin tours, and visits to the Cockscomb jaguar sanctuary. Kayaks and mountain bikes are available for guest use at no charge, and there's fine swimming off the Jaguar Reef pier. A dive shop is next door and the lodge itself offers C-Breathe, a modified scuba system for snorkelers. We also recommend a day of loafing in one's hammock, capped by a friendly game of volleyball.

Canadian owner Bruce Foerster, a one-time Arctic helicopter pilot, is constructing a lower-priced, family-oriented bungalow complex, **Jungle Sea Lodge**, down the beach from the main facility that may be open by the time of your visit. Both lodges are designed to minimize damage to the environment and a portion of profits goes to local conservation groups. You can arrange advance pickup at the Dangriga airport or bus station. All facilities and lodging here are highly recommended.

Jungle Jeanie's, north side of village; $15. Offers beach huts, camping, a restaurant, and bar as well as kayak, windsurfer, and canoe rentals. Outhouse and outdoor shower. No phone.

Ransom's Beachside Garden, on the beach; $20; 5-22889. A cabaña-style lodge that also rents bicycles and kayaks.

Sandy Beach Lodge, on the south side of the village. Operated by a group of Hopkins women as a tourism cooperative; $18; 5-22033 (community telephone). The rustic lodge's several neotraditional cabañas, built with the assistance of the Barbados-based Caribbean Council of Churches, have been open since 1987 and provide an important source of income. Meals cooked Garifuna-style by local homemakers are available for $5 or less.

Other Options

Houses in Hopkins can also be rented for about $12 a night (try **Mama Nuñez**, a friendly midwife and wonderful cook, who also has campsites). Informal **camping** along the beach costs about $5 a night, with prior consent. Inquire also at **Hopkins Guest House**, **Sand Bar Restaurant** (run by Canadian expatriate Jean Barkman), or **Lebeya Restaurant** (operated by a Swiss woman).

Locals are happy to fire up their oil-burning stoves to make meals for casual and overnight visitors, often including fresh fish, rice, beans, citrus fruit, coconut, and the ubiquitous cassava bread.

SITTEE RIVER AND POSSUM POINT BIOLOGICAL RESEARCH STATION

Location: *2 miles up the Sittee River from the Caribbean.*
Size: *About 50 acres.*
Hours and Fees: *Visitation is by prior arrangement only.*
Visitor Information: *52-2888 or General Delivery, Sittee River Village.*

About 5 miles south of Hopkins, on the banks of the wide, sinuous Sittee River, is Possum Point Biological Research Station. The 50-acre nature reserve is owned by Paul and Mary Shave, American expatriates who lease government-owned Wee Wee Caye (9 miles east) for use as a marine laboratory and education center. With a local Belizean family, the couple also oversees **Bocatura Bank Campground**, a 4-acre plot about a mile downriver from Possum Point. Although these operations cater primarily to natural-history study groups, individuals and small groups of kayakers, fishers, and birders can be accommodated on a space-available, reservation-only basis.

The Sittee is one of the biggest and most important rivers in southern Belize, and a trip up this watercourse is highly recommended. Birders can expect to see flycatchers, herons, egrets, woodpeckers, kingfishers, orioles, tanagers, parrots, and toucans along the lower reaches of the river. Its sediment-rich waters are also teeming with fish. There are several side channels that lead to wetlands and lagoons with even more flora and fauna. If you're lucky, you may see dolphins and manatees near the mouth of the river, and crocodiles and turtles upstream.

The Possum Point research station enjoys a lush setting, surrounded by broadleaf forest at a sharp bend in the river. It is named after the many opossums found here when the lab and surrounding cottages were being built in what was then thick bush. Wildlife still abounds, and birders will be especially rewarded—Possum Point has well over 100 species of "yard birds." The call of the jaguar can sometimes be heard as the cat passes through the property at night. Possum Point and Wee Wee Caye embrace studies in coral reef ecology, botany, herpetology, entomology, ornithology, and mammalogy, as well as general tropical biology.

The ruins of the 19th-century **Serdon Sugar Mill** are preserved as a park not far from the village on the road to the Southern Highway. You'll notice how the jungle has quickly reclaimed some impressive machinery, including the rusty hulk of a steam engine.

A few miles south of Sittee River along the Caribbean coast, **Sapodilla Lagoon** has an abundance of orchids and water birds. Boat trips can be arranged from Possum Point to these destinations and **Boom Creek**, a jungle tributary of the Sittee River. You can also navigate a hand-dug canal to **Anderson Lagoon**, which eventually opens on the Caribbean Sea.

Where to Stay and Eat near Possum Point

Toucan Sittee Lodge, fronts the Sittee River, Sittee River village; 5-22006 (community phone). Bungalow style, rents bicycles and canoes.

Wee Wee Caye, 52-2888, has seven cottages, and the tiny island is a wonderful place to snorkel, swim, and relax. Paul Shave, a marine biologist, has counted 46 species of coral and ten species of crab in the immediate area of Wee Wee Caye. He and his wife have taken great pains to preserve the mangroves, where a number of *wowlas* (Creole for boa constrictors) make their home, feeding on lizards, iguanas, and small birds. Bring plenty of insect repellent, as the tiny island's no-see-ums can be fierce.

COCKSCOMB BASIN WILDLIFE SANCTUARY

Location: About 20 miles southwest of Dangriga.
Size: 102,000 acres.
Fees and Registration: All tourists must register at the entrance booth in Maya Center before heading into the Cockscomb. Fee: $5 per person. Cold drinks and Mayan crafts are sold here; sales benefit Maya Center residents (many of whom were forced to relocate from the basin when it became a park).
Hours: 8 a.m. to 5 p.m. daily, 24-hours for overnight visitors.
Visitor Information: Belize Audubon Society, 2-34987 or 2-35004, or write the sanctuary at Box 90 in Dangriga.

This huge tract of Stann Creek District wilderness—locally referred to as "the Cockscomb"—encompasses a sweeping mountainside basin with an eastern edge that begins about 25 miles southwest of Dangriga. The sanctuary is the world's first-ever reserve established to protect the jaguar, one of the largest and most endangered felines in the Americas. It represents a dynamic evolution of nature's wonders as well as scientific research and conservation prowess.

The Cockscomb is highly recommended as a rewarding destination for the traveler who wants to actively support Belizean conservation while simultaneously reaping its benefits. This is one of the least expensive and most impressive locales for exploring Belize's lush broadleaf tropical forest. Wildlife and plant life are abundant, and the patient visitor will likely see some exotic creatures (and feel tiny winged ones that bite).

Visiting

From the combination registration hut and handicraft shop in the village of Maya Center (a mandatory check-in point located immediately west of the Southern Highway), you will travel about 7 miles on a rough dirt road to reach the Cockscomb visitors center, campground, picnic site, and guest huts. Stay alert—it's a favored trail of many mammals in the sanctuary, including the jaguar.

There is a small parking lot at the sanctuary's headquarters, located at the site of an abandoned lumber camp that is still littered with some of the cages used by zoologist Alan Rabinowitz during his pioneering studies of the jaguar here in the mid-1980s. Nearby are a couple of campgrounds and dormitories available for overnight travelers. There are also basic restrooms for public use.

From here you can take self-guided tours along a number of well-maintained forest trails. Brochures, maps, and signposts help identify the various local tree and plant species, which include colorful orchids and naturally buttressed hardwoods. The pathways vary considerably in their length and ruggedness, so check with the resident manager before heading out. There are some fine swimming holes where you can cool off after (or during) a strenuous trek.

History

The Cockscomb Basin's human history dates back to the ancient Maya, who left a Classic-era ceremonial site called **Kuchil Balum** deep within the forest. Pockets of fertile soil in these granite mountains helped support their milpa agriculture for many generations. The last of these Indians were relocated during the late 1980s in the interest of wildlife habitat preservation.

The Cockscomb's powers of forest regeneration are among its most intriguing qualities. The area's lushness is particularly amazing when you consider the hurricane damage inflicted on many of its tall trees, and the collective insults of slash-and-burn agriculture and tim-ber-cutting over long periods of time. If you hike along the entrance road, you may have trouble distinguishing what is left of an airstrip that was last used in 1984 to facilitate radio tracking during Rabinowitz's jaguar studies. The tropical forest has almost complete-ly taken over what was once a bare piece of land. At one end of the runway a narrow trail leads to a crash site, where a small plane still hangs from the forest canopy. The passengers (Rabinowitz, a pilot, and a cameraman) were only slightly injured.

Back at the visitors center, granitic **Victoria Peak** juts up from the back of the basin. The rocky 3,675-foot summit is capped by dark quartzite. At 4 million years of age, Victoria may be part of the oldest geologic formation in Central America. The tall peak has been a sailors' landmark for centuries and was first scaled by Europeans in 1888.

Outfitters
Nearly all major hotels and travel agencies in the Stann Creek District arrange day trips to the sanctuary. We particularly recom-mend the **Pelican Beach Resort** in Dangriga, **Turtle Inn** in Placencia, and **Jaguar Reef Jungle Lodge** in Hopkins. Such trips usually cost about $70, including transportation, a guide, and lunch.

Cockscomb Hiking Trails
Nowhere else in Belize will you find such an organized system of well-maintained trails. All are wide; most are short and level so do not involve difficult hiking. A complete trail map is posted in front of the visitors center and guest huts as well as at the main entrance road.

The **Ben's Bluff Trail** takes the more ambitious walker on a short but strenuous trek to a ridgetop from which a good part of the entire Cockscomb Basin is visible. This high point has been frequent-ly used to track jaguar via radio telemetry. Picture a researcher slowly sweeping the antennae back and forth across the dense jungle that stretches for miles before her. Or envision the sly cat, resting in the shade of a tall tropical hardwood (probably one you are unwittingly staring at) or stalking its prey along the bank of a rushing stream.

The easier **Waterfall Trail** takes you to a bank of South Stann Creek for a refreshing plunge into clear, swift water. This swimming

How the Sanctuary Came to Be

The most recent—and perhaps the most relevant—sequence of human involvement in the Cockscomb Basin is the effort to protect it. This campaign initially focused on preserving the jaguar, an "indicator species" that can serve as a good index of an ecosystem's health. Where there are large predators like the jaguar, there are likely to be hundreds of smaller animals.

The chain of events leading up to the designation of this area as a permanent wildlife sanctuary began in 1983 with a 2-year jaguar study sponsored by Wildlife Conservation Society, a division of the New York Zoological Society. Living in what is now a restricted-access warden's building, Rabinowitz carried out an intensive field study of the jaguar's range, diet, habits, and general ecology. The U.S. scientist trapped several jaguars, recorded their vital statistics, and fitted them with radio collars. This enabled him to track the felines and thus determine the size and location of their territorial ranges. Rabinowitz lived among the local Maya, employed several of them during his studies, and chronicled his many adventures—with certain embellishments—in an entertaining book entitled Jaguar.

With strong backing from the Wildlife Conservation Society and important in-country political assistance from the Belize Audubon Society, Rabinowitz recommended that the area be set aside for official protection of the jaguar. In late 1984, the Cockscomb Basin was declared a national forest reserve with a "no hunting" clause to protect the cat. The World Wildlife Fund then provided crucial financial assistance to support the basin's status as a protected area. In 1986, after much deliberation about the trade-offs involved, the government declared 3,000 acres of the 108,000-acre area as the Cockscomb Basin Wildlife Sanctuary/Forest Reserve. This made Belize the first country to protect an area specifically for jaguars.

Several Mayan families were required to move to Maya Center, where they have shifted from milpa agriculture to craftwork. Their cooperative sells the work of local artisans at the Maya Center visitors' registration booth. Some of the men transplanted from the sanctuary are employed there as managers, caretakers, and guides. The Maya-descended Belizean now in charge of the reserve, Ernesto Saqui, is one of the best-trained and most knowledgeable nature reserve managers in Central America. You pass his modest home soon after you check in at Maya Center.

In November 1990, the Cockscomb Basin Wildlife Sanctuary was expanded to include 102,000 acres of the Cockscomb Basin. This feat was accomplished through the joint efforts of the Belizean government, Belize Audubon, World Wildlife Fund, and other groups. Management by Belize Audubon has enabled the Cockscomb to emerge as a successful model of ecosystem conservation that integrates low-impact tourism with science. Wildlife habitat and ecosystem fieldwork, such as a 1990 expedition sponsored by the Belize Center for Environmental Studies, is crucial to continued success in Cockscomb management.

hole also has a picnic area beneath a shady tree. Another path heads in a westerly direction from the visitors center, past the camping area and in the direction of **Victoria's Peak**. A side trail on the left, beyond the bamboo thicket, takes you well into the forest, over a narrow suspension bridge, and past a swampy area that is a rewarding observation ground for the Cockscomb's many amphibians (bring repellent to ward off mosquitoes). Yet another trail follows switchbacks up a fairly steep hill, then zigzags down an embankment to end at one of the most gorgeous waterfalls in the sanctuary. Don't be shy—jump in!

Other Services and Reminders

Cockscomb trail maps are available at the headquarters for 50¢, rubber boots may be rented for $1.50, and guides are available and hired on-site. If there are 10 or more people in your party, the Cockscomb staff will present a slide show on the sanctuary for $25. The Belize Audubon Society has produced an in-depth guidebook in association with several individuals who know the sanctuary very well. The recommended *Guide to the Cockscomb Basin Wildlife Sanctuary* is available at the Audubon office in Belize City, at the sanctuary's headquarters, and at various gift shops throughout the country.

There are fine swimming holes in the Cockscomb, so you may wish to bring a swimsuit and towel. Long-sleeved cotton shirts, trousers, sunscreen, and hats are advisable. Tuck your pant legs into your socks to repel ticks and chiggers. Without such preparations, a visit can become very uncomfortable!

The Cats of Cockscomb

Among the main attractions for any visitor, of course, are the cats of Cockscomb. Because of their mostly nocturnal habits, however, the odds are that you will not actually see one. Still, your chances are better here than perhaps anyplace else. Besides embracing one of the highest concentrations of jaguars anywhere in the world (an estimated 30 cats in 1997), the sanctuary is home to many of Belize's four other feline species: ocelots, margays, jaguarundis, and pumas. Best bets for a sighting (early and late in the day) are along the roads and riverbanks of the Cockscomb, where the felines like to hunt. Even fleeting sightings of seldom-seen animals like the puma (which should be reported immediately to the sanctuary manager) are valued by the scientific community.

Jaguars are the third largest of its genus in the world and the most powerful land predator in Central and South America. It is called "tiger" by many Belizeans, *tigre* by local Spanish-speakers, and *balum* by

Trail sign at Cockscomb Basin Wildlife Sanctuary

the Maya. The jaguar's diet includes white-lipped peccaries, armadillos, agoutis, Virginia opossums, iguanas, deer, coatis, and kinkajous. Even if they cannot see the cats, Cockscomb visitors sometimes swear they can feel the presence of these elegant and graceful creatures.

Jaguars are not known to attack humans, except when provoked. It's not as if they are incapable of succeeding in such a foray, however. They are believed to sometimes prey on the Baird's tapir, an endangered relative of the horse (locally called "mountain cow") that may attain 650 pounds when fully grown. You can sometimes see the tapir's tracks in the muddy banks of South Stann Creek. Like the jaguar, the tapir is very shy, so this may be your closest encounter.

Howler Monkeys

During the early 1990s, an exciting collaborative effort succeeded in reintroducing black howler monkeys into their former range within the Cockscomb. Hunting, logging, a yellow-fever epidemic in the 1950s, and devastation by Hurricane Hattie in 1961 are all factors that probably accounted for the local extinction of howlers. According to Rob Horwich and his affiliated organization, Community Conservation

269

Kevin Schafer

Victoria Peak is one of the highest points in the Maya Mountains of interior Belize.

Consultants/Howlers Forever, a total of 63 howler monkeys were relocated into Cockscomb from other parts of Belize from 1992 to 1994. Hermelindo Saqui of **Maya Center**, a Cockscomb warden, diligently tracked the new howler populations for two years, with the help of radio telemetry, to provide crucial progress and distribution information. The survival rate for the relocated howlers was as high as 90 percent.

Other Wildlife

Within minutes of arrival, you will realize why the Cockscomb Basin has a reputation as a birder's paradise. At least 290 species have been recorded here, including the endangered scarlet macaw, chestnut-brown Montezuma oropendola (distinguished by its bright yellow tail), Agami heron, collared aracari, keel-billed toucan, and king vulture. In 1994 the park director and a warden recorded a flock of 10 scarlet macaws flying over Maya Center, at the Cockscomb's entrance. Another group of macaws was spotted a few days later within the sanctuary. Their continuing presence suggests a healthy, well-protected ecosystem.

The basin also provides habitat for many amphibians and reptiles. Observations by a team of Belizean conservation leaders and scientists identified over 35 species that included nine snakes, 12 lizards, 14 amphibians, and a frog known as *Smilisca phaeota*, not previously recorded in Belize. The red-eyed tree frog was also identified, and one of its major breeding areas located. The team estimated that the Cockscomb provides habitat for roughly 70 percent of Belize's non-marine reptiles.

During hikes through the Cockscomb, you may also come across the Central American river otter, a playful mammal that epitomizes an exuberant carpe diem lifestyle. Seeing one frolic or fish in the clear waters of Cockscomb's rivers is a real thrill.

Getting There

The only road in and out of the Cockscomb Basin is well-marked and intersects the Southern Highway (Mile 14) at the village of Maya Center, about 25 miles south of Dangriga. The Cockscomb's headquarters are about 7 miles up the dirt road. Walking there from the Southern Highway is possible, but no services exist en route and it can be very hot and dusty. The road has been improved in recent years but is sometimes impassably muddy during very wet weather, even for those on foot. Several buses pass the entrance each day en

Kevin Schafer

An ocelot prowls the Belize jungle.

Victoria Peak: No Longer Belize's Highest Point

*A 1996 survey determined that **Doyle's Delight**, on the main divide of the Maya Mountains, stands about 13 feet taller than Victoria Peak, the Cockscomb mountain previously believed to be the highest point in Belize. A four-member team from the Youth Environmental Action Group reached the top of Doyle's Delight after a 6-day April ascent and found it to be 1,124 meters (or 3,688 feet) above sea level. Located an air distance of 35 miles southwest of Victoria Peak, the mountain was reported to be "cool, damp, and windy" at its summit and covered with many palms, oaks, and ferns. Reaching the top required an 80-mile Land Rover trip through thick tropical forest, followed by an arduous climb over steep ridges and across treacherous creeks. The first known successful ascent of Doyle's Delight was made by British forces in 1987.*

route from Dangriga or Placencia, check locally for exact times.

Where to Stay and Eat near Dangriga
*Those who do not wish to spend the night at the sanctuary can choose from a variety of accommodations in **Maya Center**, **Dangriga**, **Placencia**, **Sittee River**, and **Independence**. Tours can be arranged from these locations, or you can be dropped off by one of the public buses that pass the entrance (ask to be let off at Maya Center) and walk in.*

Cockscomb Wildlife Sanctuary, rustic, with dorm-style rooms, $10-to-$15 a night. Campsites, $1.50 a night, are available for rent in three campgrounds near the Cockscomb headquarters. Some of the dorm accommodations have electricity (from solar panels), and the newer unit has bathrooms and showers. Dorm reservations are strongly recommended—camping is first-come, first-served—especially from November through April. Reservations are made by contacting the sanctuary (Box 90, Dangriga), the **Belize Audubon Society** office in Belize City (2-34987; Box 1001, Belize City), or the **Pelican Beach Resort** (5-22024) in Dangriga, which maintains radio contact with Cockscomb. There is fresh water, but you must bring your own food and other provisions (a kitchen is available for $2 a day). Showers and outhouses are available at no charge. Remember, insect repellent is a must!

Nu'uk Che'il Cottages and Campground, immediately west of the Maya Center registration office; $20 for basic rooms, $8 for campsites; 5-23131 or 5-22666. Sanctuary manager (and avid conservationist) Ernesto Saqui and his wife, Aurora, operate. The modest Aurora (one of the Cayo District's five famous García sisters) is a Mayan healer who sells herbs, tinctures, salves, coffees, teas, and handicrafts in the **H'men Herbal Center** next to the guest house. For $1.50, Aurora will give you a guided tour of her medicinal herb garden. Nu'uk Che'il Cottages also offers transportation to Cockscomb, Placencia, and other communities. A restaurant and day trip service may have been added by the time of your visit.

SEINE BIGHT AND MAYA BEACH
Location: 4 to 6 miles north of Placencia.
Getting There: Seine Bight and Maya Beach can be reached either via the daily Z-Line bus that runs between Placencia and Dangriga, or by private car or bicycle. Seine Bight is a pleasant 2-hour walk up the beach or dirt road from Placencia. Maya Beach is a couple more miles farther north—the bus stops here, too.
Even smaller and more laid-back than Hopkins, the Garifuna community of Seine Bight (and adjacent village of Maya Beach) is about 30 miles south of Dangriga, and about 10 miles from the Cockscomb turnoff, on the Placencia Peninsula. Until the mid-1980s, the village could be reached only by boat (a 4-hour trip from Dangriga by dugout canoe). Since then, daily buses and private auto traffic have dimmed its status as one of Belize's most isolated coastal communities. Nevertheless, the peninsula still feels like—as one visitor put it—"the island you can drive to." With more than 14 miles of adjacent beaches, this has the look and feel of the idyllic tropical paradise that so many people dream about.
    Seine Bight is said to have been founded by pirates in 1629 and later inhabited by French fishermen deported by the British from

Newfoundland when England took control of northeastern Canada. Like Hopkins, the residents occupy small palm-thatch houses atop high stilts (to keep away insects, rodents, snakes, and floodwaters). Daily duties follow traditional Garifuna patterns: women take care of children and subsistence gardens, while the men hunt and fish. Souvenir hunters will want to check out **Lola's Art**, a gallery featuring local craftwork, at the north end of the village.

Where to Stay and Eat in Seine Bight and Maya Beach

Green Parrot Beach Houses, in Maya Beach; $95; 62-2488, e-mail *greenparot@btl.net*. A Canadian couple opened this complex in 1995, offering A-frame bungalows built by local Mennonites. Recommended especially for those planning long stays or traveling with children. A superb restaurant is on-site. Day trips include snorkeling, diving, Mayan ruins, river tours, and the jaguar preserve, $30 to $65, plus reef fishing at about $200 a day. Our favorite among the numerous area beachfront accommodations. Kitchens in all rooms.

Hotel Seine Bight, in Seine Bight; $100; 62-2491. Aromatherapy massage and gourmet cuisine (16 main course choices each day!) amidst jungle-style ambiance. Some of the two-story suites have their own private balconies; day trips are easily arranged. Luxurious, small, European-run. Drumming and dancing in evening.

Nautical Inn, a short distance north of Seine Bight; $100; tel/fax 62-2310 or (800) 688-0377, e-mail *nautical@btl.net*. Upmarket restaurant, bar, dive shop, canoeing, volleyball, and air-conditioning. Built in a style that recalls New England more than the tropics.

Serenity Resort, south end of Maya Beach; $85; 62-3232. Bungalow-style lodge. Can arrange tours, snorkeling, and diving.

Singing Sands Inn, Maya Beach; $90; 62-3344 or 62-2243. Thatched beach bungalows, dive instruction, bar, and restaurant.

PLACENCIA

Location: Southern tip of Placencia Peninsula, about 30 miles south of Dangriga.
Population: 500 (1997 estimate).
Visitor Information: Belize Tourist Board, (800) 624-0686.

Straddling a sandy, palm-forested spit of land at the tip of an 11-mile-long peninsula, Placencia (also spelled Placentia) is one of the oldest continuously inhabited villages in Belize. Its residents brag that their small settlement was founded by English buccaneers in the early 1600s, and artifacts discovered beneath their homes suggest this was the location of several fierce battles between British and Spanish sailors. There is also ample evidence that Placencia was a Mayan fishing camp long before the Europeans arrived. For the last few centuries, it has been home to a close-knit cluster of mostly Creole families whose ancestry includes Garifuna warriors, freed African slaves, and Scottish pirates. Today the village seems to share only three last names: Leslie, Cabral, and Eiley.

Much of Placencia's charm can be attributed to its scenic locale. A long and gently curving beach—arguably the prettiest in Belize—graces the village's windward side. A few hundred yards opposite this wide strip of talcum-powder sand is Placencia Lagoon, a placid waterway harboring abundant marine life. Since the southernmost tip of the settlement borders the Caribbean, the illusion is that of being on a tropical island, with only the north connected to mainland Belize. Before a dirt road was hacked through the swamps, Placencia might as well have been an island, since the only access was by boat.

One unusual feature of Placencia is its main "street," a concrete sidewalk that stretches for about a mile through the center of town. (Vehicles are relegated to a single unpaved road that skirts the western edge of the village.) Placencia's unhurried ambiance is reminiscent of Caye Caulker, with smiles and friendly exchanges the norm among locals and visitors alike. With a wide range of inexpensive and reasonably good restaurants and bars to choose from, visitors will not lack for food and drink.

Along the 3-mile Placencia beachfront, dozens of guest houses, campgrounds, and lodges snuggle beneath the palm trees. The azure water is surprisingly deep here, and dolphins occasionally frolic close to shore. (The depth and tricky currents can make swimming hazardous at times.) Soothing trade winds usually keep biting insects at bay.

Placencia's one-room post office, a stone's throw from the pier, also dispenses airline and bus tickets. Janice, the friendly and well-informed postmistress, will happily place phone calls and find you a room or camping spot. If you want to charter a boat, reserve a tour, or sample some cassava bread, this is a good place to start.

Outfitters

One of the better boatman and tour guides is **Casey Eiley,** who can take you fishing or on a natural history tour, 6-23161. We also recommend **Samuel Burgess Guide Service**, next to the B&J Restaurant. For trips up the Monkey River, about $40, look for **Dave Dial**, 6-23156, at his Shell Gas Station or Tourist Trap Lodge. **Darrell Garbutt** is our recommended guide, although there are many others who do a fine job. (You may wish to pack your own lunch as restaurant food in Monkey River Town is expensive.)

The tarpon and bonefish opportunities hereabouts are superb. Several resorts and businesses now cater exclusively to anglers, and there are a number of topnotch fishing guides based in Placencia. Among Placencia's better fishing-guide services are **Kingfisher Sports**, 62-3104, which takes its *Kingfisher V* to wherever you want to go; **Pow Cabral**, 62-23132, whose wife operates **Carol's Cabañas** north of the village; and **David Westby**, 62-3234.

Recommended catamaran and snorkeling trips are offered by **Dave Dial**, based at the Shell gas station. His company charges about $15 for a half-day snorkel trip, or $25 for an all-day excursion. For diving, try the well-equipped **Rum Point Inn**, 62-3239, or **Placencia Dive Shop**, 62-3227, affiliated with Kitty's Resort (also offering snorkel and river trips). Expect to pay at least $65 for a day of diving, $200 if you charter a boat.

Kayaks are rented by several businesses in Placencia and it's possible to paddle from here to the barrier reef—or up the Monkey River as far as the Maya Mountains, many miles from the coast. We recommend Ranguana Lodge (62-3112).

Here, as elsewhere in Belize, it's best to arrange prices for tours and services *before* you set out on your trip.

Things to See and Do

There are several popular nightspots in the village, where an inexpensive bottle of local rum goes a long way. Favorites include the **Cozy Corner, Dockside Bar, Mike's Caribbean Club** (packed at happy hour), **Tentacles, Sonny's, Lagoon Saloon** (with live music on weekends), and **Kingfisher Bar**. Live music, drumming, and dancing are sometimes available weekend nights at the Cozy Corner, **Kulcha Shak,** and **Flamboyant Restaurant**.

By and large, Placencia is an informal place where you can easily fit in by doing nothing. If you change your mind, it's an excellent departure point for such lesser-known southern cayes as Colson and

Pompion, or the interior nature parks and Mayan ruins. Birding and beachcombing are especially rewarding here, and the nearby lagoon is an important breeding area for saltwater crocodiles, marine turtles, and manatees. You won't find much lobster or conch in the waters around Placencia, but some of the best snook, tarpon, and other sportfishing is available within a short boat ride.

Getting There

The hub of activity in Placencia—such as it is—can be found at the very tip of the peninsula, where the pier, marina, gas station, bus stop, pay phone, and fishing co-op are all located. A passenger ferry called *The Hokey-Pokey* leaves here for nearby Independence (a 50-minute trip for about $10), from which airplane (at Big Creek) and bus connections go both north and south. (In recent years convenient daily bus and plane service has come to Placencia, so there's little reason to make this shuttle unless you want to make faster connections.)

Both the **James** and **Z-Line** bus companies have buses heading north or south from (separate) stops in Independence. It's about $4 to Dangriga (2 hours) and a little less to Punta Gorda (3 hours). You'll pay your fare on board.

The Placencia airstrip is immediately north of Kitty's Place, about 2 miles from the village, and served by **Maya** and **Tropic Airlines**. Flying time from Belize International is 50 minutes and the 1997 fare was about $55. A taxi usually awaits deplaning passengers or you can arrange with your hotel to be picked up. We recommend some patience here; Placencia does not operate at an urban pace.

Inquire locally about direct boats from Placencia and Independence to Honduras. Once-a-week boats operated by **Charles Leslie**, 6-23104, and **Manuel Zabaneh, Jr.** (6-22131) make round-trips to Puerto Cortés for about $40 per passenger. The trip takes between three and four hours. Inquire at the BTL office, 62-3160, about occasional passenger boats from Placencia to Guatemala. Exit formalities are taken care of at the immigration office in Big Creek.

Where to Stay in Placencia

Carol's Cabañas, $20; 62-2313. Rents cabins.

Clive's Campground, at the north end of the sidewalk; $2, no phone. Clive also rents a few basic cabins.

D&L Resort, in the center of town; $25; 62-3243. A relatively modest five-room hotel.

Deb & Dave's Last Resort, on the sidewalk in the village; $20; 62-3207. Budget rooms, has shared baths, ceiling fans, and a garden setting. Recommended; co-owner Dave Vernon is an excellent local guide.

Jaguar Inn, $90; (800) 663-0775 or 62-3250. Offers several cabañas in a garden setting, with a nice bar/restaurant on the premises.

Kitty's Place, on the far north side of the village next to the airport; $45 and up; 62-3227, fax 62-3226, e-mail *kittys@btl.net*. Fishing, sailing, diving, and jungle tours, as well as accommodating campers and long-term visitors. Our first choice among moderately-priced, full-service hotels. Guests have several room options at this rambling, informal location. Offers camping on French Louis Caye ($50 per person).

Paradise Vacation Resort, $20; 6-23179. More basic than the name suggests.

The Pickled Parrot, in the middle of the village; $40; 62-3330. Two "cabins," with basic furnishings and services.

Rum Point Inn, 2 miles north of Placencia, past the airport; $225, includes meals; (800) 747-1381 or 62-3239, e-mail *rupel@btl.net*. This recommended luxury lodge is operated by Corol and George Bevier, early supporters of Belize's environmental movement and very knowledgeable tour guides. Their son, Wade, is a photographer, diver, and naturalist active in the Audubon Society. He also maintains an E-6 photo-processing lab and knows a great deal about local marine fauna. The Rum Point compound includes a gourmet restaurant (served family style after Corol "blows the conch"), a well-stocked library, 10 dome-shaped cottages, and a two-story, air-conditioned complex built in 1997. The featured attraction here is a well-equipped NAUI/PADI dive shop and a 42-foot custom dive boat, the *Auriga*, which prowls 400-square-miles of prime underwater habitat. Kayaks, Hobie-cat sailboats, and bicycles are available for rent, and a swimming pool may have been added by the time of your visit.

Sea Spray, $16; 62-3148. Run by postmistress Janice Leslie, north end of the village.

Soul Shine Resort, along a canal west of the village called Black Lagoon; $80; (800) 890-6082 or 62-3347, e-mail *soulshine@btl.net*. Modest six-cabaña complex with a swimming pool, good restaurant/bar (with the best video library in town), and day trip options. Call ahead and they'll pick up at the Placencia pier. Soul Shine offers a late afternoon "sunset cruise" on its pontoon boat to areas where manatees and dolphins sometimes beach themselves like miniature whales. The cruise include drinks and a shrimp cocktail.

The Tourist Trap (opening near Soul Shine in 1997); $35; 62-3156. Basic rooms in an octagonal structure built by tourist guide Dave Dial of Placencia Industries, who offers discounted day trips to guests as well as kitchen facilities and foodstuffs. (Entrepreneur Dial also runs the Shell gas station, Tentacles bar, and Raka Sailing Charters.)

Tradewinds Hotel, $50; 62-3122. Cabañas and rooms along 5 acres of beachfront.

Turtle Inn, north of the village; $112; 62-3244. Seven beach bungalows and a house available. You can also rent diving and snorkeling equipment here from the inn's **Hawksbill Dive Shop** (scuba certification offered). Sportfishing and other day trips start at $45. An inclusive meal program at the lodge's restaurant is about $60 per day. Skip White, the American owner, is an expert on adventure travel in Belize, having explored the back-country here since 1984.

Where to Eat in Placencia
Restaurants in Placencia tend to close early, so it's a good idea to be at your table by 8 p.m. Note that here, as elsewhere in Belize, many businesses are closed from noon to 1 or 2 p.m.

Alfredo's, on the main sidewalk, near the center of the village. Specializing in Italian dishes.

Chili's, on the south point, near the main dock. Excellent breakfasts.

Daisy's Ice Cream Parlor, in the center of town. Serves Placencia's finest homemade ice cream.

The Flamboyant Restaurant (formerly Jene's), opposite the

Seaspray Hotel. One of the friendlier social centers along the walkway. Delicious, reasonably priced meals are served under the filigree shade of a flamboyant tree.

The Galley,on the edge of the village, next to the soccer field. Some insist that this is the best food in Belize.

Green Parrot Resort, up the road in Maya Beach. Worth the trip for a truly gourmet meal.

"John the Bakerman" Whylie, behind Wallen's Market. Excellent pastries.

Kitty's Place, about 1.5 miles north of the village, next to the airstrip. Terrace dining.

Kulcha Shak, near the beach at Seine Bight. Belizean, Garifuna, and vegetarian dishes.

Miss Lilly, behind Hortense's Market. Sells delicious homemade cassava and coconut bread from her front door.

Pickled Parrot, in "downtown" Placencia behind the Orange Peel Gift Shop. The Parrot has decent food, a pleasant palapa-roof bar, and pizza specials on Friday night.

The Rum Point Inn, immediatley north of the airstrip. Family-style meals, reservations required.

Soul Shine Restaurant, along the canal. Expensive but tasty.

LAUGHINGBIRD CAYE NATIONAL PARK
Location: About 12 miles southeast of Placencia.
Size: About 10,000 acres.
Visitor Information: Friends of Laughingbird Caye, 62-3239 or c/o Rum Point Inn, General Delivery, Placencia, Belize.

A small, coconut-studded island, Laughingbird gets its name from the large number of laughing gulls that once used it as a rookery.

Overuse by humans caused the gulls to abandon the island completely, although a few have returned since 1990, along with brown pelicans, green herons, and melodious blackbirds. In recent years this has been a popular destination for day-tripping picnickers, snorkelers, divers, and sea kayakers, who placed Laughingbird on their regular route. The government has taken steps to minimize this disruption, but in the interest of conservation you may wish to drop anchor elsewhere. The island gets so crowded on some days that it's difficult to find a place to sit down. Sadly, the coral is deteriorating, and many of the fish have gone elsewhere. If you do stop here, be sure to use a mooring buoy to minimize coral damage

Laughingbird Caye, the southernmost island in the Inner Channel, is only about 120 yards long by 10 yards wide. Its unusual shape, an angular oval atoll on a continental shelf, is called a *faro*. Like true atolls, faroes are steep-sided and widely separated from other land formations. The national park that includes this faro encompasses more than 10,000 acres of the surrounding marine area.

Getting There/Outfitters

Day trips to Laughingbird Caye National Park and the nearby **Silk, Bugle, Colson, Scipio**, and **Lark Cayes** can be arranged in Placencia among the many boat charter operators. **Wippari Caye, Little Water Caye**, and **Ranguana Caye** have had overnight accommodations in recent years; with **Nicholas, Lime**, and **Hatchet Cayes** slated to host resorts by 1998. Many of the cayes on the southern part of the reef also have part-time fishing camps, and a handful have full-time residents.

BIG CREEK, INDEPENDENCE, AND MANGO CREEK

Location: About 40 miles by road south of Dangriga and slightly more miles north of Punta Gorda.
Size: The three villages encompass about 30 square miles.
Visitor Information: Belize Tourist Board, (800) 624-0686.

The small villages of Big Creek, Independence, and Mango Creek dot a 7-mile branch of the Southern Highway directly across the lagoon from Placencia.

Big Creek has been developed as an important port servicing the deep-water cargo ships that come here to load bananas, mangos, pineapples, citrus, and other cash crops. Until the late 1980s, shallow-draft boats and barges had to shuttle small loads of these exports to Puerto Barrios in neighboring Guatemala. Dredging has made this a major industrial center for Belize.

Immediately north of Big Creek are the tiny settlements of Independence and Mango Creek (many people now consider all three villages as the same community and use their names interchangeably).

Getting There/Outfitters
The Hello Hotel (a Z-Line bus stop), $45, 62-2428, is owned by Antonio and Beth Zabaneh, who also own the adjacent grocery and are experts on boat trips that can be arranged from here to Glover's Reef, Guatemala, and Honduras. (For those leaving Belize, the necessary passport stamp can be obtained from the village police station.) The slightly cheaper and faster **James Line** bus stops a short distance away, in front of María's Restaurant.

Where to Stay and Eat in Big Creek
Billbird Hotel, $60; 6-22084. Formerly Toucan Inn, a remodeled barracks for employees of Big Creek's largest banana company. The Billbird is known for its Irish food and the English pub atmosphere of its **Tipsy Toucan** bar.

María's, next to the James Line bus stop. Serves simple Belizean and Guatemalan food.

MONKEY RIVER TOWN
Location: About 10 miles south of Big Creek (and technically in the Toledo District).
Size: The village encompasses about 20 acres.
Visitor Information: Belize Tourist Board, (800) 624-0686.

This sleepy Creole fishing village is about 15 miles by boat southwest of Placencia, tucked behind mangrove forests at the mouth of the slow-moving Monkey River. This lowland waterway drains the Bladen and Swasey watersheds, which now enjoy protected status as important sources of irrigation water and sanctuaries for wildlife.

The **Paynes Creek/Monkey River Wildlife Sanctuary** and **Punta Ycacos Reserve** encompass thousands of acres between

Monkey River Town and the tiny coastal villages of Punta Negra and Punta Ycacos. The area is gradually being developed for natural history research and tourism. An overgrown dirt road (impassable in wet weather) connects the north side of Monkey River Town with the Southern Highway, about 15 miles away.

Over the years, Monkey River Town has been hard hit by disasters: a blight destroyed the banana industry (since revived), the government stopped subsidizing local rice growers, and trappers sold most of the local crocodiles for their skins. During March and April, the village briefly comes alive again with a celebration centered around the iguana egg-laying season. People from throughout the area descend on Monkey River Town to eat freshly killed iguanas (usually cooked in a stew) and their eggs, which are considered a delicacy. Efforts are now under way to develop forms of low-impact tourism that would provide jobs for residents while preserving the environment. Some residents are trying to raise wild game animals—such as the gibnut—commercially.

Outfitters

For a fee of about $40, guides from Placencia, Big Creek, or Monkey River Town will take a visitor by powerboat through a series of mangrove islands and up the largely uninhabited Monkey River for several miles. Here many species of birds and, yes, even monkeys (black howlers) can be seen. Occasionally you'll spot crocodiles and turtles sunning themselves on the river's sandy beaches, while the iguanas thrash about in overhanging trees. (There were once spider monkeys along the river, but a yellow fever epidemic wiped them out during the 1950s.) If you wish, your boatman may stop and escort you along jungle trails where the tracks of many wild animals can be seen. Lucky visitors may see the animals themselves: deer, ocelots, peccaries, tapirs, coatimundis, agoutis, and even jaguars.

Among the best local guides is life-long resident **Darrell Garbutt**, 62-2014, a former fisherman and iguana hunter who will take visitors on a jungle hike and share his astounding knowledge of the jungle river environment. Darrell is an expert at identifying water birds and animal tracks.

Tours of the Monkey River usually depart Placencia about 7:30 a.m., returning at 2:30 p.m. Bring sunscreen, a hat, and a zoom lens (if you plan to photograph wildlife). We also recommend P.I. Tours in Placencia (62-3209).

For those with a true spirit of adventure, we recommend Seattle-based **Monkey River Expeditions**, (800) 500-2175 or (206) 660-7777, e-mail *mre@halcyon.com,* which runs guided, 3-day trips up the Monkey River (camping gear provided), combined with a night in Monkey River Town and two nights camping on Ranguana Caye. Additional nights are spent in Placencia and with a rural Mayan family after a tour of the Lubaantun and Nim Li Punit ruins.

South of Monkey River Town to Punta Gorda is a relatively pristine jungle coastline now under government protection. Very few people live here and there are virtually no services. You can hire a boat and guide, however, in Monkey River Town, Placencia, or Punta Gorda.

Where to Stay and Eat in Monkey River Town
Alice's, 62-2014. The best restaurant in Monkey River Town, where you'll find savory Creole cuisine and the village's only telephone. We recommend the fish balls with fried plantains (and, of course, beans 'n rice). Camping is possible, by permission, on a sand spit at the edge of the village.

Bob's Paradise, a mile north of Monkey River Town on a coconut-studded beach called English Town. American-run bar, restaurant, and cabaña complex. No phone.

Enna's Hotel, no phone, $15. William and Enna Anderson operate this eight room hotel. Serves simple, wholesome meals. For a private bath expect to pay a bit more.

Tanya's, (no phone); $15. In 1998 this second 13-room hotel and café is scheduled to be opened by the Wellington Garbutt family. They also offer guide services (snorkeling, birding, camping, hiking, and river trips). For a private bath expect to pay a bit more.

BLADEN NATURE RESERVE
Location: About 20 miles southwest of Placencia.
Size: 97,000 acres.
Visitor Information: Access to the Bladen Nature Reserve is strictly limited to qualified scientists, archaeologists, and other designated researchers. Permission must be obtained in advance from the Belize Audubon Society, which manages the Bladen, at 2-35004 or 2-34987.

Ancient Maya in the Bladen Wilderness

The upper Bladen Branch watershed shows traces of the past presence of ancient Maya. In the early 1990s, surveys by archaeologist Peter Dunham and a team from Cleveland State University turned up four previously unknown Mayan sites. These settlements provide new evidence for a 1,000-year-old trading network in the Bladen. According to Dunham, up to 7,000 people may have inhabited the Bladen valley. A flood plain in the area called Quebrada de Oro ("the passageway of gold") contains other Mayan ruins that archaeologists have never excavated. Participants in a late 1980s field study found 18 roughly rectangular mounds here, now overgrown by vegetation. An abundance of breadfruit trees suggests that the Maya cultivated this species at Quebrada de Oro, as they did at Tikal.

There appears to have been some looting of the Quebrada ruins and at another more western site in the Bladen. In addition, just prior to the Dunham expedition, looting at one of the four newly discovered ruins resulted in the destruction of an ancient structure at this site. Unregulated visitation remains one of the biggest problems facing the reserve's managers and those concerned with protecting these and other Mayan sites throughout Belize.

One of Dunham's teams made a stunning ornithological discovery in 1994 in the Bladen—they watched a rare harpy eagle for 40 minutes as it perched in fig trees as close as 65 feet from its onlookers. This huge flying predator, which feeds on monkeys and sloths, had not been seen in Belize for 20 to 30 years prior to this date.

The 1990 designation of the **Bladen Branch** (of the Monkey River) watershed area as a nature reserve set a significant benchmark in the race to protect the earth's most biologically diverse ecosystems— broadleaf moist tropical forests—before humans destroy them. Protection of this Toledo District wilderness, sprawling across the Maya Mountains' rugged foothills, helped set the stage for an even bolder action in which Bladen became part of a vast protected area that includes **Chiquibul National Park** and the nearby **Cockscomb Sanctuary**; together the reserve encompasses some 450,000 acres of tropical forest.

The Bladen Nature Reserve provides refuge for at least 194 bird species and at least 300 plant species, in addition to such creatures as the Baird's tapir, white-lipped peccary, mountain lion, iguana, jaguar, southern river otter, greater bulldog bat, white-tailed deer, brocket deer, and Central American spider monkey. The Bladen's important birds include the king vulture, mealy parrot, slaty-breasted tinamou, ornate hawk eagle, Philadelphia vireo, and rufous-capped warbler. The area contains uninvestigated Mayan ruins, steep granite mountains, conical limestone outcrops, sinkholes, caves, underground streams, and waterfalls. Within the reserve's boundaries is **Richardson Peak**, one of the highest mountains in Belize.

Local conservation leaders had long recognized Bladen's significance as an unspoiled, remote haven for wildlife. As early as 1984, the upper Bladen watershed appeared at the top of a "wish list" of proposed protected areas. The Belize Country Environmental Profile characterized the upper Bladen Branch as almost completely undisturbed by humans. It collects water from a series of almost parallel creeks that drain the main divide of the Maya Mountains over approximately 135 square miles. The lower watershed is subtropical wet forest, while higher areas include subtropical lower montane wet forest, with cloud elfin forest on the higher peaks.

The Bladen may someday become the core of a much larger protected area through its possible designation as a **United Nations (UNESCO) Biosphere Reserve**. The government has considered protective declarations linking the Chiquibul east to the Maya Mountain Divide. Whatever the outcome, one thing is certain: the Belize government has set an international standard in protecting the existing pristine watershed. As one Belizean put it, "The Bladen is a little gem, and it shines."

TOLEDO DISTRICT

Heading south from the citrus and banana plantations of the Stann Creek District, travelers enter the most sparsely populated and undeveloped region in Belize. The Toledo District is (barely) connected to the rest of the country by a single dirt road—the Southern Highway—and one commercial airstrip at Punta Gorda. Public transportation consists of a few daily buses and a half-dozen daily domestic airline flights (Maya and Tropic). There is also daily boat service to and from Guatemala. Change is coming slowly to the Toledo District but coming nonetheless. One example of this is the ongoing improvement of the Southern Highway, which is being systematically widened and paved all the way to Dangriga.

Still, much of the area is without electricity, indoor plumbing, hot water, or roads. In fact, the majority of its residents are subsistence farmers—including about 11,000 Kekchí (sometimes spelled Ketchi) and Mopan Maya—living in wooden, thatched-roof huts or small cement-block houses. The per capita annual income here is estimated at less than $800. Obviously, a trip to the Toledo District is not for everyone. Although there are a growing number of accommodations with modern amenities, most lodges and guest houses are decidedly rustic.

Travel within the area is most manageable during the dry season (February through May) but can be problematic the rest of the year. This part of Belize averages well over 100 inches of rain annually; therefore, its many rivers and creeks can be difficult to ford during a downpour. There are few gas stations, grocery stores, or restaurants. In short, tourist services are minimal. Yet a visit to the Toledo District is a must for those who wish to get a firsthand look at the Kekchí, Mopan, and Garifuna cultures, and to experience small-scale tourism as a strategy for ecosystem conservation. The district also features Belize's only true rainforest and some of its most unusual ancient Mayan ruins and sacred caves.

There is no better time to visit the Toledo District than the present, in part because development pressures are already changing its look and character. At least 15 logging concessions reportedly have been granted by the Belize government in the Columbia and Maya Mountain forest reserves, and one Malaysian firm (Atlantic Industries) has started logging pristine rainforest at the rate of 1,200 acres per year. Local Mayan villagers, members of the Belize Audubon Society, and international conservationists have complained that Atlantic is violating terms of its contract by harvesting trees outside designated areas and destroying critical wildlife habitat, among other alleged offenses. Both the government and the logging company have denied the charges. Meanwhile, in the Caribbean about 20 miles east of Placencia, Dover Technology of Houston has sunk Belize's first offshore oil well, which is said to have leaked petroleum products into this extremely sensitive marine ecosystem.

On the positive side, work began in 1997 on a plan to protect the Punta Gorda area's endangered howler monkey population. By the time you read this, a nongovernmental reserve for the howlers (similar to the Community Baboon Sanctuary in north-central Belize) may be open to visitors in the "greenbelt" surrounding Punta Gorda.

A word to the wise should be sufficient—if you want to see southern Belize in its full pristine glory, go now!

One final caution: It should be noted that malaria and cholera were recurring problems in rural areas of the Toledo District as recently as 1996–97.

VISITING MAYAN VILLAGES

One of the greatest challenges facing the Belizeans of Toledo is the need to ensure that local people—in this case mostly Kekchí Maya, Mopan Maya, Garifuna, and Creole—benefit from increased tourism and are given incentives to protect the natural and cultural resources of the region. Complicating the matter are some daunting environmental problems facing the area's subsistence farmers. Natural habitat degradation has been especially heavy here, mainly because of new road construction and the collective impact of forest destruction by commercial logging and the kind of slash-and-burn (*milpa*) agriculture practiced by a growing native Mayan population and Guatemalan immigrants.

However, as of mid-1997, at least two noteworthy locally initiated projects were underway in Toledo, seeking to combine tourism, sustainable agriculture, cultural revitalization, and environmental conservation: the **Toledo Host Family Network/Indigenous Experience Program**, 7-22470, and the **Mayan Guest House & EcoTrail Program**, 7-22119.

These two programs both encourage foreigners to visit traditional Mayan villages, but in fundamentally different ways. The Host Family

Network places tourists in the actual homes of Mayan Indians, where guests observe and participate in daily village life. In contrast, the Guest House Program arranges visits to many of the same villages, but tourists stay in structures that are separate from Mayan homes and built specifically for use by foreigners. Under both schemes, visitors eat meals prepared by local residents and take outings guided by villagers. (Although the Maya of Belize converse among themselves in their own languages, most are also fluent in English, which is not the case in neighboring Guatemala, Honduras, or Mexico.)

"We don't look at these programs as rivals," says Alfredo Villoria, of San Pedro's **Dem Dat's Doin'** farm and one of the founders of the homestay endeavor. "We think they are complementary. Some folks want to stay in a guest house and some want to stay with families. We let them exercise that choice."

Mayan Guest House Program

Since 1991, several rural villages have constructed small guest houses, designed and marked nature trails, and started introducing travelers to Mayan customs. As of mid-1997, communal guest houses were completed and operational in five communities: San Pedro Columbia, San Miguel, Santa Cruz, San José, and Laguna. A sixth facility is scheduled to open in Barranco, on the coast. Accommodations and meals are basic, and there is no electricity or indoor plumbing, but the overall experience cannot be duplicated.

Laguna Village completed its guest house ahead of the others and offers the widest range of activities for tourists, including guided nature walks and exploration of a Mayan ceremonial cave where ancient paintings can be seen. Many villagers attended a government-sponsored "hospitality training" workshop in 1996, and 10 families have been selected to provide meals for guest house visitors.

"These people are very quiet, gentle, and vulnerable," North American visitor Louise Foster observed, in an account of her Laguna experience, published in *The Belize Review*. "They are excited about reviving their traditions and sharing them with outsiders."

Laguna is a Kekchí agricultural center located about 10 miles from Punta Gorda. The population is descended from immigrants who originated in the Alta Verapaz highlands of Guatemala and came to Belize to escape brutal oppression. The Kekchí have a strong tradition of cooperation, particularly in farming and building.

Laguna's thatch-roofed guest house accommodates up to eight visitors and includes a veranda, a separate bathhouse, and outhouses.

Guests are treated to a spectacular view of the rainforest-covered, limestone karst hills nearby. Since the lodge does not have a kitchen, visitors receive their meals in small groups at different households each day. Guides take guests on carefully tended footpaths, where the native medicinal plants are marked in various languages. A recommended stop is the arts and crafts center, where tourists can buy handmade baskets and other Mayan craftwork directly from the village cooperative.

The Mayan Guest House Program is coordinated as a profit-making venture through the Toledo Ecotourism Association, which has an office in the Belize Tourist Board information center on Front Street in Punta Gorda. The program was initiated by expatriate William "Chet" Schmidt, who owns and operates Nature's Way Guest House/Belize Adventure Travel in Punta Gorda. Schmidt has worked with local villagers to devise a system that integrates ecosystem conservation, appropriate-scale tourism, and environment-friendly farming. Its intention is to minimize stress levels on the natural and cultural resources, while employing the maximum number of villagers. Part of the profits are used to support sustainable agriculture, a community fund, local government, and the construction of clinics. Accommodation rates are about $10 a night, plus about $3 for each meal and $5 for guided tours.

The Guest House Program was originally designed to incorporate an important but controversial strategy—controlling tourists' access. In an attempt to minimize stress levels on the natural environment and not overburden local Maya with massive infusions of outsiders, organizers can arrange for individuals and small groups to be cycled in and out on a rotating basis. Each village thus gets its share of tourists, but the overall demands on local people and resources are kept low.

Toledo Host Family Network/Indigenous Experience Program

Catering to overnight visitors who wish to stay in the actual homes of villagers, the Toledo Host Family Network involves residents of **San Antonio, Santa Cruz, San José, Na Luum Ca, San Pedro Columbia, Silver Creek,** and **Santa Elena.**

After contacting village officials (or Dem Dat's Doin'/Toledo Information Center) and paying a $5 registration fee, tourists are connected with a Mayan family that will provide meals, a hammock (with sheet), illuminating conversation, and involvement in such daily activities as tortilla preparation, corn farming, "chopping bush," and land tilling. Guided trips are offered to nearby ruins, caves, and nature trails. Visitors pay their host families at a rate of about $5 a day for room and $2 per meal. Some of the money goes to host families and the rest is used for community service projects such as potable water systems and health clinics. In order to find out who coordinates the homestay in a particular village, ask for the name and address of the local *alcalde* or chair. Residents can point the way.

Keep in mind that conditions are primitive by the modern standards of the industrial world—you'll use outhouses (supplied with corncobs, not toilet paper) and wash yourself in nearby rivers, just like the Maya. There's not much to do at night and many houses lack electricity. (A favorite entertainment is watching rented videos in one of the few TV-equipped homes.) The Mayan homestay experience isn't for everyone, but your reward is getting to meet some of the warmest, friendliest people in Belize.

PUNTA GORDA
Location: *About 100 miles southwest of Belize City and 15 miles north of Guatemala.*
Population: *About 4,000 (1997 estimate).*
Visitor Information: *Belize Tourist Board, on Front Street; Toledo Ecotourism Association, 7-22119; the Toledo Visitors Information Center, 7-22470, fax 7-22199; Toledo Explorer's Club, 7-22986.*

Even in the Toledo District capital of Punta Gorda, some 200 miles south of Belize City, the pace is slow. In the middle of this sprawling town of about 2,400 people, chickens roam freely between clapboard houses and patches of uncut vegetation. Freshly caught turtles and fish are dressed on the shoreline. Wheelbarrows full of produce roll along the broad streets. Uniformed schoolchildren play in front of unpretentious churches. Adults gossip on street corners as they go about their errands. There is virtually no traffic to dodge and the silence at night can be deafening.

If you fly to "P.G.," as the community is known locally, a spectacular view of the Caribbean and, on clear days, the mountains of Guatemala and Honduras will greet you as you walk from the airport to downtown—which happen to be only a few steps apart. The five

Fallen Stones Butterfly Farm

One of the most unusual attractions in the Toledo District is the award-winning commercial butterfly farm operated by English lawyer Clive P. Farrell and tropical plant specialist Ray Harberd. Farrell, who operates butterfly parks in the U.K. and Florida, developed this operation after a similar farm of his shut down at the Shipstern Nature Reserve in northern Belize. Located in a stunning hill-top setting near the ancient Mayan ruin of Lubaantun, Fallen Stones primarily raises two species, popularly known as the blue morpho and the owl butterfly. The farm negates the need to capture these gorgeous insects in the wild, and it also returns a certain percentage of butterflies to the surrounding forests.

A tour of the facility ($5) brings you into breeding cages where dozens of butterflies feed, mate, and lay their eggs on plants that will not thrive outside the rainforest. It's an amazing experience to have these iridescent, neon-blue creatures land on your fingers and even the tip of your nose! Raising butterflies is a labor-intensive process, and thousands of caterpillars (kept in muslin-covered cups in a

tree-shaded principal streets of Punta Gorda run parallel to the coast and are unpaved. This tranquil façade belies a colorful and sometimes violent history.

Culture and Economy

Although P.G. is still an important fishing port (especially for sport anglers), it has been converted into a market town by gradual improvements in transportation and the influx of peasant farmers from nearby Guatemala. There are also many traditional farms along the coast, primarily growing cassava, beans, maize, and rice. The town

*separate room) must be fed daily by hand. A 2-acre planta-
tion of food plants is maintained a few steps from the enclosure, and other fruit and nectar sources have been developed
nearby. As a result of this activity, Fallen Stones has hired
and trained many local Maya, whose handed-down knowledge of butterfly habits is invaluable.*

*When they reach their chrysalis (pupa) stage, the dor-
mant insects are carefully packaged and shipped by air to the
U.S. and Europe, where they emerge as brand-new butterflies
within a few days of arrival. Because blue morpho and owl
butterflies typically live only a couple of weeks, there is a constant need for new pupae. The next time you visit Butterfly
World in Coconut Creek, Florida, you'll know where those
particular butterflies came from!*

The Fallen Stones Jungle Lodge, *managed separately,
offers comfortable bungalows ($80 and up), fine meals ($35
a day), and excellent guided tours of the nearby forest and
Mayan ruins. The latter are often led by Acapito Requena,
who spent many years as a chiclero (chicle-tapper) in the
adjacent wilderness.*

itself has an interesting ethnic mix that includes Maya, Garifuna,
Creole, East Indian, Chinese, European, and Lebanese residents.

According to a recent census, almost 50 percent of Punta Gorda's
population is Garifuna. These people have had a difficult time keeping
their unique culture alive, and the modern world provides few financial and social incentives for them to do so. Their rich and varied language is not taught in the schools, and the difficulty of finding steady
employment is ever-present. Farming once was a part of the Garifuna
culture in the Toledo District, but today such traditions as the baking
of cassava bread are practiced by only a few families. Many families

have at least one member now living in the U.S. or Canada and remitting income.

Until 1994 a large number of British soldiers were stationed in P.G., which bolstered the local economy. Although the Brits are mostly gone, U.S. taxpayers continue to support a large Voice of America radio station south of the town, which beams programming throughout Central America. The facility is for sale, but still operated by the U.S. Information Agency. You can see the flashing navigation lights atop the compound's 200-foot-tall antenae.

Things to See and Do
Nightlife in P.G. is limited to a handful of bars and restaurants, or you can look overhead and see one of the most amazing starscapes in the country.

Wednesdays and Saturdays are market days, and this is a good time to inspect the handcrafted wares of Mayan artisans from local villages as well as Guatemala. An amazing array of exotic fruits and vegetables is also on sale. The market is on Front Street, with booths spilling over onto adjacent Queen Street. Local handicrafts made by the **Fajina Craft Center**, 7-22470, are a particularly good value—they are of high quality, priced fairly, and their sale supports a local "self-empowerment" organization of Kekchí and Mopan women. Look for tie-tie baskets, jippy-jappa baskets, slate carvings, handwoven textiles, and embroideries. Among the more unusual craft items are reproductions of ancient Mayan symbols on handmade paper.

Punta Gorda is a good base for trips to Toledo's more than 30 Mayan villages and several major ruins (see Archaeological Sites, Chapter 10 for details), along with jungle rivers, caves, diving, kayaking, snorkeling, and sportfishing. Excursions can also be made to the southern end of the barrier reef and Glover's Reef, although the islands are so far offshore (40 miles) that it may be easier to head for them from Placencia or Dangriga.

Outfitters
Charter by Land/Sea, located at 12 Front Street, 7-72070, schedules boat and interior trips from its office. Diving is the specialty at **Orange Point Marina**, operated by an American expatriate. **Requena Boat Charters**, Main Street, 7-22070, arranges fishing, snorkeling, and nature-observation trips and provides very good guides.

Timeless Tours, (Box 11, Punta Gorda), runs 7- to 12-day camping excursions to cayes and jungle rivers aboard its 38-foot schooner *Juanita*, based in P.G. harbor. The sailboat goes as far as Wild Cane Caye (the site of a Mayan ruin), the Snake Cayes, and Livingston, a Garifuna town in Guatemala.

Visitor Information

Good sources of information include the **Belize Tourist Board**, on Front Street next to Verona's, open weekdays, 8 a.m. to 4:30 p.m. In 1997 this office also housed the **Toledo Ecotourism Association**, 7-22119, which arranges trips to local Mayan village guest houses.

The **Toledo Visitors Information Center**, open daily from 8 a.m. to 11:30 a.m., except Thursday and Sunday, 7-22470 or fax 7-22199, is operated next to the main pier by Alfredo and Yvonne Villoria of **Dem Dat's Doin'**. Besides providing extensive information on Toledo attractions, the Villorias can help arrange inland tours and boat charters. The center maintains a message center, bulletin board, and paperback book exchange as well. Information is dispensed free of charge.

Another P.G. resource is the **Toledo Explorer's Club**, 7-22986, 46 José María Nuñez Street, which answers visitors' questions and arranges custom-guided camping expeditions to remote villages, rivers, caves, and cayes. Basic accommodations are provided in the group's "clubhouse."

Getting There

As of late 1997, **Maya Airlines** had four daily flights to and from Belize City to Punta Gorda; **Tropic Air** had two flights on the same route. The plane trip from Belize City takes about 90 minutes (with two stops) and costs around $65 (one-way).

The **Z-Line** bus runs twice daily to and from Dangriga and Belize City, (53 Main St., 7-22165), and the **James Line** bus makes the same trip every day (arriving and leaving from P.G.'s main square). The trip to Belize City ($11) takes about 10 hours (Dangriga 5 hrs, $8), via the rough Southern and Hummingbird highways. A number of local buses and supply trucks carry passengers on semi-weekly schedules to surrounding villages, with the heaviest traffic on Wednesdays and Saturdays (Punta Gorda's market days). You can also simply flag down a passing vehicle; most will give you a ride. The turnoff from the Southern Highway is about 15 miles west of P.G. at a Shell gas station.

Punta Gorda's Colorful History

P.G. is believed to have been founded by Puritan traders in the 17th century, then occupied off and on by English pirates and Spanish soldiers, who gave it a name that translates as "large point," a reference to the bluff upon which Punta Gorda sits. Throughout most of the colonial era, P.G. was primarily a fishing village. In 1867, a group of disaffected Civil War Confederate Army veterans and their families settled on unoccupied land nearby and tried to re-create their Deep South lifestyle around a group of sugarcane plantations. Chinese, Creole, and East Indian laborers were brought in to cut the cane and clear the forest. Over the next 40 years, a dozen sugar mills were built. But by 1910, the Toledo Settlement, as it was known, had failed, and most of the Americans returned to the U.S. The name and townsite (plus many descendants of the conscripted laborers) remain.

Getting from Punta Gorda to Puerto Barrios, Guatemala

A relatively large but slow passenger ferry provides Tuesday and Friday boat service from P.G. to Puerto Barrios, Guatemala. The boat arrives from Guatemala at about 9:30 a.m. and leaves at noon. There are easy connections from Puerto Barrios, a major shipping port, to interior Guatemala and Honduras. (The boat no longer stops in Livingston.) The crossing takes about 2.5 hours and costs about $7.50 each way. Ferry tickets can be purchased in advance at **Godoy's Shop** in Punta Gorda, 24 Middle Street, 7-2065. Bring your own food and water; neither is available on board.

Requena's Charter Service offers much faster (1 hour) daily 9 a.m. boat service to Puerto Barrios, for about $10 one-way, one of the best bargains in Belize. If there are enough passengers (usually eight), some operators will make a trip when Requena's boats fill up. You can also try bargaining your way onto one of the supply boats that shuttle between Barrios and P.G. Cruise ships occasionally dock in Punta Gorda as well. At least once a week there is a private water taxi directly to Livingston, Guatemala, which has an immigration/ customs office. Ask around at the municipal wharf to find out when a boat is leaving.

No matter how you depart, you must have your passport stamped before embarking; the Belize immigration office is at the foot of the municipal wharf. In 1997 there was no Belize exit fee; the entry fee for Guatemala was $2.50. Boat connections to Honduras can be made from Puerto Barrios. *Quetzales*, the Guatemalan currency, can be obtained at **Grace's Shop**, from arriving ferry passengers, or the money-changer who meets boats in Puerto Barrios. The bank in P.G. does not handle quetzales, nor are Guatemalan visas available here or in Puerto Barrios.

Where to Stay and Eat in Punta Gorda

Mahung's, 11 Main St.; $14, 7-22874. A good value.

Nature's Way Guest House, south end of town at 65 Front St.; $15; 7-22119. A P.G. institution that provides many tour options and much information about the Toledo District. Quarters are basic: clean rooms with bunks and shared baths. Proprietor Chet Schmidt, an American expatriate married to a Belizean, can arrange visits to Mayan villages and a remote campsite down the coast, and has a reliable boat for trips up jungle rivers and to offshore cayes.

Punta Caliente Hotel, 108 José María Nuñez St.; $13; 7-22561.

St. Charles Inn, 23 King St.; $16; 7-22149.

The Traveler's Inn, located above the Z-Line bus station at 53 Main St.; $70; 7-22568. The most upscale place in P.G., with air-conditioning, TV, and a restaurant. Operated by the Zabadeh family, Z-Line's owners.

William Tate's Guest House, near the post office; $20; 7-22196. Air-conditioning, cable TV, owned by P.G.'s postmaster. Recommended.

Other Options

The best breakfasts in town are served at **Granny's** and **Nature's**

Way, both on Front Street. A local favorite for Belizean dishes is **Lucille's**, on Front Street, and many travelers rave about **Punta Caliente**, at 108 José Nuñez Street, near the Z-Line bus station.

We have heard consistently negative comments about the food and rooms at the **Mira Mar Hotel**, at 95 Front Street.

Where to Stay and Eat near Punta Gorda

Dem Dat's Doin', $15; 7-22470. A basic room is for rent at the San Pedro Columbia permaculture farm of Alfredo and Yvonne Villoria. Home-cooked meals are also available for a modest fee and, for $5, you can take an extensive tour of the Villoria's unusual operation. Using relatively simple, low-impact technology, the couple (who immigrated here from the U.S. in 1980) are almost completely food and energy independent. They grow fruits and vegetables (including such oddities as "flying potatoes"); capture invertebrates for scientific use; raise fish, chickens, and pigs; collect solar energy and rainwater; and generate methane gas (for cooking and refrigeration) through a "digester" fueled by animal wastes. Their frangipani and ylang-ylang flowers are pressed into perfume, and other plants are sold in a small nursery. The Villorias have transferred much of their knowledge to their Mayan neighbors, and the results are impressive. We highly recommend a visit!

Fallen Stones Jungle Lodge & Butterfly Farm, $80; 7-2216. About 45 minutes from P.G. near the Lubaantun ruins and the village of San Pedro Columbia. For those who want to experience the rainforest—with considerable creature comforts—we encourage you to try this lodge. Birding and nature tours available.

Other Options Near Punta Gorda

If you have a special interest in rainforest ecology, you can stay at one of six bungalows in the comfortable **International Zoological Expeditions** field station and lodge near Blue Creek, maintained as the private **Blue Creek Wildlife Sanctuary**, $130, including all meals; (508) 655-1461; e-mail *ize2belize@aol.com*. A special treat is IZE's canopy-level sky-walk that zigzags its way through the 100-foot-high forest "ceiling" (home to more than 80 percent of rainforest organisms, including scores of bird species). Non-IZE guests pay a small fee for use of the sky-walk. Guides can be hired (about $35 per day) for jungle hikes, cave exploration, and tours of Mayan ruins. Check the IZE Web site at *http://www.ize2belize.com*.

Although several prearranged tours, guest houses, and homestays are available, it's also relatively easy to find accommodations in the interior on your own. Many residents will take you in and feed you for about $10 a night (or less). Other options include **Bol's Hilltop Hotel** (no phone) in San Antonio and **Oh's Travelers' Farm & Lodge** (no phone) in San Pedro Columbia, where you can get basic rooms ($14) and meals. For more information, inquire among travel agencies and information services in P.G.

HOKEB HA CAVE

Recommended interior destinations include the Maya's sacred Hokeb Ha Cave (also called Blue Creek Cave), a 5-mile-long underground river system. The water flowing from this passageway is crystal clear and perfectly suited to a refreshing swim on a hot day. During the dry season it's possible to hike all the way through the cave to a nearby Mayan community. Access to Hokeb Ha is by a well-marked riverside trail from Blue Creek Village, about 21 miles west of Punta Gorda. Guests at the nearby jungle lodge operated by International Zoological Expeditions can easily arrange tours through IZE, which strongly advises against entry into the caves without an experienced guide. Recommended local guides include **Bobby Polonio** and **Alfredo Romero**, who also offer treks to sugar mill ruins and chicle camps.

KAYAKING THE UPPER MOHO

The Toledo District's kayaking options include the remote **Upper Moho River**, which drains a wilderness watershed in the southern Maya Mountains. The spectacular terrain has prompted one visitor to label this "Belize's answer to Arizona's Havasupai Falls." From December through April, **Island Expeditions,** (800) 667-1630 or (604) 452-3212, offers a six-day trip using inflatable kayaks. The cost of such a trip starts at about $1,000 per person.

TEMASH-SARSTOON NATIONAL PARK AND COLUMBIA FOREST RESERVE

If you want to see some of the tallest and oldest mangrove forests in all of Central America, a trip up the Río Temash fills the bill. This river and the neighboring Río Sarstoon are two of four major watercourses that drain into the Caribbean from the Toledo District. In

1992, the government protected much of the southeast Belize watershed through its creation of the 41,000-acre Temash-Sarstoon Nature Reserve, which later became a national park. Residents of the five villages surrounding the park are actively involved in its management, thanks to the Belize government's insistence on community responsibility in the oversight of protected areas.

As you speed southeast from Punta Gorda in a hired boat—there is no public transportation in the area—you will pass such scenic coastal landmarks as **Orange Point,** the **Moho River,** and **Mother Point**. The

The Temash River in southern Belize

Steele Wotkyns

tall forest canopy along the coast contrasts with brighter green cascades of mangrove and forest stands that have been disturbed by the periodic hurricanes that batter the mainland.

We recommend that you hire an experienced boatman and guide for this adventure. The need becomes apparent as you maneuver past dangerous sandbars and tangled mangrove thickets. In this instance, a well-informed local is also extremely helpful to the amateur naturalist once you're past the verdant tunnel entrance of the Temash's delta. Comfrey palm swamp is found around the estuary of the river, possibly the only place in the country where this habitat type exists in such abundance.

The entire area is officially classified as a tropical wet-transition to subtropical forest and harbors much wildlife. Even the usually short palmetto palms tower overhead here. The deeper you penetrate this wide river, passing Conejos and Sunday Wood Creeks, the bigger the trees become. The tangle of vines and understory is almost impenetrable. Dense stands of Santa María and sapodilla trees are broken by a swampy maze of red mangrove. And then you begin to see the river's premier natural attraction—black mangrove trees that tower above the Temash, sometimes reaching more than 100 feet.

It's believed that giant anteaters and white-faced capuchin monkeys may inhabit this area, which would be the northern limit of their range. Birds not found in other parts of Belize—including the rarely seen scarlet macaw and chestnut-bellied (or agami) heron—have also been seen here. The presence of ospreys and local anglers attest to the Temash's richness as a fishing area. Large snook and tarpon cruise in the river, which reportedly reaches a depth of more than 100 feet. Sportfishing guides in Punta Gorda and other coastal towns can arrange excursions to visit this rich aquatic environment.

Farther north, the Columbia branch of the Río Grande drains the nearly 103,000 acres of uninhabited wilderness known as the Columbia Forest Reserve, one of the last remaining large tracts of intact forest in Central America. Recent explorations of the reserve have revealed sinkholes up to 800 feet deep and ¼-mile wide, plus many sacred Mayan caves containing ancient artifacts. Access is difficult, however, and prior permission from the Department of Forestry is required.

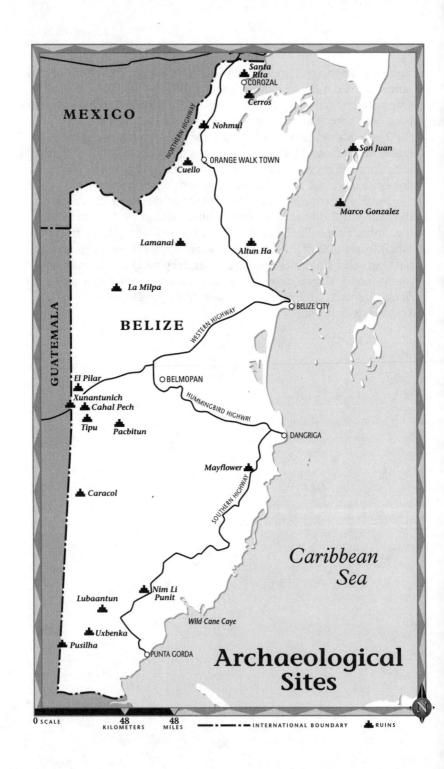

MEXICO

Santa Rita
○ COROZAL
Cerros

Nohmul

San Juan

○ ORANGE WALK TOWN

Cuello

Marco Gonzalez

Lamanai

Altun Ha

La Milpa

GUATEMALA

BELIZE

WESTERN HIGHWAY

○ BELIZE CITY

El Pilar

○ BELMOPAN

Xunantunich
Cahal Pech

HUMMINGBIRD HIGHWAY

Tipu
Pacbitun

○ DANGRIGA

Mayflower

Caracol

SOUTHERN HIGHWAY

Caribbean
Sea

Nim Li
Punit

Lubaantun

Wild Cane Caye

Uxbenka

Pusilha

○ PUNTA GORDA

Archaeological
Sites

0 SCALE   48   48
        KILOMETERS MILES   ▬ ▬ ▬ INTERNATIONAL BOUNDARY   ▲ RUINS

N

10

ARCHAEOLOGICAL SITES

Neither archaeologists nor government officials know exactly how many ancient Mayan sites there are in Belize, but certainly the number is in the thousands. The remnants of Mayan occupation—ranging from microscopic vegetable pollen found in the dust of pot shards to sky-scraping temples poking through the forest canopy—are found from border to border. Such artifacts are even commonplace on the offshore islands. It is now widely acknowledged that Belize was once at the very heart of the lowland Maya civilization.

Experts speculate that this relatively small territory may have easily supported as many as 1 million or more Maya, several times the present population of about 220,000. In 1997, one prominent archaeologist speculated that 2 million Maya may easily have lived within the present borders of Belize a dozen centuries ago.

Yet despite their clear domination of the area for hundreds of years, precious little is known about these early residents. Formal excavation of the largest ruins is relatively recent, and much of the early archaeological work is now regarded as amateurish and slipshod. Many important sites have remained virtually untouched, and others have received only cursory field research. Even Caracol, the country's biggest known Mayan complex, saw no serious investigation until the mid-1980s.

PRESERVATION AND EXPLORATION

Although many foreign agencies and universities are now helping the Belizeans study and preserve their Mayan relics, many precious artifacts have already been lost to looters, farmers, collectors, and the vagaries of nature. A great threat continues to exist, as impoverished and/or unscrupulous people plunder sites in the hope of finding valuables that can be sold for prices that start at about $300 per pot (equal to more than a month's salary for many a Belizean).

Unlike Mexico and Guatemala, Belize has lacked sufficient funds to restore its major Mayan cities, and only a handful of caretakers are looking after them. Informed guides are rare; literature on the individual sites is nonexistent or hard to come by. Access to many locations is difficult and only improving slowly. In some cases, the ruins are on private property.

Yet underdevelopment has its advantages. Even during the peak tourist season, it is not uncommon to find yourself alone at one of Belize's Mayan ruins, or in the company of a single resident manager. If you are patient, you may find that you're surrounded by wildlife.

COLLECTING ARTIFACTS

Keep in mind that under Belize law, all "ancient monuments" (defined as those structures over 100 years old) and "antiquities" (human-made articles crafted more than 150 years ago) are the property of the state. Their removal, destruction, or possession is expressly forbidden without the permission of federal authorities. The collecting, buying, and selling of such artifacts is also illegal, and anyone engaged in such activity is subject to stiff fines and a jail term. Nevertheless, looting continues to be the single biggest threat to the integrity of Mayan sites here, as elsewhere.

Be advised that a thriving business exists in imitation artifacts, and many travelers spend good money on cheap fakes. Trading in these items is not illegal, but without proper documentation the items may be seized by customs officials when leaving the country.

WHEN TO GO AND WHAT TO TAKE

Because of the sites' varying degrees of isolation, it is best to visit during the drier months (February through May). Remember that it can rain at any time and place in Belize, and waterproof boots or shoes are advisable. Lightweight, comfortable clothing should be worn, and a hat or raincoat may be useful. It is also a good idea to bring along insect repellent, sunscreen, and drinking water.

Few of the Mayan sites allow overnight visits, and only a handful have restrooms. All visitors must register and fees are usually between $1.50 and $5 per person, although these are not always collected. Children under 12 are admitted free, as are all Belizean nationals on Sundays. For further information, call the Department of Archaeology in Belmopan at 8-22106, fax 8-23345.

OUTFITTERS

A handful of U.S.-based tour companies specialize in trips to Mayan ruins. We particularly like **Far Horizons**, operated by archaeologist and conservationist Mary Dell Lucas, who has lived in Belize and helped excavate several sites. Trips organized by Far Horizons are led by well-informed archaeologists and deliberately kept small to minimize disruption of research teams and rural communities. Part of each trip fee funds the archaeology project visited. Based in Albuquerque, New Mexico, Far Horizons can be reached at (800) 552-4575 or (505) 343-9400.

ADVANCE READING

For travelers with an interest in the Mayan history of Belize, we suggest some background reading before setting out (see Appendix B for suggested books). The best local guidebook is *Warlords and Maize Men: A Guide to the Maya Sites of Belize*, which contains detailed travel instructions and maps, plus photographs and archaeological histories for each location. Another good resource is *The Belizean Bullet*, an infrequent publication of the Department of Archaeology that provides detailed information about ongoing research. The internationally distributed *Archaeology* magazine also reports often on Mayan sites in Belize.

PRINCIPAL SITES

Ancient Mayan archeological sites in this chapter are listed by district, in what is roughly a descending order of their size and accessibility.

CAYO DISTRICT

CARACOL

Until 1992, this largest Mayan site in Belize was one of the most difficult to reach. Located in the Cayo District's rugged back country, Caracol is in the middle of the remote Chiquibul National Park, only 7 miles east of the Guatemalan border. The complex—which covers at least 55 square miles—is a bumpy 2- to 3-hour journey (in good weather) by four-wheel-drive vehicle from San Ignacio via the Mountain Pine Ridge community of Douglas De Silva (formerly Augustine), about 30 miles distant.

The most extensive known Mayan ceremonial center in the country, Caracol's central core covers 30 square miles of thick, high-canopy forest and comprises a Classic-period complex that includes many pyramids, five plazas, and an astronomical observatory. The main plaza is linked by causeways to a number of outlying ruins. Overall, the network of structures is at least three times denser and 85 percent larger than nearby Tikal. Although estimates of Caracol's size are being revised upward, in 1997 it was estimated that 180,000 or more people lived in this area at the city-state's peak, around A.D. 700. The site has ruins of an estimated 35,000 buildings, with more discovered each year.

History

Caracol (Spanish for "snail"; a reference to the numerous land-snails found here) remained unknown to the outside world until the early 1930s, when a local woodcutter stumbled upon its mysterious mounds while searching for mahogany and chicle. Loggers cut timber in the area over the next two decades—crushing many valuable artifacts in the process—and it was not until 1950 that archaeologists began mapping Caracol. The ruin was mistakenly considered a small site and left to loggers, looters, and army patrols for some time. It began receiving considerable attention in 1985, after husband-and-wife archaeologists Diane and Arlen Chase began making annual research pilgrimages from the University of Central Florida.

In 1986, while planting a plot of corn at the site, Caracol caretaker and guide Benjamin Panti made a major discovery. He chanced upon a well-preserved stone ball-court marker that contained a startling carved hieroglyphic record of a military victory by an underdog leader, Lord Water of Caracol, over the mighty warlords of Tikal, some 60 miles to the northwest. This A.D. 562 conquest was apparently the culmination of many years of fierce fighting between the two powers. Caracol did its best to humiliate the royalty of Tikal and the neighboring city-state of Naranjo (conquered by Caracol in A.D. 631) during Caracol's 140 years of domination, possibly even sacrificing its high-ranking captives in demeaning public executions.

Carved stela at Caracol

Richard Mahler

Excavations at the outskirts of Caracol suggest that the ancient Maya were not divided exclusively into elite and peasant classes, as previously believed. By studying ancient garbage, archaeologists believe that the city's sizable middle class apparently had access to jade, polychrome pottery, ritual vessels, and even fancy burial tombs. Experts conclude that Caracol grew rapidly for quite a while before suffering a period of decline, possibly caused in part by an equalization in social power that destroyed the influence of Mayan royalty.

Clues contained in the hieroglyphics of circular stone altars now unearthed at Caracol may eventually help the Chases determine why the Maya fled. "We know that when they finally left, they left fast," Diane Chase told an Associated Press reporter in 1993, noting that buildings were burned and the body of a child was abandoned on the floor of a palace.

Another riddle not yet solved is why a city as large as Caracol was built on a plateau that has almost no reliable water supply during four or five months of relatively dry weather each spring. Mayan engineers managed to overcome the limitations of nature by painstakingly building reservoirs, aqueducts, and gardening terraces that optimized use of rainfall. Nevertheless, their ingenuity does not explain the reason for locating such a large population here in the first place. Even today, 2,000 years after Caracol's founding, visitors are advised to bring with them all the water they will need during their stay. (A Mayan reservoir fulfills the needs of the research team during its February to June encampment.) It is speculated that Caracol may have been a good location for trading with other Mayan communities spread throughout present-day Guatemala, Honduras, and Mexico, or that such prized plants as cacao grew here.

Another major discovery at Caracol was the bones of a woman in a royal tomb at the top of the highest pyramid. The find suggests that, in the absence of a male heir, females may have periodically ruled Mayan city-states, although this skeleton also could be that of a ruler's wife or close relative.

The most visually striking structure here is Caana ("sky palace"), a temple towering 140 feet above the plaza floor. It is 2 meters higher than El Castillo at the site of Xunantunich, previously regarded as the tallest man-made structure in Belize. (Modern hotels in Belize City now compete for this honor.) Visitors can climb to the summit of Caana and enjoy a sweeping view of the Vaca Plateau's tall forests, which extend for as far as the eye can see. Looking west and southwest from the temple, dozens of unevaluated building mounds up to 70 feet in height are evident all the way to the horizon.

In the first four years of digging, Caracol yielded 54 burial tombs, twice as many as have been found in all the decades of searching at Tikal. The project's directors estimate there are as many as 4,500 structures at the core of Caracol, compared to 2,300 mapped in the center of Tikal. The archaeological richness of this site, one of the five largest Mayan cities anywhere, is expected eventually to result in a much better understanding of the civilization, particularly since many of Caracol's tombs and monuments clearly indicate the year of their initial construction.

The Belizean government has expanded the Caracol Archaeology Reserve to the borders of the surrounding (and much larger) Chiquibul National Park. The region's high-canopy forest, much of it in pristine condition, is an important habitat for several species of cat and the endangered howler monkey, plus such rare birds as the keel-billed motmot, thought to be extinct in Guatemala, Mexico, and Honduras. Endangered ocellated turkeys and other large birds strut among the ruins with impunity, though they have vanished from most of the rest of Belize. A wide variety of orchids, vines, and trees (many as tall as 120 feet) are found in the area. One enormous ceiba tree, at least 700 years old, towers above the epicenter of Caracol. The Maya considered ceiba trees sacred because they connected the underworld, the earth, and the sky.

Road Conditions

A check of road conditions from the Forestry Department's western division in Douglas DeSilva is advised prior to any rainy season visit to Caracol. Forestry officials grant access based on road conditions, since the last 30 miles into Caracol are rough—especially during or after wet weather.

Getting There/Outfitters

High-clearance four-wheel-drive vehicles are recommended. The nearest gas station and mechanic are in San Ignacio, about 65 miles from the site. There is no public transportation to Caracol, and few taxis will make the trip. Rather than attempting a visit on your own, we recommend checking with local resorts for guided tours to the site. **Chaa Creek**, **Maya Mountain Lodge**, and **Mountain Equestrian Trails** are among the recommended operators. Since road improvements were made in 1992, tour companies no longer schedule regular horseback trips to Caracol. Such trips can be arranged, however, and during the wet season they may be the only access.

Where to Stay and Eat in Caracol

There are no overnight accommodations at Caracol and camping is allowed only with special permission from the Department of Archaeology. The nearest campground is in Douglas De Silva and the nearest lodges are in the Mountain Pine Ridge. Remember to bring your own food and water. A solar-powered telephone is available for emergency use only.

Fees

The $5 visitor's fee is payable upon registration at the site.

Guides

On-site workers are fairly knowledgeable about the archaeology and wildlife of the area—some, like Benjamin Panti, have worked here for many years—and they will provide guided tours when archaeologists are not available. Fluency in Spanish is helpful. When researchers are encamped, archaeologist-led tours are given at specified times. Check with tour operators or hotels for the current schedule.

XUNANTUNICH

In contrast to remote Caracol, Xunantunich (the Mayan "x" is pronounced like a cross between an English "s" and "z") is one of the most accessible ancient Mayan sites in Belize. The ruins are near the confluence of the Belize and Mopan rivers, on a naturally occurring limestone bluff above the Western Highway, about 7 miles west of San Ignacio.

This is a Late Classic period ceremonial center of impressive height but relatively small size. It is just across the Mopan River from the Mayan village of San José Succotz and only a few miles east of the Guatemalan border. The temple complex, occupied from about A.D. 700 until at least A.D. 1000, is surrounded by forest that is gradually being whittled away by local farmers.

Because of its commanding presence and proximity to populated areas, Xunantunich has been visited by a lengthy parade of archaeologists stretching back to 1894. In 1959, experts speculated that the site had been partially destroyed in an earthquake during the Late Classic era and reasoned that this incident may have shaken the faith Mayans had in their leaders, who claimed an intimate relationship with the gods. In recent years, however, this theory has been discredited by some archaeologists.

Dominating the entire topography of Xunantunich ("maiden of the rock") is a spectacular 135-foot monolith known as **El Castillo** (The Castle). In typical Mayan fashion, the corbel-vaulted temple at the summit is actually built on the rubble of several earlier temples constructed one atop the other over the centuries. Visitors can climb nearly to the top of this impressive tower, which affords a sweeping view of the steamy jungle and overlooks the three adjacent plazas and various corbel-arched buildings that surround them.

Visible on the east side of El Castillo's lower temple is a restored stucco frieze, restored in 1972, showing symbols of the sun, moon, Venus, and days of the week. Also included is a headless man, apparently decapitated for some long-forgotten transgression against the royal rulers. Originally the frieze continued all the way around the structure, and its highest point was probably topped by a roof comb. An excavated stairway continues to a small chamber in the upper temple of El Castillo. Near the structure's base is a wide terrace that once supported several smaller temples.

The grass-covered mounds surrounding the three primary plazas are the remains of ancient residential buildings and on the west side, near the restrooms, is a flat, narrow rectangle believed to be a ball

Kevin Schafer

*This restored Mayan frieze decorates the temple
of El Castillo at the ancient city of Xunantunich.*

court, used in a deadly form of basketball developed by the Mayan
hierarchy. Also visible is a room with a built-in stone bench and some
walls bearing ancient Mayan graffiti.

Judging from the jewelry, tools, semiprecious stones, and weaving
materials found here, archaeologists believe Xunantunich was once
an important and well-ordered city. No one is sure why this site was
abandoned, or why it flourished so late in the Mayan epoch.

The University of California-Los Angeles is involved in an eight-
year field study here, and you may encounter UCLA archaeologists
and researchers during your visit. On the west side of El Castillo, the
team has uncovered a spectacular plaster frieze, one of the largest
man-made structures in Belize. Thirty feet long, the frieze was made
between A.D. 800 and 900, a time when most other Mayan cities were
collapsing. Archaeologists are also uncovering small homesites and
farms along the length of a *sacbé*, a very old Mayan road.

Fees/Guides

The $5 admission fee is collected by resident caretaker Elfego Panti,
himself of Mayan descent and very knowledgeable about the history
of Xunantunich. He is happy to point out structures of interest and is

311

familiar with local wildlife and plants. Drinking water and restrooms are also available near his office.

Getting There

Heading west about 10 minutes from San Ignacio on the Western Highway, the tower of El Castillo is suddenly visible on the western horizon. As you enter the village of San José Succotz, look for a sign and bus shelter marking the turnoff on the right-hand side of the highway. You will cross the Mopan River on a tiny, hand-cranked ferry (that handles two cars at a time) secured to a steel cable. There is no charge, as this is a public right-of-way. Follow the dirt road for about one-half mile up the hill to a small parking lot, then walk into the Xunantunich plaza. The access road can be very slippery when wet. If you decide to proceed on foot, it takes about 40 minutes to walk up the hill from the ferry.

Besides passenger cars and package tours, visitors can take taxis to the Xunantunich ruins from Benque Viejo or San Ignacio for about $5. An alternative is to take a bus from either town and ask the driver to stop at the ferry crossing. Xunantunich is an easy half-day trip from the resorts of the Cayo District or the hotels of San Ignacio.

EL PILAR

This is a 100-acre, Classic-era ceremonial center being studied by researchers from the University of California-Santa Barbara. Occupied from about 500 B.C. to A.D. 1000, it is one of the largest unconsolidated Mayan ruins in the country, located in a cultivated part of the Cayo District near the Belize River, about 16 miles directly north of Xunantunich and 12 miles north of San Ignacio.

Archaeologists are especially intrigued by a causeway that extends from the east side of Pilar across the Guatemalan border into the dense Petén jungle. The 25 plaza groups include many temples and palaces that were built over the many centuries when this was an administrative center for the Belize River valley.

El Pilar sits on an undulating series of ridges that rise more than 900 feet above the surrounding countryside, largely covered with lush vegetation through which a few trails have been hacked.

Known officially as the **El Pilar Archaeological Reserve for Maya Flora and Fauna**, the management plan for this site calls for the involvement of local residents (with input from archaeologists) in protecting the ruins and surrounding forest as well as sharing their knowledge of the region's history and ecology. A great effort has been made to preserve the natural environment during the archaeological survey of this site. The name itself derives from the Spanish *pila* (wash basin), an apparent reference to the natural water drainages near El Pilar.

There are plans for on-site educational and tourism facilities—as well as access to the Guatemalan side of El Pilar—but at present there are limited improvements at the ruins beyond five marked nature trails. A caretaker is on hand to show you around, and archaeologists are usually working here from February through June. Archaeologist Annabel Ford says her goal is to "show that the people who walk in the Maya's footsteps can benefit from ancient methods to produce a sustainable and economically viable solution to the area's needs." For information about these efforts, contact the **BRASS/El Pilar Project**, MesoAmerican Research Center, University of California, Santa Barbara, CA 93106, (805) 893-8191.

Getting There/Outfitters
Drive to the village of **Bullet Tree Falls** and ask area residents for directions to the Pilar Road. Future plans call for an El Pilar visitors center at Bullet Tree Falls, which would offer handicrafts, food, drinks, and guiding services. In wet weather the ruins are best reached by horseback; high-clearance vehicles can make it here during dry weather. By the time you read this, plans to improve the road may have been realized. **Fred Prost** of nearby **Parrot Nest Riverside Treehouses** is a good resource and leads guided tours of the area regularly. From San Ignacio, the trip takes about an hour. Parrot Nest also runs trips to chicle camps in the nearby jungle.

CAHAL PECH
The ridgetop ruin of Cahal Pech, practically within the town limits of San Ignacio, underwent extensive excavation and restoration during the early 1990s by San Diego State University, the University of Oregon, Canada's Trent University, and the Belize Department of Archaeology. Some visitors may be surprised—and even put off—by the overlay of limestone plaster on much of these ruins, but supervising archaeologists insist that such restoration is historically accurate. We are not used to seeing smooth plaster surfaces on ancient Mayan buildings, the experts point out, because it has almost entirely eroded over the years.

Cahal Pech derives its Mopan Maya name, "place of the tick," from the large number of bovine parasites found here when the area was used as a cattle pasture. The ruins were not mapped until 1950 and were periodically looted until a complete survey was made in 1988.

This ceremonial complex of what was once a medium-size Mayan settlement and political center consists of 34 structures spread across several acres. There are seven courtyards, plus a central plaza, a number of ball courts, stelae, family tombs, and temple pyramids. The tallest building is 77 feet high. The site reportedly functioned as a kind of royal castle, standing guard over the nearby confluence of the Mopan and Macal Rivers. Cahal Pech is believed to have been closely associated with nearby Buena Vista and Xunantunich, both of which date from the same era.

Preliminary analysis indicates that Cahal Pech was occupied during the Late Classic period from at least 900 B.C. to about A.D. 1100, reaching its greatest strength around A.D. 600. Notable findings here include an altar, a mosaic mask, and what appears to have been a sweat lodge. Research supports the theory that the famous Classic Maya "collapse" of the ninth century came neither swiftly nor easily, at least at Cahal Pech. Based on new evidence of lingering squalor and decay, it appears that the breakdown of the civilization dragged on for as long as 100 years, until the early tenth century.

Getting There

Visitors are welcome at Cahal Pech, which is a pleasant 20-minute walk (or 5-minute drive) west of downtown San Ignacio. Look for a sign pointing to the ruins at a point where the Western Highway makes a sweeping turn just west of San Ignacio. The site is on the south side of the road, out of view in a cluster of trees.

Fees/Services

A worthwhile museum and visitors center are at the entrance to the site, open daily from 8 a.m. to 4 p.m. An informative, free pamphlet about Cahal Pech is distributed here, and the $5 admission fee is collected. A hardback book about the site, published by San Diego State University, is sold at the museum and various bookstores around Belize.

On top of a hill, a few hundred yards from the ruin, is the Cahal Pech Tavern, a popular bar and dance hall that's worth a visit. Vendors sometimes sell drinks and snacks near the entrance to the ruins.

PACBITUN

Located on a dirt road near San Antonio Village, about a 45-minute drive south of San Ignacio, Pacbitun (meaning "stones set in the earth") is one of the most enduring Middle Pre-Classic Mayan ruins in the country. Archaeologists believe it was first occupied in 1000 B.C. and abandoned around A.D. 900. The location was known for many years by local residents but not registered by the Belize Department of Archaeology until 1971. Trent University excavated and partially reconstructed this ceremonial site during the 1980s. Findings include a number of Mayan altar stones and ball courts, as well as ancient musical instruments, such as ocarinas, fashioned out of carved and molded pottery. Pacbitun has at least 24 temple pyramids, the largest standing 60 feet tall. Two thousand years ago this was apparently a wealthy trading center with fancy homes, elevated walkways, a ball court, and raised irrigation causeways up to a half-mile long.

Getting There

The Pacbitun site is on private farmland, but owner **Fidencio Tzul** welcomes and guides visitors for a small fee. His family home is at the well-marked turnoff to Pacbitun one-half mile east of San Antonio. The ruins are about 3 miles farther down the side-road. Tzul will be happy to answer any questions. There have been persistent rumors that the Belize government will one day purchase Pacbitun and relocate the Tzul family, so access may have changed by the time you read this.

BELIZE DISTRICT

ALTUN HA

The ancient Mayan ruins of Altun Ha are 31 miles north of Belize City on the old Northern Highway that passes through Maskall. (The new Northern Highway continues in a more westerly direction toward Crooked Tree Lagoon, reconnecting with the old highway at Carmelita.) The Altun Ha site, 8 miles from the sea, was an important Mayan trading and ceremonial center. Here the sun was a focus of worship; Mayan priests were buried within one of the tallest structures, known as the **Temple of the Sun God**. Altun Ha means "stone water" in Maya, and this name refers to nearby Rockstone Pond, an ancient water catchment ingeniously dammed and lined with clay for irrigation purposes. Near this pond stands a temple in which archaeologists found artifacts the Maya obtained from the faraway city of Teotihuacán, on the outskirts of present-day Mexico City.

During its seventh-century height, Altun Ha became a focal point for the sacrifice of such valuables as jade jewelry and carved pendants, as well as offerings of copal resin. At the top of the **Temple of the Masonry Altars**, such precious items were smashed into small pieces and cast into an intense fire. Like many Mayan rituals, the origin and purpose of this sacrificial offering remain unclear.

Thirteen structures surround two main plazas at the site. The two tallest temples, Temple of the Sun God (the structure depicted on Belikin beer bottles) and Temple of the Masonry Altars, rise 60 feet above the grassy plaza floor. Altun Ha covers an area of about 5 square miles and includes an extensive swamp north of the plazas. It's believed that up to 10,000 people lived here during the Classic period of Mayan civilization, as late as A.D. 1000.

Visitors interested in birds are likely to be rewarded here. Brilliant green Aztec parakeets often streak by in tight formation, level with the tops of the temples. Ringed kingfishers rest on the summit of the Mayan structures before returning to the nearby Rockstone Pond to fish. There are also trails into the bush for birders driven by the constant chorus of calls that echo around the two main plazas.

Altun Ha was first excavated by A. H. Anderson in 1957 and by W. R. Bullard in 1961, undergoing some of the most extensive field-work of any Belizean ruin. This rich ceremonial center remained archaeologically quiet until 1963, when quarry workers unearthed an elaborately carved jade pendant. This discovery triggered an intensive archaeological excavation from 1964 to 1971, spearheaded by David Pendergast with support from Canada's Royal Ontario Museum.

Perhaps Altun Ha's most famous historical footnote is Pendergast's discovery of a huge jade head replica of **Kinich Ahua, the Sun God**, in one of the last tombs to be excavated. The effigy was made in about A.D. 600 and owned by an elderly priest. At the time of its discovery, this priceless relic was the largest of its type ever recorded in the Mayan world—almost 6 inches tall and weighing nearly 10 pounds. The jade head can be viewed in the Department of Archaeology's vault in Belmopan. On rare occasions the Kinich Ahua replica is taken on exhibition tours with other artifacts; eventually it will be displayed in Belize's long-planned National Museum. Jade found at Altun Ha probably came from Guatemala's Sierra de las Minas, since this stone does not occur naturally in Belize. Altun Ha's obviously important religious function as a sacrificial site remains unexplained.

Getting There

From Belize City, take the Northern Highway about 20 miles and turn right just north of the village of Sand Hill, at the junction of the old Northern Highway (the sign is marked "Maskall and Orange Walk"). Proceed about 11 miles and turn left (just past Cowhead Creek) at the sign for the 2-mile connecting road to the Altun Ha parking lot. The drive from Belize City takes approximately 45 minutes. There is no regular bus service to the site, although it is possible to hire a taxi or hitch a ride with a truck that brings goods to market in Belize City from the village of Maskall, which is located about 10 miles north of Altun Ha.

Fee

An admission fee of $5 per person is collected at the visitor registration center.

Outfitters

G & W Holiday Tours, has an office at the International Airport, 25-2461, e-mail *gholiday@btl.net.* Winston Seawell is a wealth of information about Belize, has reliable transportation, and gives an informative tour of Altun Ha. **S & L Travel Services & Tours** (2-77593) is a good choice for some of the best Belizean guides. If you're coming by water from Ambergris Caye, your boatman will likely serve as your guide—and many are excellent.

Where to Stay and Eat near Altun Ha

There are no accommodations at Altun Ha, but camping is allowed with permission from the caretaker, who also permits overnight RV parking.

Maruba Resort & Jungle Spa at Mile 40.5 on the old Northern Highway; $110; 3-22199, in the U.S. (713) 799-2031. Maruba Resort boasts a restaurant and bar, an open-air Japanese-style hot tub, swimming pool, massages, cabaña-style accommodations, birding, horseback riding, tours of Altun Ha and Lamanai, and scuba or snorkeling trips. Although not recently visited by the authors, some guests have made allegations of consistently poor service and unjustly high prices at Maruba.

Several low to moderately priced guest houses are available in nearby Crooked Tree Village; we recommend these for visitors who want to see both Altun Ha and the Crooked Tree Wildlife Sanctuary. **The Paradise Inn** is our favorite.

MARCO GONZALEZ

This is a late Pre-Classic era (A.D. 1100 to 1300) residential and sea-trading center that was active for hundreds of years. Located in the thick mangrove swamp at the south end of Ambergris Caye, its ruins have been studied by the Royal Ontario Museum, which found no intact structures. It's believed that most buildings were constructed of seashells, particularly conch. Pottery, obsidian, and jade, as well as basalt grinding tools, stelae, and temple mounds, were unearthed here. Access to Marco Gonzalez, which has been heavily looted, is by foot trail from the town of San Pedro.

SAN JUAN

Excavated by a Texas archaeological team, this small site is at the north end of Ambergris Caye (now the Bacalar Chico National Park headquarters) and dates from the Pre-Classic period. It is one of about a dozen Mayan sites pinpointed on the island, all largely abandoned by A.D. 1000, as trading patterns shifted to overland routes. Many of the other cayes and atolls have similar sites and middens, the equivalent of Mayan trash heaps. The site is accessible by boat from San Pedro.

CHAU HIIX

This is a small Classic Maya site currently under excavation near Crooked Tree Village, about 35 miles northwest of Belize City. The forest-covered site is accessible by trail from the village, and there is much wildlife (including spider monkeys) in the area. Archaeologists believe Chau Hiix was occupied before and during the arrival of Spanish clerics in the 16th century.

COLHA

The Colha site is located on the Rancho Creek Farm, about 7 miles north of Maskall on the (old) Northern Highway, roughly 40 miles northwest of Belize City in the Belize District. Permission of the landowner is required to see this small ceremonial site. Colha shows occupation as early as 2400 B.C., making it one of the oldest Mayan sites. It is under excavation by the University of Texas, which is also exploring the nearby Blue Creek site.

ORANGE WALK DISTRICT

LAMANAI

While the towering temples of Xunantunich and Caracol are impressive by any measure, a different kind of beauty awaits visitors making the scenic journey to Lamanai, which is variously translated as "the submerged crocodile" or "the drowned insect." These intriguing ruins are about 70 miles northwest of Belize City, on a patch of high ground that looms over the west bank of the shimmering New River Lagoon, the country's biggest lake.

Lamanai is unusual in that it was occupied longer than almost any other known Mayan site, from about 1500 B.C. (or earlier) until at least A.D. 1650—and for varying intervals to the present day. As an important trading center and ceremonial site, its history extends from the formative years of the civilization until well after Franciscan friars arrived from Spain in the 1540s to convert Lamanai's "heathens." The city enjoyed its greatest strength during the Pre-Classic era of A.D. 200 to 900, and Lamanai's major pyramid—referred to as the **Southern Temple** or **N10-43**—was completed around 100 B.C., then modified several times before A.D. 600.

Some of Lamanai's ruins are among the oldest surviving buildings from the Pre-Classic period, dating back to 700 B.C. Pollen samples show that corn was being cultivated here at least 800 years earlier. There are over 700 buildings in the complex, which is believed to have supported as many as 35,000 people. Only about 5 percent of the known structures have been excavated.

Thanks to records kept by early Catholic missionaries, we know that Lamanai is a Spanish corruption of *Lamanain*, the original Mayan name for this place (most other sites were named by their European discoverers). The term is fitting, since the lagoon nearby was—and is—perfect crocodile habitat. Many representations of the reptile have been found here, including ceramic decorations and plaster masks, some of which may be seen in the excellent on-site museum. A figure wearing a crocodile headdress, found in many forms throughout the area, is thought to represent one of Lamanai's important rulers.

Although it is possible to drive here (about 2 hours from Belize City), many visitors prefer to come to Lamanai by boat up the New River, exactly as the ancient Maya did. After navigating through miles

of constantly dividing tributaries and closed-in landscape (full of waterbirds and
their predators), a pyramid-
shaped temple (N10-43)
suddenly looms 112 feet
above the New River
Lagoon. When the temple's
crown was placed in about
100 B.C., this was probably
the tallest building in the
Mayan world. At the apex of
its considerable power, this
well-situated city-state is said
to have had a wide trading
influence that extended over
much of present-day Mexico,
Guatemala, and Honduras,
plus all of Belize.

The site's central core
covers about one square
mile, with residential structures and smaller buildings

Carved face at Mayan ruin of Lamanai

Kevin Schafer

spread over another thousand acres. Vegetation makes it difficult to
get an adequate perspective on the ground, so a hike to the summit of
one of the temples is a good idea: three are over 100 feet tall.

In one section, accessible by a short path, are a few crumbling
walls that remain from a 16th-century Catholic mission, one of the
few reminders of Spanish occupation extant in all Belize. Conversions
of the Maya to Christianity began here in 1544 and the Spanish
remained until 1641, when the Indians rebelled and burned their
church to the ground as part of a regional uprising that included
Lamanai's sister city of Tipú, on the Macal River (later destroyed
when a citrus plantation was put in). A second chapel was built at
Lamanai using stones from one of the Maya's most sacred temples,
which contributed to the friction between Europeans and Indians. In
fact, a Mayan stela (still visible) was erected in front of this church
after its destruction, containing a written message firmly disavowing
any allegiance to Christianity. A figurine found in the ruins of the second church has gaping jaws at either end with a god coming out of

one of these mouths. It is thought to be a Mayan warning along the lines of, "Beware, this could happen to you!"

Virtually no one lived here when the British loggers arrived with their Jamaican slaves in the 18th century to extract mahogany and other trees. Chinese and East Indian laborers were imported about ninety years later to work in the local sugarcane fields, but they did not react well to the demanding climate and debilitating diseases; most of the plantations were soon abandoned. The ruin of a 19th-century sugar mill, with ficus-strangled flywheel and boiler, is still visible. It was built in 1866 and burned by the Maya (along with other European constructions) the following year. A corroded molasses storage chamber, now home to bats, lies a short distance from the abandoned mill.

Because of the ruin's protected status as an archaeological reserve, the number of black howler monkeys and other endangered mammals living here has been on the rise. In 1993, researcher Hal Markowitz of San Francisco State University began a long-term study of the behavioral ecology of howlers here. Volunteers may work alongside the primate experts through arrangement with Oceanic Society Expeditions (800-326-7491). Participants help in all aspects of non-invasive data collection and live in double-occupancy cabañas at the site. OSE also offers Lamanai trips in which participants help researchers identify and record birds. The goal is to collect as many tropical bird songs as possible for laboratory study.

Vegetation here is lush. Common trees at Lamanai include the guanacaste, mahogany, rubber, cohune palm, poisonwood, and ficus. The adjacent lagoon, fed by a maze of underwater springs and aquifers, is teeming with fish and virtually unpolluted. Waterbirds thrive here. On the western bank stretch miles of swampy savannas that are an important habitat for jaguars and other cats.

The wide array of artifacts found suggests that Lamanai's residents were enthusiastic and successful merchants. One ancient pottery vessel contained several small offerings floating in pools of liquid mercury, their purpose a mystery. Other oddities include an unusually small Mayan ball court and an extraordinarily preserved carved offering stone that now lies under a protective palm thatch. It is believed that this carving escaped destruction because it apparently fell face-forward to the ground during a Mayan fire ceremony and was therefore left unmolested for fear the event itself portended evil. The stone's outstanding depiction of the Lamanai priest-king Lord Smoking Shell (whose reign began about A.D. 608) clearly shows his open-mouthed-serpent head-dress and other accoutrements. He holds a ceremonial bar in his arms, symbolizing his royal authority.

The museum at Lamanai contains incense burners (censers), burial urns, and chalices discovered here, along with eccentric flint carvings, tools, and many ceramic objects. If you are fortunate enough to visit while the well-informed Mayan archaeologist and curator **Nasario Coo** is on-site, you can obtain a thorough account of Lamanai's fascinating history. Coo may provide a guided tour if his schedule allows.

Getting There/Outfitters

Public transportation to Lamanai is limited to taxis (from Orange Walk Town), rental cars, supply trucks, and hired boats. A dirt road, occasionally impassable during the wet season, extends to the site from Orange Walk Town via the village of San Felipe. Watch for the signs directing you to Indian Church Village and/or Lamanai.

Most visitors arrange a day trip through local hotels, travel agencies, or package tour operators, traveling from as far away as San Pedro, Belize City, and San Ignacio. We recommend **Jungle River Tours** (3-22293) or **Carlos Godoy Tours** (3-22969), which both offer a fine New River/Lamanai archaeological tour.

Another approach is to drive as far as Tower Bridge, Guinea Grass, or the Mennonite community of Shipyard, then head up the New River by locally hired boat. (There is no public transportation to Guinea Grass or Shipyard.) Boats can usually be rented on the spur of the moment in any of these riverside villages or can be arranged in advance through large hotels, such as the **D'Victoria** (3-22518) in Orange Walk Town, or the **Maruba** in Maskall (3-22199).

The boat trip is very pleasant, affording opportunities for swimming and other water sports along the way. Many orchids and other flowering plants are visible in the trees overhead. Hollowed-out trunks along the riverbank provide a daytime home to a small, fish-eating bat. Many kinds of birds and animals live along the banks of the lagoon and are easily glimpsed en route to Lamanai. The **Crooked Tree Wildlife Sanctuary** is only eight miles to the east, and many species are present in both locations. Jabiru stork, snail kite, northern jacana, squirrel cuckoo, blue-crowned motmot, limpkin, cormorant, and night heron, along with huge flocks of parrots, are among the birds recorded near Lamanai. You also may see crocodiles, although the noise of powerboats tends to scare them away.

Where to Stay and Eat

Lamanai Outpost Lodge, 2-33578, one-half-mile away from the ruins in Indian Church, accommodations (and restaurant). Rooms are also available in Orange Walk Town, about 20 miles to the northeast. Camping is not allowed at Lamanai, and no food or drink is sold here.

The site has restrooms, a picnic area, and several trails cut through the forest. Besides curator Nasario Coo, the resident caretakers can answer basic questions about the site. The structures are not well marked, however, and no literature is available. Bring your own guide or a map, as well as the usual sunscreen and insect repellent. A swimsuit is also a good idea; New Lagoon ranks as one of the best swimming holes in Belize.

Richard Mahler

Ruin of the old sugar mill at Lamanai

CUELLO

Cuello is located on private land, and permission is needed to visit this ancient site, a minor ceremonial center and settlement area about 4 miles southwest of Orange Walk Town on Yo Creek Road. Arrangements can be made by calling the **Cuello Rum Distillery**, the site's owner, during business hours at 3-22141. Tours of the distillery, which bottles sugarcane spirits under the "Caribbean" label, can also be scheduled. Permission can usually be obtained by simply showing up; the facility is open Monday through Saturday. Ask to speak with Hilberto or Oswaldo Cuello. Their biggest concern is that visitors not disturb their cattle, which are pastured near the ruins.

Although not well developed for visitors, Cuello is one of the most exciting discoveries in the Mayan world. Before the exploration of this site in 1973 by Cambridge University (and later Boston University), most experts believed the Mayan civilization had its start around 600 B.C., which was the earliest date of any previously known settlement.

Applying state-of-the-art carbon dating techniques to ancient maize fragments and wooden posts, it was determined that occupation by the Maya began here around 1000 B.C., possibly even earlier. Thus, the "start date" of the civilization was pushed back substantially. Subsequent findings at the Colha and Pulltrouser Swamp sites in northern Belize have set that date back to as early as 2500 B.C.

Other findings at Cuello raise more unanswered questions: Why did a mass slaughter of at least 32 individuals take place here about 400 B.C.? Why were earthenware pots placed over the heads of the deceased in some of Cuello's burial chambers? Did the Maya originate their pyramid-plaza architectural style here, as many have suggested?

One certainty is Cuello's continuous occupation for thousands of years, until as recently as A.D. 1500. The site has yielded evidence that the Maya may have been able to build the strength of their city-state empire partly through the development of more productive strains of corn, their principal crop.

Actually, there is not a lot for the casual visitor to see at Cuello, which lies in a forested compound of the distillery. Norman Hammond and his Cambridge research team continue to conduct research at the ruin, but they fill in excavated areas after completing their studies. Still, this is an important historical site for any serious student of the Maya.

Getting There
Cuello can easily be reached by taxi ($6) or private car via Yo Creek Road, which begins in Orange Walk Town as Baker's Street. No information or guides will be found at the site, although the Department of Archaeology can provide background materials in Belmopan.

About 25 miles down the same road are traditional and modern Mennonite farms and settlements that fan out from Blue Creek Village. By heading through August Pine Ridge and San Felipe, you will eventually reach the Mexican border crossing (pedestrians only) at La Unión. This is also the preferred route for those driving to Chan Chich Lodge, the Programme for Belize lands, and the Río Bravo Conservation Area.

NOHMUL
Nohmul is a major ceremonial center spread among privately owned sugarcane fields near the village of San Pablo, about 7 miles north of

Orange Walk Town. Permission from the property owner is required before visiting. The site—located on a limestone ridge and dominated by a massive acropolis atop which a pyramid has been built—consists of two groups of buildings incorporating ten plazas and connected by a raised causeway.

Nohmul (Mayan for "great mound") was occupied first during the Pre-Classic era (350 B.C. to A.D. 250) and again during the Late Classic period (A.D. 600 to 900). At its height, the community was the seat of government for an area encompassing eight square miles and including the nearby settlements now known as **San Esteban** and **San Luis**.

The dominant ceremonial structure at Nohmul, a large limestone-block rectangle, was built during the late Pre-Classic era with several modifications in subsequent years. Interestingly, this acropolis seems to have lost its religious significance over time and to have been converted into residential quarters by the end of Nohmul's Mayan occupation.

Thomas Gann first recorded the large mound as a Mayan site in 1897 and conducted digs here over the next 39 years. He and his wife found jade, seashells, flint, obsidian, pottery, and human bones. Much of this material was removed from burial tombs and sent to the British Museum in London. Neglect, looting, and the use of ancient buildings as road construction material took their toll on Nohmul before full-scale excavation could begin in 1982.

Getting There

Nohmul is about 1 mile west of the village of San Pablo, which straddles the Northern Highway midway between Orange Walk Town and Corozal Town, both about 8 miles distant. The site's owner, **Esteban Itzab**, should be contacted before proceeding to the ruin. He lives in the house directly across the street from the community water tower.

There are no facilities or services. Buses pass through the village hourly en route to Orange Walk Town or Corozal Town. Nohmul can also be easily reached by private car or taxi from either of these communities in about 20 minutes. Part of the ruin can be seen from the Northern Highway.

LA MILPA

A mostly unrestored ceremonial center, these ruins (said to the third-largest Mayan site in Belize, after Caracol and Lamanai) are on private property within the protected **Río Bravo Conservation and Management Area** in northwest Belize. Located near a biological field station in the middle of the 250,000-acre Río Bravo tract, La Milpa (sometimes called Las Milpas) comprises more than 85 structures scattered throughout thick forest. Two dozen courtyard groups have been counted, plus an elaborate system of reservoirs and causeways. Four pyramids rise to around 70 feet and a "great plaza" here has been judged to be one of the civilization's biggest. There are many other constructions, including two ball courts, believed to be associated with ritual sacrifice as well as recreation.

Stelae and other artifacts indicate major occupation during the Early and Late Classic periods, although the Maya were still a force in the area until the early 19th century, when they attacked nearby mahogany camps. La Milpa was "rediscovered" in the 1930s but extensive mapping did not get under way here until 1990, after extensive looting in the 1970s. Thanks to ongoing study by Boston University, a better picture of La Milpa is gradually emerging. In 1996, the unlooted tomb of a Mayan ruler called Bird Jaguar, who died in about A.D. 450, was found by archaeologist Norman Hammond. Bird Jaguar was among the first Mayan lords to undergo ceremonial burial (the ritual included placement of a cherry-sized jade bead in his mouth), a practice that began about 50 years before his death.

Getting There/Where to Stay

La Milpa is located in a remote area, about 15 miles east of the Guatemala border, that is inaccessible by road during wetter months. Most visitors arrive by private plane via the **Gallon Jug** airstrip and stay at **Chan Chich Lodge**, 2-75634, located in the plaza of another Mayan ruin. Lodge bookings and archaeological tours are arranged through Programme for Belize offices in Belize City and the U.S. Arrangements should be made as far in advance as possible.

Visitors who have obtained a permit from Programme for Belize can drive to the site in about 4 hours from Belize City (during dry weather) via Blue Creek Village in the Orange Walk District. Overnight visitors are housed (with advance permission only) in the dormitory of the Río Bravo Project's field station. Meals and guide services can also be arranged there (2-75616).

COROZAL DISTRICT

CERROS

About 20 miles northeast of Cuello, on an uninhabited stretch of Caribbean coastline overlooking Corozal Bay, are the ruins of Cerros (also known as Cerro Maya, or Mayan Hill). During the dry season, the site can be reached by a dirt road via Chunox, Progreso, and Copper Bank, but it is more commonly visited by boat from Corozal Town, Sarteneja, or Consejo Shores. On a clear day, especially at sunset, the profile of the ruins is clearly visible from the opposite side of the bay.

Cerros is a late Pre-Classic era (350 B.C. to A.D. 250) complex with virtually no construction after A.D. 100. Experts believe it was an important center of maritime commerce, probably handling much of the seagoing trade headed up the nearby New River to Lamanai and the Río Hondo to the Yucatán. Its early demise may have been caused by a gradual Early Classic period shift in Mayan trading patterns in favor of overland routes between the lowland and highland city-states. During this time, inland population centers such as Tikal and Caracol became established.

Although the archaeological reserve is small (53 acres), it includes three large structures that loom above several plazas and a few pyramid-like buildings. The tallest temple is 72 feet and provides a sweeping view across the water. Cerros probably reached its peak around the time of Christ's birth. During this period it appears to have shifted from an economy dependent on fishing, hunting, and farming to one reliant on the importation of pottery, salt, jade, and obsidian by dugout canoe. It was almost certainly linked to the many smaller trading sites on the Belizean cayes and atolls farther south.

Ancient ball courts, quasi-religious tombs, elegant residences, farming terraces, and boat canals have been found at Cerros, indicating that its social structure was once highly developed. Surrounding the site is a man-made drainage canal that was nearly a mile long, 20 feet wide, and 6 feet deep. The immediate area has been uninhabited for some time, and part of the original complex is now underwater as a result of a rise in sea level over the last 2,000 years.

Some of the buildings at Cerros display large painted stucco masks, up to 13 feet high, that depict images of humans and animals. Unfortunately, because salt-air speeds erosion and no money is available for restoration, most of the masks have been plastered over to prevent further decay. The pyramid known as **5C**, however, still has four masks: two identified as the sun and Venus, the others unknown. Some feel that the presence of these large friezes demonstrates that the divine Mayan elite were in power by the end of the Pre-Classic era, or about A.D. 250.

Fees and Services
Largely unrestored, much of Cerros appears to the casual visitor as little more than a series of low mounds, with only the tallest ceremonial structures hinting at past grandeur. Cerros remains without accommodations or services, and camping is not allowed. A caretaker will collect the $2 entrance fee and provide an informative tour of the ruin.

Getting There
The roundabout road from Corozal Town passes by pastoral lagoons and Mestizo fishing villages, but this route cannot be recommended during wet weather.

By easily chartered private boat at the Corozal Town public pier, Cerros is about 5 miles (20 minutes) across Corozal Bay and slightly longer from Sarteneja. Transport can be arranged by Corozal's **Caribbean Village Resort** or boatman **Manuel Hoare**, 4-22744; or Sarteneja boatman **Fernando Alamilla**, 4-32085. Expect to pay at least $75 for the round-trip. Because of the ruin's close proximity to the mouth of the New River and adjacent wetlands, insect repellent and long-sleeved clothing are advised.

SANTA RITA
Amateur archaeologist Thomas Gann, a turn-of-the-century British physician living in Corozal, was perhaps the first European to recognize Santa Rita and Cerros as ancient Mayan sites. Located directly across the bay from the latter ruin and northeast of the Corozal Town center (now encircled by private homes and businesses), Santa Rita flourished off and on from at least 1800 B.C. until the arrival of the Spanish in the 1530s. Some might convincingly argue that since part of the present-day town is built atop Santa Rita, human habitation has continued here without interruption since at least 18 centuries before the birth of Christ!

Gann theorized that Santa Rita was one of an important series of coastal towns strategically located so that signal fires could be used to send messages up and down the Yucatán peninsula. Although this theory has never been conclusively proven, there is plenty of evidence that Santa Rita was in fact one of the region's most powerful Mayan communities and even regained some of its prominence after the disintegration of the civilization as a whole. Its strategic placement within a few miles of the Río Hondo and New River trade routes was one key to its long survival.

Santa Rita's location, on a limestone plateau overlooking the Chetumal and Corozal bays, immediately attracted the attention of Spanish conquistadors, who seized the city-state under the leadership of Alfonso Davila in 1531 from the Mayan lord Nachacan. Although they were eventually routed by the Indians, the Spanish simply relocated farther north (at what is now the Mexican city of Chetumal) and managed to sever the remaining trade routes that fueled Santa Rita's prosperity. Within a few years the community was almost completely abandoned. The modern town of Corozal was subsequently established on the ruins' foundations in 1858 by survivors of the famous massacre at Bacalar, Mexico.

Despite its long and impressive history, only one visible structure remains at Santa Rita: a 55-foot-high, partially restored pyramid-shaped tomb, where two important burials were excavated. This site includes several chambers and an offertory niche. One of the rulers found buried here wore a kind of gold earring reserved only for the highest noblemen, another hint of Santa Rita's importance not only as a city, but as a terminus for trade with other rich communities. Not incidentally, the discovery of gold objects here is believed to have prompted the first attack by the Spanish.

Like nearby Cerros, Santa Rita appears to have been an agricultural center long before the seagoing trade boom hit. Once its boats got under way, however, Santa Rita found eager markets for the prized commodities gathered or cultivated nearby, including cacao, vanilla, honey, and spices. Unlike Cerros, Santa Rita thrived through the Classic period and was still stockpiling turquoise and gold from the Aztecs long after more-distant Mayan cities had collapsed. Relics from Santa Rita's tombs even include pottery made in the Andes mountains of far-off Peru.

Gann uncovered several burial sites, along with sculptured friezes and stuccoed murals. Much of this material has subsequently been lost—Indians deliberately destroyed six murals in 1900 before Gann could copy them—but some of the doctor's meticulous notes and drawings survive. Among important discoveries made here over a seven-year period beginning in 1979 was a skeleton adorned with jade and mica ornaments. Many of these findings are now held in the Archaeology Vault in Belmopan.

Sadly, since the founding of Corozal Town some 150 years ago, a good part of Santa Rita has been systematically looted, paved over, or built upon. Hundreds of ancient structures and artifacts here have been lost forever.

Getting There/Fees

The last ancient building at Santa Rita, known as **Structure** 7, is an easy walk or car ride from the plaza of Corozal Town. Local residents will be happy to point you in the right direction: turn left at the Hilltop Bar and follow the road to the Coca-Cola bottling plant. No services are available at the site, although the caretaker (who once lived in one of the tombs) is very helpful and knowledgeable. He collects a $2.50 fee during Santa Rita's hours of admission, 8 a.m. to 5 p.m. daily, except Sunday. Be sure to lock your car, as some visitors have reported thefts during their visit.

STANN CREEK DISTRICT

MAYFLOWER

This is a fairly recent "discovery" (1976) about 20 miles east of Dangriga on upper Silk Grass Creek. The remote Classic Maya site is being surveyed by Harvard and Tulane Universities. Nearby are two impressive waterfalls: **Antelope** and **Hummingbird**. You can hire a local guide to tour the unrestored ruins or arrange a trip through the **Jaguar Reef Jungle Lodge** in Hopkins or **Pelican Beach Resort** in Dangriga.

TOLEDO DISTRICT

LUBAANTUN

Lubaantun is modern Mayan for "place of the fallen rocks," which aptly describes this Late Classic ceremonial center, noted for an unusual style of construction that is unique to southern Belize. The large pyramids and residences observed here are made of crystalline limestone blocks with no visible mortar binding them together, not unlike constructions by the Inca civilization in the high Andes of Peru and Ecuador. This means that every hand-cut stone was carefully measured and shaped to fit together with the adjoining stone. (Remember, the Maya had no stone tools and used the wheel only in toys.) The effect of their masterful dressed stonework looks a bit like marble. Some speculate that the Maya had destroyed the nearby forest, making it impossible to fuel the high-temperature limestone kilns needed to created mortar. The forest long ago renewed itself, and today's Lubaantun visitors include pumas, ocelots, deer, coatimundi, and parrots.

Unlike most other Mayan ceremonial sites, the buildings that were then placed on top of these pyramids were made from perishable materials, such as tree limbs and palm fronds, and obviously no longer remain. We can only guess at what they looked like.

The austerity of this site—Lubaantun is now essentially a stone acropolis—is reminiscent of Quiriguá, located about 100 miles away in southeast Guatemala, and there may have been close contact between the two city-states. Curiously, Lubaantun has yielded impressive stone architecture, but virtually no carved stone stelae and only a handful of painted pottery vessels. Yet nearby **Nim Li Punit** and **Uxbenka** have plenty of sculpted rock monuments but no large masonry structures. This suggests to some authorities that a diverse social organization once prevailed in this area and that each site served a distinct purpose.

At Lubaantun, 11 large pyramid-platform structures are built around five main plazas and three ball courts. The tallest of the pyramids rises 45 feet above the jungle. There are 13 smaller plazas and a number of other structures, including a large stadium that may have been used for the observation of sacred ceremonies. Several burial tombs have reportedly been found here as well.

It is believed that carvings and other types of building decorations commonly fashioned out of stone at other Mayan sites were made out of wood at Lubaantun, located in one of the most rain-soaked and densely forested corners of Belize. One theory persists that Lubaantun was an important religious, administrative, political, and commercial center, yet only for a brief time—two centuries at most, but perhaps as few as 20 years. No one knows what led to abandonment around A.D. 900, or why the hilltop site was not leveled before construction began, in the traditional manner. Instead, workers simply filled in gaps with stones and mortar.

It is thought that the greatest wealth of Lubaantun came from the harvest and trade of wild cacao—the modern source of chocolate—

which was so highly prized by the Maya that they used it as a form of currency. The area is still considered prime cacao-growing country, and the 1970 discovery of a ceramic musician wearing a cacao-pod pendant lends credence to the notion that the prized beans were grown here in the eighth century. Cacao, used to make a drink prized by Mayan royalty, was probably traded for jade and obsidian.

The best-known discovery at Lubaantun is the remarkable **Crystal Skull**, supposedly unearthed in 1926 by Anna Mitchell-Hedges (daughter of archaeologist F. A. Mitchell-Hedges) on her seventeenth birthday. This artifact demonstrates superb artistry and workmanship; it is perfectly carved from an eight-inch-cube of pure rock crystal and shows virtually no tool marks. The treasure appears to have been modeled after a specific human head, but the identity of that individual—and the Crystal Skull's significance—remains unknown. Some believe the skull was brought from somewhere else for a "staged" birthday discovery at Lubaantun; others are convinced it is linked to the lost continent of Atlantis. Archaeologist Norman Hammond believes the skull is not a Mayan creation. The relic remains in Canada and its aged owner reaffirmed during a 1996 visit to Lubaantun that she has no intention of returning it to Belize.

Getting There
Lubaantun perches on ridge immediately north of the Columbia River, about 1.5 miles by dirt road past the village of San Pedro Columbia (turn right at the church and left after you cross the river bridge). This route is about a 45-minute walk. A steep short-cut path leads to Lubaantun from the banks of the Columbia; ask one of the local boys to show you the way. Yet another option is taking the public bus (which runs Monday, Wednesday, Friday, and Saturday) to San Miguel to the Lubaantun turnoff, which is marked by a directional sign to the ruins. The last mile of road is slippery when wet.

Accommodations and Services
Accommodations and service are available in San Pedro Columbia through both the "indigenous experience" homestay and guest house program (see chapter 9, Southern Belize, for details). The operators of **Dem Dat's Doin'**, Alfredo and Yvonne Villoria, rent a room at their San Pedro permaculture farm by advance arrangement. You can also overnight at **Fallen Stones Jungle Lodge** (1.5 miles away) or **San Antonio Village** (5 miles distant). Camping at the ruin is not allowed.

Several hotels and travel agencies in the Toledo and Stann Creek districts arrange tours to Lubaantun and other nearby Mayan ruins. There are restrooms and a picnic area here but no drinking water, food, or literature. The setting is peaceful and birds abound. A Mayan caretaker, **Santiago Coc**, answers questions and sometimes waives the $1.50 entrance fee. Santiago is very knowledgeable, having worked with archaeologists here in 1970.

NIM LI PUNIT

Located about 25 miles north of Punta Gorda off the Southern Highway, this Late Classic ceremonial center remained hidden from outsiders until oilworkers stumbled upon it in the early 1970s. Since then, excavations have revealed 25 stelae, at least eight of which are carved, including the tallest (at 31 feet) carved stone monument in Belize. The site's name is Mayan for "big hat" and refers to a head-dress-adorned figure on the tallest stela.

Archaeologists believe Nim Li Punit may have been affiliated with nearby Lubaantun, which flourished around the same time and is architecturally similar. Digging did not start here until 1983, after the site had been badly looted. Nevertheless, an impressive stele and royal tomb were uncovered in 1986. UCLA archaeologist Richard Leventhal continues to oversee excavations.

There are several tall structures (up to 40 feet high) around two plazas and the remains of a fairly large settlement. More than two dozen monuments have been identified at Nim Li Punit, many of an unusually long and low design. One building, for example, is only 9 feet high but 215 feet long. It is believed that the site may have been a funerary cult center that acted as a kind of service community to the local elite, who were probably headquartered in Lubaantun. The true function of Nim Li Punit and its relation to other Mayan centers remains unclear.

Although it is small, Nim Li Punit has hieroglyphics and many interesting carvings on its ceremonial stones. As is the case at many Mayan sites, there is an enormous ceiba tree (next to the caretaker's hut) and many flowering plants. The friendly resident caretaker, **Placido Pec**, will answer questions, direct you to the guest registry, and collect the $1.50 entrance fee.

Getting There/Services

Nim Li Punit is about ½-mile northeast of the Southern Highway at Mile 75 near the Mayan village of Indian Creek. It is not directly accessible by public transportation, although daily **Z-Line** and

James Line buses pass by on their way to and from Punta Gorda and Dangriga (the drivers will pick you up and let you off here).

A well-marked track leads visitors to the site from the highway in about 20 minutes. The trailhead is not far from a handicrafts stand and Whitney's Grocery Store (if you pass Whitney's Lumber Mill, heading south, you've gone too far). The nearest accommodations are in Silver Creek and Big Falls. We recommend **Rav's Guest House**, next to one of the only known hot springs in Belize. You can also stay in Punta Gorda (25 miles south), San Antonio (10 miles south), or one of the Mayan villages participating in the regional guest house and homestay programs. Several hotels and tour operators in the region make trips here, often in combination with Lubaantun.

The ruins overlook a mixture of second-growth jungle and milpa plots. Local Maya use the nearby streams to bathe and are friendly to tourists, sometimes approaching them with handicrafts for sale. Except for a small sun/rain shelter, there are no facilities at Nim Li Punit.

UXBENKA

Local Maya have known about Uxbenka—"the old place" in their local dialect, also spelled "Uxbentun"—for centuries. But the outside world only learned officially of the small site's existence in 1984, when reports of looting filtered back to Belmopan. On further investigation, archaeologists learned that indeed this was a very ancient settlement and, yes, parts of it were being carted off for private sale.

One of the seven carved stelae found here dates from the Early Classic period, the earliest archaeological date yet recorded in southern Belize, but most of the sculpted stones are too badly eroded to read. An additional 13 uncarved stelae have been unearthed at Uxbenka, which also features a couple of unexcavated pyramids and a small plaza, plus some overgrown structural mounds. There's been virtually no restoration work here and, in truth, there's not much for the casual visitor to see.

The site perches on a ridge overlooking the foothills and valleys of the Maya Mountains. The nearby hillsides have been faced with cut terrace stones, a form of agricultural masonry not found outside the Toledo District. The Uxbenka caretaker lives nearby in Santa Cruz Village and may or may not be present when you visit. A map of the ruins was produced with help from the British Army, but you'll have to ask around in order to find a copy.

Getting There

Uxbenka is on the outskirts of Santa Cruz Village, about 3 miles west of San Antonio and 20 miles from Punta Gorda. Besides private vehicle, you can get here on the Wednesday/Saturday bus that shuttles between Punta Gorda and Pueblo Viejo, or take the P.G. bus to San Antonio and hitch a ride (or walk) the rest of the way. Other transportation for visitors is by arranged tour from Punta Gorda or via the supply trucks that come through the area once or twice a week. There is a guest house in San Antonio and overnight accommodations can be arranged with Mayan families in Santa Cruz. Camping is not permitted.

Nearby Attractions

Be sure to check out the soothing waterfall and swimming hole just east of Santa Cruz. Several caves are also worth visiting in the hills to the north, near San José Village. A local guide is helpful in finding these destinations.

GUATEMALA

TIKAL

The famous ancient Mayan ruin of Tikal is located about 50 miles (2 to 3 hours) northwest of the Belize border in Guatemala. Set in a lush high-canopy jungle, the site encompasses at least 3,000 buildings, including a handful of impressively tall temples that loom above the forest. At its peak some 1,500 years ago, Tikal was home to an estimated 100,000 Maya. Yet this city-state was virtually forgotten by the outside world until its "rediscovery" in 1848. Because it is so close to Belize, many travelers make a side trip to Tikal, which is one of the most impressive in the entire Mayan world. For a detailed discussion of Tikal and other nearby ruins, see Richard Mahler's *Guatemala: Adventures in Nature*, (Santa Fe, N.M.: John Muir Publications).

Getting There

If traveling to Tikal on your own, you can obtain Guatemalan visas and/or tourist cards ($2.50) either in Belize City or at the frontier, and formalities at the border are straightforward. (If you travel from Belize to Tikal in a package tour, paperwork and fees are usually taken care of by the operator.) The border is open daily from

8 a.m. to noon and 2 p.m. to 6 p.m.; crossing during off-hours is sometimes possible for an extra fee.

The international boundary runs along the east bank of Mopan River between the towns of Melchor de Mencos, Guatemala, and Benque Viejo, Belize. If you are driving a vehicle, be sure to have your registration and insurance papers in order, and expect to pay a few dollars to have the car fumigated with insecticide on the Guatemalan side (this is required by law and is one reason almost no Belizean companies allow their rental cars to enter Guatemala).

Bus passengers usually have to stop on the Belize side of the crossing and walk or take a taxi a few hundred yards into Melchor de Mencos, where Guatemalan buses (about five a day) pick up westbound passengers. The same thing happens going the opposite direction, although there are some bus companies that drive their vehicles in both countries. Belizean taxi drivers often intercept passengers as they descend from buses on the Guatemala side and take them all the way to San Ignacio, for a fee of about $7 per traveler.

Services

If you simply want a quick glimpse of Guatemalan life, Melchor de Mencos is the place to find it. There is a colorful market where handicrafts are sold and a bank where Belize dollars can be exchanged for quetzales (moneychangers at the border offer slightly better rates). The hotels are inexpensive, and several offer reasonably priced tours to local Mayan ruins, including Tikal. Try the **Hotel Melchor Palace** on the Mopan River, which has a restaurant, a travel service, and a car rental agency. Operator Marco Gross also owns the **Arts & Crafts of Central America** store in San Ignacio, 9-22823, where reservations for the Melchor Palace can be made. Another option is the **Hotel Palque**, also on the river.

The entrance to **Tikal National Park** is northwest of Melchor de Mencos via 2 hours of poor road, then a half-hour of paved surface to the ruins themselves. The $6 admission fee to Tikal National Park is good for the date of entry only. Because the site is so large, a good guidebook and/or map greatly enhances the experience. Well-informed, English-speaking Guatemalan guides can be hired at the site (By law, Belizean guides are not allowed to escort visitors through the ruins). We recommend **Raul Calvillo**, of Jades J.C., who also arranges tours to the El Mirador ruin via horseback.

You'll need two days to take in the majority of structures here, but the highlights can be seen in a few hours. Be sure to spend some time in Tikal's **Silvanus G. Morley Archaeological Museum** ($3 admission), where many artifacts recovered by researchers are on permanent display, including relics from a ruler's tomb.

Travel Tips
En route to the park, you may be stopped by the Guatemalan military and asked to show your passport or other identification. The political situation in Guatemala is improving, but parts of the Petén wilderness are still controlled by outlaws. There are reports of tourists being robbed by gunmen en route to Tikal from Belize, therefore you should take only as much money as you expect to need during your visit. Better yet, fly from Belize City (if you can afford it).

As tourism has increased in Belize, the number of alternative ways for getting to Tikal has also increased. Several scheduled flights are offered each week between Belize City and Flores/Santa Elena (about 40 miles south of the ruins) by Tropic Air, Aerovías, and Aviateca. Expect to pay about $125 round-trip. Charters can also be arranged from Belize City and San Pedro for around $200 and up. From the Flores/Santa Elena airport there are frequent minibuses to Tikal, or a car can be rented for the short drive.

Both **Novelo's** and **Batty's** bus services carry passengers from Belize City to Melchor de Mencos, dropping passengers there for connections to Tikal and/or Flores. If you are heading directly to Tikal you will need to get off at El Cruce, an intersection about 20 miles south of the ruins. From there you can take a public bus or hitch the rest of the way, but there is a risk of getting stranded. Bus schedules being what they are, you will probably need to spend a night in Flores or Santa Elena to catch the early morning public bus or a private minibus to the ruins.

Package Tours
The most popular, and in many respects the easiest, way to visit Tikal from Belize is as part of a package tour. Most of the Cayo lodges arrange such trips (by van or airplane) on a weekly or even daily basis, often including the services of a knowledgeable guide. Similar tours can be arranged from Belize City, San Pedro, and other towns. Prices for package tours of Tikal vary, depending on the number of persons traveling and the duration of the trip. Expect to pay at least $50 per person, however, depending on the size of your group. Bear in mind that a one-day overland round-trip means being inside a vehicle for 5 hours or more.

Overnight visits require lodging and meals in Flores, Santa Elena, or Tikal National Park. Popular hotels in greater Flores include the **Petén, Posada Tayasal, San Juan,** and **Itzá.** Some of these places are very picturesque, situated beside the large lake that dominates this Spanish colonial town, built on the site of an ancient Mayan city. Also recommended is the modern and luxurious (but environmentally friendly) **Hotel Camino Real,** located about 25 minutes (15 miles) west of Tikal on the eastern shore of **Lake Petén Itzá.** This resort has many amenities, including a gift shop and pool.

There are three basic guest houses at Tikal National Park: the **Jaguar Inn,** the **Jungle Lodge,** and the **Tikal Inn.** The latter is recommended because of the conservation orientation of its owners, the Ortíz family. (Ask Mike Ortíz for directions to Tikal's various nature trails.) Rates start at about $35 a night. There is also one campground, which charges about $6 a night for tent, hammock space, or overnight parking. Showers and cooking facilities are included in the fee. Water is scarce, so bring your own. Several undistinguished restaurants and overpriced gift shops are also near the Tikal ruins. There is a post office, but no telephone, and electricity is only produced by generators (turned off from 10 p.m. to 6 a.m.). An overnight visit to the park is highly recommended because of the tremendous amount of wildlife, including monkeys, deer, foxes, agoutis, and cats. Birders will be particularly rewarded. Because the area has been protected since the mid-1950s, many of the animals show little or no fear of humans.

APPENDICES

APPENDIX A
TRAVEL BASICS

BELIZE BASICS

If you have already spent time in Mexico or Central America, you're in for some surprises when you first visit Belize. First of all, almost everybody speaks English. A linguistic island in a sea of Spanish and Native American dialects, much of Belize looks and feels more like the relaxed, post-colonial British Caribbean than Latin America. And for travelers accustomed to the extremes of poverty, overcrowding, corruption, and militarism that are typical of some destinations, the comparative tranquillity and prosperity of Belize will come as a welcome change. Its singular status as the only non-Spanish-speaking nation between Mexico's Río Grande and South America's Guyana explains some of Belize's eccentricities.

Reservations for airline tickets and hotel rooms are often needed and recommended during the "high season" in Belize, which begins just before Christmas and continues through April. It's customary to provide a first-night's payment or a credit card number to hold a room reservation.

A growing number of travel agents specialize in Belize and most of the country's larger tourism businesses can easily be reached by telephone, fax, or e-mail.

Climate

As a subtropical country that is close enough to North America to be subject to its seasonal air currents, Belize has a warm and wet summer/fall (June through November) followed by relatively cool and dry winter/spring (December through April). There is often also a dry spell in August. The driest months are February and March, although rain can (and does) fall at any time of the year. Belize is hottest in April and May. Humidity is fairly high no matter what the season. Trade winds tend to keep things less sticky along the coast, although this area is subject to sudden squalls. Winds are generally calm in midsummer (except for those pesky hurricanes).

Most visitors prefer to travel to Belize in the Northern Hemisphere's winter months. Daytime coastal temperatures during this period are in the 70s and 80s (20°-to-30°C). Even during summer months, shade temperatures seldom rise above 90 degrees F (38°C). During the "cold" spells of December and January, the thermometer sometimes falls below 55 degrees F (13°C). Extremes are greater inland, even dropping into the low 40s in the highlands. The average temperature throughout the year is 79 degrees F. Water temperatures along the barrier reef range from the mid-70s to mid-80s.

Rainfall in Belize increases from north to south. About 50 inches a year falls near the Mexican border in Corozal, 65 inches in Belize City and the Cayo District, 95 inches in Dangriga, and 120 inches around Punta Gorda, across the Bay of Honduras from Guatemala.

Hurricanes are rare but can threaten Belize at any time between June and November. After Belize City was twice destroyed by severe storms earlier this century, a warning system was set up, and hurricane shelters were established throughout the country. You should be warned well in advance if a potentially destructive storm is expected in Belize, which seems to happen once every 15 years or so. The last big hurricane struck in 1979.

Cuisine

There are relatively few distinctive Belizean dishes, which is why you've probably never heard of any. The most popular meal by far is rice and beans, with or without stewed chicken and frequently spiced by habañero pepper sauce. A typical Belize breakfast might include fried jacks, a puffed pastry similar to a Mexican sopapailla that is often smothered with tropical fruit jam, and johnny cakes, a sweet pancake. The best local recipes are compiled in the *Belize Hospital Auxiliary Cookbook*, sold at local bookstores.

Currency, Banks, and Credit Cards

Although the U.S. dollar is widely accepted—particularly on Ambergris Caye—the preferred currency is the Belize dollar, stabilized at a fixed exchange rate of $2 Belizean to $1 U.S. Coinages from 1 to 25 cents are in use.

The best rates of exchange for foreign currencies are at the borders, with Mexican pesos sometimes obtaining an especially good rate. Belizean banks charge 3 percent for the exchange of foreign currency or traveler's checks, so it may be preferable to make such transactions with merchants, hotels, or individuals, who will almost always make a straight two-for-one swap for U.S. dollars.

The Belize Bank and Barclays, among others, will draft cash on VISA and MasterCard accounts, for a fee. A maximum of $200 may be withdrawn in cash, with any higher amounts in traveler's checks (you may be asked to show your onward ticket). In 1997 there were no ATMs in the country. Money can be telexed to the larger banks in Belize. There is no black market, as financial rates are generally uniform from one institution to another.

All banks are open Mondays through Thursdays from 8:00 a.m. to 1:00 p.m. and reopen from 3:00 p.m. to 6:00 p.m. on Fridays. After closing time, moneychangers can often be found in the vicinity of major banks. They offer fair exchange rates for most major currencies. Credit cards have long been welcome in the larger hotels and are becoming increasingly acceptable among tour operators and other businesses that cater to foreigners, although a credit card "fee" of five percent or more is often added automatically. The American Express agent is Global Travel, 41 Albert St., Belize City (2-77185).

Electrical Current
Electical current is the same in Belize as in the U.S. and Canada: 110 volts A.C.

Holidays, Festivals, and Business Hours
Normal business hours are 8:00 a.m. to noon and 1:00 p.m. to 5:00 p.m. Some stores are open during the morning only on Wednesday and Saturday, or evenings from 7:00 to 9:00. Few establishments open on Sundays, and regular bus and airline schedules may be canceled or curtailed. Banks, shops, and government offices may be closed on the following national holidays:

New Year's Day–January 1
Baron Bliss Day–March 9
Good Friday–date varies
Holy Saturday–date varies
Easter–date varies
Easter Monday–date varies
Labor Day–May 1
Commonwealth Day–May 24
National (St. George's Caye) Day–September 10
Independence Day–September 21
Pan American (Columbus) Day–October 12
Garifuna (Settlement) Day–November 19

Christmas Day–December 25
Boxing Day–December 26

An increasing number of special events and annual festivals take place in Belize. Among the more interesting are the Baron Bliss Regatta (March 8), Crooked Tree Cashew Festival (early May), Caye Caulker Coconut Festival (late May), San Pedro Sea & Air Festival (midsummer), Belize City Festival Grand Market (mid-September), and Hike & Bike for the Rainforest (a countrywide athletic competition in late October that benefits environmental conservation).

Internet Access in Belize

Visitors seeking Internet access from Belize had limited options as this book went to press in late 1997. Eva's Restaurant in San Ignacio (22 Burns Ave.) had a cybercafé with e-mail and Internet accessibility. E-mail them at *evas@btl.net* to find out more. The Corozal Central Guesthouse near Corozal Town's bus station offers free e-mail for its guests (*Vince@btl.net*) as does Cayo's Maya Mountain Lodge (*maya_mt@btl.net*). Some other tourist-oriented businesses will allow you to log on using their own local accounts. Bear in mind that as recently as 1995 it was virtually impossible to access Belize via the Internet, so things could have changed by the time you read this.

Language

English is the mode of instruction in all Belizean schools and is the official language of government and commerce. Spanish is widely spoken (many of the nation's newest immigrants speak little or no English) and about one-third of the people speak a Creole dialect not unlike the accented patois of Jamaica and other former British colonies of the Caribbean.

An estimated 60 percent of the population is bilingual (mostly Spanish/English) and at least 40 percent regard Spanish as their mother tongue. The 10 percent of Belizeans identified as Garifuna speak their own language, as do the 12 percent who are Mayan (mostly Mopan, Kekchí, or Yucatec). Most of the country's 6,000 Mennonites converse in an archaic Low German dialect, although most of the men (and a smaller percentage of the women) speak English and many speak Spanish.

Mail Service

Mail service is inexpensive and reliable. Cards or letters sent from Belize usually reach overseas destinations within a week (U.S. and Canada) or two (Europe, Asia, Australia). Stamps are available at many large hotels.

Belize is known among collectors for its beautiful postage stamps, many of which depict the country's flora and fauna. A special department for stamp collectors is located at the main post office in Belize City.

Taxes and Tipping
In larger hotels and restaurants, a service charge is sometimes added to the bill. If not, tips are based on the quality of service, usually ranging from five to 10 percent, although many Belizeans do not tip at all in restaurants, and only Americans seem to tip 15 percent. Taxi drivers and boatmen are tipped at the discretion of the individual, but the practice is less common than in the U.S., since taxi fares are fixed. A seven percent government room tax is automatically added to any bill for overnight accommodations and is usually not included in the quoted rate. A value-added tax (VAT) of 15 percent was introduced in 1996 and applies to most goods and services.

Telephone Service
There are few public telephones in the country, but most Belizean hotels will allow visitors to make calls at fixed rates. The larger of these will also make their telex and fax facilities available. Direct-access long-distance service is available at some hotels and the international airport.

In most large towns there is a Belize Telephone Ltd. (BTL) long-distance office where operator-assisted calls can be made. The BTL office in Belize City (1 Church St.) offers fax, telex, telegraph, and telegram service (8:00 a.m. to 9:00 p.m. Monday through Saturday). Some of the island and jungle lodges can be reached only by shortwave radio or radio-telephone, which can be problematic. Keep trying—and remember that your conversation is often being overhead by others who belong to this "party line" system.

Direct-dial calls to and from Belize are not difficult—remember to always dial 011 from the U.S. to get an overseas circuit. Belize's international country code is 501, followed by a one- or two-digit region code that varies with each district. When calling direct from the United States or Canada, dial 011-501, drop the first zero from the local number, then dial the remaining numbers. Within the country, it is sometimes necessary to dial a zero before the local number. Remember, 800 numbers in Canada and the U.S. cannot be accessed from overseas telephones.

Time Zone
Belize follows Central Standard Time. Daylight savings time is not observed.

WHAT TO BRING

Visitors to Belize are allowed to bring virtually anything they might reasonably be expected to need during their stay, including fishing gear and diving equipment. Light, informal clothing is recommended. Firearms are prohibited without prior clearance. Pets are allowed into the country only with proof of rabies vaccination and a certificate of good health signed by a veterinarian. Up to 200 cigarettes, 20 ounces of liquor, and one bottle of perfume may be brought in duty-free.

In contrast to most other Central American countries, Belize is a relatively expensive country to visit. Almost everything, including food, is imported and subject to substantial duty and/or value-added taxes. Therefore, it's best to bring along all the clothing, equipment, film, books, maps, diapers, and toiletries you think you'll need. If not, you can expect to pay much more than you would at home for such items, provided they are available. If you wish to make friends among the locals, bring along gifts of fishhooks and small tackle items for men, cosmetics for women, books and small toys (e.g., balloons, pens, and magnifying glasses) for children.

No matter where you travel in Belize, you'll want to carry insect repellent, sunscreen, and drinking water. It's also advisable to have an old pair of tennis shoes or Reefwalkers if you'll be on the beach and reef.

ENTRY AND EXIT REQUIREMENTS

Required for entry:
•passport
•sufficient funds (currently a $50 per day minimum), and
•ticket out of the country.

Visas are not required from citizens of the United States, Canada, Mexico, Germany, France, the United Kingdom, British Commonwealth countries, and most members of the European Economic Community. Visa requirements vary, so check with a travel agent or Belizean authorities if in doubt.

In recent years, the last two requirements (sufficient funds and a ticket out of the country) have not been strictly enforced, although there are occasional reports of authorities turning away individuals whose appearance was deemed unsavory and/or who carried less than $30 per day for the duration of their intended visit. Don't be surprised if an immigration or customs official asks exactly where you will be staying and precisely how much cash you have, especially if you are a long-haired backpacker. For stays longer than 30 days, an extension must be obtained (for a $12.50 fee) from the Immigration Office at 115 Barracks Road in Belize City.

Visas

Visas (not required for citizens of the U.S., Canada, Mexico, and most members of the EEC), may not be purchased at the border, although they can be obtained for $10 from the Belizean consulate in Chetumal, Mexico, just north of the international crossing. These documents can also be arranged at Belizean embassies in Mexico City, Washington, D.C., and other capitals, and, in some instances, through British consulates. Free transit visas are available at the border for periods of 24 or 48 hours, and visas are sometimes not needed if the visitor has an onward ticket in hand. If visiting other countries after leaving Belize, travelers should obtain visas before arriving in Belize. Guatemala now has both an embassy and a consulate in Belize, for visitors needing a Guatemalan visa or tourist card.

Tourist Permits

Tourists are initially granted 14- or 30-day permits to visit Belize, which can be renewed for up to six months. (After six months, travelers must exit the country for at least 24 hours.) As tourists, visitors may not do any kind of work (paid or unpaid) without first obtaining a permit from the Department of Labor. With domestic unemployment hovering around 20 percent, permission is not easily obtained.

HEALTH AND SAFETY

Immunization and Health Precautions

No immunizations are required for entry, and public health standards in Belize are generally good.

Tropical diseases are reasonably well-controlled in Belize, but mosquito-borne malaria and dengue fever are still reported. Yellow fever, cholera, and tuberculosis are rare but do occur. The cautious traveler who plans to spend extended time in the interior may want to take antimalarial drugs or obtain hepatitis A and B vaccinations, as well as oral typhoid immunization, tetanus inoculation, and a tetanus booster (usually combined with diphtheria). Ask your physician for advice or call the Center for Disease Control's "traveler hot line" at (404) 332-4559. As of mid-1997, there were no reports of chloroquine-resistant strains of malaria in Belize, as there are in parts of South America and other continents. Outpatient medical attention in Belize is free at government clinics and hospitals, and there are a number of private physicians' offices throughout the country. A brand-new hospital opened in 1994 in Belize City.

The most common health problem among travelers is diarrhea, usually caused by unfamiliar intestinal bacteria and treatable with Pepto Bismol (or any medication containing bismuth), Bactrim, Cipro, or Doxycycline. If symptoms worsen or persist, see a doctor (and always drink plenty of non-contaminated water).

Since well-stocked Belizean pharmacies are sometimes hard to find, bring along your regular medications and items such as contact lens solutions or prescription eyeglasses.

Outdoor pests such as mosquitoes and biting flies are common, especially during the rainy season, and it is advisable to carry repellent at all times: Cutter's, Jungle Juice, Repel, and other preparations with a high DEET content. Some travelers report excellent results from Avon Skin-So-Soft lotion, citronella oil, and the consumption of garlic. Rubbing alcohol will soothe itching. Since most insects cannot fly well in a breeze, a fan is also useful.

Snakes are found in much of Belize, so be careful when hiking or walking off the road. Only nine of the country's 54 snake species have enough venom to seriously threaten a human, but the roster includes the deadly tommygoff (also called fer-de-lance), as well as several varieties of coral snakes and rattlers. Scorpions, spiders, ticks, biting flies, and carnivorous ants are also fairly common.

At the seaside, on the reef and cayes, the most common problems are overexposure to the sun, scratches from sharp coral or sea urchins, and the annoying bites of such otherwise harmless flying insects as no-see-ums and sand fleas. Stepping on stingrays can cause extremely painful wounds that are potentially deadly if not treated. The scorpion fish and jellyfish are an infrequent hazard. Barracuda, eels, and sharks are common in these waters (especially the non-aggressive lemon and nurse sharks) but almost never attack humans unless provoked or drawn by bleeding wounds, including those of speared fish. Do not touch these animals—it may trigger an aggressive response.

Fair-skinned visitors should wear shirts when snorkeling (to protect their backs from sunburn) and water-resistant sunscreen. Bring along a hat, a long-sleeved cotton shirt, cotton trousers, and sunglasses for midday hours.

An altogether different sort of hazard is posed by powerboats. Several tourists have been badly injured and even killed in recent years while swimming in areas where fast-moving boats regularly travel. The most dangerous areas are off Ambergris Caye near San Pedro and in or near the "split" at Caye Caulker. Before you swim, dive, or snorkel, ask about powerboat hazards and stick to designated areas.

Food and Drinking Water Safety
Public water supplies in most large communities are chlorinated, although there have been some reports of tap water contamination. Many travelers take the added precaution of drinking only bottled water and/or other beverages. A drop of iodine or bleach can be added to each liter of local water for purification, although stronger chemical solutions such as Bactrim and Metronidazole may be needed to kill some parasites and especially virulent bacteria.

Food is generally safe in established hotels and restaurants. As in any underdeveloped country, some risk is involved in eating at roadside stands and sidewalk vendors, particularly where unrefrigerated meat, uncooked fish, and unwashed fruits or vegetables are concerned. Bottled drinks are safe.

Remember that cooking seafood does not destroy ciguatera toxin, which has been occasionally found in barracuda in Belize. Symptoms range from nausea and numbness to diarrhea and heart arrhythmia. Check locally about any reports of ciguatera poisoning, which also may occur in large red snapper, hogfish, and grouper.

Crime and Drug Issues
Several urban centers, notably Belize City, Caye Caulker, and Orange Walk Town, have acquired reputations as being "unsafe" and even downright inhospitable to tourists. In each of these communities, there are persistent reports of street crime in certain neighborhoods and some degree of drug trafficking. Production of marijuana and transshipment of cocaine are big businesses in Belize, despite aggressive attempts by the United States, British, and Belize governments to squelch such illicit activity. Visitors should inquire before setting out on foot into areas that seem questionable, particularly at night. In Belize City, we recommend you go with a friend and take taxis. The most common harassment is strictly verbal, and the perpetrators will usually leave you alone if you ignore them, politely turn down their solicitation, or banter good-naturedly. Anything beyond this should be reported to the authorities immediately.

As in many other countries, it is a good idea to keep your expensive jewelry, flashy watches, and other signs of wealth at home. Tote your camera only when you plan to use it. Carry money and important documents in a money belt hidden under your clothes. Keep only as much cash in your wallet or purse as you expect to spend that particular day. Make sure you have a duplicate of valuable papers (including front pages of your passport) and keep a list of traveler's check identification numbers separate from the originals. It's also prudent to leave a copy of these items with a friend or relative back home.

Immediately report any theft to local police and get a written report from them. To reach the police, dial 911. For the fire department or ambulance service in Belize, dial 90. The U.S. State Department is a good source of up-to-date information about safety conditions in Belize and other foreign countries; contact the Office of Overseas Services at (202) 647-5225.

TRANSPORTATION

Arriving by Air

Phillip Goldson International Airport is in Ladyville, about 20 minutes northwest of Belize City. Immigration and customs procedures are straightforward and relatively efficient. Taxi rates are regulated by the government and tipping is not customary. The cost is $15 to $20 for the 9-mile ride into town. (Taxis are identified by their green license plates.) Some hotels and resorts will arrange private pickup by van or cab, but there are no shuttle buses. Cars can be rented at the terminal building or in Belize City. There is a money exchange desk at the airport.

When leaving the country, bear in mind that Belize bans the export of marine curios, turtles, and turtle products, as well as such national treasures as Mayan artifacts and endangered plants or animals. A maximum of 20 pounds of fish may be taken out of the country, but visitors are urged to either release their catches or consume them while in Belize.

Anyone tempted to fly out of Belize with cocaine or other illegal drugs should be aware that baggage inspections are quite thorough, and even a small amount of marijuana can yield a stiff fine and/or jail term.

A $15 departure tax/screening charge must be paid for all international air departures (either in U.S. or Belizean dollars); if the individual has spent less than 24 hours in the country, there is no fee. Airline overbooking is common, so it's a good idea to reconfirm international flights three days ahead and to arrive at least two hours before departure.

Air Service

In 1997, Belize was served from the U.S. by three U.S. carriers and one

Central American airline via the international airport near Belize City. Belize can be reached most directly from Miami (American, United, Taca), New Orleans (Taca), San Francisco (American, Taca), and Houston (Taca, Continental).

Taca also flies to Belize from San Pedro Sula and Tegucigalpa, connecting to San José, Guatemala City, San Salvador, and Panama City. The Guatemalan airlines, Aviateca and Aerovías, have biweekly schedules from Flores/Santa Elena and Guatemala City to Belize City. A domestic carrier, Tropic, flies twice a week between Flores/Santa Elena and Belize City. Bonanza Airlines flies between Belize City and Chetumal, Mexico, with connections from there to Mérida, Cancún, and Mexico City. Jamaica Air has regular service between Belize City and both Jamaica and the Cayman Islands.

There is currently no direct service to Europe, although this could have changed by the time you read this book. Most European visitors transfer at one of the American gateway cities, in Cancún, or in Guatemala City.

From Belize City's international and municipal airports (about 15 miles apart), frequent flights to smaller towns are offered by Tropic Air, Maya Airways, Sky Bird, Su-Bec, Javier's, and Island Air. Tropic, Maya, and others will also arrange charters to Mexico, Guatemala, and Honduras, as well as to destinations within Belize.

Most airlines now maintain World Wide Web sites on the Internet that provide information on schedules, seating arrangements, and luggage restrictions. You can often make your own reservations via Internet and sometimes take advantage of last-minute, on-line discount prices offered by carriers eager to fill their seats. The Alliance of Central American Airlines is a coalition of five regional airlines that maintains a "webport" with "Hot Deals" section at *http://www.flylatinamerica.com.* Websites for some individual Belize carriers include: *http://www.americanair.com* (American Airlines) and *http://www.flycontinental.com* (Continental Airlines).

International Airlines Serving Belize
Aerovías
2-75445 or (305) 885-1775
Semiweekly flights to and from Flores and Guatemala City.

American Airlines
U.S.A. (800) 433-7300
Canada (800) 433-7300

Belize City 2-32522
Daily flights from Miami with connections to other cities.

Aviateca
International Airport
Belize City
(800) 327-9832
Semi-weekly flights to and from Flores, Guatemala City, and Cancún.

Continental
32 Albert Street
Belize City
U.S.A. (800) 231-0856
Canada (800) 525-0280
Belize City 2-78309
Daily flights from Houston with connections to the rest of the U.S. and
Central America; actively supports conservation work in Belize.

TACA
41 Albert Street
Belize City
2-77363, fax 2-75213,
U.S./Canada (800) 535-8780 (except Quebec, 800-263-4063, and
Ontario, 800-263-4039)
Daily flights from Houston, Miami, and New Orleans, with connections to
New York, Washington, San Francisco, and Los Angeles; also connections
to the rest of Central America, including Roatan and Guatemala City.

United
(800) 222-8333
Daily flights from Miami, with connections to other cities.

Domestic Airlines and Air Charter Services
*Note: Most of Belize's domestic flights and charters originate at the
Municipal Airport in Belize City, on Barracks Road, about 15 miles east
of the International Airport.*

Cari-Bee Air Service
Belize City
2-44253
Charters.

Island Air
General Delivery
San Pedro, Ambergris Caye
2-62180, fax 2-62192
Daily flights to and from San Pedro, Caye Caulker, Caye Chapel,
Municipal airport, International airport, plus charters.

Javier's Flying Service
Municipal Airport
Belize City
2-45332, fax 2-32731
Charters and M-W-F flights to Gallon Jug.

Maya Airways
6 Fort Street
Belize City
2-45968, 2-44032, or 2-62611, fax 2-30585
(504) 522-2311 or (800) 552-3419
Daily flights to and from seven airports in Belize; charters available to
other destinations; semi-weekly flights to Guatemala.

Sky Bird
Belize City
2-32596 or 2-52045, ext. 515
Daily flights between Belize City and Caye Caulker.

Su-Bec Air Service
Belize City
2-44027 or 2-62170, fax 2-30389
Charters.

Tropic Air
P.O. Box 20
San Pedro, Ambergris Caye
2-62012, fax 2-630807 or 2-62338
in Belize City 2-45671
in U.S.A. (800)447-2931, except Texas (713) 449-5230
Daily flights to and from seven airports in Belize, plus twice weekly to
Flores/Santa Elena in Guatemala. Charters available to Cancún, Mérida,
Cozumel, Cayman Islands, and Roatan.

Arriving by Boat

If you arrive in Belize by private vessel, you must report your arrival to police or immigration immediately. No permits are required, but you need the usual official documents, clearance from the last port, and manifests for crew, passengers, stores, and cargo. Allowable points of entry are Belize City, Dangriga, Corozal/Consejo, San Pedro, Barranco, and Punta Gorda.

Private boats can be arranged between Corozal, Sarteneja, and other northern villages to Mexico's Yucatán. They can also be hired from Belize City, Placencia, Punta Gorda, and other places for trips into Guatemala and Honduras.

A passenger ferry provides regular, twice-weekly (Tuesday and Friday at noon) service from Punta Gorda to Puerto Barrios, Guatemala, with connections there to interior Guatemala and Honduras. The crossing takes about 3 hours, and you must have documents in order before embarking, 7-22065. Tickets are about $7 one-way, and it is best to purchase them in advance at Godoy's Shop in Punta Gorda. The ferry no longer stops in Lívingston, Guatemala. It arrives from Puerto Barrios around 10 a.m. Tuesdays and Fridays.

A weekly ferry (actually, a large motor-powered canoe) also operates between Dangriga and Puerto Cortes, Honduras. It leaves Wednesday mornings from the north side of Stann Creek, by the bridge. The trip takes about 10 hours, and you can clear immigration at the office on Commerce Street. Ask at The Hub restaurant/hotel in Dangriga for details.

Many boats ply the waters between Belize City, Caye Chapel, Caye Caulker, and Ambergris Caye. Remember to agree on your fare in advance and pay at the end of the trip. The *Andrea I* and *Andrea II* leave the Bellevue Hotel dock (5 Southern Foreshore) for San Pedro at 4:00 p.m. weekdays, 1:00 p.m. Saturdays. The return crossing is at 7:00 a.m. Trips take about 1 hour and 15 minutes to Ambergris, 45 minutes to Caulker. An efficient water taxi service operates from the Belize City marine terminal, immediately east of the Swing Bridge on N. Front Street, providing reguarly scheduled passenger service to Caulker and Ambergris. The one-way fare to Caulker is about $8 and to Ambergris about $12. Check with your travel agent about cruise ships that may stop in Belize.

Arrival by Car or Bus

While the Belizean road infrastructure is improving, only one (the Western Highway) is smooth and well maintained. All others vary in quality, ranging from rough dirt track to potholed pavement. Foreign aid money was obtained in 1995, however, to upgrade and pave many miles of road, including the notoriously rough Southern Highway.

Overland entry to Belize by foreigners is permitted only from eastern Guatemala (at the Western Highway crossing between Melchor de Mencos and Benque Viejo) or Mexico's Yucatán peninsula (where the Northern Highway crosses the Río Hondo at Santa Elena and Chetumal). A small Mexican crossing is sometimes open (for foot traffic only) at La Unión, a village northwest of Orange Walk. The 1300-mile drive from south Texas to Belize takes from two to seven days, depending on the number of hours spent driving and the road conditions. Belizean buses—many purchased secondhand from U.S. and Canadian public schools—run regularly between Chetumal, Mexico, and Belize City. Seats can be reserved in advance, and ticket prices are reasonable. Passengers may pay on board. Batty Brothers and Venus are the two main companies, both charging about $8 for the four-hour trip. From Chetumal it is a 220-mile bus ride to Cancún, where there are many inexpensive flights each day to the U.S. and Europe.

By Bus from Guatemala

Crossing into Belize from Guatemala is bit more problematic than from Mexico. Few public buses cross the border; therefore, it is sometimes necessary to walk about 50 yards from one side to the other to buy an onward ticket and change vehicles. The crossing is open from 6:00 a.m. to midnight and is sometimes closed for the midday siesta (noon to 2:00 p.m.). Guatemala assesses a $2.50 fee for entering the country by land. There is no charge to land travelers as they exit Belize. Guatemalan and Belizean tourist cards are issued at the border, but visas usually are not. There is a Guatemalan consulate in Belize City, however, and a Belizean consulate in Guatemala City.

Bus Companies

Note: Most Belize City bus terminals are near the intersection of Orange and Collett Canal Streets, not a safe area at night. All addresses and phone numbers listed are in Belize City.

Batty Bus Service
15 Mosul Street
2-72025
Points north and west.

Novelo's Bus Service
West Collett Canal
2-77372
Points west.

Venus Bus Service
Magazine Road and Vernon Street
2-73354 or 2-77390
Points north.

Z-Line Bus Service
Magazine Road and Vernon Street
2-73937 or 6-22211
Points south.

Car Rental

While it is possible to rent a private car in Belize, many travelers are put off by the high cost (typically $65 or more per day for a small car, $100 and up for a mid-size vehicle, plus about $15 a day for insurance) and limited selection (mostly Suzuki Samurais). If you're traveling to remote areas, a four-wheel-drive with spare tire and jack is advisable. Some tourists have complained about unscrupulous rental companies that have allegedly overcharged them for insurance and unnecessary repairs. Overbooking is also a problem. Only a few rental agencies will allow Belizean vehicles to travel into Guatemala and vice versa. It is possible to rent a car in Mexico and drive it into Belize, but agents will charge more if informed that this is your destination. If your Mexican car breaks down in Belize, you may have to pay for it to be towed back to Mexico for repairs and spare parts, both hard to find in Belize. Gas is expensive in oil-poor Belize (about $2.60 U.S. per gallon in 1997) and sometimes difficult to find because of spot shortages.

Driving in Belize

International Driver's Licenses may be used in Belize, but domestic equivalents are acceptable. Drivers should carry valid licenses and vehicle registration documents if driving their own cars. If your vehicle is not going to be sold in Belize, you must obtain a temporary permit at Customs Control waiving the otherwise hefty import duty.

Third-party insurance is compulsory and can be purchased at border crossings or in major towns for about $70 a month. There is an exit fee of $2.50 per car. Visitors are permitted to use a Canadian or U.S. driver's license for 90 days, after which they must obtain a Belizean license ($20, plus photos and a medical examination report).

Car Rental Companies

Ace
12 N. Front Street
Belize City
2-31650, fax: 2-31586

Avis Rent-A-Car
International Airport or
Radisson Ft. George Hotel
Belize City
2-31987 or 2-78637

Budget Rent-A-Car
771 Bella Vista Road
Belize City
2-32435, fax 2-30237, e-mail: jmagroup@btl.net
Well-run operation with a good selection of dependable cars.

Crystal Auto Rental
1.5 Mile, Northern Highway
Belize City
2-31600, fax 2-31900
Rents used cars and arranges driveaway trips from Houston; valid driver's license and damage deposit required; all major credit cards accepted.

ECO-Kar Rental
Northern Highway
Ladyville
25-2797
Conservation oriented and low cost, based near International Airport.

Hertz Rent-A-Car
Bella Vista Road
Belize City
2-32710

Jaguar EcoTours
Ebony and Pine Streets
Belize City
2-73142, fax 2-70397
Twenty-four-hour auto rental service

Alistair King
Texaco Station
Far West Street
Punta Gorda
7-2126, fax 7-2104
Four-wheel-drive available; valid driver's license required; offers tours.

Maxima Car Rental
Maxima Hotel
Hudson Street
San Ignacio
92-2265

Melmish Mayan Rentals
International Airport
Belize City
2-45221, fax 2-77681

National Car Rental
International Airport
Belize City
2-31586, fax 2-52272
Mostly Suzuki Samurais, mostly in excellent shape.

Safari Car Rental
International Airport
Belize City
2-35395, fax 2-30268, e-mail: safari@btl.net
Four-wheel drive Isuzu Trooper specialist.

Arriving by Railroad
Belize no longer has any railroads. The few railways established during colonial days for logging and citrus have been dismantled, and today the nearest railhead is in Mérida, Mexico.

APPENDIX B
ADDITIONAL RESOURCES

TOURIST INFORMATION

An excellent source of background information is Angelus Press (2-35777, fax 2-78825), a publisher and distributor of books, maps, and videos about Belize. Ask for their free catalogue or check out their website (*http://www.belize.net.com/angelus*, e-mail: *angelus@btl.net*).

Belize Tourism Industry Association
Box 62
Belize City
2-75717, fax 2-78710

Belize Tourist Board
Box 325
Belize City
2-77213 or 2-73255, fax 2-77490, e-mail: *BTBB@btl.net*.

Belize Tourist Board
New York Office
421 Seventh Ave., Suite 1110
New York, NY 10001
(800) 624-0686 or (212) 563-6011, fax (212) 563-6033
Website: *www.belizenet.com*

Belize Embassy
2535 Massachusetts Ave. NW
Washington, DC 20008
(202) 332-9636, fax (202) 332-6888. *Belize has consulates in New York, Miami, Washington, Chicago, New Orleans, San Francisco, and Houston.*

BELIZE ON THE INTERNET

Belize has a strong presence on the World Wide Web and many hotels and other tourist businesses have websites and e-mail, most of them through *btl.net*, a service of the government's telephone monopoly, Belize Telephone Ltd. You may also wish to contact entrepreneur Ian Cawich, who keeps track of many Belize web connections (*imcawich@life.uams.edu*).

One of the best websites is **Belize by Naturalight**, created by Tony Rath, of Dangriga's Naturalight Productions and Pelican Beach Resort. The website carries information about hotels, guide books, tour operators, Belize EcoTourism Association members, weather, and natural history destinations at *http://www.belizenet.com*. The Belize Tourist Board sponsors a "virtual tour" of Belize on the Naturalight web page and the BTB can be sent e-mail at *BTBB@btl.net*.

The Belize Online Tourism and Investment Guide has an extensive set of fact-filled pages at *http://www.belize.com*. This site includes their email address (*itm@belize.com*), a helpful newsgroup forum where visitors can post appropriate comments or make inquiries; a thorough booklist page, with links for background on specific places in Belize; and a handy general orientation map of the country. The Belize government has selected Belize Online as its official Internet home at *http://www.belize.gov.bz*.

Another popular Belize-oriented website is offered by The Turquoise Group, which posts an on-line edition of Lan Sluder's excellent *Belize First* magazine at *http://www.turq.com/belizefirst*. The tourist industry on Ambergris Caye maintains a website at *http://www.ambergriscaye.com* and the Belize Tourist Board at *http://www.turq.com*.

An especially helpful interactive on-line publication focusing on natural history tourism and adventure travel in Belize (and neighboring countries) is *La Planeta Platica* (*http://www.planeta.com*), edited by Ron Mader (author of *Mexico: Adventures in Nature* and co-author of *Honduras: Adventures in Nature*, both published by John Muir Publications, 1998).

One of Belize's weekly newspapers, *The Reporter*, receives e-mail at *report@btl.net* and reprints some of its pages at *http://www.belize.com/reporter.html*.

The *Green Arrow Guide to Central America* provides information on countries throughout the region, lists tours that can be booked on-line, and answers travel questions: *http://www.greenarrow.com*. A website for sea-kayaking and adventure travel enthusiasts is posted at *http://www.slickrock.com* (e-mail: *slickrock@slickrock.com*) by Slickrock Adventures.

RECOMMENDED TOUR COMPANIES

Belize City Tour Companies

Belize Global Travel Service
41 Albert Street
2-77185, fax 2-75213
Full service: tickets, tours, hotels.

Belize Land, Air, and Sea Tours, Ltd.
58 King Street
Tel./fax 2-73897
Charter boat, land, and diving tours.

Caribbean Holidays Ltd.
81 Albert Street
2-72593, fax 2-78007
Full service, also works with students, senior citizens.

Ricardo Castillo Tours
59 N. Front Street
2-44970 or VHF marine ch. 68
Offshore and inland tours, cottages on Bluefield Range.

G & W Holiday Travel & Tour Agent
Box 820
Belize City
2-31979 or 25-2461, cellular 14-8756, e-mail: *gholiday@btl.net*
Air-conditioned van; car rental referral; archaeology tours, nature tours; historical sites; bookings for other tours, air charters, and resorts.

Jal's Travel and Tours
148 N. Front Street
2-45407, fax 2-78852
Full-service travel agency; specializes in trips to see manatees; caving, bird-watching, and Mayan ruins.

MayaWorld Safaris
Box 997
Belize City
2-31063, fax 2-30263

Boat trips on New River from Orange Walk Town to Lamanai, tours of Mayan ruins and other sights.

Mesoamerica Tours Ltd.
Fiesta Hotel (formerly Ramada Royal Reef)
Barracks Road
2-30625, fax 2-30750
Custom and individual tours; destinations include Altun Ha, Crooked Tree Wildlife Sanctuary, Community Baboon Sanctuary, Xunantunich, Belize Zoo, Lamanai, Mountain Pine Ridge, Tikal.

Tubroos Tree Adventures
146 Barracks Road
2-33398, fax 2-30385

Cayes Tour Companies

Amigo Travel
San Pedro, Ambergris Caye
2-62180, fax 2-62192
Full-service agency, scooter and bike rental, snorkeling, reef and interior tours.

Travel and Tour Belize, Ltd.
San Pedro, Ambergris Caye
26-2031, fax 26-2185
Diving, snorkeling, fishing, archaeology.

Cayo District Tour Companies

Pine Ridge Lodge
Chiquibul Road
Mountain Pine Ridge
92-3310 or (216) 781-6888
Caving, nature treks, equestrian, birding, and archaeology tours.

Alwyn Smith
Bullet Tree Road
San Ignacio
92-2155 or -3077
Taxi service and tour guide; Mayan ruins, Cayo, Tikal, Mexico.

Windy Hill Tours
Mile 68 Western Highway
San Ignacio
92-2017, fax 92-3080, e-mail: *windyhill@btl.net*
Affordable, all-inclusive Tikal trips; other archaeology tours.

Yute Expeditions
San Ignacio
92-2979, fax 92-2076
Trips to Tikal; birding and other natural history and archaeology tours in Cayo.

Corozal District Tour Companies

Manuel Hoare
13 G Street South
Corozal Town
4-22744, fax 4-23375
Belizean archaeology expert and boatman.

Menzies Travel and Tours, Ltd.
Caribbean Village Resort
South End
Corozal Town
4-22725, fax 4-23414
Agent for Tropic Air; tours in northern Belize; archaeology tours; Mexico and Guatemala guided tours.

Orange Walk District Tour Companies

Godoy & Sons
4 Trial Farm
Orange Walk Town
3-22969
Specializes in orchids and bromeliads of Belize, boat trips up New River to Lamanai and beyond.

Jungle River Tours
20 Lovers Lane
Orange Walk Town
3-22293, fax 3-22201
River trips, jungle tours; Lamanai; strong Belizean archaeology expert.

Lamanai Outpost Lodge
Box 63
Orange Walk Town
Tel./fax 2-33578
Windsurfing, boat trips, canoeing on New River Lagoon in Orange Walk District.

Atilano Narvallez
Guinea Grass
3-22081
Boat rental; jungle river tours of Lamanai.

Stann Creek District Tour Companies

Allen Andrewin
Gales Point
5-22087
Jungle and boat tours; guide services.

Dalton Eiley
Placencia
6-2046, ext. 119
Natural history tours, guide to cayes, fishing, diving, boating.

Jorge Rosado Tours
35 Lemon Street
Dangriga
5-2020 or 5-22119
Nature trips, reef charters and accommodations, Mayan village and cave tours.

David Vernon
Placencia Inland Tours
6-2046, ext. 116
Natural history, river trips, ruins, Cockscomb Basin Wildlife Sanctuary.

Toledo District Tour Companies

Dem Dat's Doin'
Box 73
Front Street at the Wharf

Punta Gorda
7-22470
Tourist information service, permaculture farm, bed and breakfast.

Nature's Way Guest House/Belize Adventure Travel
65 Front Street
Punta Gorda
7-22119
Mayan villages guest house and Garifuna model village contact; boat trips to cayes.

Julio Requena's Charter Service
12 Front Street
Punta Gorda
Boat trips to cayes, rivers; scheduled trips to Puerto Barrios, Guatemala; tours to caves, ruins, indigenous villages.

U.S.-Based Belize Tour Companies

Belize Services
2480 Times Boulevard
Suite 210
Houston, TX 77005
(800) 880-MAYA, fax (713) 528-6292
Belize travel specialists, including nature, reef, and Mayan ruin tours; hotel and airline bookings; car rental; special knowledge of Corozal and Orange Walk districts.

Belize Tradewinds
8715 W. North Avenue
Wauwatosa, WI 53226
(800) 451-7776 or
(414) 258-6687
Hotels; fishing and dive tours.

Belize Travel Representatives
5 Grogans Park, Suite 102
The Woodlands, TX 77380
(800) 451-8017 or (281) 367-3386, fax (281) 298-2335
Owner Tommy Thomson can arrange any kind of trip you want.

Explore the World
672 Las Gallinas Road

San Rafael, CA 94903
(800) 735-9520, fax (415) 454-6188
Hotel and airline booking; nature, diving, fishing, and snorkeling.

Magnum Belize
Box 1560
Detroit Lakes, MN 56502
(800) 447-2931 (U.S. and Canada), fax (218) 847-0334
Travel planners for Belize visitors at every budget and interest level; including "jungle experience," Mayan ruins, and rainforest tours.

Ocean Connection
16734 El Camino Real
Houston, TX 77062
(800) 365-6232, fax (713) 486-8362
Diving, fishing, snorkeling, sailing, tours, hotels, airfare.

BELIZE CONSERVATION GROUPS

Belize Audubon Society
Box 1001, 12 Fort Street
Belize City
2-35004 or 2-34987
e-mail: *base@btl.net*

Belize Center for Environmental Studies
Box 666, 55 Eve Street
Belize City
2-45739, fax 2-32347

Belize EcoTourism Association
Box 1129
Belize City
25-2806
e-mail: *betalin@btl.netday*

Belize Natural History Society
Gallon Jug
Orange Walk District
No phone.

Belize Tropical Forest Studies
P.O. Box 208

Belmopan
92-3310
e-mail: *tfs@pobox.com*

Belize Zoo & Tropical Education Center
Mile 30, Western Highway
Box 1787, Belize City
8-13004

Ix Chel Tropical Research Foundation/Traditional Healers' Foundation
Ix Chel Farm
San Ignacio, Cayo District
9-23870

Programme for Belize
Box 749
Belize City
2-75616, fax 2-75635

Slate Creek Preserve
Mile 8 Mt. Pine Ridge Road
Central Farm P.O.
Cayo District
92-3310, fax 82-3361, e-mail: *tfs@bcsl.com.bz*

International Tropical Conservation Foundation
c/o Papiliorama
Marin-Centre
Case postale 31
CH 2074 Marin-Neuchâtel
Switzerland
(032) 7534350

Wildlife Conservation Society
New York Zoological Society
185th Street and So. Boulevard Bldg. A
Bronx, NY 10460
(212) 220-5155

World Wildlife Fund—U.S.
1250 24th Street, NW
Washington, DC 20037
(202) 293-4800

EMBASSIES AND CONSULATES (PARTIAL LIST)

Canada
85 North Front Street
Belize City
2-31060

Costa Rica
2 Sapodilla Street
Belmopan
8-22725

Guatemala
6-A Saint Matthew Street
Belize City
2- 33150, fax 2-35140

Honduras
91 North Front Street
Belize City
2-45889

Mexico
20 North Park Street
Belize City
2-30193

United States
Hutson Street and Gabrouel Lane
Belize City
2-77161

SUGGESTED READING

World of the Maya

The Blood of Kings: Dynasty and Ritual in Maya Art, Linda
Schele and Mary Ellen Miller. Ft. Worth: Kimbell Art Museum, 1986.

The Complete Visitor's Guide to Mesoamerican Ruins,
Joyce Kelly. Norman: University of Oklahoma Press, 1982.

Guide to Ancient Maya Ruins, C. Bruce Hunter. Norman:

University of Oklahoma Press, 1986.

Time Among the Maya, Ronald Wright. New York: Weidenfeld & Nicholson, 1989.

Warlords and Maize Men: A Guide to the Maya Sites of Belize, Byron Foster, ed. Belize City: Cubola Publications, 1989.

Nature and the Environment

A Belizean Rain Forest: The Community Baboon Sanctuary, Robert Horwich and Jon Lyon. Gay Mills, Wisc.: Orangutan Press, 1990.

A Guide to the Birds of Mexico and Northern Central America, Steve N. G. Howell and Sophie Webb. Oxford University Press, 1995.

Belize: A Country Environmental Profile and Field Study, Robert Nicolait and Associates. San José, Costa Rica: Hnos Sucs, S.A., 1984.

Belize: An International Travel Map, Vancouver: International Travel Maps, 1995.

Birds of Mexico and Central America, Steve Howell and Sophie Webb. New York: Oxford Press, 1993.

Caribbean Reef Ecology, William S. Alavizon. Pisces Books, 1994.

Checklist of the Birds of Belize, Wood, Leberman, and Weyer. Pittsburgh: Carnegie Museum of Natural History Special Publication No. 12.

The Diversity of Life, Edward O. Wilson. Cambridge: Belknap Press of Harvard University Press, 1992.

Guide to Corals and Fishes, Jerry Greenberg. Miami: Seahawk Press, 1972.

Guide to Community-based Ecotourism in Belize, Community Conservation Consultants, Gays Mills, WI. (A report on six major projects where Belize villages are actively involved in managing local protected areas)

Jaguar, Alan Rabinowitz. New York: Arbor House, 1986.

Jungle Walk: Birds and Beasts of Belize, Katie Stevens. Belize City: Angelus Press, 1989.

A Neotropical Companion: An Introduction to the Animals, Plants, and Ecosystems of New World Tropics, John C. Kricher. Princeton: Princeton University Press.

Macdonald Encyclopedia of Butterflies and Moths, Mauro Daccordi, Paolo Triberti, and Adriano Zanetti. Macdonald & Co Ltd. 1988.

Marine Plants of the Caribbean: A Field Guide from Florida to Brazil, Diane Scullion Littler, Mark M. Littler, Katina E. Bucher and James N. Norris. Washington: Smithsonian Institution Press, 1989.

Neotropical Rainforest Mammals: A Field Guide, Louise H. Emmons. Chicago and London: University of Chicago Press.

One Hundred Birds of Belize, Carolyn M. Miller. Washington: International Council for Bird Preservation.

Orchids of Guatemala and Belize, Oakes Ames and Donovan Stewart Correll. New York: Dover, 1985.

Preliminary Faunal Surveys at Tapir Mountain Nature Reserve, Bruce and Carolyn Miller. Wildlife Conservation Society, 1994.

Rainforest Remedies: One Hundred Healing Herbs of Belize, Rosita Arvigo and Michael Balick, Twin Lakes: Lotus Press, 1993.

Reef Coral Identification, Paul Humann. New World Publications, 1994.

Reef Fish and Reef Creatures, Paul Humann. Jacksonville: New World Publications.

Reef Fish Identification, Paul Humann. New World Publications, 1989.

Sastun: My Apprenticeship with a Maya Healer, Rosita Arvigo with Nadine Epstein. San Francisco: Harper Collins, 1994.

Snorkeling Guide to Marine Life, Paul Humann. New World Publications, 1995.

History and Culture

Creole Proverbs of Belize, Colville N. Young. Belize City: National Printers Ltd., 1988.

Hey Dad, This Is Belize, Emory King. Belize City: Tropical Books, 1984.

Inside Belize: A Country Guide, Tom Barry. Albuquerque: Inter-Hemispheric Education Research Center, 1992.

I Spent It All in Belize, Emory King. Belize City: Tropical Books, 1986.

On Heroes, Lizards and Passion, Zoila Ellis. Benque Viejo, Belize: Cubola Publications, 1989.

Profile of Belize, Society for the Promotion of Education and Research. Belize City: Cubola Publications/SPEAR Press, 1990.

Spirit Possession in the Garifuna Community of Belize, Byron Foster. Benque Viejo, Belize: Cubola Publications.

PUBLICATIONS AVAILABLE IN BELIZE

Belize Business & Travel Directory, Henson & Associates. Belize City: Angelus Press, 1988.

Emory King's Driver's Guide to Beautiful Belize, Emory King. Belize City: Tropical Books, 1990.

Magazines and Newspapers

Amandala
(weekly; independent newspaper)
3304 Partridge Street
Belize City

Belize Currents
(semi-annual; general interest magazine)

2159 Summer Avenue
Memphis, TN 38112

Belize First
(quarterly; general interest magazine with travel orientation)
280 Beaverdam Road
Candler, NC 28715

Belize Magazine
(quarterly; general interest and conservation magazine)
Box 803283
Dallas, TX 75380

Belize Natural History Society Papers
c/o Bruce Miller
Gallon Jug, Orange Walk District

Belize Times
(weekly; PUP newspaper)
Box 506, 3 Queen Street
Belize City

Belize Today
(bimonthly; free; business-
oriented)
Belize Information Service
Box 60
Belmopan

Chac Nol Newsletter
(journal of the Central American Institute of Prehistoric and
Traditional Cultures)
Box 59
San Ignacio

Chamber Update
(monthly; business magazine)
Belize Chamber of Commerce
Box 291, 63 Regent Street
Belize City

San Pedro Sun
(weekly; independent
newspaper; also publishes

Belize Sun, a country-wide weekly)
Box 35
San Pedro, Ambergris Caye

People's Pulse & Beacon
(weekly; UDP newspaper)
7 Church Street
Belize City

Reporter
(weekly; independent)
Box 1217
Belize City

SCIENTIFIC NAMES OF FLORA & FAUNA
Note: This is not a comprehensive list of Belize's flora and fauna. Those species listed below, with the exception of insects and crustaceans, are only those mentioned in the text.

Birds
American coot *(Fulica americana)*
American redstart *(Setophaca ruticilla)*
Aztec parakeet *(Aratinga astec)*
azure-crowned hummingbird *(Amazilia cyanocephala)*
bare-throated tiger heron *(Tigrisoma mexicanum)*
barred antshrike *(Thamnophilus doliatus)*
barred forest falcon *(Micrastur ruficollis)*
belted kingfisher *(Megaceryle alcyon)*
black-and-white warbler *(Mniotilta varia)*
black-bellied whistling duck *(Dendrocygna autumnalis)*
black catbird *(Melanoptila glabrirostris)*
black-chinned hummingbird *(Archilochus alexandri)*
black-headed saltator *(Saltator atriceps)*
black-headed trogon *(Trogon melanocephalus)*
black rail *(Laterallus jamaicensis)*
blue-black grosbeak *(Cyancompsa cyanoides)*
blue-crowned motmot *(Motmotus momota)*
blue-gray tanager *(Thraupis episcopus)*

blue grosbeak *(Guiraca caerulea)*
blue-winged teal *(Anas discors)*
boat-billed heron (*Cochlearius cochlearius*)
brown-hooded parrot *(Pionopsitta haemotosis)*
brown jay *(Psilorhinus morio)*
brown pelican *(Pelicanus occidentalis)*
chestnut-bellied (agami) heron *(Agamia agami)*
citreoline trogon *(Trogon citreolus)*
collared aracari *(Pteroglossus torquatus)*
collared forest falcon *(Micrastur semitorquatus)*
common wood nymph *(Thalurania furcata)*
crested guan *(Penelope purpurascens)*
emerald toucanet *(Avlacorhynchus prosinus)*
eye-ringed flatbill *(Rhynchocyclus brevirostris)*
gray-breasted crake *(Laterallus exilis)*
great blue heron *(Ardea herodias)*
great curassow *(Crax rubra)*
great kiskadee *(Pitangus sulp huratus)*
green-backed heron *(Butorides striatus)*
green heron *(Butorides virescens)*
green-winged teal *(Anas crecca)*
hooded oriole *(Icterus cucullatus)*
harpy eagle *(Harpia harpyja)*
jabiru stork *(Jabiru mycteria)*
keel-billed motmot *(Electron carinatum)*
keel-billed toucan *(Ramphastos sulfuratus)*
king vulture *(Sarcoramphus papa)*
least grebe *(Tachybaptus dominicus)*
least tern *(Sterna albifrons)*
limpkin *(Aramus guarauna)*
lineated woodpecker *(Dryocopus lineatus)*
little blue heron *(Florida caerulea)*
little tinamou *(Crypturellus soui)*
magnificent frigatebird *(Fregata magnificens)*
mangrove warbler *(Dendroica erithacorides)*
mealy parrot *(Amazona farinosa)*
Montezuma oropendola *(Psarocolius montezuma)*
northern jacana *(Jacana spinosa)*
ocellated turkey *(Agriocharis ocellata)*
olivaceous cormorant *(Phalacrocorax olivaceus)*
orange-breasted falcon *(Falco deiroleucus)*
ornate hawk eagle *(Spizaetus ornatus)*
osprey *(Panion haliaetus)*

Philadelphia vireo *(Vireo philadelphicus)*
plain chachalaca *(Ortalis vetula)*
prothonotary warbler *(Protonotaria citrea)*
pygmy kingfisher *(Chloroceryle aenea)*
red-billed azurecrown *(Amazilia cyanocephala)*
red-capped manakin *(Pipra mentalis)*
reddish egret *(Dichromanassa rufescens)*
red-footed booby *(Sula sula)*
red-lored parrot *(Amazona antumnalis)*
red-throated ant-tanager *(Habia fuscicauda)*
ringed kingfisher *(Ceryle torquata)*
roadside hawk *(Buteo nitidus)*
roseate spoonbill *(Ajaia ajaja)*
roseate tern *(Sterna dougalli)*
rose-throated becard *(Pachyramphus major)*
rough-winged swallow *(Stelgidopteryx ruficollis)*
ruddy woodcreeper *(Dendrocincla homochroa)*
rufous-browed peppershrike *(Cyclarhis gujanensis)*
rufous-capped warbler *(Basileuterus belli)*
rufous-tailed hummingbird *(Amazilia tzactl)*
scaly-throated foliage gleaner *(Anabacerthia variegaticeps)*
scarlet macaw *(Ara macao)*
scissor-tailed flycatcher *(Muscivora forficata)*
slaty-breasted tinamou *(Crypturellus boucardi)*
smoky-brown woodpecker *(Venilorus fumigatus)*
snail kite *(Rostrhamus sociabilis)*
sooty tern *(Sterna fuscata)*
spectacled owl *(Pulsatrix perspicillata)*
squirrel cuckoo *(Piaya cayana)*
tropical mockingbird *(Mimus gilvus)*
vermiculated screech-owl *(Otus guatemalae)*
vermillion flycatcher *(Pyrocephalus rubinus)*
white-bellied emerald *(Amazilia candida)*
white-capped noddy *(Anous minutus)*
white-collared seed eater *(Sporophila torqueola)*
white-crowned parrot *(Pronis senilis)*
white-crowned pigeon *(Columba leucocephala)*
white-fronted parrot *(Amazona albifrons)*
white hawk *(Leucopternis albicollis)*
white ibis *(Eudocimus albus)*
white-necked jacobin *(Florisuga mellivora)*
wood stork *(Mycteria americana)*
yellow-billed cacique *(Amblycercus holosericeus)*

yellow-headed parrot *(Amazona ochrocephala)*
yellow-lored parrot *(Amazona xantholora)*
yellow-throated euphonia *(Euphonia hirundinacea)*
Yucatan jay *(Cyanocorax yucatanicus)*

Mammals
agouti *(Dasyprocta punctata)*
armadillo *(Dasypus novemcinctus)*
Atlantic bottlenose dolphin *(Tursiops truncatus)*
Baird's tapir *(Tapirus bairdii)*
black howler monkey *(Alouatta pigra)*
brocket deer *(Mazama americana)*
Caribbean manatee *(Trichechus manatus)*
Central American river otter *(Lutra longicaudus)*
Central American spider monkey *(Ateles geoffroyi)*
coati *(Nasua nasua)*
fishing bat *(Noctillo leporinus)*
giant anteater *(Myrmecophaga tridactyla)*
gray four-eyed opossum *(Philander opossum)*
gray fox *(Urocyon cinereoargenteus)*
hog-nosed skunk *(Conepatus semistriatus)*
jaguar *(Panthera onca)*
jaguarundi *(Felis yagouaroundi)*
kinkajou *(Potos flavus)*
margay *(Felis wiedii)*
ocelot *(Felis paradalis)*
paca *(Agouti paca)*
puma *(Felis concolor)*
silky anteater *(Cyclopes didactylus)*
spinner dolphin *(Stenella longirosrus)*
tamandua *(Tamandua mexicana)*
tayra *(Eira barbara)*
Virginia opossum *(Didelphis virginiana)*
West Indian manatee *(Trichechus manatus)*
white-lipped peccary *(Tapirus pecari)*
white-tailed deer *(Odocoileus virginiana)*

Reptiles
boa constrictor *(Constrictor constrictor)*
fer-de-lance *(Bothrops atrox)*
hawksbill turtle *(Eretmochelys imbricata)*
hickatee *(Dermatemys mawii)*
iguana *(Iguana iguana)*

loggerhead turtle *(Staurotypus triporcatus)*
Morelet's crocodile *(Crocodylus moreletii)*

Fishes
Atlantic sailfish *(Istiophorus albicans)*
banded butterflyfish *(Chaetodon striatus)*
black durgon *(Melichthys niger)*
black grouper *(Mycteroperca bonaci)*
bluehead wrasse *(Thalassoma bifasciatum)*
blue marlin *(Makaira nigricans)*
blue-striped grunt *(Haemulon criurus)*
blue tang *(Acanthurus coeruleus)*
bonefish *(Abula vulpes)*
four-eyed butterfly fish *(Chaetodon capistratus)*
gray angelfish *(Pomancanthus arcuatus)*
great barracuda *(Sphyaena barracuda)*
hogfish *(Lachnolaimus maximus)*
horse-eye jack *(Caranx latus)*
indigo hamlet *(Hypoplectrus indigo)*
king mackerel *(Scomberomorus cavalla)*
lane snapper *(Lutjanis synagris)*
longspine squirrelfish *(Holocentrus rufus)*
permit *(Trachinotus falcatus)*
schoolmaster *(Lutjanus apodus)*
sergeant major *(Abudefduf saxatilis)*
Spanish mackerel *(Scombermorus maculatus)*
spotfin butterflyfish *(Chaetodon ocellatus)*
spotted moray eel *(Gymnothorax moringa)*
stoplight parrotfish *(Sparisoma viride)*
tarpon *(Tarpon atlanticus)*
wahoo *(Acanthocybium solandi)*
white marlin *(Tetrapturus albidus)*
yellowhead wrasse *(Halichoeres garnoti)*
yellowtail damselfish *(Microspathodon chrysurus)*
yellow-tail snapper *(Ocyurus chrysurus)*

Trees
allspice *(Pimienta dioica)*
balsa *(Ochroma lagopus)*
banak *(Virola koschnyi)*
barba jolote *(Pithecellobium arboreum)*
black mangrove *(Avicennia)*
black poisonwood *(Metopium brownei)*

breadnut *(Brosimum alicastrum)*
bullhoof *(Drypetes brownii)*
buttonwood *(Conocarpus erecta)*
ceiba *(Ceiba pentandra)*
coconut *(Cocos nucifera)*
cohune palm *(Orbignya cohune)*
copal *(Protium copal)*
Cortéz *(Tabebuia chrysantha)*
give and take palm *(Crysophila argentea)*
grande Betty *(Cupania belizensis)*
guanacaste *(Enterolobium cyclocarpum)*
hairy palm *(Colopothrinax cookii)*
ironwood *(Dialium guianense)*
kaniste *(Pouteria campechiana)*
logwood *(Haematoxylon campechianum)*
mahogany *(Swietenia macrophylla)*
mamee apple *(Pouteria mammosa)*
mapola *(Bernoullia flammea)*
mylady *(Aspidosperma cruenta)*
negrito *(Simarubra glauca)*
palmetto palm *(Acoellorhaphe wrightii)*
quamwood *(Schizolobium parahybum)*
red breadnut *(Trophis racemosa)*
red gumbolimbo *(Bursera simaruba)*
red mangrove *(Rhizophora mangle)*
Santa María *(Calophyllum brasileinse var. rekoi)*
sapodilla *(Manilkara zapota)*
Spanish cedar *(Cedrela odorata)*
waika chewstick *(Symphonia globulifera)*
wild mammee *(Alseis yucatanensis)*
yemeri *(Vochysia hondurensis)*
ziricote *(Cordia sebestena)*

INDEX

Titles from John Muir Publications

Rick Steves' Books

Asia Through the Back Door, 400 pp., $17.95

Europe 101: History and Art for the Traveler, 352 pp., $17.95

Mona Winks: Self-Guided Tours of Europe's Top Museums, 432 pp., $18.95

Rick Steves' Baltics & Russia, 160 pp., $9.95

Rick Steves' Europe, 576 pp., $18.95

Rick Steves' France, Belgium & the Netherlands, 304 pp., $15.95

Rick Steves' Germany, Austria & Switzerland, 272 pp., $14.95

Rick Steves' Great Britain & Ireland, 320 pp., $15.95

Rick Steves' Italy, 224 pp., $13.95

Rick Steves' Scandinavia, 192 pp., $13.95

Rick Steves' Spain & Portugal, 240 pp., $13.95

Rick Steves' Europe Through the Back Door, 512 pp., $19.95

Rick Steves' French Phrase Book, 192 pp., $5.95

Rick Steves' German Phrase Book, 192 pp., $5.95

Rick Steves' Italian Phrase Book, 192 pp., $5.95

Rick Steves' Spanish & Portuguese Phrase Book, 336 pp., $7.95

Rick Steves' French/German/Italian Phrase Book, 320 pp., $7.95

City•Smart™ Guidebooks

City•Smart Guidebook: Austin, 224 pp., $12.95

City•Smart Guidebook: Cleveland, 208 pp., $14.95

City•Smart Guidebook: Denver, 256 pp., $14.95

City•Smart Guidebook: Indianapolis, 224 pp., $12.95

City•Smart Guidebook: Kansas City, 248 pp., $12.95

City•Smart Guidebook: Memphis, 224 pp., $12.95

City•Smart Guidebook: Milwaukee, 224 pp., $12.95

City•Smart Guidebook: Minneapolis/St. Paul, 232 pp., $14.95

City•Smart Guidebook: Nashville, 256 pp., $14.95

City•Smart Guidebook: Portland, 232 pp., $14.95

City•Smart Guidebook: Tampa/St. Petersburg, 256 pp., $14.95

Travel+ Smart™ Trip Planners

American Southwest Travel + Smart Trip Planner, 256 pp., $14.95

Colorado Travel + Smart Trip Planner, 248 pp., $14.95

Eastern Canada Travel + Smart Trip Planner, 272 pp., $15.95

Florida Gulf Coast Travel + Smart Trip Planner, 224 pp., $14.95

Hawaii Travel + Smart Trip Planner, 256 pp., $14.95

Kentucky/Tennessee Travel + Smart Trip Planner, 248 pp., $14.95

Michigan Travel + Smart Trip Planner, 232 pp., $14.95

Minnesota/Wisconsin Travel + Smart Trip Planner, 232 pp., $14.95

New England Travel + Smart Trip Planner, 256 pp., $14.95

New York State Travel + Smart Trip Planner, 256 pp., $15.95

Northern California Travel + Smart Trip Planner, 272 pp., $15.95

Pacific Northwest Travel + Smart Trip Planner, 240 pp., $14.95

Southern California Travel + Smart Trip Planner, 232 pp., $14.95

South Florida Travel + Smart Trip Planner, 232 pp., $14.95

Adventures in Nature Series

Belize: Adventures in Nature, 408 pp., $18.95

Guatemala: Adventures in Nature, 392 pp., $18.95

Other Terrific Travel Titles

The 100 Best Small Art Towns in America, 256 pp., $15.95

The Big Book of Adventure Travel, 400 pp., $17.95

The Birder's Guide to Bed and Breakfasts: U.S. and Canada, 416 pp., $17.95
Costa Rica: A Natural Destination, 416 pp., $18.95
Indian America, 480 pp., $18.95
The People's Guide to Mexico, 608 pp., $19.95
Ranch Vacations, 632 pp., $22.95
Understanding Europeans, 272 pp., $14.95
Watch It Made in the U.S.A., 400 pp., $17.95
The World Awaits, 280 pp., $16.95

Automotive Titles

The Greaseless Guide to Car Care, 272 pp., $19.95
How to Keep Your Subaru Alive, 480 pp., $21.95
How to Keep Your Toyota Pick-Up Alive, 392 pp., $21.95
How to Keep Your VW Alive, 464 pp., $25.00

Extremely Weird® Series

Each is 32 pages and $5.95 paperback, ages 6 to 10.
Extremely Weird Animal Defenses
Extremely Weird Animal Disguises
Extremely Weird Animal Hunters
Extremely Weird Bats
Extremely Weird Birds
Extremely Weird Endangered Species
Extremely Weird Fishes
Extremely Weird Frogs
Extremely Weird Insects
Extremely Weird Mammals
Extremely Weird Micro Monsters
Extremely Weird Primates
Extremely Weird Reptiles
Extremely Weird Sea Creatures
Extremely Weird Snakes
Extremely Weird Spiders

Kidding Around® Travel Series

Each is 144 pages and $7.95 paperback, ages 6 to 10.
Kidding Around Atlanta
Kidding Around Austin
Kidding Around Boston
Kidding Around Cleveland
Kids Go! Denver
Kidding Around Indianapolis
Kidding Around Miami
Kidding Around Milwaukee
Kidding Around Minneapolis/St. Paul
Kidding Around San Francisco
Kids Go! Seattle
Kidding Around Washington, D.C.

Kids Explore Series

Written by kids for kids, each is $9.95 paperback, ages 8 to 12.
Kids Explore America's African American Heritage, 160 pages
Kids Explore America's Hispanic Heritage, 160 pages
Kids Explore America's Japanese American Heritage, 160 pages
Kids Explore America's Jewish Heritage, 160 pages
Kids Explore the Gifts of Children with Special Needs, 128 pages
Kids Explore the Heritage of Western Native Americans, 128 pages
Kids Explore Kids Who Make a Difference, 128 pages

Ordering Information

Please check your local bookstore for our books, or call **1-800-888-7504** to order direct and to receive a complete catalog. A shipping charge will be added to your order total.

Send all inquiries to:
**John Muir Publications
P.O. Box 613
Santa Fe, NM 87504**

ABOUT THE AUTHORS

Richard Mahler is a writer and broadcast journalist who has reported on conservation and nature topics for more than 25 years. The author of five published books, he has written for more than 100 magazines and newspapers, including the *Los Angeles Times, Christian Science Monitor, Miami Herald, Outside, Great Expeditions, Mother Jones,* and *New West.* He has been a freelance correspondent for National Public Radio since 1973 and covers environmental matters for the public radio series *Living on Earth,* reporting on such issues as rainforest destruction and preservation of Native American sacred sites. Mahler's writing and radio productions have received awards from the Associated Press, PEN USA, and the Radio-TV News Directors Association. As an advocate of natural history tourism and conservation activism, he has worked on behalf of numerous environmental organizations in the American West and Latin America. A longtime resident of New Mexico, Mahler is based in Santa Fe.

Steele Wotkyns has worked to help protect the environment in the United States, Belize, and five other Central and South American countries. He is a featured speaker and a regular source for media interviews on conservation topics. An outdoor sports enthusiast with a journalism degree from Colorado State University, he is also a member of the Society of Environmental Journalists. He lives with his wife, Rita, and his cat, Viento, in Santa Fe, New Mexico.